D1552221

Watching Films

Watching Films:
New Perspectives on Movie-Going, Exhibition and Reception

Edited by
Karina Aveyard and Albert Moran

intellect Bristol, UK / Chicago, USA

First published in the UK in 2013 by
Intellect, The Mill, Parnall Road, Fishponds, Bristol, BS16 3JG, UK

First published in the USA in 2013 by
Intellect, The University of Chicago Press, 1427 E. 60th Street,
Chicago, IL 60637, USA

Copyright © 2013 Intellect Ltd

All rights reserved. No part of this publication may be reproduced,
stored in a retrieval system, or transmitted, in any form or by
any means, electronic, mechanical, photocopying, recording, or
otherwise, without written permission.

A catalogue record for this book is available from the
British Library.

Cover designer: Holly Rose
Copy-editor: Sue Jarvis
Production manager: Melanie Marshall/Tom Newman
Typesetting: Contentra Technologies

ISBN 978-1-84150-511-4
EISBN: 978-1-78320-042-9

Printed and bound by Hobbs the Printers Ltd, UK

Dedication
For David Bordwell and Kristin Thompson
who have done so much to help us all see.

Contents

Contents

Foreword

This collection of new essays on watching films engages in a conversation with a new research direction in cinema studies, one that focuses less on the form and content of films and instead explores their circulation and consumption, and that considers the cinema as a site of social and cultural exchange. Borrowing concerns about both distribution and reception from work in other areas of media studies, this trend is underpinned by a strengthening recognition that if we intend to address the social and cultural significance of cinema, we must find ways to write about its audiences, not as imaginary spectators but as civic agents who invest time in incorporating commercial fantasies into the continuities of their everyday lives.

The recognition that audiences go to the movies for a complex mix of reasons to do with family, workplace and community must be matched by an acknowledgement of the transitory nature of any individual film's exhibition history. Since their industrial beginnings, motion pictures have been understood as consumables: viewed once, disposed of and replaced by a substitute providing a comparable experience. Encouraging and sustaining audiences' habits of cinema-going as a regular and frequent social activity has required a constant flow of film products, ensuring that the evanescent images on the screen have formed the most expendable element of the experience of cinema.

The project of writing what Jeffrey Klenotic (2007) terms 'a people's history of cinema' will also lead us to produce a more market-focused account of the existence of individual films – an account that pays attention to the global traffic of their circulation, the variations and regularities in the patterns of their consumption, and the ways in which the resilient parochialism of individuals and communities accommodates the passing content occupying their screens to their local concerns.

Giving consideration to the economics of distribution or the behaviour of audiences inevitably displaces the films themselves from their conventionally central place in the history of cinema, by asking questions that cannot be answered by formal analysis. These questions can, however, engage researchers from other disciplines who have not been schooled in the professional orthodoxy that the proper business of film studies is the study of films. For geographers, demographers, economists or anthropologists, the observation that cinemas are sites of social and cultural significance will unproblematically have as much to do with patterns of employment, urban development, transport systems and leisure practices that shape cinema's global diffusion as it does with what happens in the brief encounter between an individual audience member and a film print.

The events at which these encounters between the everyday and the extraordinary take place are themselves ephemeral: each such encounter is at the same time unique, quotidian and reiterated. The event of cinema – the screening – is a social experience in which every spectator contributes and in which they share as part of the temporary existence of an audience. But each movie audience is an unstructured social agglomeration, assembled for that event and afterwards dissolved, less durable even than the shadow images it watches. Screenings embody Fernand Braudel's (1982) metaphor for the historical event: the phosphorescent firefly that glows and goes out 'without piercing the night with any true illumination'. Because movie screenings leave only residual, contextual traces of their existence, even the idea of studying them presents researchers with a range of evidential and methodological challenges. Some of these challenges can be addressed by using the computational apparatus of databases, spatial analysis and geovisualization to compile information that was previously too time-consuming and labour-intensive to acquire. They also present opportunities for film studies to escape the confines of textual analysis, overcome the self-perpetuating insularity of middle-level accounts of film's medium-specificity, and begin at last to speak with other disciplines in the humanities and social sciences, in the expectation that the study of cinema should be more than an entertaining diversion decorating the margins of other discourses, and that it has something of substance to contribute to our broader understanding of social and cultural practice.

The evanescence of these events is, however, also essential to their existence as cinema – and indeed to the existence of cinema studies. Every aspirational encounter with cinema's dreams of abundance is a particular act of individual imagination, taking place in the particular circumstances of the Great Dark Room, where cinema exists in the transient space between the audience and the screen. Accounts of the cinematic equation that pay more attention to the audience than they do to the screen – such as those in this book – are no less accounts of cinema because of that emphasis.

Richard Maltby

References

Braudel, F. (1982), *On History*, Chicago: University of Chicago Press.
Klenotic, J. (2007) 'Four Hours of Hootin' and Hollerin': Moviegoing and Everyday Life Outside the Movie Palace', in R. Maltby and M. Stokes (eds), *Going to the Movies: Hollywood and the Social Experience of Cinema*, Exeter: University of Exeter Press.

Figures and Tables

Figures

Tables

Acknowledgements

We would like to warmly thank all of the chapter authors for supporting this project and for their innovative and highly engaging contributions. We are grateful also to Richard Maltby for his thoughtful Foreword. Further, we are indebted to Intellect for its interest in the collection and in particular Melanie Marshall and Tom Newman, who have been so helpful through all the different stages of the process. We also thank Sue Jarvis for her invaluable copy editing work on the manuscript and compilation of the index.

Griffith University has long been a leader in the field of film and media studies, and the majority of the work for this collection was conducted at this institution. We are indebted to the School of Humanities at the Nathan campus in Brisbane for its assistance and encouragement on this project. Karina also expresses thanks for more recent and highly valued support provided by the School of Film, Television and Media Studies at the University of East Anglia. Further, we gratefully acknowledge the Australian Research Council, the National Film and Sound Archive and Screen Australia, who together provided the Linkage Grant that has underpinned our cinema research work over the past four years.

Karina would like to thank Peter Reuter for his love, support and advice throughout this project.

Albert also expresses personal thanks to his wife Noela for her love, advice and support, and his daughter Kate, who provided research assistance along the way.

About the Contributors

Eylem Akatav is a Senior Lecturer in Film and Television Studies at the University of East Anglia. She is the author of *Women and Turkish Cinema: Gender Politics, Cultural Identity and Representation* (Routledge, 2012) and the editor of *Directory of World Cinema: Turkey* (Intellect, 2012).

Louise Anderson worked at the British Film Institute before taking up an Arts and Humanities Research Council studentship in collaboration with the Tyneside Cinema in Newcastle. Having gained her doctorate in 2011, Louise now works as a freelance researcher.

Karina Aveyard is a Lecturer in the School of Film and Television Studies at the University of East Anglia. Her research interests include rural cinemas, and film exhibition and distribution and Australian film.

Daniel Biltereyst is Professor in Film and Media Studies at Ghent University, Belgium, where he is Director of the Centre for Cinema and Media Studies. His work has been published in many journals and edited volumes. He is the editor, with Richard Maltby and Philippe Meers, of *Explorations in New Cinema History* (Wiley-Blackwell, 2011) and of *Cinema, Audiences and Modernity* (Routledge, 2012). His latest volume is *Silencing Cinema: Film Censorship around the World* (Palgrave Macmillan, 2013), edited with Roel Vande Winkel.

Lucy Faire is an Honorary Fellow in the Centre for Urban History at the University of Leicester. She specializes in the twentieth-century history of home, leisure and behaviour. She is the co-author of *The Place of the Audience: Cultural Geographies of Film Consumption* (British Film Institute, 2003) and the co-editor of *Research Methods for History* (Edinburgh University Press, 2011).

Kathryn Fuller-Seeley is Professor of Communication at the University of Texas at Austin. Her work focuses on the history of film, radio and television and audiences. She is co-author of *One Thousand Nights at the Movies: An Illustrated History of Motion Pictures, 1895–1915* (Whitman Publishing, 2013) and the editor of *Hollywood in the Neighborhood: Historical Case Studies of Local Moviegoing* (University of California Press, 2008).

Douglas Gomery is a Professor Emeritus at the University of Maryland and is currently Resident Scholar at its Library of American Broadcasting. His prize-winning publications include *Shared Pleasures* (University of Wisconsin Press, 1992) and *Who Owns the Media?* (Routledge, 2000). His latest publication is *Patsy Cline: The Making of an Icon* (Trafford, 2011).

Ian Goode teaches film and television in the School of Culture and Creative Arts at the University of Glasgow. His research interests include rural cinema and cinema-going, film exhibition, and documentary and non-fiction film and television.

Stuart Hanson is a Senior Lecturer in Media and Communication at De Montfort University, Leicester. He is author of *From Silent Screen to Multi-screen: A History of Cinema Exhibition in Britain Since 1896* (Manchester University Press, 2008) and also co-edited two collections of *CCCS Selected Working Papers* (2007).

Ian Huffer is a Lecturer in Media Studies at Massey University, New Zealand. His current research explores the economic, social and cultural relations articulated through film exhibition in New Zealand. Work from this research can be found in *Studies in Australasian Cinema*, 5: 3 and 6: 2.

Mark Jancovich is Professor of Film and Television Studies at the University of East Anglia. He is the author of several books on cinema, including *Horror* (Batsford, 1992), *The Cultural Politics of the New Criticism* (Cambridge University Press, 1993), *Rational Fears: American Horror in the 1950s* (Manchester University Press, 1996) and *The Place of the Audience: Cultural Geographies of Film Consumption* (with Lucy Faire and Sarah Stubbings, British Film Institute, 2003).

Janna Jones is Professor of Communication at Northern Arizona University. She is the author of *The Past is a Moving Picture: Preserving the Twentieth Century on Film* (University of Florida Press, 2012) and *The Southern Movie Palace: Rise, Fall, and Resurrection* (University of Florida Press, 2003). Her other published works focus on cinema-going practices, amateur film, the history of the film archive and theatre preservation.

Jeffrey Klenotic is Associate Professor of Communication Arts at the University of New Hampshire. Recent publications include 'Space, Place and the Female Film Exhibitor: The Transformation of Cinema in Small Town New Hampshire in the 1910s' in J. Hallam and L. Roberts (eds), *Locating the Moving Image* (Indiana University Press, 2013) and 'Putting Cinema History on the Map: Using GIS to Explore the Spatiality of Cinema' in R. Maltby, D. Biltereyst and P. Meers (eds), *Explorations in New Cinema History* (Wiley-Blackwell, 2011). More details about his research, including the Geographic Information System 'Mapping Movies', are available at http://jeffklenotic.com.

Julia Knight is Professor of Moving Image at the University of Sunderland, and co-editor of *Convergence: The International Journal of Research into New Media Technologies*. Before entering academia, she was co-manager of Albany Video Distribution, and was subsequently a member of the management committee of Cinenova, the surviving women's film and video distributor in the United Kingdom. She has published widely on various aspects of moving image culture, including a co-authored (with Peter Thomas) book, *Reaching Audiences: Distribution and Promotion of Alternative Moving Image* (Intellect, 2011), and an accompanying Film and Video Distribution Database (fv-distribution-database.ac.uk), which makes available a selection of primary research material.

Geoff Lealand is an Associate Professor in Screen and Media Studies at the University of Waikato in New Zealand. Further information about his research interests can be found at http://cinemasofnz.info. He is an avid film-goer, and has a bottom-line target of seeing at least 52 films at the cinema every year, which must include a good helping of Australian and New Zealand titles.

Kathleen Lotze is a doctoral candidate and member of the Visual Studies and Media Culture Research Group at the University of Antwerp, Belgium. Her PhD research is centred on film exhibition and reception in Antwerp (1945–95), and includes a focus on the Rex-cinema group. She has published articles on local cinema culture in Flanders, Dutch film culture in the 1960s, as well as on subversive film practice in East-Germany in the 1980s.

Adrian Mabbott Athique has lectured in sociology, screen, media and cultural studies in the United Kingdom, Australia and New Zealand. His research interests include the social practice (and malpractice) of film exhibition, the impact of new technologies on media distribution and the transnational reception of media in Asia. Adrian is author of *The Multiplex in India: A Cultural Economy of Urban Leisure* (with Douglas Hill, Routledge, 2010), *Indian Media: Global Approaches* (Polity Press, 2012) and *Digital Media and Society* (Polity Press, 2013).

Richard Maltby FAHA is Matthew Flinders Distinguished Professor of Screen Studies and Executive Dean of the Faculty of Education, Humanities and Law at Flinders University, South Australia. His publications include Hollywood Cinema (2nd edn, Blackwell, 2003), *'Film Europe' and 'Film America': Cinema, Commerce and Cultural Exchange, 1925–1939* (with A. Higson, University of Exeter Press, 1999) and seven books on the history of movie audiences and exhibition history, the most recent being *Explorations in New Cinema History: Approaches and Case Studies* (Wiley-Blackwell, 2011).

Alan McKee is a Professor at Queensland University of Technology (QUT), and an expert on media and healthy sexual development. He leads the Promoting Healthy Sexual Development Research Group at QUT, and is Project Leader for the Queensland Government-funded

NIRAP grant, 'Developing Improved Sexual Health Education Strategies'. He has published on healthy sexual development, the effects of pornography on young people and entertainment education in the area of healthy sexuality, in journals including the *International Journal of Sexual Health,* the *Journal of Sex Research* and *Sex Education.*

Philippe Meers is an Associate Professor in the Department of Communication studies at the University of Antwerp and Deputy Director of the Visual Studies and Media Culture Research Group. He has published recently on historical and contemporary film cultures in *Screen* (2010), *The Handbook of Political Economy of Communications* (2010), *Javnost – The Public* (2011) and *Communications* (2011). Together with Richard Maltby and Daniel Biltereyst, he edited *Explorations in New Cinema History: Approaches and Case Studies* (Wiley-Blackwell, 2011) and *Cinema, Audiences and Modernity. New Perspectives on European Cinema History* (Routledge, 2012).

Albert Moran is a Professor in the School of Humanities at Griffith University. He is a pioneer contributor to the critical study of Australian film and television history, and founded the international TV studies sub-field of program formats. Recent books and collections include *Cultural Adaptation* (with Michael Keane, –Taylor & Francis, 2010) and *TV Format Mogul: Reg Grundy's Global Career* (Intellect, 2013).

Alan O'Leary is Associate Professor in Italian at the University of Leeds. His monograph *Tragedia all'italiana: Italian Cinema and Italian Terrorisms, 1970–2010* was published by Peter Lang in 2011, and he has co-edited two volumes on similar themes. *Fenomenologia del cinepanettone,* his study of the Italian Christmas film, is published by Rubbettino (2013). He co-founded the annual Film Issue of the *Italianist* and edited the issue between 2009 and 2013. He also co-edited 'Thinking Italian Film', the influential special edition of *Italian Studies,* with Catherine O'Rawe (2008).

Catherine O'Rawe is Senior Lecturer in Italian at Bristol University. She is the co-editor of *The Femme Fatale: Images, Histories, Contexts* (Palgrave, 2010), and of the special issue of *Italian Studies* on 'Thinking Italian Film' (2008). She has articles published and in press on contemporary popular Italian cinema, and on Italian cinema of the 1940s.

Clara Pafort-Overduin teaches film and television history in the Department of Media and Culture Studies at Utrecht University. Her research concerns the popularity of Dutch films in the 1930s. She is interested in social, economic and cultural aspects of film popularity, and published about this with economic historian John Segdwick and marketing economist Jaap Boter. Together with Douglas Gomery, she wrote the second edition of *Movie History: A Survey* (Routledge, 2011).

Tom Phillips conducted his AHRC-funded PhD research at the University of East Anglia, examining the online community of Kevin Smith fans. His research interests include fan studies, film and television comedy, and contemporary celebrity. His work has been published in *Flow, Participations* and *Transformative Works and Cultures*.

Sarah Stubbings obtained her PhD, 'From Modernity to Memorial: The Changing Meanings of the 1930s Cinema in Nottingham', from the University of Nottingham in 2003. Since then she has worked in education at the University of Nottingham and for a literacy charity, and is currently a manager at the National College for School Leadership.

Deb Verhoeven is Professor and Chair of Media and Communication at Deakin University, Melbourne. Her most recent book is *Jane Campion* (Routledge, 2009). In addition to her publications, Verhoeven has focused her attention on the development of online research resources, particularly the development of databases and the introduction of digital research methodologies in film and media studies. In 2010, this work was recognized by the Australian Teachers of Media (Best Tertiary Education Resource Award for *bonza: an online film and TV research resource*).

Mike Walsh is an Associate Professor in the Department of Screen and Media at Flinders University, Adelaide. He is also a programmer for the Adelaide Film Festival. He has published on Australian and Asian cinema in numerous anthologies and journals. He is currently working on a history of the South Australian Film Corporation.

Introduction: New Perspectives on Movie-going, Exhibition and Reception

Karina Aveyard and Albert Moran

In the film *Sullivan's Travels* (1941), writer-director Preston Sturges presents a comedy about Hollywood. The protagonist, John L. Sullivan, is himself a highly successful writer and director of comedy films. However, he has come to regard comedy as meaningless. He has hopes to direct a film with a more socially uplifting 'message' about the poor, which he has entitled *O Brother Where Art Thou?* Criticized by his staff as having no experience of what it is like to be 'down and out', Sullivan decides **to** take to the road, pretending to be a hobo. By chance, he ends up in prison, working on a chain gang in the Deep South of the United States. One night, he and his fellow prisoners are taken to an Afro-American church where the curtains are drawn, a sheet is hung as a screen and a projector is set up. He and the other convicts are treated to a light-hearted program of cartoons beginning with *Mickey Mouse*. Sullivan finds himself howling with laughter, as do his fellow prisoners. A simple narrative ruse sees Sullivan released from prison and returned to his Hollywood workplace, where he announces to the surprise of his aides that he plans to return to comedy and will not direct the script of *O Brother Where Art Thou?*

Over half a century later, the Coen brothers released a film of exactly that name (2000). This was another feature comedy with another protagonist on the run after escaping from a Southern chain gang. However, apart from the use of the fictional John L. Sullivan's unfilmed script as its title, there is no other overt reference to the Preston Sturges film in the Coen brothers' movie. There are, though, many references and homages to other works of art – including a literary one to Homer's *Odyssey* and a cinematic one to *Cool Hand Luke* (1967).

A DVD dust jacket for the film begins its background notes as follows: 'This masterpiece by Preston Sturges is perhaps the finest movie-about-a-movie ever made'. Maybe … But for our purposes, its interest lies elsewhere. John L. Sullivan's travels are in fact the fieldwork undertaken by a media professional as a means of further informing his craft. Like the good anthropologist that he is, he 'goes native', becoming a participant observer of the milieu that he seeks to represent. He returns to Hollywood at the end of the film a more reflective practitioner, more aware and responsive to his dispersed and unseen audience.

That was 1941. However, when the Coen brothers released their version of Sullivan's fictional script, *O Brother Where Art Thou?*, in 2000, they could assume a greater cinematic (and literary) sophistication on the part of their audience. Their film fiction was able to dispense entirely with the narrative machinery of a movie-within-a-movie even though it too displays an even higher degree of filmic knowingness than the Preston Sturges film. Thompson and Bordwell date the onset of this enhanced cinematic sophistication and knowingness back to the 1960s, seeing it as part of a more profound socio-cultural shift in western society whereby mass culture displaced older frameworks of meaning that had been based primarily on the Bible (2010: 661–92).

The path traversed from *Sullivan's Travels* to *O Brother Where Art Thou?* forms part of the background to *Watching Films*, a collection that offers new bearings on film audiences, movie-going, exhibition and reception. This book assembles a series of chapters that look at the social, economic and cultural formations that have influenced the circulation, presentation and consumption of film from the early twentieth century to the present day. The analyses range from micro-studies of particular locations and events through to reflections on national and even global scales.

New bearings require new approaches. *Watching Films* is anchored in the innovative, open and interdisciplinary practice of film-related inquiry established over the past decade by such scholars as Richard Maltby, Robert Allen, Daniel Biltereyst, Douglas Gomery, Mark Jancovich and Philippe Meers. The key shift within this field of 'new cinema history' (Maltby et al. 2011) has been the move away from the text as the primary focus of investigation. Instead, what this development has brought sharply into view is the importance of the institutional and geographic frameworks that direct and control the film viewing experience and the wider socio-cultural situation of the audience. Collectively, this research has made a major contribution to expanding our understanding of what cinema is and the almost infinite possibilities of what the act of film consumption can mean.

While many of the chapters in this collection have strong conceptual and methodological links to new cinema history, they also take us further by delving into new subjects and introducing further innovative approaches to analysis and interpretation. We see this work as contributing to expanding critical discourse in three significant ways. First, by integrating contemporary and historical perspectives, it draws attention to and helps address the significant gaps in knowledge that exist around the experience of film screening and viewing in spaces outside the cinema. Second, this volume explores the matter of how greater attention to the role of the film as a text might productively contribute to the widening scope of movie viewing studies. Third, the collection helps to highlight how little we know about the meaning of the modern popular film experience.

Before turning to the significance of the contemporary research showcased in this volume, one clarification is in order. This concerns history and the fact that it is possible to regard all cinema scholarship as historical. Until something has happened – a film is made and/or screened to however small an audience – it is arguable that the preconditions for investigating its meaning and impact do not exist. However, some events are clearly more recent than others, and have a greater relevance for and impact on current industrial and viewing practices. For the purpose of this discussion, we distinguish the trends of the past two decades from earlier chronological periods by referring to them as contemporary.

Viewing outside the cinema

One of the most significant changes to have occurred in film consumption over the past century or so has been the development and widespread adoption of home and mobile viewing technologies. Domestic audiovisual technologies have been with us for a considerable period – popular television since the 1950s, home video since the early 1980s and the Internet since the mid-1990s. Their presence in the home has become commonplace and integral to the leisure and entertainment activities of many households. Non-theatrical windows, such as video, DVD, cable and broadcast television, now represent as much as 70 per cent of the revenues generated by Hollywood studio films (Belton 2002: 107). In Australia, for example, the value of retail DVD sales surpassed cinema box office revenues for the first time in 2003, and has exceeded it every year since (Screen Australia 2011a, 2011b).

Essays in this volume by Janna Jones and Julia Knight in particular, directly address movie circulation and consumption in these 'other' situations. Contributors including Douglas Gomery and Mike Walsh offer new perspectives on the wider industrial and economic factors that have shaped the integration of new formats into the viewing landscape.

The place of the film

As we have outlined, the critical shift that has taken us beyond textually centred analysis of films and their reception has greatly enhanced and expanded the field of cinema studies. In our enthusiasm for the rich new perspectives that have emerged from this shift, however, the role of the film as an integrated part of the viewing experience has become somewhat obscured. Part of the explanation for this may be attributed to the findings that have emerged from cinema memory research. These studies have demonstrated that audiences do not tend to anchor their cinema-going memories around individual films. Annette Kuhn explains that films texts are often not useful for the purpose of recounting narratives of life events, which tend to figure prominently in memories of cinema-going (1995: 166). In a similar vein, Richard Maltby asserts that films 'do not seek out landmark status for themselves but are designed to fade back into the overall field of our cultural experiences' (2011: 11).

Several of the chapters in this volume suggest that these arguments are also relevant in contemporary contexts. Adrian Mabbott Athique notes that among audiences at multiplex cinemas in India, the programming tends to be far less important than the quality of seats and the person whom one sits alongside. Similarly, Janna Jones' study of the viewing experiences of Gen Y audiences in the United States indicates that film viewing was perhaps most significant for the role it played in enhancing family relationships than for the movies that were consumed.

However, the fact that movies do not figure prominently in reconstructions of viewing experiences does not necessarily mean they were not important at the time they were consumed. Several of the chapters in this volume, including those by Albert Moran and

Eylem Akatav, widen the scope of this speculation by presenting structural and experiential perspectives on viewing that more closely integrate on-screen and off-screen factors. More overtly, Clara Pafort-Overduin reasserts the place of the film in her chapter as follows:

> Much as we should avoid a too film centric approach, we should also not fall into the trap that the film is not important at all. Though viewers may not remember much about the films they watched (Kuhn, 2002) and the measurable effects these might have had on their worldview, ultimately, they do represent a positive decision. Even in a one cinema town, there is always the choice between entering and passing by.

The popular film experience

This collection helps bring into focus a third key issue for critical inquiry: the blind spot that exists in relation to studies of the contemporary popular film experience. Cinema research has embraced the institutions and audiences of popular film in historical contexts, but there has been considerably less engagement with its contemporary incarnations, particularly insofar as audiences are concerned. Most of what we know about popular film viewing has instead come from the fields of reception and cultural studies (e.g. see Barker and Mathijs 2008; Storey 2003: 72–86; Tinkcom and Villarejo 2001; Sandler and Studlar 1999; Barker and Brooks 1988).

The proliferation of large, multi-screen movie theatres has received some attention, although most of this work has been focused on the multiplex's economic and structural implications for the film industry (e.g. see Gomery 1992: 103–18; Acland 2003; Allison 2006), or on its implications for non-Western cinema-going (see Athique and Hill 2010; Falicov 2007). With regard to multiplex audiences in other contexts, the major study by Phil Hubbard of cinema-goers in the UK city of Leicester has been highly influential (2002, 2003). In one of the few detailed investigations of Western multiplex audience behaviour to date, Hubbard emphasizes two key features of the experience. First, the main attraction of the multiplex is its predictability and its isolation from the streetscape, which is able to shield patrons from the potential hazards of less-regulated public spaces. In this respect, Hubbard frames a visit to the multiplex as an exercise in 'risking the riskless' (2003: 267). Second, Hubbard contends that the commercial transactions and socialization that go on among multiplex patrons is relatively superficial; it is a place where patrons 'can interact "lightly" without too much riding on the outcome' (2003: 267). The implication is that multiplexes are not places where audiences can expect to be challenged, confronted or find too much excitement.

This conceptualization of the unadventurous and duped consumer has also found a place within broader concerns about the degeneration of once-dynamic town centres, the rise in banal suburban shopping malls, and the standardization and increasing corporatization of retail and leisure activities (e.g. see Odenheimer 2006; Voyce 2006; Sit et al. 2003; Jones

2003). Within these studies of urban trends, there is a tendency to see the rise of the mall and its cinemas as an undesirable and negative development – one that has eroded the social vibrancy and cultural meanings of commerce and entertainment.

But such a viewpoint is surely too reductionist, given that multiplexes – and shopping centres more broadly – attract millions of consumers from such a diverse range of backgrounds. It is entirely possible for sentient consumers to buy goods at a mall that fulfil a useful, practical purpose, even if these are influenced by marketing spin. It is also equally possible to have an enjoyable and even memorable time watching a film in a multiplex cinema. In the absence of more detailed and wide-ranging research on the popular film experience, it is premature to dismiss multiplexes as places for 'indulgence in trash' and as soulless 'film supermarkets' (Barker and Brooks 1998: 195; Edmonson in Scarano 2009). In doing so, we risk culturally devaluing the way in which the majority of people – at least in western countries – experience the cinema. Another concern within this discourse is the implied audience passivity – a concept in relation to viewing that many scholars rejected decades ago. As Barker and colleagues assert, 'nobody ever just "happens" to watch a film at the cinema' (2008: 14).

Crystallizing this argument, the chapter by Alan O'Leary and Catherine O'Rawe explores the cultural significance of popular Italian film from the perspective of the spectator. While these films have become a focus for distaste and reproach among film critics, mainstream audiences flock to see them. Moving beyond the culturally loaded assessment of these as 'bad' films, the authors instead consider the significance and impact of these movies on the everyday lives of those who enjoy them. Chapters in this volume by Geoff Lealand and Stuart Hanson also contribute to expanding our horizons on the detail and meaning of the popular cinematic experience.

We turn now to a more systematic presentation of the contents of this volume.

Watching films: the collection

In framing this volume, we began with four key questions: Who watches films? Under what circumstances? What consequences and affects follow? And what do these acts of consumption mean? These propositions echo Harold Lasswell's classic approach to content analysis – 'who says what, to whom, why, to what extent and with what effect?' (1971). Our initial questions proved a useful starting point for structuring perspectives around the activity of movie consumption. However, on more detailed reflection, the apparent isolation and autonomy of these categories – at least so far as the activity of watching film is concerned – began to break down. 'Who', for instance, concerns not only those who create content but also those involved elsewhere in the media industries, in production, distribution, programming and exhibition. Similarly, audiences engaged in perceiving the 'what' of film are not simply absorbing a predetermined spectacle. They are actively filtering and reimagining what they are seeing. In doing so, viewers construct individual patterns and personalized meanings from such materials.

Thus, we shifted back to our four questions, which we reworked as five categories. These more usefully and accurately reflect the fluidity and cross-referencing of the original research queries. Part I: Theoretical Perspectives, is concerned with how we (scholars) interpret and account for industry and viewing practices. It also offers some reflections on the practice and inherent value of critical research. From there the volume is notionally divided into two parts. Part II: The Film Industry: Systems and Practice and Part III: Movie Theatres: From Picture Palace to the Multiplex are concerned with how the film industry and its attendant institutions attempt to regulate and control the framework of mainstream viewing. The remaining two parts (Part IV: On the Margins and Part V: Just Watching Movies?) centre on exploring the various indirect, unconscious and deliberate attempts by movie-goers and other industry participants to fix the experience of film watching outside the confines of commercial imperatives.

Part I: Theoretical perspectives

The interest of this first section is prefatory. It presents philosophical and conceptual considerations as a springboard to critical thinking about film viewing. Such reflection might once have been bracketed under the label of 'theory', but such a name here would create false expectations for the closely interrelated research activities of reflection and detailed investigations that are common to many of the chapters in the following parts. Instead, the aim in this part is to offer some middle-range theory-building. What unites the five chapters here is the fact that they are more explicitly concerned with preliminary matters of knowledge construction than others in the volume. They should be read against a background of reflexive interrogations such as: What, in this instance, is to count as knowledge? How might that knowledge be identified and labelled? How might such considerations be investigated and researched? and How might such awareness be presented, circulated and developed?

We begin in Chapter 1 with Daniel Biltereyst's re-examination of the link between cinema and early twentieth-century modernization. Prioritizing the film audience and pointing to their role as both agents and consumers of change, Biltereyst highlights many of the conceptual complexities and contradictions within the ongoing cinema-modernity debate. The title of Chapter 2 by Deb Verhoeven recalls André Bazin's famous inquiry even as it suggests how such an interrogation might be reconstituted in the present age of the digital. 'Closure' and 'change', Verhoeven suggests, are of constitutive importance as critical tools for rethinking our defining assumptions about cinemas as a collective entity and as a cultural and social institution.

Chapter 3 by Albert Moran focuses on analysis of popular American films of the 1940s, the object being to identify a body of feature films that might provide clues to later historians about the ideological landscape of the time. Chapter 4 by Louise Anderson follows and reflects on the fluid and interdisciplinary practice of cinema memory research – in this case, into newsreel audiences.

The final chapter in this section, by Alan McKee, sets about answering the startling question posed in the title of his contribution. His considered analysis sits in contrast to the often overly emotional inquiries by government and social agencies. Instead, critical inquiry as practised by McKee – and, indeed, by all the other contributors to this volume – subjects itself to rigours of method, context, reference and peer review, thereby opening itself up to necessary tests of corrigibility and more robust conclusions.

Part II: The film industry – systems and practices

Part II also focuses on matters that are more empirical and pragmatic. Its aim is to locate the activity of film viewing within a much larger landscape, which we term 'the industry'. Media industries are powerful money-making and cultural entities located within an even more impressive landscape comprising political, regulatory, commercial, social and even religious institutions that can all have a determining effect on conditions under which audiences look at films.

Chapters 6 and 7 take historic moments of industry change as opportunities to contemplate the peculiar pressures that are brought to bear on exhibition. Chapter 6 by Kathryn Fuller-Seeley examines the use of movie-star personalities to promote films in the first decade of twentieth century, and looks at how this helped create the cult of the picture personality that was later centralized and used to great effect by Hollywood. Mike Walsh's Chapter 7 deconstructs a number of the key industrial assumptions to do with the introduction of television broadcasting in Australia in the 1950s.

Geoff Lealand's Chapter 8 considers the film audience in New Zealand. His study is wide ranging and informative, and incorporates an industry-wide approach to the particular subject of exhibition. He notes the anomaly that although the film production industry was only established (or re-established) in the 1970s, it is far better known and studied than the exhibition sector.

The mega forces indicated in this section can also affect film viewing at the local, micro level. Hence, in Chapter 9, Eylem Akatav adopts a case study approach, taking the distribution story of the film *Certified Copy* as her object of inquiry. Her chapter suggests that a film's meanings for audiences are not necessarily fixed and stable, but can be recontextualized by such mechanisms as film press kits and reviews.

Part III: Movie theatres – from picture palace to the multiplex

One crucial consideration was bracketed out in the previous discussion of the film industry: the relevance of geography, an issue that is taken up in this part of the book. Watching films in commercial theatres is inevitably and unavoidably tied to the physical places and cinematic spaces in which it occurs. This group of chapters traces the contours of the major cinema developments from the emergence of the grand picture palaces of the early twentieth century to the forces driving the more recent multiplex construction boom. They demonstrate how particular geographic places, with their unique social, cultural and economic forces, have contributed to shaping the possibilities and characteristics of film exhibition in the past and the present.

The first two chapters in this section focus on the early decades of cinema, and in particular on the impact of the national theatre chains that emerged in the United States from the 1920s. In Chapter 10, Douglas Gomery examines exhibition in the Shenandoah Valley of Virginia. He details the entry of Warner Bros into the local market in the late 1920s and the coexistence and conflict that arose between this major company and the region's independent operators. Jeff Klenotic's study of the Paramount Theatre in Springfield in Chapter 11 further enriches our understanding of picture theatre development in the United States outside the major cities. Looking at the entry of the national chain exhibitor Paramount-Publix into the local market in Springfield, Klenotic demonstrates how the theatre was welcomed by residents, offering them greater access to films and functioning as a luxurious, aspirational social space, as well as helping the community to come to grips with urban modernization.

Across the Atlantic, in the United Kingdom, Mark Jancovich, Lucy Faire and Sarah Stubbings examine the regional significance of cinema construction in Nottingham in the late 1910s and 1920s in Chapter 12. This material is drawn from their larger study of movie-going developments in the city over the course of the twentieth century – a pioneering project that made a major contribution to broadening the scope of cinema studies (2003).

In Chapter 13, Kathleen Lotze and Philippe Meers guide us into the post-World War II period with their examination of cinema culture in Antwerp, Belgium in the middle decades of the twentieth century. Concerned with situating exhibition within its wider spatial contexts, Lotze and Meers utilize cinema programming data, information about theatre infrastructure and audience memories to construct a multi-faceted view of movie-going in the city. Taking up the most recent phase in the development of public cinema, in Chapter 14 Stuart Hanson looks at the development of multiplexes in Britain since the 1990s. This analysis details the way in which the construction of multi-screen cinemas has intrinsically been linked to changes within city centres and their shifting focus as a site for retail activity.

In Part IV, we shift focus from the mainstream to the periphery – film places and economies that exist outside the interests of large corporations.

Part IV: On the margins

As the chapters in the previous part highlight, the activity of film viewing is highly contested. On the one hand, it posits the rigid frameworks of the film industry and other institutions against the more fluid and reactive dynamic of socio-cultural forces. While at the populist centre the corporatized processes of production, distribution and exhibition are able to maintain their hold, towards the periphery they become inherently less stable. Alongside mainstream theatres and popular movies, there have always existed groups of would-be film viewers unable or unwilling to participate in cinema under the terms set by the mainstream. The chapters in this part explore how various non-mainstream interests have attempted to structure different conditions of engagement with the medium of film.

In Chapter 15, Ian Goode examines the origins and workings of the publicly funded Highlands and Islands Film Guild in rural Scotland from the late 1940s. Examining non-mainstream cinema as a site of identity and cultural differentiation, in Chapter 16 Ian Huffer surveys the contemporary independent cinema exhibition environment in Wellington, New Zealand, exploring how the city's non-aligned movie theatres tap into a distinctive market by consciously setting themselves against the mainstream.

Turning to the question of how non-mainstream films reach an audience, in Chapter 17 Julia Knight examines the business history of niche distribution company, Cinema of Women, which operated in the United Kingdom during the 1980s. While the company handled specialist feminist films, it pursued its education and empowerment agenda by working hard to place its product in mainstream cinemas and with major television broadcasters. Finally, in Chapter 18 Tom Phillips examines the social dynamics of movie fandom among online followers of US cult filmmaker Kevin Smith. Based on detailed ethnographic research, Phillips identifies an interesting trend away from Smith as a media producer towards the notions of fans as a (self-defined) community.

Part V: Just watching movies?

At its most straightforward, film viewing is an act of engagement with an audio-visual text. As reception studies have demonstrated, this interaction can be profound, multi-layered, complex and superficial. However, it can be both reductive and limiting to see consumption only in these terms (Jancovich et al. 2003: 3–4, Morley 1992: 157–58). Watching a film is also about the people with whom the experience is shared, as well as the moment in time and the place in which it occurs. Studies that have embraced this wider conceptualization of viewing have been central to the development of the 'new cinema history' field of research, and instrumental in widening our perception of what 'watching' means.

In Chapter 19, Clara Pafort-Overduin explores how audiences historically have engaged with popular films. Drawing upon extensive and detailed research of cinemas and films in 22 Dutch cities, this chapter examines distribution patterns, regional demographic and differences in cinema aesthetics. Expanding the analysis of popular film, in Chapter 20, Alan O'Leary and Catherine O'Rawe interrogate the negative critical and academic attitudes that exist towards mainstream cinema and its audience in contemporary Italy. Looking in detail at two popular genres – the teen film and Italian Christmas comedies (also known as *cinepanettoni*) – the chapter contends that these films and their viewers are a central, if repressed and maligned, part of Italy's cinematic imaginary.

Continuing the focus on popular film experiences, in Chapter 21 Adrian Mabbott Athique examines social stratification at multiplexes in India. He explores the place of these cinemas as sites of middle-class aspiration. Based on richly detailed material emanating from student essays, the final chapter in the collection, by Janna Jones, investigates and lays bare some myths about Gen Y movie audiences. Her analysis offers an important counter-perspective to narratives wedded to the notion of the isolated and disconnected youth consumer.

In summary, these chapters bring together a thoughtful, stimulating and rich series of insights about the activity of watching films that range widely in approach as well as in terms of time and place. The collection expands the field of cinema viewing research, poses new questions and opens new horizons to this fascinating area of practice and study. Audiences very often do their film watching in the dark, but there is no excuse for critical investigators to remain fog-bound in a similar situation.

References

Acland, C.R. (2003), *Screen Traffic: Movies, Multiplexes and Global Culture*, Durham, NC: Duke University Press.

Allison, D. (2006), 'Multiplex Programming in the UK: The Economics of Homogeneity', *Screen*, 47: 1, pp. 81–90.

Athique, A. and Hill, D. (2010), *The Multiplex in India: a Cultural Economy of Urban Leisure*, London and New York: Routledge.

Barker, M. and Brooks, K. (1998), *Knowing Audiences: Judge Dredd, its Friends, Fans and Foes*, Luton: University of Luton Press.

Barker, M., Egan, K., Jones, S. and Mathijs, E. (2008), 'Researching *The Lord of the Rings*: Audiences and Contexts', in M. Barker and E. Mathijs (eds), *Watching The Lord of the Rings: Tolkien's World Audience*, New York: Peter Lang.

Barker, M. and Mathijs, E. (eds) (2008), *Watching The Lord of the Rings: Tolkien's World Audience*, New York: Peter Lang.

Belton, J. (2002), 'Digital Cinema: A False Revolution', *October*, 100 (Spring), pp. 98–114.

Edmonson, R. interviewed in Scarano, A. (2009), *Electric Shadows: The Story of a Cinema*, documentary film, Canberra: Ronin Films and Scarnett, at time code 10.15.

Falicov, T. (2007), *The Cinematic Tango: Contemporary Argentine Film*, London: Wallflower Press.

Gomery, D. (1992), *Shared Pleasures: A History of Movie Presentation in the United States*, Madison, WI: University of Wisconsin Press.

Hubbard, P. (2002), 'Screen-shifting: Consumption, "Riskless Risks" and the Changing Geographies of Cinema', *Environment and Planning A*, 34, pp. 1239–58.

——— (2003), 'A Good Night Out? Multiplex Cinemas as Sites of Embodied Leisure', *Leisure Studies*, 22: 3, pp. 255–72.

Jancovich, M. and Faire, L. with Stubbings, S. (2003), *The Place of the Audience: Cultural Geographies of Film Consumption*, London: British Film Institute.

Jones, J. (2003), *The Southern Movie Palace: Rise, Fall and Resurrection*, Gainesville, FL: University Press of Florida.

Kuhn, A. (1995), *Family Secrets: Acts of Memory and Imagination*, London: Verso.

—— (2002), *An Everyday Magic: Cinema and Cultural Memory*, London and New York: I.B. Tauris.

Lasswell, H. (1971 [1948]), 'The Structure and Function of Communication in Society', in W. Schramm and D.F. Roberts (eds), *The Process and Effects of Mass Communication*, Urbana, IL: University of Illinois Press, pp. 84–99.

Maltby, R. (2011), 'New Cinema Histories' in R. Maltby, D. Biltereyst and P. Meers (eds), *Explorations in New Cinema Histories: Approaches and Case Studies*, Malden: Wiley-Blackwell, pp. 3–40.

Maltby, R., Biltereyst, D. and Meers, P. (eds) (2011), *Explorations in New Cinema Histories: Approaches and Case Studies*, Malden: Wiley-Blackwell.

Morley, D. (1992), *Television, Audiences and Cultural Studies*, London: Routledge.

Odenheimer, M. (2006), 'The End of Public Space: Israel's New Shopping Malls', *Tikkun*, 21: 1, pp. 29–30, 62–64.

Sandler, K. and Studlar, G. (eds) (1999), *Titanic: Anatomy of a Blockbuster*, Piscataway, NJ: Rutgers University Press.

Screen Australia (2011a), 'Cinema Admission and Key Events 1901–2009', http://www.screenaustralia.gov.au/research/statistics/wchistsince1900.asp. Accessed 5 March 2011.

—— (2011b), 'Units and Value of Video Product (DVD, Blu-ray and VHS) Sold', 1998–2009, http://www.screenaustralia.gov.au/research/statistics/wvprodretail.asp. Accessed 22 January 2011.

Sit, J., Merrilees, B. and Birch, D. (2003), 'Entertainment-seeking Shopping Centre Patrons: The Missing Segments', *International Journal of Retail & Distribution Management*, 31: 2, pp. 80–94.

Storey, J. (2003), *Cultural Studies and the Study of Popular Culture*, 2nd edn, Athens, GA: University of Georgia Press.

Thompson, K. and Bordwell, D. (2010), *Film History: An Introduction*, New York: McGraw Hill.

Tinkcom, M. and Villarejo, A. (eds) (2001), *Keyframes: Popular Cinema and Cultural Studies*, London and New York: Routledge.

Voyce, M. (2006), 'Shopping Malls in Australia: The End of Public Space and the Rise of "Consumerist Citizenship"?', *Journal of Sociology*, 42: 3, pp. 269–86.

PART I

Theoretical Perspectives

Chapter 1

Cinema, Modernity and Audiences: Revisiting and Expanding the Debate

Daniel Biltereyst

I was struck by how little the audience or even exhibition featured in the received film history ... film history had been written as if films had no audiences or were seen by everyone and in the same way.

(Allen 1990: 348)

Introduction: audiences and the institutional turn

In his frequently cited *Screen* article on audiences and film history, written in the early 1990s, Robert C. Allen makes an appeal for a more thorough and empirically oriented inquiry into film audiences and reception. Hoping that 'no film scholar would write a serious film history with the near elision of the audience', Allen perceived reception to be more than merely including references to audience figures or exhibition contexts (1990: 348). Reception encompassed the confrontation between the semiotic and the social – or, in a similar phrasing, the tension between the film text on the one hand and the historical conditions and mechanisms of reception on the other. For Allen, this dichotomy implies that film historical scholarship requires the acknowledgement of 'what generalizable forces help to account for the unstudiable and for any individual investigator, incomprehensibly numerous and diverse instances of reception' (1990: 355–56). Likewise, scholars such as Janet Staiger (1992) and Michèle Lagny (1994) compellingly voice this necessity for a more ambitious research agenda on historical audiences, and their interrelationship with broader societal forces. Lagny insists on the importance of conceiving cinema as an open field, 'where different forces (economic, social, political, technical, cultural or aesthetic) come into being and confront each other' (1994: 41). Although film is 'an essential tool' for understanding the 'period ranging from the end of the 19th century and the time in the 20th century during which it had been the most important form of visual mass entertainment', Lagny argues that 'political and social conflicts, economic structures and circumstances leave institutional traces which are more relevant than film' (1994: 26). Lagny's ideal conception of film history, which leaves ample space to wider institutional histories, includes 'an articulation among three types of analysis, dealing with cultural objects, with the framework of their creation, making and circulation, and finally with their consumption' (1994: 27).

Two decades later, one might assert that this call for a more zealous and empirically grounded research curriculum on audiences and reception has been heard. Over the past 15 years, a wide range of studies on historical film audiences appeared in journals, monographs and edited volumes, all explicitly aiming to get beyond the screen and textual interpretations of films in order to understand cinema as a more complex social phenomenon (e.g. Biltereyst et al. 2012; Fuller-Seeley 2008; Kuhn 2002; Stokes and Maltby 1999). In the introduction to a recent volume on 'new cinema history', Richard Maltby argues that in recent years a shared effort has engaged 'contributors from different points on the disciplinary compass, including history, geography, cultural studies, economics, sociology and anthropology, as well as film and media studies' in order to examine the circulation and consumption of films, or cinema 'as a site of social and cultural exchange' (2011: 3). Other recent volumes, which aim to display ways of conducting film history and film historiographic methodologies, now clearly contain sections on audiences, reception or consumption (e.g. Chapman et al. 2007; Lewis and Smoodin 2007).

This emerging international trend of historical film audience and reception studies encompasses the usage of a wide variety of methods, theoretical underpinnings, temporal and spatial limitations. In an attempt to grab the historical audience, scholars make quantitative analyses of box-office revenues (e.g. Sedgwick, 2011); they use corporate reports or other recordings and testimonies on the audience coming from the industry (e.g. Sullivan 2010); researchers turn to programming analyses in order to understand what cinemagoers saw in what kind of theatres in what kind of locations (e.g. Biltereyst et al. 2011); they examine letters and other traces left by historical film fans; they use questionnaires or started to interview older cinemagoers (e.g. Taylor 1989). There has been a move away from the idea of the nationwide survey or the mass audience, stimulating the examination of more local forms of film culture or city-related social experiences of movie-going (e.g. Moore 2008). Research into film audiences and reception now includes the examination of top-down institutional and corporate strategies, as well as bottom-up experiences, reminiscent of the intellectual tradition of cultural and memory studies, thereby using sophisticated oral history methods (e.g. Kuhn 2002).

This redirection of film studies has brought forward many new insights on exhibition, distribution and programming strategies, as well as on different levels of the social experience of cinema-going and audience engagement with films. Besides difficulties related to multi-methodological work, one could raise the question of how these case studies on all those levels can be integrated into a more coherent explanation of some of the key issues within film history and theory. One of these issues relays to the connection between cinema, modernity and the experiences of metropolitan urbanity (Gunning 2005). As well as addressing questions about the temporal and spatial confines of the cinema-modernity debate, this chapter will revise and expand this debate by bringing in some of the insights coming from recent historical audience and reception research. Questions of audience engagement with cinema, we argue, are crucial to better understanding the socio-historical and cultural role of cinema in mediating modernity.[1] When discussing cinema's role in modernity and the audience's engagement with it, it is also necessary to relate questions of audiences or human agency to broader issues of structural determinacy and institutional control.

Revisiting the cinema, modernity and metropolis debate

Since the end of the 1980s, an interesting debate has emerged within film studies on the intertwining of the cinema and modernity. Drawing on the work of Charles Baudelaire, Georg Simmel, Walter Benjamin, Siegfried Kracauer and other early writers on everyday life in modern society (Schwartz and Przyblyski 2004), a whole series of film scholars – including some of the most prominent writers in the field (e.g. Casetti 2005; Charney 1998; Charney and Schwartz 1995; Doane 2002; Gunning 1998, 2005, 2006; Keil and Stamp 2004; Singer 2001) – has claimed that early cinema embodied the idea of modernity produced by urban cultural change. Arguing that cinema emerged as a technology and grew as a popular mass medium at the time of massive technological and societal change (mediated communication, urbanization, transportation, electrification, commodification, the growth of consumer capitalism and society, and individualization), scholars tried to understand this interrelationship in terms of a similar experience of modernity. As a new technology of reproduction, representation and perception, cinema was not only a contingent part and a consequence of modernity, it was also a vital component of modernization – an emblem and a catalyst of modern life characterized by a culture of novelty, shock, distraction and thrills (Singer 2001). Tom Gunning suggests that early films reflected modernity's disruption of social order by representing 'the experience of urban life with its threats and danger', embracing 'modern technology or new environments', focusing on 'female subjectivity' and emphasizing 'the heightened involvement of a viewer in a visual illusion combined with motion' (1998: 266). Referring to modernity as a culture of shocks and cinema as a reflection of this, Gunning's understanding of the cinema of attractions identifies a type of filmmaking that solicited spectator attention through visual curiosity, exciting spectacle, surprise, fragmentation, speed, shock, brevity and confrontation, promoting a particular gaze or perception.

In the 1990s and 2000s, this body of work stimulated a debate on the characteristics of early films, the kind of spectatorship they included and the perceptual changes they might have stimulated. Many of these arguments were heavily criticized – also by some of the leading scholars in the field, like David Bordwell, who identified the position as advancing the 'modernity thesis' (1997: 143). One level of the criticism relates to the thesis's thoughts about changes in human perception brought about by the condition of modern life and the role played in this process by motion pictures – matters, Noël Carroll argues, that are 'better left to experimental investigation rather than to armchair speculation' (2001: 16). Questions were also raised about the attempts to tie modern experiences and the fragmentation of urban life to stylistic aspects of early cinema (Bordwell 1997: 143–46). Claiming that the advocates of the thesis tend to exaggerate the reflection of urban modernity in movies and pay less attention to alternative styles of film, Joe Kember provides examples of early film-makers demonstrating a 'fascination with bucolic rural life', with 'exotic locations' and with 'the wilderness' (2009: 18). In his exploration of an institutional account of the early film industry, Kember forcefully argues that film institutions tended to *market* modernity and otherness by explicitly promoting cinema's capacity to offer spectacular and disruptive material. Early film shows, he maintains, tried to stitch themselves 'into the fabric of everyday life', and a 'substantial part of the enterprise of such shows involved a revalidation of existing concepts of selfhood and community on behalf of audiences'. Rather than breaking down traditional notions of community, Kember proposes, the film industry 'participated fully in modernity's fascination with, and repackaging of, very traditional social forms' (2009: 213–14). As a result, 'early cinema needs to be seen as a dynamic, responsive environment which developed multiple relationships – sometimes at the same time – with its varied audiences, and which therefore proliferated experiences of intimacy, empathy, curiosity, reassurance and mastery for individual spectators in place of those it was widely accused of undermining' (2009: 213).

A key topic in the cinema-modernity debate, which is central to this chapter, relates to the audience. One might argue that, in general, the modernity thesis starts from an apparatus-led and textually constructed spectator who, according to Francesco Casetti, is absorbed and 'immersed in the spectacle and the environment' (1998: 166). The cinematographic apparatus 'encourages a fusion between subject and object and between subject and environment', so that it renders 'subjects – particularly their bodies – "docile"' (1998: 176). This conceptualization of the spectator and the new sensory and bodily experiences of cinema is mostly closely linked to the metropolitan experience of speed, surprise, visual curiosity and the practice of seeing without being seen (Charney 1998: 75). It is also connected with Baudelaire's view of the *flâneur* in the city, so that the 'perfect *flâneur* is the passionate film spectator' (Bruno 1999: 49).

It is precisely here, at this level of the emphasis on the urban environment – the apparatus-inspired conception of the spectator and the cinematic experience – that recent empirical film audience research brings in more nuanced and critical insights. A first criticism relates to the urban environment where, as Allen (2006: 64) argues, film historians tend to be obsessed 'not just with the urban experience of cinema but the metropolitan experience'. This 'Manhattan myopia', as Allen (1996) calls it, ignores the fact that most Americans in the early period 'lived in rural and not urban settings' (Allen 2006: 63). In recent years, a large number of studies have examined the emergence of cinema in non-urban and rural areas; these have mostly reached the conclusion that the metropolitan experience is unique rather than prototypical, and that the canonical views of early cinema are not applicable to the majority of smaller cities and rural areas. The centrality of the metropolitan experience, so to speak, denies the cultural and social geographies that existed and that were related to regional and local variations. There is a recognition that, next to metropolitan versions, there were also substantial processes of modernization in non-metropolitan areas, and that cinema played a role in them (Allen 2006; Fuller-Seeley 2008). Exploring cinema's role in mediating, marketing and informing audiences about provincial and rural modernity contains the acknowledgement of specific societal configurations here, in terms of political-economic, demographic, class, race, gender and other differences (Meers et al. 2010). Apart from the examination of specific rural, small-town and regional-town geographies of film culture, a more dynamic view on a situated social history of cinema was also developed within the big city, where conditions of film consumption varied widely according to the venue and the neighbourhood, and where class-related differences played a key role (e.g. Biltereyst et al. 2011). Finally, the relationship of exchange and mutual influence between the metropolis, small towns and rural environments might offer a more nuanced view of the different particularities of local film exhibition cultures and consumption patterns (Jernudd 2012).

Another key criticism of the cinema-modernity thesis deals with its conceptualization of spectatorship – which, as Kathryn Fuller-Seeley and George Potamianos (2008: 5) claim, tends 'to transform viewers and their culture, the surrounding theaters and streets, into a vast, anonymous, homogeneous, mass audience'. Even in relation to the early period, contemporary observers underlined the more competent, active, selective and even sometimes rebellious character of film consumption. A case in point is the way the French surrealist writer André Breton gives a description of early cinema-going in his landmark novel *Nadja* (1928). The image Breton offers of movie houses in popular areas of Paris is one where people went to the cinema without really looking at what was on the program, where people talked loudly, gave their opinions about what was happening on the screen, and where cinemagoers could openly eat and drink while consuming a picture. This view, which is far away from grand theories on spectatorship, corresponds to recent research on spectatorial practices and the cinema as a lively and interactive social space, where cinema-going was very much part of the social fabric of everyday life. Cinema-goers were not only active and selective, they even became self-confident film connoisseurs who, as Andrea Haller argues, interpreted films according to their own preferences, 'laughing when others were crying', while they playfully 'embraced the various attractions on offer without fainting or becoming hysterical' (2012: 134–35).

In recent years, proponents of the cinema-modernity thesis have argued for a more complex redefinition of modernity and started to re-evaluate conceptions of cinematic style, cinema's influence on perception and spectatorship, and its reflection of and relation to modernity at large. While maintaining the central thesis that early cinema can still be understood as an essential part of the experience of modernity as a culture of speed, novelty and shock, authors like Gunning (2005, 2006) and Ben Singer (2009) recognize that this frame does not supply the total explanation for film style and the cinema-going experience. In a strong article on the paradoxes in the discourse on modernity and cinema, Singer rightly explores a more dialectical view upon modernity, suggesting that modernity is best understood as a heterogeneous arena where modern and counter-modern impulses meet – a position shared by broader sociological and other theories on modernity. The recognition of this ambivalence – or this 'ambimodernity' – is central, Singer argues, for 'expanding the model' in order to 'yield a more complex and ambiguous view upon modern culture' (2009: 38).

We will return to these 'counter-forces of antimodern sentiment' and their implications for audiences' cinema-going experiences, but Singer's proposal to expand the debate and to include the modernity sceptics' criticism suggests a more sophisticated model for understanding early cinema audiences. Rather than suggesting that the recent empirical audience and reception studies should be seen as a revisionist anti-thesis, it might be more fruitful to strive for a dialectical view where analyses of spectatorship are joined by empirical studies on the social experience of cinema. From this perspective, a multifaceted view of reception and the audience emerges, one that comprises insights on how movies might encourage, as Mary Ann Done (2002: 132) claims, 'spectatorial absorption and submission', along with understanding how audiences look at and deal with what was on the screen and what happened beyond it, in and around the site of the cinema. Next to expanding the cinema-modernity debate with more grounded empirical evidence on the reception of cinema and on cinema-going practices, it might also be fruitful to include a political-economic perspective on how film and other societal institutions have tried to guide, influence or impose constraints on movie-going practices (Biltereyst and Meers 2011). This multiplicity of the audience provides better tools for understanding, for instance, claims about the standardization or homogenization of cinema-going practices along bourgeois rules of conduct in the transitional era, or the argument that cinema in modern society underwent a gradual process of silencing and disciplining through capitalist and bourgeois notions of social order, elitism and cultural distinction (e.g. Sullivan 2010: 164–66).

Cinema, multiple modernities and institutions

Looking back at this debate on cinema and modernity, one cannot escape the idea that, even by expanding it as we suggested, a quite restricted view is taken of modernity. Besides the temporal restriction to early cinema and the transitional era, modernity was most often conceived from a rather Eurocentric, liberal, free-market perspective. Issues of cinematic modernism or the construction of modernity in movies in other regions and other social systems have been treated, of course, but again little attention has been paid to audiences. However, it might be interesting to look at some of these studies focusing on the question of how audiences in non-western environments dealt with forces of modernization or those looking at the role cinema played as a gateway to understanding the transition from a traditional to a modern society. Some of those studies insist on underlining the importance of cinema as a didactic tool, one that also has a democratizing potential. This was, for instance the case of Mexico where, as Andrea Noble writes, the cinema was 'where one went to learn how to be modern' (2006: 508). Noble argues that cinema 'mediated the effects of modernity by providing its audiences with models of modern values with which to identify and which were, moreover, reflected in the urban landscapes, technologies and patterns of consumption that played out on the screen' (2006: 510). Following Miriam Hansen's (1991) view of cinema as a potentially alternative public sphere, Noble maintains that in this intensely hierarchical

Mexican society, the cinema was 'one of the few public spaces in which different sectors of society would have encountered one another in their leisure time' (2006: 509).

Examining the cinema–modernity relation from this non-Eurocentric perspective throws up other questions like those dealing with cultural imperialism, dependency and the influence of massively imported Western mass culture. Again, though – much in line with debates on the relativist stance of empirical audience studies in other domains of media research – often actual audiences appear to have been more competent, active and selective consumers than is conceived by theoretical spectator positions. A case in point is Charles Ambler's (2001) research on movie-going in post-war Northern Rhodesia. Although the experiences of cinema in this part of the world appear to have been very different from those in western industrialized countries, Ambler comes to the conclusion that audiences 'were by no means passive consumers of cinema' (2001: 87). Audiences on the Copperbelt 'absorbed exotic images' coming from Hollywood, but they also 'appropriated and reinterpreted film images and action in their own terms'. Hollywood films even 'comprised a crucial repertoire of images through which to engage notions of modernity' (2001: 87). Even though cinema was heavily censored by the British colonial powers, movies remained a potentially dangerous medium because 'African audiences often disturbed European officials by the ways they used material from films to make judgments about the outside world, the nature of imperialism, and the character of European culture' (2001: 100).

Locally produced movies also appeared to have been important resources for audiences to develop an understanding of modernity and processes of modernization, which were often – as Dilek Kaya Mutlu (2010: 428) argues for the Turkish case – identified as a sort of Westernization. In her analysis of audiences' engagement with local melodramas and film stars, Mutlu indicates how local melodramas articulated the desire of (a typically Turkish version of) modernity, which consisted of a negotiation between traditional and 'civilized' modern values. In her analysis, Mutlu insists that in their engagement with these popular movies and their stars, audiences also negotiated between those values, and that they 'reworked and appropriated stars' off-screen images in terms of their own values, lifestyles, and dispositions'. Cinema then becomes a 'critical site where audiences meet, negotiate, and appropriate modernity … in their own terms' (2010: 48).

The Turkish case is interesting because it emphasizes the fact that in the twentieth century (and eventually today) there was more than just one modernity. The coexistence of various sorts of modernities refers to different ways of conceiving the transition from a traditional to a modern society – with differences in terms of timeframe, culture, political or ideological system. If we want to understand the importance of cinema in mediating, informing and negotiating modernity, it is necessary to acknowledge these differences, which – following Shmuel Eisenstadt's concept of 'multiple modernities' (2000) – include the simultaneity of various types of counter- or alternative forms of modernity – modernities that cinema often played an active role in helping to construct and imagine (e.g. on film policy, audiences and Fascist inspired modernity, see Manchin 2012; on film and Socialist modernity, see Skopal 2012).

As these critical variations indicate, modernity was a highly contested field and a site of struggle; this was also the case in Western liberal democracies, where forces representing counter- or even anti-modern values tried to discipline trends that were seen as dangerous or reprehensible. This view of a more ambiguous modernity (cf. ambimodernity – see Singer 2009), and the coexistence of heterogeneous tendencies within it, is closely linked to the workings of societal institutions. In this respect, we suggest that it is necessary to look more firmly for sociological theories on the role of institutions in modernity. A key theorist here is Anthony Giddens (e.g. 1991), who insists on the importance of social institutions as one of the main features distinguishing the traditional social orders from the modern ones. Institutions like the nation-state, the law, and political and economic institutions are closely linked to their capacity for promoting a system of surveillance, or the supervisory control of populations through bureaucratic means. Criticizing theoretical dualisms between structure/agency and society/individual, Giddens emphasizes that institutions and structures are not external to personal identity and human action, but rather are integrally involved in everyday practices and routines. According to Giddens, modernity's dynamism is built around the duality of structure in modern institutions, which sees institutions simultaneously constraining and enabling their subjects to act.

A crucial consequence of Giddens' view of modernity for the interrelationship with cinema relates to the power of institutions in controlling the making and consuming of movies (Kember 2009: 29–39). Looking back at film history from this perspective, one is struck by the sweeping resistance to the emergence of the medium and to its connotation for being a dangerous tool for modernization. At the risk of being accused of blatant media-centrism, one could argue that cinema has probably been among the most systematically and bureaucratically controlled institutions in the twentieth century, leading to the creation of institutions that, in almost all parts of the world, systematically scrutinized every movie for public screening. Cinema has been the object of harsh control, either in the straightforward form of censorship or in other, more sophisticated forms of discipline. In very different historical contexts, a consortium of various societal forces tried to discipline not only the production but also the free distribution and exhibition of movies, along with attempts to 'guide' audiences in their cinema-going habits and eventually tastes. Although these interventions were often inspired by local imperatives, many of the intervening forces responded to wider anxieties occasioned by cinema's modernity and its possible threat to the social order, thereby deploying discourses mostly preoccupied with the protection of children and the defence of traditional values and norms, with the aim of restoring traditions and community life, as well as with feelings of nationalism or national belonging. Much attention has been given to film-censorship institutions, government interventions and diplomatic actions; however, religious groups, grassroots, workers' and other progressive movements were also often extremely active in disciplining cinema, along with actions and censorious reactions from the film industry itself (e.g. Cronin 2009; Biltereyst and Vande Winkel 2013).

Disciplining spectatorship and audiences

If the guiding role of institutions and their attempts to constrain human action are central features of modern life, one might wonder to what degree these efforts to discipline cinema-going and audiences' experiences with movies actually were successful. It is clear that there is no clear-cut answer to this question, but again we think that recent empirical audience studies are instrumental in nuancing some of the most evident arguments in favour of confirming institutional disciplining strategies. Without going into detail, one might distinguish different levels of control and constraints on audiences' film experiences, ranging from the film text itself and its construction of a particular spectatorship to the role of advertising, the promotion of the star system and the creation of fandom as a means to influence the audience's tastes. Another level deals with the various types of film censorship and content regulation, mostly originating from the industry itself, police departments, and city or state film boards. A further level relates to strategies to put material constraints, limiting the physical capacities of viewers within and around the film venue (Kember 2009: 33). Although the film industry often promotes discourses on the consumer's sovereignty and power, various instruments of social control were developed in order to create manageable viewing habits. These means were mostly initiated by the industry, but also state regulations influenced the physical behaviour and the place given to viewers. In fact, in many countries the first legal regulations on cinemas dealt with the movie theatre's physical environment, mostly related to hygiene and the (fire) safety of the venue, along with attempts to discipline the audience's conduct. This was, for instance, the case in China, where in 1905 the Police Department of Beijing started to regulate cinema, stating that movie-goers had to conduct themselves in a civil and courteous manner and be seated separately according to their gender (Xiao 2013). A final instrument of guiding audiences, closely linked to social institutions, relates to all sorts of spatial segregations, or the process of separating people spatially as a way of making and fixing absolute differences. Much attention has been given to forms of racial segregation, especially in an American context (Stewart 2005; Allen 2006); however, as Grace Elizabeth Hale points out other forms of 'spatial mediations of modernity' existed (1998: 6). These included attempts to separate audiences along religious cleavages (see Vezyroglou 2004 on the role of the Catholic Church and the growth of parish cinema halls in France), gender (Haller 2012), political, ideological and other differences (see Jernudd 2012 on the Swedish grassroots movements and cinema).

Due to a lack of space, it is not possible here to examine all the consequences of these constraints, nor can we discuss in great detail how audiences reacted. Obviously, we might argue that this was neither a clear-cut, top-down, nor a fully bottom-up story. Empirical studies on historical film audiences, however, indicate that strategies of control might have set boundaries to how movie-goers engaged with cinema, but many examples also illustrate the degree to which viewers seemed to ignore or avoid these constraints in an everyday life context, up to the point of developing tactics of resistance. This might sound like a romanticist position, but a recurrent item in audience studies relates precisely to cinema-goers' active engagement with what was shown on the screen. Movies provided audiences with raw material that offered them building bricks, which they read and discussed in their own terms, and used to understand the world (e.g. Amber 2001). Arguments were given in order to underline the use of movies as a tool for identity construction – or at least experimenting with identity scenarios. In her work on female film fans, Haller (2012) indicates how women were both attracted by stars and tried to imitate them, but equally transformed the mythologies of stardom for purposes of self-definition and the formation of a (temporary) self-identity.

The engagement with cinema was not only a matter of the ideal spectator and the individual viewer, lively submerged in and negotiating with the world of moving pictures. Cinema-going was also a part of the routines of social life and, as Annette Kuhn writes, one that appeared 'to have been less about particular films, or even films in general, than about experiences surrounding and part of the activity of "going to the pictures", about the place of this activity in the context of their daily lives, interactions with family and friends, and comings and goings within and beyond the neighbourhoods in which they lived' (1999: 539). Notwithstanding various forms of segregation, cinema-going offered a 'kind of communal experience' (Noble 2006: 510) where, for instance, as Jacqueline Stewart (2005) indicates, Chicago's African American audiences were actively engaged, in several senses, with the pictures as a modernizing force.

Audiences were active in many more respects, even up to the point of resisting distribution and exhibition strategies – as in the case of post-war communist Czechoslovakia, where audiences at some point resisted by staying away from cinemas (Skopal 2012). Another example is China, where Hollywood's stigmatizing portrayal of Chinese society infuriated audiences and forced censors to react (Xiao 2012). This case illustrates Kuhn's (1988) Foucauldian-inspired view upon censorship as one consisting of fluid interrelations between audiences, movies and the censorial institution. In other cases, audiences seemed to have been well aware of, and trying to be resistant to, censorship. The existence of film censorship had a potentially productive effect – for instance, stimulating an inverse effect by promoting censored or age-restricted movies. Oral history research on audiences' awareness of censorship in Belgium, for instance, shows that, following Michel de Certeau's terminology, cinema-goers sometimes deployed various tactics in their attempt to circumvent authorities' control or to be attentive to what was forbidden (Biltereyst et al. 2012). These tactics frequently remained innocent and playful, rather than constituting a conscious act of resistance. Summarizing, it could be argued that the tension between institutional constraints and these everyday life tactics of audiences illuminates the classical trope of structure versus agency.

Discussion

This chapter – which admittedly raises more questions than results – began by revisiting and confronting the cinema-modernity debate, with insights coming from recent empirical studies on the historical film audience. We argued that, rather than seeing this research trend as an anti-thesis, it might be more fruitful to assume a dialectical position resulting into a multifaceted view of the film audience. It is assumed that, to a certain degree, the audience comprises both citizens and consumers, both individuals and members of larger ensembles of people, differentiated by gender, age, race, class, varieties of cultural and economic capital. Viewers are in part constructed by the movie's textual repertoires, as well as being selective, reflective and resistant. This recognition of the audience's multiplicity must not be seen as a forced effort of reconciling divergent views upon what film studies should be looking for. It is only by acknowledging this multiplicity of the audience that a more nuanced view of cinema's societal role will be developed.

The same 'realistic' approach to the workings of modernity – in terms of multiplicity, heterogeneity, ambiguity and resistance – brings forth a more balanced view of the different roles cinema played in mediating, informing or giving audiences tools to understand the implications of modernization. If one lesson has to be learned from examining empirical studies of historical film reception, it is that these do not deny or minimize cinema's role in everyday life, in people's personal trajectories and in their growing understanding of the world and their place in it. Paraphrasing Maltby, we might argue that the empirical encounter with the situated social history of the audience 'frees us from the obligation to assume that people living through periods of rapid change naturally felt disorientated; this liberation may enable us to develop a more nuanced understanding of cinema's various relations with "modernity" in the early twentieth century' (2011: 12).

In order to reach this stage, more research is needed, because there is so much we do not know about the cultural and social complexities of cinema-going (Allen 2006). Next to paying attention to audience diversities, the issue of the interrelation with institutions remains crucial to any attempt to understand the principal societal forces that tried to refrain (or stimulate) modernizing tendencies. Finally, more work is necessary outside the western hemisphere, along with more comparative work in other historical, cultural and political locations. This reminds me of the research agenda formulated by Garth Jowett at the end of a very personal journey through his life as a cinema-goer:

> I am now a champion for the study and understanding of the place of movies in societies not only by looking at the number of tickets sold at the box office, or other viewing statistics, but by examining the collected individual memories which go to make up the shared experience, and extrapolating from that hypotheses about the impact of movie-going in a wide variety of cultures and settings. (2006: 18)

References

Allen, R.C. (1990), 'From Film Exhibition to the History of Film Reception: Reflections on the Audience in Film History', *Screen*, 31: 4, pp. 347–56.

—— (1996), 'Manhattan Myopia; Or, Oh!', *Cinema Journal*, 35: 3, pp. 75–103.

———— (2006), 'Relocating American Film History: The "Problem" of the empirical', *Cultural Studies*, 20: 1, pp. 48–88.

Ambler, C. (2001), 'Popular Films and Colonial Audiences: The Movies in Northern Rhodesia', *The American Historical Review*, 106: 1, pp. 81–105.

Biltereyst, D., Maltby, R. and Meers, P. (eds) (2012), *Cinema, Audiences and Modernity: New Perspectives on European Cinema History*, London: Routledge.

Biltereyst, D. and Meers, P. (2011), 'The Political Economy of Audiences', in J. Wasko, G. Murdock and H. Sousa (eds), *The Handbook of Political Economy of Communication*, Malden, MA: Blackwell, pp. 415–35.

Biltereyst, D., Meers, P., Lotze, K. and Van de Vijver, L. (2012), 'Negotiating Cinema's Modernity: Strategies of Control and Audience Experiences of Cinema in Belgium, 1930s–1960s', in D. Biltereyst, R. Maltby and P. Meers (eds), *Cinema, Audiences and Modernity: New Perspectives on European Cinema History*, London: Routledge, pp. 186–201.

Biltereyst, D. and Vande Winkel, R. (eds) (2013), *Silencing Cinema: Film Censorship Around the World*, London: Palgrave Macmillan.

Bordwell, D. (1997), *On the History of Film Style*, Cambridge, MA: Harvard University Press.

Breton, A. (1928/1960), *Nadja*, London: Grove Press.

Bruno, G. (1999), *Streetwalking an a Ruined Map*, Princeton, NJ: Princeton University Press.

Carroll, N. (2001), 'Modernity and the Plasticity of Perception', *The Journal of Aesthetics and Art Criticism*, 59: 1, pp. 11–17.

Casetti, F. (1998), *Inside the Gaze: The Fiction Film and Its Spectator*, Bloomington, IN: Indiana University Press.

———— (2005), *Eye of the Century: Film, Experience, Modernity*, New York: Columbia University Press.

Chapman, J., Glancy, M. and Harper, S. (eds) (2007), *The New Film History: Sources, Methods, Approaches*, Basingstoke: Palgrave Macmillan.

Charney, L. (1998), *Empty Moments: Cinema, Modernity, and Drift*, Durham, NC: Duke University Press.

Charney, L. and Schwartz, V.R. (eds) (1995), *Cinema and the Invention of Modern Life*, Berkeley, CA: University of California Press.

Cronin, T. (2009), 'Media Effects and the Subjectification of Film Regulation', *The Velvet Light Trap*, 63: 3–21.

Doane, M.A. (2002), *The Emergence of Cinematic Time: Modernity, Contingency, the Archive*, Cambridge, MA: Harvard University Press.

Eisenstadt, S.N. (2000), 'Multiple Modernities', *Daedalus*, 129: 1, pp. 1–29.

Fuller-Seeley, K.H. (ed.) (2008), *Hollywood in the Neighborhood: Historical Case Studies of Local Moviegoing*, Berkeley, CA: University of California Press.

Fuller-Seeley, K.H. and Potamianos, G. (2008), 'Introduction: Researching and Writing the History of Local Moviegoing', in K.H. Fuller-Seeley (ed.), *Hollywood in the Neighborhood: Historical Case Studies of Local Moviegoing*, Berkeley, CA: University of California Press, pp. 3–19.

Giddens, A. (1991), *Modernity and self-identity: Self and Society in the Late Modern Age*, Cambridge: Polity Press.

Gunning, T. (1998), 'Early American Film', in J. Hill and P. Church Gibson (eds), *The Oxford Guide to Film Studies*, Oxford: Oxford University Press, pp. 255–71.

—— (2005), 'Modernity and Early Cinema', in R. Abel (ed.), *Encyclopedia of Early Cinema*, London: Routledge, pp. 439–42.

—— (2006), 'Modernity and Cinema: A Culture of Shocks and Flows', in M. Pomerance (ed.), *Cinema and Modernity*, New Brunswick, NJ: Rutgers University Press, pp. 297–315.

Hale, G.E. (1998), *Making Whiteness*, New York: Pantheon.

Haller, A. (2012), 'Diagnosis: Flimmeritis: Female Cinema-going in Imperial Germany, 1911–18', in D. Biltereyst, R. Maltby and P. Meers (eds), *Cinema, Audiences and Modernity: New Perspectives on European Cinema History*, London: Routledge, pp. 130–41.

Hansen, M. (1991), *Babel & Babylon: Spectatorship in American Silent Film*, Cambridge, MA: Harvard University Press.

Jernudd, Å. (2012), 'Spaces of Early Film Exhibition in Sweden, 1897–1911', in D. Biltereyst, R. Maltby and P. Meers (eds), *Cinema, Audiences and Modernity: New Perspectives on European Cinema History*, London: Routledge, pp. 19–34.

Jowett, G. (2006), 'Apartheid and Socialization: Movie-going in Cape Town, 1943–58', *Historical Journal of Film, Radio and Television*, 26: 1, pp. 1–20.

Keil, C. and Stamp, S. (eds) (2004), *American Cinema´s Transitional Era*, Berkeley, CA: University of California Press.

Kember, J. (2009), *Marketing Modernity: Victorian Popular Shows and Early Cinema*, Exeter: University of Exeter Press.

Kuhn, A. (1988), *Cinema Censorship and Sexuality, 1909–1925*, London: Routledge.

—— (1999), 'Cinema-going in Britain in the 1930s: Report of a Questionnaire Survey', *Historical Journal of Film, Radio and Television*, 19: 4, pp. 531–43.

—— (2002), *An Everyday Magic: Cinema and Cultural Memory*, London: I.B. Tauris.

Lagny, M. (1994), 'Film History: Or History Expropriated', *Film History*, 6: 1, pp. 26–44.

Lewis, J. and Smoodin, E. (eds) (2007), *Looking Past the Screen*, Durham, NC: Duke University Press.

Maltby, R. (2011), 'New Cinema Histories', in R. Maltby, D. Biltereyst and P. Meers (eds), *Explorations in New Cinema History: Approaches and Case Studies*, Malden, MA: Wiley-Blackwell, pp. 3–40.

Maltby, R., Biltereyst, D. and Meers, P. (eds) (2011), *Explorations in New Cinema History: Approaches and Case Studies*, Malden, MA: Wiley-Blackwell.

Manchin, A. (2012), 'Imagining Modern Hungary Through Film: Debates on National Identity, Modernity and Cinema in Early Twentieth Century Hungary', in D. Biltereyst, R. Maltby and P. Meers (eds), *Cinema, Audiences and Modernity: New Perspectives on European Cinema History*, London: Routledge, pp. 64–80.

Meers, P., Biltereyst, D. and Van de Vijver, L. (2010), 'Metropolitan vs Rural Cinema-going in Flanders, 1925–1975', *Screen*, 51: 3, pp. 272–80.

Moore, P.S. (2008), *Now Playing: Early Moviegoing and the Regulation of Fun*, New York: State University of New York Press.

Mutlu, D.K. (2011), 'Between Tradition and Modernity: Yeşilçam Melodrama, Its Stars, and Their Audiences', *Middle Eastern Studies*, 46: 3, pp. 417–31.

Noble, A. (2006), 'Vino todo el pueblo: Notes on Monsiváis, Mexican Movies and Movie-Going', Bulletin of Latin American Research, 25: 4, pp. 506–11.

Schwartz, V.R. and Przyblyski, J.M. (eds) (2004), The Nineteenth-Century Visual Culture Reader, New York: Routledge.

Sedgwick, J. (2011), 'Patterns in First-Run and Suburban Filmgoing in Sydney in the Mid-1930s', in R. Maltby, D. Biltereyst and P. Meers (eds), Explorations in New Cinema History: Approaches and Case Studies, Malden, MA: Wiley-Blackwell, pp. 140–58.

Singer, B. (2001), Melodrama and Modernity: Early Sensational Cinema and Its Contexts, New York: Columbia University Press.

—— (2009), 'The Ambimodernity of Early Cinema', in A. Ligensa and K. Kreimeier (eds), Film 1900: Technology, Perception, Culture, New Barnet: John Libbey, pp. 37–50.

Staiger, J. (1992), Interpreting Films: Studies in the Historical Reception of American Cinema, Princeton, NJ: Princeton University Press.

Skopal, P. (2012), 'The Cinematic Shapes of the Socialist Modernity Programme', in D. Biltereyst, R. Maltby and P. Meers (eds), Cinema, Audiences and Modernity: New Perspectives on European Cinema History, London: Routledge, pp. 81–98.

Stewart, J.N. (2005), Migrating to the Movies, Berkeley, CA: University of California Press.

Stokes, M. and Maltby, M. (eds) (1999), American Movie Audiences from the Turn of the Century to the Early Sound Era, London: British Film Institute.

Sullivan, S. (2010), 'Child Audiences in America's Nickelodeons, 1900–1915: The Keith/Albee Managers' Reports', Historical Journal of Film, Radio and Television, 30: 2, pp. 155–68.

Taylor, H. (1989), Scarlett's Women: Gone With The Wind and its Female Audience, London: Virago.

Vezyroglou, D. (2004), 'Les Catholiques, le cinéma et la conquête des masses', Revue d'histoire moderne et contemporaine, 51: 4, pp. 115–34.

Xiao, Z. (2013), 'Film Censorship in China', in D. Biltereyst and R. Vande Winkel (eds), Silencing Cinema: Film Censorship Around the World, London: Palgrave Macmillan, pp. 109–130.

Note

1   'Modernity' and 'modernism' are notoriously complex concepts. We will return to describing 'modernity' in this chapter, but in general modernity will refer to a particular era (mostly situated from the end of the nineteenth century onwards) and the experience of this era, which is characterized by the transition from a traditional society to one with substantial (and continuous) technological, social, cultural and ideological changes. Modernism refers to an arts-related movement and arts practices, often related to the twentieth-century artistic avant-garde.

Chapter 2

What is a Cinema? Death, Closure and the Database

Deb Verhoeven

Death is surely one of the rare events that justify the term … cinematic specificity.

– André Bazin (2003: 30)

Not everything can be described, nor need be.

– Mark Doty (2010: 116)

Introduction: 'cinemapocalypse'

The spectre of death haunts the cinema – again. And, as an almost inevitable consequence, there proliferate accompanying stories of its rekindling, of a continued, albeit stuttering, afterglow. Angela Carter may have quipped in 1980 that, 'the *fin* has come a little early this *siècle*', but it is now equally apparent that, where the cinema is concerned, it lingers still (Carter 1992: 155).

The film-maker Peter Greenaway has famously and specifically identified the cinema's date of death as 31 September 1983.[1] On this day, he says, 'the remote control was introduced to the living rooms of the world. Bang. That's the end' (van Leer 2007). Speaking at the Pusan Film Festival, he elaborated: 'If you shoot a dinosaur in the brain on Monday, its tail is still waggling on Friday. Cinema is brain dead … Thirty-five years of silent cinema is gone, no one looks at it anymore. This will happen to the rest of cinema. Cinema is dead' (Coonan 2007).

Greenaway is the latest in a long line of film-makers who have, at various times in its history, laid claim to the cinema's unwary end. Godard and Truffaut, for example, repeatedly declared the end of cinema in the 1950s and 1960s (on Godard, see Milne 1972: 210 and Habib 2001; and on Truffaut see de Baecque and Toubiana 2000: 109). And film-makers have not confined their apprehension of cultural catastrophe to the page. There have been many significant films that consider the 'death' of the cinema in one way or another, from the coming-of-age movie that is entwined with an end-of-an-era commentary, *The Last Picture Show* (Bogdanovich 1971), to Wim Wenders' meandering almost-documentary portrait of the last moments of small German cinemas in *Im Lauf der Zeit/Kings of the Road* (1976), the nostalgic reminiscences of *Cinema Paradiso* (Tornatore 1988) and perhaps the finest of them all, Tsai Ming-Liang's (2003) masterpiece, *Bu San/Goodbye Dragon Inn* – a film of the most unrelenting funereal introspection, in which one of the few lines of dialogue is the mournful comment, 'No one goes to the movies anymore'.

In its contemplation of a film audience as threadbare as the seats it occupies, *Goodbye Dragon Inn* explicitly asks; Do the 'phantoms' and shadows of the cinema belong to the screen or to its spectators – is the cinema material or metaphysical, or somehow both? In this film, the sagging proscenium of an almost abandoned venue is also the setting for an incipient philosophical debate about the ontology of cinemas. The question of what a cinema *was* also poses questions about what a cinema *is*, and what it *might be*. These speculations themselves are founded in an 'apocalyptic thinking' that encompasses both a particular approach to the temporality of cinema technologies and a particular figuration of the entanglement of matter and meaning.

Apocalyptic thinking is not isolated to particular film-makers' explicit contemplation of the film industry's diminished circulation. For example, Paul Arthur has observed a techno-apocalyptic taint to a number of celebrated films of the 1990s, which he suggests that on closer examination presents a thinly disguised, self-concerned allegory of the battle between electronic and traditional film production technologies: 'Of late Hollywood has been haunted – at times quite profitably so – by the specter of its own demise' (2001: 342).

This question of the cinema's ghostly existence, its contemporary continuance as a 'trace', is also present in a great deal of writing around a perceived paradigmatic shift in practices of film consumption. Robert C. Allen, for example, recently noted:

> More and more movie theatres now serve as haunted houses – places where, on Friday nights, Hollywood studios summon the ghost of a bygone epoch in an attempt to suffuse their products with an aura of cinematic glamour strong enough to survive for a few months in the decidedly unglamorous domestic settings where they eventually will be housed. (2011: 81)

Writing as the cinema celebrated its hundred year anniversary, Laura Mulvey invoked a similarly ghoulish image when she confidently asserted: 'Certainly, the cinema is inhabited increasingly by spectres' (2006: 196). For Mulvey, what is at stake in the mortification of the cinema is a realignment of its defining difference. For example, instead of the structuring clarity of oppositional differences, 'film and photography are now producing new relations and connections to each other, sequentially or simultaneously, out of which new oscillating, shifting, representations of time may be experienced' (2006: 196). Mulvey correctly identifies the question of temporality and differentiation at the heart of apocalyptic pronouncements. For Mulvey, however, it is the binary logic of the digital that must bear the brunt of culpability for the cinema's most recent bereavement:

> The resonance of ageing, and of death, associated with the cinema's centenary coincided with the arrival of a technology that created a divide between the 'old' and the 'new' media. However significant the development of video had been for film, the fact that all forms of

information and communication can now be translated into binary coding with a single system signals more precisely the end of an era. The specificity of cinema, the relation between its material base and its poetics, dissolves while other relations, intertextual and cross-media, begin to emerge. (2006: 18)

Like Tsai Ming-Liang, Mulvey perceives the cinema's specific 'end' on the one hand as a reproductive crisis, observed in the dissolution of an originating coupling of matter and metaphysics. New audio-visual technologies, on the other hand, are comparatively promiscuous – indiscriminate and formless in their 'single system' of indifferent binaries.

Echoes of this form of thinking resonate through the walkways of film criticism. Mahnola Dargis (2010), reviewing the digital release of *Carlos*, finds a regretful finality at the end of celluloid film exhibition. For Dargis, film, with its 'rich textural density', gives us contact with a metaphysical world, 'Digital, by contrast, just gives us data: ones and zeroes'. For Dargis, like Mulvey, new technologies exist outside the dualism of matter and metaphysics that characterized pre-digital cinema viewing. 'The digital' is doubly deficient, lacking both the metaphysicality and the materiality of film; it neither matters nor is matter.

Dargis's apocalyptic thinking regarding film technology infers that its value lies only in its role as a tool for the completion of a greater metaphysical project. The digital – a proxy for 'the end of film' – is without a temporal dimension of its own, existing only as the evidence of a larger ontological crisis. Dargis (2010) diminishes time to her thinking of it, rather than acknowledging the ways in which the technical – in this instance, digital technologies – might open up time and be constitutive of a type of 'event-ness'.

In his landmark study of apocalyptic literature, Frank Kermode (1968) argues that *apocalyptic thinking* is a form of 'temporal geometry' through which we figure our notions of historical transition and crisis. Apocalyptic thinking 'depends on a concord of imaginatively recorded past and imaginatively predicted future' (1968: 8) and creates a 'satisfying consonance with the origins and the middle' (1968: 17). Apocalyptic thinking disavows the multiple contingencies of time, condensing time and ending into an impossibly totalizing coincidence. The types of terminal punctualities recited above fasten the empirical to the transcendental, variously aligning changes to audience viewing practices, shifts in production technologies and the material closure of (some) cinemas, for example, with 'death'.

'For God's sake, it's only a cinema'

Now the Bijou, the Globe, the Luxor, the Roxy and the Star are bingo palaces. Old ladies with thick stockings holding veins like knots of worms, and men whose eyes are duller than clay alleys dream other dreams and watch the numbered screen, killing time, hoping for a win. The Empire is a supermarket now, a freezer full of TV dinners where the Gents once stood. (Harding 1990: 18)

Yet another chapter in the never-ending story of the cinema's decline, demise and defence recently surfaced over the closure of Sydney's Academy Twin Cinemas. A rental dispute led to the withdrawal of the lessee, Palace Cinemas. Public debate particularly centred around not the dimming of the screens (which were swiftly replaced by the Palace in a nearby venue), but the statement of the landlord, the president of the Greek Orthodox Community, Harry Danalis: 'These are commercial decisions for us, there's no emotion or drama in this. For God's sake, it's only a cinema … What do you do? We have obligations to our members and the various charities that we run … and they're a lot more beneficial to society than a cinema' (Morgan 2010).

Public response to the Danalis's indifference was swift. For one respondent, Danalis had clearly committed a capital offence:

WE ALL STILL MISS THE VALHALLA & THE WALKER ST CINEMAS. AND THEY'RE NOT 'JUST CINEMAS' – THEY'RE A PART OF OUR CULTURE. IT'S ALL JUST HAEMORRAGING AWAY AND NO ONE WHO CARES CAN REALLY DO ANYTHING MUCH ABOUT IT … PEOPLE WILL JUST BE GOING TO SAUSAGE FACTORY MULTIPLEXES BEFORE TOO LONG. JUST STOP IT! (Dennison 2010).

In the face of the cinema's death is the 'evidence' of its persistent transience. This is perhaps most shocking when it involves the loss of what we assume are its most enduring and 'concrete' of assets: the buildings themselves. The chair of the National Film and Sound Archive of Australia weighed in, arguing that the owners of cinema buildings hold a particular indebtedness to the community:

I presume Mr Danalis would be outraged if some developer decided the Theatre of Dionysus Eleuthereus on the slopes of the Acropolis, or Polykleitos's theatre at Epidauros, was to be bulldozed to make way for a fast-food outlet … The Academy Twin is so much more than 'only a cinema'; it is a critical part of our cultural patrimony. (Puplick 2010)

For these commentators, the Academy Twin is not a commercial enterprise, but a meaningful community and cultural 'place' that accommodates a type of film spectatorship that is also a proxy for a sense of community (sensibilities apparently not found in multiplexes or fast-food outlets), and which must at all costs be preserved. For these commentators, both 'the cinema' (as a set of cultural and commercial practices) and 'cinemas' are interchangeable. A sense of this conflation is captured by the documentary *Into the Shadows*, examining the spate of recent Australian venue closures:

I'm a big supporter of independent cinema in terms of, not art-house films, but cinemas actually owned by people. There was a great tradition in Australia, and all over the world actually, where you'd have cinemas that were owned in country towns and the Dad would be the projectionist and Mum would be tearing tickets out the front, and there was real showmanship in what was coming into a town … So there was a certain personality in what you did. That is dying – dying because major distributors and major exhibitors are pushing those smaller players out of the market. (Film distributor Troy Lum, in Scarano 2009)

Contemporary film industry practice is characterized as lacking human feeling and personality, as being inherently counterposed to the specificity of past cinema experiences. New business practices, and the digital cinema technologies on which they rest, are placed in the realm of the inhuman, figured as some sort of post-human form of existence (such as ghosts) or as a generalized sense of the technological (and sometimes both).

For the most part, these various stories of the cinema's long-anticipated demise cross paths with a wider, omniscient narrative that connects the arrival of new technologies with a cultural decline. These are Darwinian tales in which lithe, rampantly reproductive mobile technologies rise up to mercilessly devour their lumbering anachronous heritage-media antecedents. They are desolate stories of an authenticity lost, of specificity submerged beneath the soulless swell of the technological tsunami. The end of the cinema 'as we know it' is attributed to the increasing presence of new dehumanizing technologies, the large-scale attrition of content afforded by format shifts, the observation of multiple crises in the digital production of films and the resulting closure of dearly remembered but nevertheless empty cinemas. The digital, it seems, spells doom.

In this context, I want to argue that the most pressing task of the (new) cinema historian is to be mindful of a more complex relationship between the transcendental and the empirical, and to develop a thinking of the digital that does not easily lapse into metaphysical positivism. One way forward is to reflect on how the technical (often abridged as the digital) might also be attributed a temporality, ensuring it does not simply 'follow' a pre-existing claim for the truth. Proposing the end of *film* exhibition as somehow commensurate with the 'end of cinema' explicitly refuses the digital this temporal dimension. So, rather than repeat instrumentalist and reductive accounts of new technologies, we might consider instead how technology itself participates in the definition of various historical and cultural forms of humanization; how the 'inhuman', the technical, might already exist *within* the 'human'. By relocating time to the 'inhuman' of the technological, we can examine in detail its contribution to our thinking of time and history, as well as to our conceptualization of the cinema itself and to our practices as film scholars. These are particularly salient issues for those of us developing new digital film history methodologies, such as those based on working with large collaborative datasets.

The Cinemas and Audiences Research Project (CAARP) database

> The digital is not only a new technique of post-production work and a new delivery system or storage medium, it is the new horizon for thinking about the cinema. (Elsaesser and Hoffman 1998: 227)

The Cinemas and Audiences Research Project (CAARP) database is a fully searchable relational database that incorporates the use of Wiki-style information fields to enable the addition and searching of detailed data and discursive commentary specific to a venue, company, film or film screening. The database provides a framework for research and analysis concerned with the history of film exhibition and distribution in Australia, and currently houses information about more than 11,000 films, 1700 companies, 2,000 venues, and in excess of 400,000 film screenings.

CAARP (http://caarp.flinders.edu.au) is intended to be both a reference work and a research tool. It was designed specifically to enable creative interrogation of its holdings. A web application was created to allow entry of data, controlled searching of the entered data and an advanced mining tool, allowing direct select statements to be performed on the database. For example, registered researchers are able to save and retrieve complex Structured Query Language (SQL) statements. A download facility allows search results to be saved as a Comma Separated Values (CSV) file for importation into a spreadsheet or other database application. For casual visitors, there is also a simple search allowing for the straightforward name exploration of film title, company name and venue name. And there is also a more nuanced search screen incorporating optional information filters.

The programming language used in the CAARP application is Perl, built on a framework called Catalyst. The venue screen in particular also uses a Javascript library called JQuery to allow data entry elements to call back and forth from the database. The database itself is a MySQL database. CAARP is housed on an Apache server running on Linux. Collectively, these technologies combine to form the acronym LAMP: Linux, Apache, MySQL, Perl.

The CAARP database was established in 2004 as part of an Australian Research Council (ARC)-funded research project (DP0560144 *Regional Markets and Local Audiences: a History of Australian Cinema Consumption*, researchers Richard Maltby, Mike Walsh, Kate Bowles, Deb Verhoeven). From the outset, the database was intended to address a major deficit in Australian and to some extent international cinema studies. However, establishing an all-of-project dataset was no small challenge. In order to unite extensive research from a variety of smaller studies (specifically on diasporic cinema-going in Victoria, cultural memories of cinema attendance in rural and regional New South Wales and data about the transition from silent to sound projection in South Australian cinemas), the database needed to encompass a wide variety of historical periods and practices, thematic emphases and methodologies. Our approaches included film history (based on archival research sources); the cultural and commercial analysis of the consumption of cinema (based on available and inferred quantitative data); and audience analysis (based on oral histories).

These diverse research practices and their attendant information sources presented a number of challenges that we had to address when we initiated the CAARP database:

- Databases typically exist to formulate, collate and retrieve information in accessible ways. How might a database encapsulate idiosyncratic and affective aspects of social and personal experience (especially when these may be in conflict with other documented or personal accounts)? How might a database manage information that 'dissembles' as much as it assembles the historical record?
- To date, research databases have usually been developed for a well-defined audience – for example, 'scholars' or 'fans' – with a common information literacy. How might a database that incorporates information about social experience be designed in such a way as to be useful for professional academics and researchers, *and* casual historians or community members?
- The multidisciplinary nature of the project provided an additional challenge – specifically the research group's own disparate levels of instructional and information literacy.

For the database designers (Strategic Data), the Cinema and Audience Research Project also posed a number of challenges to traditional approaches to information systems development. The academic team was geographically dispersed and loosely affiliated (through a large, multi-institutional ARC grant). In addition, while the project was broadly centred on cinema and audience research, our respective research approaches (and therefore the data we required) ranged from the collection and qualitative analysis of oral histories to narrowly defined quantitative measures such as theatre location and capacity. Finally, there were the usual timeline and budgetary restrictions that constrained the potential choices of development methodology and software expenditure.

In order to deal with the dispersed nature of the group, the designers suggested that the first phase of the project should involve setting up a collaborative online workspace where specifications could be documented and revised when people had time. Teleconferences were scheduled to focus the academic team on the evolving content and make final decisions. The software chosen for this task was Twiki (http://www.twiki.org), an open source form of Wiki.

Furthermore, while some members of the research group had very specific and well-defined information requirements, others were in a more formative stage in terms of identifying the data they thought would be useful. It became increasingly evident that the development of the database would need to be evolutionary or 'iterative' in nature, with an initial version of the system providing useful experience that would then drive progressive enhancements and requirements.

Even when the kinds of data required became apparent, the specific information formats were not necessarily clear. Database development usually requires explicit definition of each item that is to be stored, retrieved and manipulated. The more mutable requirements of the research did not fit well with that approach. Strategic Data looked at using a more Wiki-like (free-form) design, but this didn't suit the requirement for the quantitative data that were to be collected, searched for and summarized. Specifically, we wanted to develop better tools to manage our growing library of transcribed oral histories, classifying whole texts down to small passages with various interlinked themes as determined by research priorities. Likewise, a traditional database model forced decisions to be made arbitrarily about the best format for certain data before the researchers had time to explore what worked and what did not.

Ultimately, Strategic Data developed a hybrid model. Data that were clearly structured and could be captured in the rigorous form required by a traditional database would be entered into discrete fields. The more speculative or qualitatively derived commentaries would be added to an integrated Wiki component. The combination of these two elements provided the necessary balance for the project to progress while we learned more about our requirements and developed new ones. It also meant that future, as yet undetermined, questions could be asked of the data, as both the specified data fields and the Wiki components of CAARP were searchable.

In this way, CAARP acknowledges Alun Munslow's (2003) appeal for an 'epistemic relativist' approach to historical resources. CAARP is specifically designed to allow adaptive responses to an expected variety of usage situations and interpretive ends. The database recognizes the validity of empirical records, but also enables the inclusion of alternate forms of analysis and documentation through the inclusion of oral history extracts and comments fields, for example. These are specifically intended to incorporate non-academic interpretations of attributes and information in the dataset. Through the inclusion of the Wiki, with its diverse approach to content, navigation and information retrieval, CAARP invites researchers to create contextual information and reassemble sequences of data in a multitude of ways.

New cinema history and the digital

> The ultimate goal of film history is an account of its own disappearance or its transformation into another entity. (Cherchi Usai 2001: 89)

Despite our careful efforts to ensure that CAARP incorporated flexible frameworks that could handle future data sources and forms, practical obstructions continued to arise. Thus in 2008, mid-stream in its development, the database was subject to a seismic reconsideration. In seeking to describe detailed information about cinema venues, a series of seemingly insurmountable challenges had arisen. The venue data tables, which contained information about specific cinemas, originally were designed in a way that did not easily allow for changes to be recorded throughout the lifetime of the venue. In relational databases such as CAARP, a 'table' is a set of data elements that is organized using a model of vertical columns that are specified by name and an unlimited number of horizontal rows of information. Venue records provided opportunities to record 'technical' information about the venue, organized in a table (such as location data, seating capacity, number of screens and so on), as well as descriptions from period publications, information about screening policy, nearby businesses, more recent commentary about the venue and critical assessments of the quality and provenance of the information by members of the research team captured in the Wiki fields (see Figure 2.1). The venue tables were formed as a two-tier hierarchical structure with the top level acting as a container element, allowing generic information about the venue to be recorded such as a common name for the venue, i.e. a sequence of known names, and comments. The next level comprised a table to store a defined set of details (attributes) about the venue; Address details (Street, Suburb/town. Postcode, State) and Operation Dates (From and To), Status (City, Suburban, Country), Company (to record a single company associated with the venue), Primary Purpose, Capacity, Number of Screens. In this way, specific data fields organized as a table captured information about cinemas as if they were easily identified 'entities', unique *a priori* objects.

However, this structure did not allow for viewing all the various changes to the venue over time. Each time a significant change occurred, we were forced to create a new table of records to store new information about a venue. So, for example, if a cinema changed address this could only be captured by the database as if one venue had closed and another,

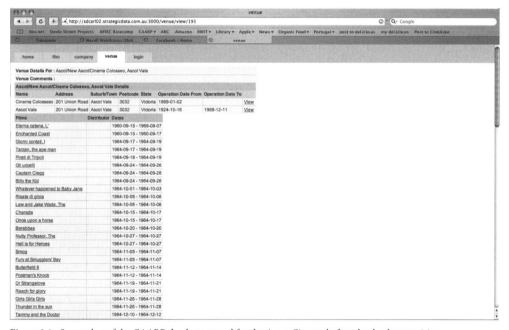

Figure 2.1: Screenshot of the CAARP database record for the Ascot Cinema before the database revision.

with the same name, reopened shortly afterwards. This process was highly impractical for describing the realities of cinema venue businesses, which are subject to constant change. For example, the structure was limited in its capacity to accurately represent venues that operated under the same name and simultaneously from multiple locations (such as in the country town of Myrtleford for a period), or venues that moved location but remained in all other respects the same enterprise (such as the Valhalla in Melbourne, which moved from Richmond to Northcote, and the Curzon in Adelaide, which moved from the city to Goodwood), or cinemas that closed and then reopened under new management with entirely new programming policies (as the Sydney Chauvel recently did).

Rather than imagining venues to be operating in different ways at different times, the data structure required us to express changes to a venue's operations as a 'closure'. If new data was to be recorded, it required an entirely new entity table to be generated with newly ascribed attributes. As researchers, we were often confounded by which circumstances (or attribute changes) we should consider significant enough to define the 'closure' of a venue within the database. Cinema venues rarely die neatly or promptly. How long did a cinema need to be dark before it could be deemed lifeless? How could we better describe a lingering death – or indeed an opportune revivification? If a cinema was relocated, was it also by definition reborn? Similarly, should changes of ownership, programming policy or primary purpose necessitate a new designation? The Astor cinema in St Kilda (Melbourne) began as a venue for popular Hollywood films. In the post-war period, it screened programs for Melbourne's burgeoning Greek community before turning its attention to repertory double-bills in recent years. Do any of these programming shifts in the ongoing operations of a venue necessarily define a cinema's death *per se*, however dislocating they may be for a loyal audience? What – or, better, who – in these circumstances is in fact responsible for killing cinemas?

The inflexibility of this data schema could not reconcile the layering of change that typified and in some historical periods necessitated a cinema's ongoing sustainability (such as physical changes to accommodate new projection technologies), nor could it satisfactorily describe the complexity of a cinema's demise. Operation dates simply do not neatly align with every noteworthy modification in a venue's activities. For instance, a venue may continue to operate despite changes to seating capacity. On the other hand, sweeping changes to programming policy such as switching to the screening of foreign language films, could be perceived by the cinema's erstwhile audience as a 'closure' of sorts.

As a result of these descriptive challenges, and in order to encapsulate our rethinking of the constitutive 'DNA' of a cinema, the database was reconceived and with it came a new definition of a cinema.[2] This new conceptualization moved away from the assumption that cinemas are 'entities', characterized by the selection and organization of a defining and stable set of details. Instead, it turns more on the idea that cinemas are constituted explicitly through the changeability of myriad 'events'. A new set of tables was created to store the venue information, allowing dates to be attached to each of the elements of change, producing an overlapping timeline of events for the life of a venue (see Figure 2.2). To accommodate these changes, two new tables were created: an event table, which captures the date of the event

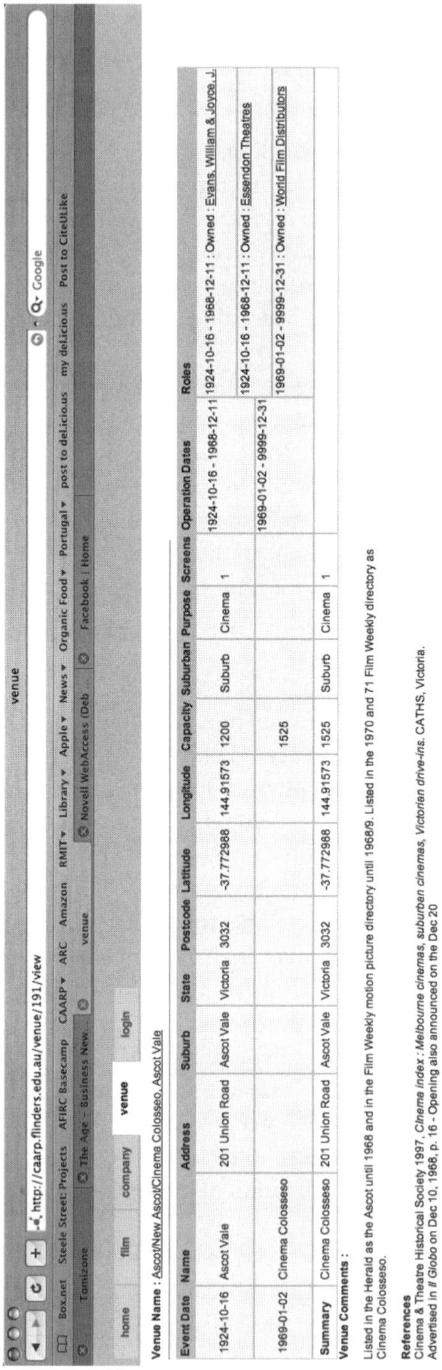

Figure 2.2: Screenshot of the CAARP database record for the Ascot Cinema after the database revision showing different events in the cinema's timeline.

and provides a link to the venue and an attributes table which links to the events table and stores the name and value of the attribute and the date (day, month or year) associated with the change in attribution. These attributes (which include venue data such as name, address, capacity, screens and which can be expanded to include new data) exist only when a date is applied to them, to identify their place in the venue timeline.

These changes to the database structure had profound repercussions for our broader research. *Rather than describing the cinema venue as a place where film events happen, we realized it could just as easily be imagined in the converse, as a series of events where 'places' happen.* In the reorganization of CAARP, each venue attribute is recognized as being subject to change, with these attribute changes occurring according to different rhythms and temporalities.

The move away from describing venues as assembled entities and towards understanding them as dissembling events (made up of multiple, related, contingent attributes) allows for a necessary fluidity in the definition of a venue for which the 'evidence' is not simply physically grounded, present and locatable. In attending specifically to the mutability of cinemas, we can think aporetically about them, as somehow *both* material and meta-physical, empirical and transcendent, a construction both concrete and conceptual; a thinking of the condition of cinemas that is enabled rather than disavowed by a 'thinking' technically through the database. The cinema database itself can then be understood as both a tool and as a surface for inscribing the world.

In turn, questioning what a cinema was, is and might be prompted a reconsideration of what the database is. Robert Allen (2008) hints at the cinema's non-foundational ontology when he describes the cinema venue as, "not so much a fixed place as a process — a "coming together" (as the etymology of the word suggests) of physical location, agency (individuals, groups, and institutions responsible for regulating, arranging, and authorizing a film exhibition), and event (the experience of at least one instance of movie exhibition)."

However, if cinema venues are fully understood as an event-in-process, then the cinema cannot be isolated from its surroundings or from its networks (of audiences, films, amenities and so on). In fact, these transactions with the cinema's environment shape its definition, ensuring that it is not misidentified or conflated with its milieu. Cinemas are articulated in relational terms, both in contrast to and connection with their specific location. The same relationships that allow us to differentiate an individual cinema – that enable us see it distinctly – also point to its defining connectivity. Instead of trying to grasp the cinema by using the individual venue as a starting point, we need to think about how cinemas simultaneously emerge from and constitute a system of differentiation that we know more broadly as 'the cinema'. In this context, time is the expression of the cinema's dimensionality, as it is constantly differentiated – as it *eventu*ates.

Similarly, the information housed in a database is not relative to a unique and homogenous *a priori* reality, but exists between different realities. This is because data, as the signification of a unit of difference, can only emerge through the establishment of a set of relations (a system of meaning). The descriptions entailed in establishing a research database do not simply reinscribe the already known. Databases are combinatory environments, which provide templates guiding the formation of connections. *The relationality of the database is contemporaneous with the data whose existence it supports. Data may appear to 'belong' to a cinema, but the cinema venue is in fact constituted though the relations of data (with other data and within interrogative frameworks).*

The digital film historian establishes a cinema's 'difference' at both an epistemological level (through our detailed descriptions of cinemas) and the ontological level (describing the operation of the cinema in the world). The database is founded in the asking: How many differences? In what relationships? It is the granular, relational nature of these specific differences that constitutes a 'cinema' and that does not precede, but rather results from, its interconnectedness. If the defining feature of a revised and expanded approach to the study of cinema histories is, as Robert C. Allen (2006) has famously called it, 'the problem of the empirical', then we must be equally attendant to the implications of this revision for the metaphysical dimensions of our studies, recognizing that the technological and the metaphysical bear an aporetical relationship for instance.

Online databases offer the promise of establishing new discursive and relational possibilities for the cinema. Digital research technologies invite us to rethink the cinema because, by incorporating the cinema within them, it is fundamentally changed. At an atomistic level, venue information is organized, manipulated, segmented, recombined and delivered in modular and multifarious ways – which potentially can enable contradictory and alternative interpretations of cinemas to appear. Working with databases moves us away from the moralizing hermeneutics of film studies (with its accent on articulating the 'truth') and creates instead an openness to contingencies, to piecing the puzzle of how things fit (and don't fit) together, to the questions of belonging and not-belonging that underlie the social enterprise of the cinema.

Databases such as CAARP challenge the idea of research purity. If the objects they describe are inherently relational, then their meaning and significance will always evade the scholarly researcher. Harald Kramer describes this digital research as the 'accumulation of information with the aim of comprehensiveness but without a sense of the whole' (2007: 196). Epistemological uncertainty is 'built into' the system, but also exists in the broadening of expectation that results from the range of researchers and other database users. Like the data with which we are working, we need to envisage ourselves as part of larger collaborative, cross-disciplinary, multi-institutional, cross-sector networks. Through their emphasis on the social dimensions of information creation and exchange, online databases such as CAARP realign the familiar hierarchy of information retriever and recipient, recognizing the dynamic social, creative and analytical dimensions of contemporary research and information management. *So in recognizing the unforeseen relations of the cinema, we also reorganize and expand our own relations with others.*

In creating research systems that enable relationship mapping, and contribute to wider knowledge systems through reorchestrating and remixing data, the researcher also opens herself in a disciplinary sense. Computer scientists, database engineers, programmers, information managers and designers, archivists, librarians, curators, experts and buffs all contribute to the success of a digital data collection. Digital research proceeds via the formation of distributed teams of specialist researchers rather than the humanities convention of lone operators single-handedly building personal 'life's work' archives. Challenges to research achievement will lie in the management of metadata and frameworks – such as the establishment of globally agreed standards and protocols for the attribution of authority files, the creation of shared digital ontologies and common commitments to interoperability between domain-based datasets.

Tom O'Regan, noting at the end of the millennium a plethora of doomsday film academics, describes in pointed self-reflection his own sense of undoing and ultimacy:

> Part of the reason some of us have a sense of the impending 'end of the cinema as we know it' is that we see a crisis in the institutional reproduction of ourselves. We cinephiles can feel like dinosaurs separated by a gulf of affect, enthusiasm and cultural archive from a younger generation of movie-goers. We can feel part of the old mechanical cinema economy and not the new electronically-mediated economy, part of the *ancien* analogue regime and not the digital republic. (O'Regan 2000: 74)

Ultimately for O'Regan, if it is the end of the world 'as we know it', it is not because of the collapse of entire industries of film exhibition, but rather a recognition of epistemological tremors occurring beneath these apocalyptic presentiments. The 'world' may not be ending *per se*, but the ways in which it is and can be known are definitely shifting.

The power of apocalyptic thinking rests on the belief that films, venues and even film historians and cinephiles are realized entities, pre-existing the world with which they are faced and that is somehow external to them. To challenge the cinema's long apocalypse is not to deny or dissipate the influence of its transformations, but to propose another way of thinking the cinema's 'temporal geometry', to challenge the underlying certitude of its difference as an *a priori* state and to propose instead a non-foundational ontology of cinemas. Interrogative forms of conceptualization such as those proposed by databases like CAARP might offer such an alternative.

Conclusion: digital film history

Doom and gloom predictions shouldn't dissuade us from looking at the palpable effects of the comprehensive industrial changes that have occurred in the cinema over the past ten years, including the digitization of production, delivery and projection, but also extending to the adaptive reuse of cinema spaces for the presentation of digitally streamed events, the uneven conversion to 3D and the proliferation of platforms for distributing and accessing film content. These very same digital technologies that are transforming the production and consumption of cinema can also prompt us to reconsider the ways in which we understand cinema at the most fundamental level.

There are substantial evidential, methodological and philosophical consequences that arise from undertaking a cliometric approach to cinema studies. Rather than ask how we make cinema research more digital, we might rephrase the question and ask instead how the digital changes 'cinema', and more specifically 'cinemas' (including for film researchers). This question is not simply concerned with how digitization changes the work of film archivists and historians, but goes to the heart of how interpretation must acclimatize as the winds of change sweep through our archives, altering the shape and presence of our primary sources. Finally, and most importantly, we might ask how the digital changes the way we understand change itself. How will the increasingly rapid advances in film consumption *and* research technologies contribute to their own alienating effect – making prior research technologies and their content obsolete? How will the ubiquity of digital sources and evidence challenge any aspiration for empirical diligence? How might research databases like CAARP, in their defining incompleteness, serve to remind us even more sharply of the underlying sense of loss and absence, specificity and abstraction that has also come to define our cinema experiences?

If we persist with an apocalyptic thinking of digital technology – a thinking that extends to databases but also the contemporary cinema itself, and that rests on simply understanding these as a tool for the completion of a prior metaphysical project – then we fail to grasp the most creative aspects of our work as cinema historians. If, as historians, we fail to acknowledge the temporality of the technical, then we will fail to appreciate how cinema databases such as CAARP are both resources and resourceful. By moving away from instrumentalist accounts of digital technologies to the consideration of how these technologies themselves participate in the formation of cultural and historical experiences, we not only expand our understanding of our own relationship to the cinema but we also embrace and participate in the possibility of a projected future.

Acknowledgements

Aspects of this chapter were delivered in conference papers at the Film and History Association of Australia and New Zealand conference 2008 and Edinburgh International Film Audiences Conference 2009 prior to being submitted in 2011 for this publication. I would also like to thank Jenny Anderson, Adam Thick and Olympia Szilagyi for their assistance in the preparation of this chapter.

References

Allen, R.C. (2006) 'Relocating American Film History: The "Problem" of the Empirical', *Cultural Studies*, 20: 1, pp. 48–88.
——— (2008), 'Going to the Show: What is a Venue?', http://docsouth.unc.edu/gtts/about-venue.html. Accessed 20 December 2011.

―――― (2011), 'Reimagining the History of the Experience of Cinema in a Post-Movie-going Age', *Media International Australia*, 39, pp. 80–87.

Arthur, P. (2001), 'The Four Last Things: History, Technology, Hollywood, Apocalypse', in J. Lews (ed.), *The End of Cinema as We Know It: American Film in the Nineties*, New York: New York University Press, pp. 342–55.

Assayas, O. (2010), *Carlos*, France/Germany: Films en Stock, Egoli Tossell Film, Arte France, Canal +.

Bazin, A. (2003), 'Death Every Afternoon', trans. Mark A. Cohen, in I. Margulies (ed.), *Rites of Realism: Essays on Corporeal Film*, Durham, NC: Duke University Press, p. 30.

Bogdanovich, P. (1971), *The Last Picture Show*, United States: Last Picture Show Productions; BBS Productions.

Carter, A. (1992), 'Grace Paley: The Little Disturbances of Man and Enormous Changes at the Last Minute', in A. Carter, *Expletives Deleted: Selected Writings*, London: Chatto & Windus, pp. 155–58.

Coonan, C. (2007), 'Greenaway Announces the Death of Cinema – and Blames the Remote-control Zapper', *The Independent*, 10 October, http://www.independent.co.uk/news/world/asia/greenaway-announces-the-death-of-cinema--and-blames-the-remotecontrol-zapper-394546.html. Accessed 20 December 2011.

Cherchi Usai, P. (2001), *The Death of Cinema: History, Cultural Memory and the Digital Dark Age*, London: British Film Institute.

Dargis, M. (2010), 'Cinematic Change and the End of Film', *New York Times*, 10 May, http://artsbeat.blogs.nytimes.com/2010/05/21/cinematic-change-and-the-end-of-film. Accessed 20 December 2011.

Dennison, M. (2010), Online comment, *Encore*, 28 June, http://www.encoremagazine.com.au/its-only-a-cinema-3339. Accessed 21 December 2011.

de Baecque, A. and Toubiana, S. (2000), *Truffaut: A Biography*, Berkeley, CA: University of California Press.

Dibbets, K. et al. (2011) *Cinema in Context* database, http://www.cinemacontext.nl. Accessed 21 December 2012.

Doty, M. (2010), *The Art of Description: World into Word*, Minneapolis, MN: Grey Wolf Press.

Elsaesser, T. and Hoffman, K. (1998), *Cinema Futures: Cain, Abel or Cable? The Screen Arts in the Digital Age*, Amsterdam: Amsterdam University Press.

Habib, A. (2001), 'Before and After: Origins and Death in the Work of Jean-Luc Godard', *Senses of Cinema*, 16, http://archive.sensesofcinema.com/contents/01/16/godard_habib.html#b5. Accessed 20 December 2011.

Harding, M. (1990) [No title] in I. Breakwell and P. Hammond (eds), *Seeing in the Dark: A Compendium of Cinema-going*, London: Serpents Tail.

Kermode, F. (1968), *The Sense of an Ending: Studies in the Theory of Fiction*, Oxford: Oxford University Press.

Kramer, H. (2007), 'Art is Redeemed, Mystery is Gone, The Documentation of Contemporary Art', in F. Cameron and S. Kenderdine (eds), *Theorizing Digital Cultural Heritage: A Critical Discourse*, Cambridge, MA: MIT Press, pp. 193–222.

Milne, T. (ed.) (1972), *Godard on Godard*, London: Secker & Warburg.

Morgan, C. (2010), 'No Hollywood Ending for Battle to Save Cinema', *Sydney Morning Herald*, 24 June 2010.

Mulvey, L. (2006), *Death 24x a Second: Stillness and the Moving Image*, London: Reaktion Books.

Munslow, A. (2001) 'Review of *The New Nature of History: Knowledge, Evidence, Language* by Arthur Marwick', *Discourse on Postmodernism and History*, https://www.history.ac.uk/resources/discourse-postmodernism/munslowonmarwick-paper. Accessed 20 December 2011.

O'Regan, T. (2000), 'The End of Cinema? The Return of Cinema?', *Metro*, 124/125, pp. 64–75.

Puplick, C. (2010), 'Cinema, and Cinemas, are Vital to Our Culture', Letter to the Editor, *Sydney Morning Herald*, 26 June, http://www.smh.com.au/national/letters/women-in-power-are-no-different-from-the-men-20100625-z9lu.html. Accessed 20 December 2011.

Scarano, A. (2009), *Into the Shadows* (documentary), Scarnett Productions, Canberra.

Tornatore, G. (1988), *Nuovo Cinema Paradiso/Cinema Paradiso*, Italy/France: Cristaldi Film, Les Films Ariane, Rai Tre, TF1 Films Production, Forum Pictures.

Tsai, M.-L. (2003), *Bu San/Goodbye Dragon Inn*, Taiwan: Homegreen Films, Council for Cultural Affairs.

van Leer, R. ('Westframe') (2007), 'Peter Greenaway, Cinema – Dead', 29 June, http://www.youtube.com/watch?v=-t-9qxqdVm4. Accessed 20 December 2011.

Verhoeven, D. et al. (2011), *Cinema and Audiences Research Project Database* (CAARP), http://www.caarp.flinders.edu.au.

Wenders, W. (1976), *Im Lauf der Zeit/Kings of the Road*, Germany: Wim Wenders Productions.

Notes

1   It is useful to remember when considering Greenaway's specificity that there are only 30 days in September.
2   The idea that databases disclose the DNA of film culture belongs to Karel Dibbets et al., *Cinema in Context* database, http://www.cinemacontext.nl. Accessed 20 December 2011.

Chapter 3

A Poetics of Film-audience Reception? Barbara Deming Goes to the Movies

Albert Moran

The critical analysis of popular film in the United States received a boost in the 1940s, with six sets of notable studies occurring. Parker Tyler published three of these – *The Hollywood Hallucination* (1944), *The Magic and Myth of the Movies* (1947) and *Chaplin: The Last of the Clowns* (1948). There were also several one-offs: Siegfried Kracauer's *From Caligari to Hitler: A Psychological History of German Film* (1947), Martha Wolfenstein and Nathan Leites' *Movies: A Psychological Study* (1950) and Barbara Deming's *Running Away from Myself: A Dream Portrait of America* (1969), drawn from the films of the 1940s. All of these studies appeared in that decade, with the exception of Deming's book. Her analysis has suffered neglect and misunderstanding, especially compared with the other 1947 Kracauer and 1950 Wolfenstein and Leites studies. The object of this chapter is to argue that Deming's study represents a significant achievement in terms of its intelligence, imagination, comprehensiveness, elegance and richness. Even beyond these qualities, I argue that the study constitutes an engaging and important exercise in the poetics of film reception. My discussion falls into seven parts. The first is preliminary and deals generally with poetics, especially with the idea of approaching film reception and audience understanding as one kind of cinema poetics. Then follows a biographical outline of Deming's career that touches on the institutional, practical and personal contexts of her film writing. Even while involved in film analysis at the Library of Congress in the later years of World War II – work that would, a quarter of a century later, give rise to her book-length study of popular American films of the 1940s – Deming published a thoughtful, suggestive article in 1944 concerning the methodology underlining a film archiving exercise then underway, in which she was involved. This article is discussed as a useful introduction to the book *Running Away from Myself*.

A major part of the chapter is concerned with Deming's book. The discussion traces continuity and changes between the 1944 article and the book, examines the methodology at work in one of the book's chapters, and uses this as springboard to suggests how Deming's audience poetics works as a whole. She and her fellow analysts' work at the Library of Congress Film Project had early support from another film researcher, the German *émigré* Siegfried Kracauer, and the last substantial section of the chapter takes the opportunity to consider *Running Away from Myself* alongside the Kracauer's *From Caligari to Hitler* as a means of further commending Deming's significance as an excursion into film-audience poetics. A short set of conclusions ends the chapter, reiterating Deming's interest and importance for scholarship in the field of film reception and audience involvement.

A poetics of reception?

Poesis is a Greek term referring to the making of an artefact. In turn, following Greetham (1999), I understand the term poetics to refer to a system of ordering and classification of human knowledge and experience of one kind or another (1999: 1–12). Broadly speaking, it is a structure of elements whereby some matters or procedures relating to cultural artefacts are included and others excluded, where some conventions are accepted and others rejected. The exercise of a poetics involves the observation of general tendencies of a medium or phenomenon with a litany of specificities that helps define its range of possibilities. This practice is not dependent on a fixed or preordained object of scrutiny so that, over time, there has been a thoughtful set of extensions to matters subjected to poetic scrutiny. Aristotle, for instance, was concerned with a poetics of Greek tragic drama, Todorov has developed a poetics of prose while Greetham has been concerned with the poetics of the literary archive. Additionally, the object of a poetics needs not to be large in scale. Bordwell (2005), for example, notices that the English poet W.H. Auden was concerned with the poetics of the literary detective story while French-born film critic André Bazin directed his attention to a historical poetics of film style (2005: 14–15), thereby reminding us that a poetics is not invariably concerned with a singular or recurring object.

Bordwell offers two additional suggestions in the same essay, whereby the notion of a poetics of cinema is elaborated (2005: 12–56). First, he suggests that poetics may be principally focused on three different, although interrelated, subjects: the finished object or artefact, the makers of that artefact and those who are the intended recipients of the artefact (2005: 14–15). Texts and contexts are important not only for the artist who crafts an object with some design or purpose in mind, but also in terms of an intended effect for a recipient or an audience. Because the idea of a poetics refers to an approach or method rather than a necessary subject, its application can be seen to possibly apply to three different although connected domains of craft. These are what is made, those doing the making and those for whom the making is intended (2005: 14–16).

Bordwell notes that, in the case of cinema, various projects involving poetics may be undertaken, including the study of the operation of film form and style at different times; the changing guidelines offered to practitioners in manuals and formal courses of instruction and training; and the scrutiny of various circumstances of film viewing and reception (2005: 15–16). In turn, each of these three emphases throws up further opportunities for the exercise of different poetics. Hence the period about which Deming writes, the 1940s, saw the operation of one kind of audience-oriented poetics in the shape of the set of production regulations, variously known as the Hays Code or the Breen Code, the voluntary code of self-censorship operated by the major Hollywood motion picture production companies (Jowett 1976: 238–60). Similarly, as we shall see, Deming's anatomy of popular films of the 1940s codified another set of conventions operating across a large corpus of films with regard to audience recognition of recurring themes and narrative arrangements.

Mention of Deming's project brings us back to Bordwell's second useful suggestion about poetic projects in general. This is his notion that traditional poetics distinguishes between three domains of investigation: thematics, large-scale form and stylistics (2005: 14–7). The first line of inquiry focuses on subject-matter as disclosed by motifs, iconography and theme as audience effects triggered by constructed principles. The second studies large-scale form, such as prologues and epilogues, story development and endings, and the orchestration of alternative narrative lines of action. Stylistics is the third component of this triangle and relates to the range of lower order artistic choices available in the creation process. Emphasizing the extent to which her poetics is concerned with audience understanding and reception, Deming's analysis has much to say regarding the first and second of these domains and very little to add regarding the third. With these considerations in mind, let us turn to the biographical figure of Deming and an article in which she anticipates some of the argument of her book.

Biographical outline

Barbara Deming was born in 1917 to middle-class parents in New York City, where she attended Quaker school and college (Deming and Meyerding 1984: 1–12). She worked as an editorial assistant, studied literature and theatre at Bennington College, took a Masters degree from Case Western Reserve University, practised drawing with George Grosz, directed stock company plays, taught dramatic literature and held a variety of 'pink collar' jobs in New York City. In 1942, she was hired as a film analyst for a Library of Congress national film library undertaking. This was the Library of Congress Film Project, which was based at the Film Division of New York's Museum of Modern Art (MoMA).

Working conditions at MoMA were privileged, with the five film analysts employed on the film project able to watch films especially projected for them with various controls over both the viewing and the note-taking situation. Deming had been trained in shorthand, and this was invaluable in making notes about a film during its projection, including recording details of action and setting as well as lines of character dialogue. The project was completed in 1945, but hopes for further employment of this kind were quashed when a Republican Congress cut the budget of the Library of Congress; among other measures, this caused it to postpone its plan to establish a permanent Film Division (Jones 2007: 40).

Undeterred, Deming continued to work on the study of popular feature film of the time, heroically taking notes in theatres, writing these up and analysing contemporary American films as these played to popular audiences. By 1949, she had completed a book manuscript entitled *A Long Way from Home: Some Film Nightmares of the Forties*. However, unlike two other studies of film audiences of the time – those by Siegfried Kracauer, and Martha Wolfenstein and Nathan Leites – Deming had no institutional benefactors or cultural network of consequence so she was unable to secure a publishing contract. Instead, the magazine *City Lights* published the first two chapters of Deming's manuscript in instalments between 1953 and 1955. *City Lights* then ceased publication, so no further instalments of *A Long Way from Home* appeared in magazine form.

The book manuscript sat in a desk drawer for 20 years (Deming 1969: 1–3). Meanwhile, Deming was following a personal pathway in the direction of peace activism, non-violent protest and radical feminism. She spent a year in India looking in detail at Gandhi's methods of resistance through non-violence, and was active in civil rights, the anti-nuclear movement and peace marches in the United States in the 1960s, spending time in prison with other demonstrators (Deming 1966). As a writer, Deming had published a small handful of literary works in the 1950s, including short stories, essays and poems; in the 1960s, however, she redefined herself as a political journalist, analysing the immediate political events and situations in which she was a participant. Many of these writings were collected together, and gave rise to Deming's first book of political essays, *Prison Notes*, which was published by a sympathetic New York publishing house, Grossman, in 1966.

In turn, this publication caused Deming to revisit her unpublished book manuscript. She found that even though that study dealt with films of the 1940s, the manuscript had a clear relevance to the operation of American political ideology and Hollywood films in the 1960s (Deming 1969: 1–12). Grossman Publishers would have been aware of the international publishing boom in film-related books that had got underway in 1966 (Whittaker 1970: 152–53) and would probably have been sympathetic to a second manuscript from the author. The late 1940s study was lightly revised, a Foreword was written, film stills were collected and *Running Away from Myself: A Dream Portrait of America Drawn from the Films of the Forties* appeared in 1969. Belatedly, it joined the two other studies of dream psychology in film and society of the forties already mentioned: Kracauer's (1942) analysis of German film entitled *From Caligari to Hitler: A Psychological History of the German Film*, and Martha Wolfenstein and Nathan Leites' (1950) *Movies: A Psychological Study*.

However, beyond the satisfaction of finally seeing her manuscript into print, Deming probably gave little consideration to its likely place in the annals of American film scholarship. Her advocacy work continued, although a car accident was to curtail her physical movement in the next decade (Deming and Meyerding 1984: 3–14). She maintained her political activism and journalism despite this drawback.

Barbara Deming passed away in 1983. A collection of her writings was published posthumously by New Society Publishing the following year under the title *We Are All Part of One Another: A Barbara Deming Reader* (Deming and Meyerding 1984). The fact that it anthologizes part of Chapter 4, 'Success Boy', from *Running Away from Myself* seems to indicate her continued satisfaction with the achievement of the book.

Deming's 1944 article

Running Away from Myself had its origins in an idea that developed in the minds of others in a series of institutional settings dating back to as early as the 1930s. The idea was a simple one: that films were worth collecting and archiving as indices of the climate of ideas abroad at their time of production and exhibition. Deming would give distinct expression to this idea in 1944, and would proceed to recast it by 1969 when *Running Away from Myself* appeared in print.

In late 1944, Barbara Deming published a long article entitled 'The Library of Congress Film Project: Exposition of a Method', which appeared in a newly established quarterly journal of the Library of Congress on acquisitions. The historical and institutional background to the essay has usefully been outlined by Jones (2007) – although, as I will suggest, she appropriates the article to a narrative of dramatic struggle between two venerable US organizations, the Library of Congress and MoMA. Since at least as early as 1934, the *National Archives Act* had established that, as well as books and other documentary materials, films should be preserved for 'historical purposes and study'. To that end, the Library of Congress would establish preservation vaults and a projection room (Jones 2007: 37). Practically, the Act led to the (slow) development of the Motion Pictures and Sound Recordings Division at the Archive.

A more important matter was postponed for the time being: the question of what kinds of films might be accepted and archived. The Act related primarily to films relating to the government of the United States, including the Congress, executive, judiciary and Administration; however, depending on interpretation, there might also be room for other films, including features from Hollywood. In fact, an early director of the division proceeded with a more catholic and inclusive archiving policy than might otherwise have been the case on the basis that the film collection should aim to be 'a reflection of the American scene' (Jones 2007: 36–9).

Under the direction of the poet, Archibald MacLeish, who served as Librarian of Congress from 1939 to 1944, the Library's commitment to film collecting and archiving advanced considerably (Jones 2007: 40–42). There already existed a film library at MoMA in New York, so there were now two important public institutions that collected films and supported the notion that films were worthy objects of study in their own right as well as for historical purposes. Among his many other activities, MacLeish set up a collaboration between MoMA and the Library of Congress, under which a five-member panel from MoMA's Film Division would, on behalf of the Archive, select the most significant films made each year (2007: 43). For instance, in 1942 a total of 104 films were selected for preservation from 1400 films deposited for copyright purposes (2007 44). MacLeish inclined towards film collecting criteria that emphasized the factual, the explicit and the utilitarian. Barbara Deming was a member of that five-person team of film analysts working at MoMA, and her 1944 article suggests that the MoMA film analysts diverged significantly from MacLeish's view of the criteria that should govern the film-selection process (Jones 2007: 45).

Jones sees Deming's article as elaborating an epistemology and a selection procedure that implicitly challenged the principles elaborated by MacLeish. The methodology was one that was far more concerned with the artistic mechanisms and effects of film – especially feature film – and it was one that had been in operation at MoMA's Film

Division over the previous decade under the directorship of British-born Iris Barry. As Jones puts it:

> Deming's essay neatly unravels MacLeish's collecting mission and reveals their [the team's] commitment to Barry's guiding principle of film collecting for art's sake, for the scholar's sake ... Her essay is a discursive collision between two major institutions ... forming the national collection was surely a schizophrenic process. (Jones 2007: 49)

I would not disagree with this account of an institutional clash at the heart of the film collecting and archiving process at MoMA on behalf of the Library of Congress at this time, as it neatly demonstrates Jones' larger point that archives – including film archives – are not self-selecting, but can be shaped by the push and pull of different principles of choice.

On the other hand, I would take issue with the authorship of the 1944 essay, which Jones sees as a collective document despite citing no supporting evidence for such a claim beyond the fact that Deming's article must have covered the activities, and that she thought of herself and other members of the MoMA team. Deming's name is the only one appended to the article, and there is no statement of collective authorship. In fact, she slips into using the first-person singular pronoun in some footnotes. Other facts also militate against Jones' suggestion (e.g. see Jones 2007: 31–2). There appears to be no trace of the subsequent research career of the other members of the MoMA team, whereas Deming continued to write and publish the film research already underway in the article, first in the pieces printed in the magazine *City Lights* and then in the book *Running Away from Myself.*

Article to book

Let us now turn to the book, using continuities and differences between the 1944 article and the 1969 book as a point of departure. Three recurring features and three variations sum up the relationship between the two. First, there is the broad observation that Deming's overall approach remains the same – namely, to examine a number of films selected so as to reveal common narrative and thematic threads that are clues to the ideological universe inhabited by the US film audience in the 1940s. As Deming puts it: 'It is in a wise selection of a time's most powerful film daydreams that the historian will find evidence of issues and of attitudes not talked of, not professed, but felt in the bones.' (1944: 20) Additionally, the methodology also remains the same, with a single film being seen as capable of representing a larger clutch of films. In turn, such a film's formal narrative processes are examined by means of full story synopsis – witness the scrutiny of the plot of such films as *Mr Lucky* (1944) and *Hail the Conquering Hero* (1942). A third continuity has to do with a number of narrative storylines and themes developed in the book, which had already been identified in the article. These include a concern with the 'success boy' and with 'animated cartoons ... with the theme of a disordered world … [that] frequently ends in an explosion. Or it may end simply by interrupting itself … to spill one realm of reality into another' (1944: 18).

On the other hand, significant variations appear in *Running Away from Myself*. For instance, new themes and storylines have been identified and added to the various ideological currents seen to be at work in the United States in the 1940s. One of these categories involves the 'tough guy' – often a private detective who courts danger and destruction not only because of his code as a professional but also to prove to himself that he has the capacity to survive. A second variation lies in the fact that in the book there is far less emphasis laid on the paradigm of cognitive psychology (with its recurring vocabulary of dream, nightmare, daydream, hallucination and so on). Instead, a more amorphous vocabulary appears that, *inter alia*, refers to dream but also to the veil, the magic circle, substitution, translation and sleight of hand among other terms.

A third shift has to do with the more intricate interweaving of ideological discourses that Deming sees at work as a collective effect of the films that she examines. In the 1944 article, she describes these as a 'constellation', whereas *Running Away from Myself* stresses their interconnection. We will now examine Deming's book in more detail.

Form and themes

Running Away from Myself runs to a little more than 200 pages organized into ten chapters. The first and last chapter are general, so eight chapters investigate a total of 99 feature films. Each of these chapters is concerned with examining a series of films that disclose a particular theme and an accompanying formal narrative arrangement whereby that theme is elaborated and qualified. Chapter 2 of the book can usefully introduce us to the emphasis laid on film form and film theme. Deming's point of departure is an extended synopsis, a careful retelling of the plot of *Casablanca* (1942). This film had already been mentioned in the 1944 article, but here it is given an extended summary that amounts to a little under half the chapter.

One reviewer of *Running Away from Myself* complained that the book was top-heavy with film synopses (Whittaker 1970: 152–53), while even a more sympathetic account notes this same tendency towards synopsis (Bordwell 1989: 74–76). There are certainly plenty of film summaries in the book, but Deming is aware of the possible charge of too much story description. She rebuts the accusation by noting that a film synopsis can help serve as a substitute if the film itself is unavailable to the book's reader (Deming 1969: 7). This was certainly the case in 1944 when she wrote her article, and it was still the case in 1969 when *Running Away from Myself* was published. I would also add the important methodological point that a written film synopsis is also a necessary way for Deming to introduce the reader to the process of meaning-making in a particular film. An extended, accurate retelling of a film serves as a token of its emotional and durational experience in terms of its development, its ongoing orchestration of story and situation, its interweaving of plot and character, and its progression from part to part through to its ending.

The extended synopsis of *Casablanca*, the longest in the book, can serve here to demonstrate in detail how Deming sees form and theme operating to establish an ideological landscape for an audience to inhabit. The extended outline, including its registration of key shifts and changes, also allows more truncated recital and analysis of other films elsewhere in the book. Although she does not use the term, Deming is aware that *Casablanca* – like many feature films then and since – operates with a double plotline that constantly intersects: a war story and a love story. The film's setting and time are quite specific – an occupied French colonial city in early December 1941. Its protagonist is bitter, emphatic that he is not a patriot; he will let others do whatever fighting needs to be done. Deming describes an early flashback revealing that Rick (Humphrey Bogart) was also a jilted lover, whereupon the woman in question enters the film in the present, along with her husband, a French patriot wanted by the Nazis. There follows a succession of events relating to the war story, the love story or both, which ends with the protagonist now committing himself to the war and the fight although he loses the woman. Deming draws attention to the process by which the presence of one plotline allows a thematic sleight of hand to occur in the other plotline:

> Look where the film has brought us out … [It] has permitted a most disturbing figure to take shape (the war objector), and there before our eyes has comfortably recruited him … without even leaving us with the sense that we have witnessed a remarkable translation … The love story has borne the brunt of the work: it is the guise of the jilted lover that has allowed the figure to take shape at all and utter his bitter cries; and it is the scene in which he regains his lost faith in the beloved that enables us to cancel out those cries and believe in his entry into the fight. (Deming 1969: 22–23)

The analysis of this film then becomes a springboard for the investigation of seven other films of the early to mid-1940s. What these films have in common is the theme picked up from Casablanca of the reluctant warrior or patriot who undergoes a narrative conversion to the fight and to the cause. Obscuring this commonality with *Casablanca* in other films is the fact that the protagonist may be played by a different actor while the setting and situation may also be different. But it is even more important to consider what other plotlines and themes have 'borne the brunt of the work in such thematic reversals' (Deming 1969: 29). Table 3.1 summarizes Deming's examination of this other group of films in Chapter 2, which – following *Casablanca* – has introduced a protagonist who was initially cynical about fighting for a cause only to undergo a conversion late in that particular film wherein he becomes a fighting patriot.

It can be seen from Table 3.1 that in all the films offered by Deming in Chapter 2, following her analysis of *Casablanca*, all the protagonists undergo a similar kind of conversion, leading their heroes not only to take up arms but even to encounter death. In turn, this outline of the micro procedures at work in Chapter 2 allows us to grasp Deming's poetics project in the book as a whole. Here we need to understand the overall structure, the processual logic, at work in the chapters of *Running Away from Myself*. The development underlying the

Table 3.1: Recurring themes and plotlines in 'war hero' films

Films	Themes and storylines
Passage to Marseilles (1944)	C A R
The Imposter (1944)	C A I O S
Mr Lucky (1943)	C R I O
China (1943)	C R S
To Have and Have Not (1944)	C R A S
Reunion in France (1942)	C R S

Key abbreviations of themes and plotlines

C   The protagonist converts to the cause, to a sense of duty, to the good fight.

R   The protagonist falls in love or reconfirms his love for a woman.

I   The protagonist takes on the identity of another man.

O   The protagonist has an ordinary, everyday background and moves away from humble or even criminal origins.

A   The protagonist leads himself and, sometimes, others through perilous and dangerous adventures.

S   The protagonist is stoic or even suicidal in the face of physical challenges.

succession of the chapters is not random; rather, the moves are cumulative and intricate, with the chapters complexly catching these up like the gears of a mountain bike. The emerging pattern is increasingly complicated and broad.

As already mentioned, Chapters 1 and 10 can be set aside as explanatory and general, so we need only attend to eight intervening chapters. As already noted, Deming's point of departure is a theme related to the war, concerning a (male) 'war hero' with his characteristic cry 'I'm not fighting for anything anymore – except myself'. This protagonist soon drops his cynicism in favour of a patriotic commitment to the 'Cause', becomes a warrior prepared to fight the good fight. As we have also seen, some of the films examined in the chapter also involve romantic storylines. Hence, in the next chapter of her book, Deming focuses on a particular kind of 'love story', and especially on the protagonists – female as well as male – deployed in a series of other films of the time. These feature 'strong' positive women, whereas the male love interests tend to be damaged goods – whether as the result of war or other circumstances. Deming also notices a second, less-demanding woman figure so that, in effect, these films have elements of a love triangle situation.

In Chapter 4, *Running Away from Myself* returns to the figure of the male, although this is one who appears to be the opposite to the damaged male protagonists of the previous two chapters. This other male is a mythic American hero – 'the success boy' – but he is revealed in 1940s films to display the same shattered self as some of those other male heroes of Chapters 2 and 3. Indeed, there is also a dark version of the figure. This is a variant of the 'success boy', who reveals the figure to sometimes be a villain planning to kill a beloved because the latter knows too much about him. Detachment and questing ('I keep running away from myself') are common themes assembled around the very complex protagonist of 1940s American films taking shape in the book, so that Chapter 5 addresses a series of 'restless ones', 'rolling stones' poised between possibly never leaving home on the one hand and questing into the unknown and even into oblivion on the other.

In turn, Chapter 6 offers an even more composite figure, who sums up all the thematic tendencies noted to this point, pursuing an object that turns out to be illusory and empty. Here, Deming introduces a more historical emphasis by noting such an implicit focus in two wartime 'love' films and a more brutal consideration in several melodramas from the immediate postwar period that feature danger, intrigue and even murder. Nevertheless, even if the attainment is a hollow one in these latter films, the protagonist can still affirm his own survival in the pursuit of a goal or objective.

This act of avowal ('I'm still alive') serves as pretext for Chapter 7, which examines the 'tough boy' private detective hero of noir crime melodrama. Women are a dominant part of the labyrinth that surrounds the hero, but even when they turn out to be on the right side of the law, the real test for the hero lies in his own endurance, his own capacity to survive. Chapter 8 resumes the figure of the reckless one of Chapter 5, who was ready to plunge into disengagement – even oblivion. Examining a small handful of films, beginning with *Double Indemnity* (1944) and *The Postman Always Rings Twice* (1945), allows Deming to focus on the figure of the nihilist, a particular version of the composite protagonist of *Running Away from Myself*. This character is bent on getting free of all commitments, risking annihilation but also possibly gaining transcendence. The latter possibility is further probed in Deming's last chapter, which concerns a specific version of the composite figure as a whole. This particular protagonist is a comic one; not really a member of this world, this figure can see it fall asunder, be superseded by a kind of cosmic humour. Deming links this hero back to the tough guy protagonist of Chapter 7, maintaining that they are the only ones who 'manage in a broken world to hold themselves intact, if precariously' (1969: 200).

Deming's US audience and Kracauer's German audience

We can follow up this outline of Deming's poetics of film audience reception by considering it alongside another that was underway at approximately the same time. Jones mentions another element at work in Deming's 1944 article (and, I would add, in *Running Away from Myself*) (Jones 2007: 42). This was the influence of German Jewish *émigré* intellectual Siegfried Kracauer, who became a kind of mentor to Deming, with the relationship repeatedly acknowledged in the article's footnotes, in the Preface of Kracauer's *From Caligari to Hitler* and in repeated asides in *Running Away from Myself*. The connection has more than anecdotal interest for my argument, for a juxtaposition of the two books further enhances the claim of Deming's poetics.

First, though, the historical connection. Working alongside each other at MoMA between 1942 and 1945, the two developed a regard for each other's projects. The young woman found inspiration both in the middle-aged émigré's method of close analysis of film plot and motif and in the grand scale of his project, while the German exile noted a flattering complementarity of sorts in the Library of Congress Film Project's team investigation of contemporary US films. Kracauer had arrived in the United States in 1941 and obtained sponsorship from the Film Division of MoMA. Subsequently, he secured grants from the Rockefeller, Guggenheim, Bollingen and Mellon Foundations. In 1942, he published *Propaganda and the Nazi War Film*, and this helped him to secure backing for a larger project on the history of German film (Jay 1985: 169–72). He worked on this project at MoMA between 1942 and 1947, when his research culminated in the book *From Caligari to Hitler: A Psychological History of the German Film*. The institutional support that had come his way continued, with the book being published by Princeton University Press.

Kracauer argued that a close analysis of German films – especially from the end of World War I – revealed a consistent desire for and fascination with a superman figure controlling and manipulating affairs. However, as Jay notes, *From Caligari to Hitler* also 'bitterly condemn the German people as a whole with little effort spent on determining which film appealed to which audience' (1985: 170). As a sympathetic biographer of Kracauer's intellectual achievement, Jay does not press this point, although he notes that critics at the time of the book's publication and in the four decades since then had been divided in their assessment of the book's achievement. The nub of the matter was just how valid it was to infer the political and social actions of a people on the basis of an examination of the cultural artefacts of the time.

Jay's study appeared in 1985. Coinciding in that same year with the publication of his analysis of German émigré intellectuals in America during World War II and afterwards (Jay 1985) came another study that delivered a final *coup de grace* to the validity of Kracauer's 'psychological history' of German film. This was Thompson's (1985) *Exporting Entertainment: America in the World Film Market, 1907–1934*, an analysis of the international distribution of Hollywood feature films across much of the period covered by *From Caligari to Hitler*. Thompson does not mention the latter study and its hypothesis about the German film audience. Instead, by means of careful scholarship using trade records, she shows that American films – shorts, silent films and sound features – were highly popular in many overseas film markets in the 1920s and 1930s, including that of Germany.

Kracauer's study takes no account of this variety of local and imported films being shown in German film theatres at the time. For his thesis of ideological reflection or mediation to be at least plausible, his unstated assumption is that German film audiences were watching nothing other than the films that he examines in *From Caligari to Hitler*. Thompson's study shows that this was not the case. Some audience members may have seen only the films discussed in his book, but many more would have seen these alongside many others in many genres imported from elsewhere, most especially from Hollywood. Once this realization is taken on board, Kracauer's thesis about a

German's public growing disposition towards submission to a superman becomes even more implausible. In other words, *From Caligari to Hitler* may, finally, tell us little about German popular opinion and social outlook in the 1920s and 1930s, an assumed *zeitgeist* of the time, and tell us a lot more about the ideological spectacles worn by a German émigré intellectual watching a batch of films from his native country at MoMA between 1942 and 1947.

Deming's poetics never takes on the grand ambitions of Kracauer's project. Instead, the approach is more open-minded and agnostic, far less apocalyptic than that of the German. Admittedly, the pattern revealed in Deming's analysis is a more complex one than is unearthed in the German films of the earlier time. Reminding herself that films were multivocal, she finds a complex recurring structure of ideological discourses at work in contemporary American films dealing, as we have seen, with protagonists ranging from the war hero to the comic figure. Instead of one recurring ideological discourse, there is discovered a fluid, shifting series of voices with no one voice permanently in the ascendancy. Where Kracauer is not in doubt about the message that German audiences historically derived from films of the 1920s and 1930s, Deming deliberately stops short of assuming how such tropes and motifs from American films of the 1940s were actually received and understood by different audiences. As she comments on this gap between perceived meanings and audience effects, 'the films that have found an orientation among the sensed realities of the time, that demonstrate most vividly the difficulties of belief today ... We are, for the moment, not quite sure where we live' (Deming 1969: 36). In effect, her poetics does not require her to go any further, and she does not do so.

Conclusions

The main conclusion will already be clear: that Deming's book *Running Away from Myself* is a notable achievement in the field of audience-oriented poetics of cinema. Interpretation and criticism do not come to the fore in its account of how films worked to create a landscape of meaning for their audience. Nor is the book concerned with cultural value judgements that would promote the claim of one film over another in terms of aesthetic achievement, morality of outlook, technical breakthroughs, artistic significance and so on. For that matter, the study does not deal with the history of film in the 1940s, whether focusing on the production industry or as one affected by larger social, political and other concerns and events. Instead, Deming's aim is to describe a mental landscape cumulatively created and maintained by films of the 1940s that audiences of the time inhabited to a larger or a lesser extent. Repetition and variation were key mechanisms in the audience's viewing experience, so filmgoers could identify recurring story situations, narrative sleights of hand, frequent plot developments and endings, character relationships, protagonist dilemmas, verbal formulas and slogans, character convictions and aspirations, familiar statements and claims, and so on – even as they also enjoyed various inventive touches within such an ideational terrain. This kind of meaning-making was and is a recurring process, a matter of renewed activity each time an audience watches one of these films – hence the importance of the story synopsis in Deming's account of how these films work as meaning-makers for audiences.

Poetics is not a popular field of critical inquiry, so we can also deduce why the book has received little attention over the past 40 years. As we have seen, *Running Away from Myself* was published almost 20 years after its time, so far as film scholarship was concerned. By 1969, cognitive psychology no longer provided a master discourse for the analysis of film. The paradigm was already waning by the early 1950s, and was massively supplanted as film discourse by auteurism in the 1960s. This shift meant that the book was destined to struggle to find an appreciative readership. *Running Away from Myself* deserves more attention than it has received, but not as a 'classic' or historical curiosity. Instead, the book remains just as lively, interesting and relevant today as an excursion into the mostly uncharted region of film-reception aesthetics as when it was first conceived and begun back in the 1940s. It deserves to be far better known than it is. Accordingly, my prime concern here has been to identify just what kind of book Barbara Deming has given to later generations of film scholars.

References

Bordwell, D. (1989), *Making Meaning: Inference and Rhetoric in the Interpretation of Cinema*, Cambridge, MA: Harvard University Press.

——— (2005), *Poetics of Cinema*, New York: Routledge.

Deming, B. (1944), 'The Library of Congress Film Project: Exposition of a Method', *Library of Congress Quarterly Journal of Current Acquisitions*, 2: 1, pp. 1–38.

——— (1966), *Prison Notes*, New York: Grossman.

——— (1969), *Running Away from Myself: A Dream Portrait of America Drawn from the Films of the 1940s*, New York: Grossman.

Deming, B. and Meyerding, J. (ed.) (1984), *We are All Part of One Another: A Barbara Deming Reader*, Baltimore, MD: New Society Publishing.

Greetham, D. (1999), '"Who's In, Who's Out": The Cultural Poetics of Archival Exclusion', *Studies in the Literary Imagination*, 32: 1, pp. 1–38.

Jay, M. (1985), 'The Extraterritorial Life of Siegfried Kracauer', in M. Jay, *Permanent Exiles: Essays in the Intellectual Migration from Germany to America*, New York: Columbia University Press, pp. 165–97.

Jones, J. (2007), 'The Library of Congress Film Project: Film Collecting and a United State(s) of Mind', *The Moving Image*, 6: 2, pp. 30–51.

Jowett, G. (1976), *Film: The Democratic Art*, Boston: Little Brown and Co.

Kracauer, S. (1942), *Propaganda and the Nazi War Film*, New York: Museum of Modern Art.

——— (1947), *From Caligari to Hitler: A Psychological History of the German Film*, Princeton, NJ: Princeton University Press.

Thompson, K. (1985), *Exporting Entertainment: America in the World Film Market, 1907–1934*, London: British Film Institute.

Tyler, P. (1944), *The Hollywood Hallucination*, New York: Creative Age.

—— (1947), *Magic and Myth of the Movies*, New York: Henry Holt.

—— (1948), *Chaplin: Last of the Clowns*, New York: Vanguard Press.

Whittaker, R. (1970), 'Book Review: *Running Away from Myself* by Barbara Deming', *Journal of Aesthetic Education*, 4: 4, pp. 152–53.

Wolfenstein, M. and Leites, N. (1950), *Movies: A Psychological Study*, Glencoe, IL: The Free Press.

Chapter 4

The Porous Boundaries of Newsreel Memory Research

Louise Anderson

B etween 2006 and 2009, the Arts and Humanities Research Council in the United Kingdom funded a unique research project to investigate cinema audiences' memories of newsreels on Tyneside (north-east England) in the 1940s.[1] Interviews were conducted with older people across Newcastle-upon-Tyne and its surrounding districts, collecting their memories in oral history-style interviews.[2] The research sought to establish how newsreels, as a distinctive cultural phenomenon, are remembered. These hitherto undocumented audience memories are crucial to a more complete understanding of the newsreels as a vital part of both the historic cinema-going experience and as the cultural expression of a particular wartime generation. Based in oral history, the research focused on the processes of remembering the newsreels, referred to here as 'newsreel memory'. In doing so, the research revealed a great deal about how personal memory operates within the constraints of society and culture.[3] This chapter explores the particular challenges of conducting research into newsreel memories that appear to linger on the porous boundaries of personal memory, cultural memory and history. It also looks at the questions that are posed as newsreel memory work takes place in the spaces between a number of disciplines and methodologies. It examines how the different 'types' of newsreel memory expressed by the Tyneside research participants revealed, first, how newsreels are remembered both as simply part of the backdrop to cinema-going and as an important source of epoch-defining news and, second, that newsreel memory is expressed as if these remembered news events had been witnessed at first hand. Finally, this chapter also considers how the over-exposure of a limited number of iconic newsreel images has impacted upon personal memory, as individuals both lived through the events they recall from the 1940s *and* have subsequently been repeatedly exposed to mediated representations of the period.

Newsreels

It is worth reminding ourselves that British cinema programmes of the 1940s were much more than one feature film: for audiences 70 years ago, a typical cinema programme included both A and B pictures, a newsreel and at least one additional short item, which could include a travelogue, a comedy, a cartoon, a topical novelty or a public information film – additional elements that are so often forgotten in film histories. However, it is this 'cinematic surround' that completes the history of cinema-going itself. Despite the historical importance and social impact of newsreel viewing in the 1940s, beyond a passing acknowledgement that there were factual elements of the regular cinema programme, film histories pay little attention to the newsreels. In addition, although the number of empirical research projects investigating the distant memories of the cinema audience is steadily increasing, there remains an apparent lack of scholarly interest in audience perspectives on the newsreels.[4] Indeed, to date, cinema memory studies have decisively ignored newsreel memories, which remain virtually undocumented.[5] This is regardless of the fact that they were an integral part of virtually every cinema programme – including, in some cases, children's cinema clubs – and, of course, at a small number of dedicated news theatres.[6] We know a great deal about regular cinema-goers, and a number of authoritative contemporary studies have told us much about the habits and preferences of cinema audiences during the 1940s (e.g. see Box 1946; Box and Moss 1946; Mayer 1948). However, we know virtually nothing about what these vast audiences thought of, or how they now remember, the newsreels.[7]

To fully appreciate the complexities of newsreel memory, we must first be clear about what newsreels were, and what they were not. Historian Nicholas Pronay (1976) identifies cinema's economic basis – its ability to produce mass entertainment relatively cheaply – as the feature that defined the newsreels. He argues that the development of film journalism was inextricably linked to the development of film as an entertainment industry (1976: 96). All five of the British sound newsreels, *Pathé Gazette* (later *Pathé News*), *Gaumont-British News*, *British Paramount News*, *British Movietone News* and *Universal News*, were produced and distributed by companies affiliated with successful British and American feature film companies, thus ensuring both financial backing and/or distribution to the parent company's exhibition circuit.[8] Newsreels were designed from the outset to be screened in regular cinemas – the first British newsreels were produced by Pathé in 1910 – and we should remind ourselves that they served a specific purpose: they were not primarily a source of news (a role reserved for newspapers and radio news coverage), but provided an entertaining package of news and events already in the public domain.[9] In essence, British newsreels illustrated the news rather than attempting to analyse or interpret it, instead providing audiences with a breezy round-up of news and topical items. According to film historian Rachel Low, newsreels

> were part of the entertainment industry and did exactly what they set out to do, which was to present a light magazine about current events similar to the more popular papers, and to avoid antagonising anyone ... Editorial comment or a balanced picture of world events were somebody else's business. (1979: 43)

In addition, the newsreel companies appeared to be responding to audiences' preferences. Quoting figures from a 1927 survey of Odeon patrons, historian Nicholas Hiley reveals that although an impressive majority of the audience may have responded positively when asked about newsreels, their length (typically six to ten minutes) and their position within the cinema programme (as a filler between the features) suggested something rather different. 'British cinema-goers wanted entertainment, not news,' he writes (1998: 59). Nevertheless, in the 1940s the newsreels' recognition factor was undoubtedly high, with newsreels and their particular style of reporting familiar to most of the British population. Indeed, they were designed for audiences who were familiar with their format, and were shown to audiences who would have missed them if they had been dropped, but who would not tolerate them taking more than ten minutes out of the cinema programme (1998: 62).

Of course, the situation was somewhat different in news theatres, where initially newsreels made up the bulk of the programme. However, by the mid-1930s, even within this specialized sector, it was becoming clear that news theatre programmes were moving away from their news-only beginnings by including cartoons, among other things, in an effort to attract customers. In 1934, the trade paper *Kinematograph Weekly*, observed that only a third of the average news theatre programme was made up of current news, the rest being animated cartoons, two-reel comedies and travelogues, and suggested that a more suitable description for news theatres would be 'interest theatre' (cited in Young 2005: 229).

Everyday newsreel memories

Given their ubiquity within the regular cinema programme, it is perhaps unsurprising that much of the remembered pleasure associated with newsreel viewing was its reassuring character, its oft-repeated format, familiar title music and well-loved commentators. Indeed, perhaps because of the familiarity of the newsreel encounter, its memory is often rendered in the vaguest of terms: 'It was simply part of the fabric of cinema-going,' according to 72-year-old research participant Steve Whitley. The act of newsreel viewing was recalled by many of the research participants as a secondary activity, a precursor to the main activity of the cinematic experience – that is, the feature film they had gone to see. The inclusion of the newsreel in the regular cinema programme became just one small part of the cinema-going routine or ritual. Further, a great deal of the newsreels' content was in fact simply light entertainment, demanding minimal attention or engagement. As 75-year-old Patricia Charlewood recalled:

> I think when you're just going to be entertained it would just be sort of information wouldn't it, 'and today the King went and did this, that and the other and the Queen did this'. So it wouldn't be anything too serious.

Although, as discussed below, a handful of momentous historic events are remembered with great clarity, to recollect in substantive detail an everyday experience from 60 years ago is particularly challenging as one works at the limits of living memory.[10] Even when recalling their wartime newsreel memories, research participants presented them as little more than inventories or catalogues of named momentous events, described in the broadest of terms.

In this way, newsreel memories become part of a wider historical discourse, a meta-narrative of events in British history from the period 1939–45. For example, 76-year-old Ted Moralee said: 'That was the main thing, the war in news.' Despite participants' obvious desire to share their newsreel memories, spontaneously recalled memories of specific news events featured in the newsreels were few and far between. As participant Steve Whitley expressed it: 'Sorry my recollections are fairly slender – they [newsreels] were just part of the backdrop to going to the cinema. As I say, I can't recall anything in particular.' Mr Whitley's use of the term 'in particular' is revealing; when participants were asked whether they could remember any specific newsreels, many struggled to recall any in detail. For example, 88-year-old Harry Lenthall recalled that newsreels were: 'Well, anything that was topical at the time.' Here the recollection of a rather vague generic memory impression of the newsreels is not enough to sustain a detailed response. As 96-year-old Rose Johnson put it: 'You'll find it [newsreel memory] pretty general I would think.'

Thus newsreel memory appears to differ from other cinema memory in a number of respects precisely because of what we might refer to as a particular kind of disengagement. While traditional cinema memory studies focus on fans of a particular star or genre (Barker and Brooks 1998; Fiske 2000; Lewis 1992; Stacey 1994; Taylor 1989), allowing scope for participants to recall their own special, 'treasured' cinematic memories – moments invested with personal meaning and importance – newsreel memories are often characterized by their vagueness or 'lack' of personal memory.

'Types' of newsreel memory

Given the complexity of newsreel memory, it would be useful at this juncture to distinguish between two distinct 'types' of newsreel memory. The first 'type' recalls the significance of the newsreels as a cultural form. Eighty-two-year-old participant Yvonne Edwards recalled how important the newsreels were to a generation of film-goers: 'Well they really were a lifeline or an information line you know … you got a good grounding of the news that was going on.' The research participants were unanimous, despite the recognition in hindsight of bias or World War II propaganda, that the newsreels were a significant cultural form. Ironically, many participants recalled the triviality of much newsreel content, yet insisted that the newsreels were an important source of news and information. It was the perceived, and now mythologized, evidential status of the newsreel image that came to the fore in memory. The opportunity to see moving images of news and historic events imbued the newsreels with significance as a form of cultural knowledge despite misgivings, either at the time or in hindsight, about the veracity or truthfulness of the images they contained. The second 'type' of newsreel memory recalls the newsreels as chronicler of a limited number of specific historic events, triumphs and tragedies – and here, perhaps, lies the defining feature of newsreel memory. When asked to describe their memories, participants often talked of the news event itself, referring to it as if they had witnessed the event itself at first-hand. Examining the memory of these vicarious experiences of secondary witnessing leads to a better understanding of how newsreels have become part of our shared cultural heritage, with resonance far beyond the audiences who first saw them.

Undoubtedly, the investigative focus on memory as historical evidence raises ongoing epistemological concerns about its reliability and veracity. As all historical audience research acknowledges, what audiences tell researchers is shaped by many factors, all of which are formed, to some degree, by memory itself. Of course, in a sense all ethnographic approaches to film audiences deal with memory; it is in fact simply the 'gap' between the experience and the recollection of that experience that widens or narrows, depending on the period being studied. Noting the positivist tendency for scholars in the social sciences to regard oral histories as impossibly subjective, Maynes and colleagues maintain that it is precisely this characteristic 'that has opened up space for new understandings of the relationship between the individual and the social' (2008: 6). In this regard, the work of oral historians Luisa Passerini (1987), Michael Frisch (1990) and Alessandro Portelli (1991) has been particularly influential in highlighting the need to interpret individual stories within wider cultural frameworks, and to explore the complex ways in which meanings are negotiated between the individual and the public consciousness. Portelli, for example, distinguishes oral histories from their written counterparts, in that the former tend to reveal more about the meaning of events and rather less about the events themselves. Importantly, he maintains that 'subjectivity is as much the business of history as are the more "visible" facts' (1991: 51). An integral part of studying the past is the role that both the mythologizing of popular memory and the specificity of individual experience play in the formation of personal recollection. Memories are formed within the constraints of particular cultural conventions, discourses, nostalgias and mythologies about the past – even for those who lived through it. Thus the interviews conducted for the Tyneside research revealed less about the relationship between audiences and newsreels than they did about the ways in which a particular type of cinematic memory is formed.

Mnemonic communities

Focusing on the processes of remembering through oral testimony, we can analyse the practices and processes of memory at the level of the individual, but perhaps more importantly, look at how individual memory operates within society and culture. Much recent reception and memory-focused research is based on the communal nature of reception practices, and in the Tyneside study – although it was based principally on individual narrative – communities of memory emerged strongly.[11] These are the groups – to which all of us as individuals belong – that frame our memories and which provide a context within which individual memories are formed and in which recollection takes place.

For example, talking about the extraordinary impact of newsreel footage from the German concentration camps released in 1945, 78-year-old research participant Frank Knaggs recalled: 'There was a different kind of sensibility in those days. Nowadays we're so hardened to this kind of thing.'

The Tyneside study focused on the analysis of the collective remembering of a particular mnemonic community: the wartime generation in the city of Newcastle-upon-Tyne and its surrounding districts. For this group of individuals of varying class, political and familial backgrounds, the shared experience of having lived through 'the war' remains central to their sense of both cultural and personal identity – and crucially, in this context, to their memory. Indeed, the popular mythology surrounding the British resolve and defiance against the odds ('the Dunkirk spirit') during World War II (1939–45) appears to exert enormous influence on their individual newsreel memories, which is both enabled and limited by the popular discourses of history.[12] It was clear that the gathered memories were a negotiation between lived experience and the imagined and mythologized, but that these myths are integral to the creation and survival of both individual and collective identity.

In this regard, the research examined the manifestation of social interactions and collective structures within the individual memories gathered and the extent to which newsreel memories at these different levels (the individual and the social) are interwoven. In analysing the memories of the newsreels from the 1940s, the study revealed that newsreel memories represented the place where personal and social memory met. What became apparent was the extent to which major historical events were anchored within the personal and the autobiographical. In the following interview extract, 70-year-old participant Jack Barrie recalls his father's response to newsreel images of the liberation of the Bergen-Belsen concentration camp:

> I do remember when the war was at an end, *Paramount News* covered ... when the Belsen prisoner of war camp was liberated you know. And some of the shots there I can still remember them and it was really bad. In fact me father had to come out ... couldn't, he couldn't watch it.

Remembering their distant newsreel viewing allowed participants to negotiate different configurations of identity: national, local, generational, personal and at times political, as in their sometimes critical analysis of wartime newsreel propaganda. As revealed through the gathered narratives, the relationship between past and present selves – a process that Portelli calls 'shuttlework' (1991: 65) – is dynamic and constantly shifting, persisting as a delicate negotiation or dialogue between an individual's past and present selves. It is what Nancy Huggett refers to as the 'narrated self' (the young remembered self) and the 'narrating self' (the older speaking self) (2002: 208), as illustrated here by research participant Steve Whitley: 'I now realize it was terrible propaganda but nevertheless then I thought they [the newsreels] gave a true picture of what was going on.'

The past, then, is produced in the act of remembering. The newsreel memories generated for the research were inevitably affected by present-day attitudes, views and concerns, the intervening 70-odd years, repeated exposure over those years to archive newsreel material and the specific research context within which participants were asked to recall their memories. Nevertheless, it is their relation to lived historical experience that constitutes memories' specificity, and we should not forget that oral histories are embodied in a real person, 'with a real history and psychology, and living and changing through time' (Maynes et al. 2008: 41). At the very heart of the study was the interpretation of individual stories or autobiography within wider cultural frames of meaning, utilized in order to elucidate the relationship between newsreel memory formation, familial influences, and national and generational identity. The cultural history of the newsreels is not simply about their consumption, but about how these encounters were integrated into the very fabric of everyday life. Often recollections were framed within a familiar context of habitual cinema-going or news theatre-going, as 74-year-old research participant Christopher Beadle explained:

> During the war we'd come into Newcastle [from] time to time for shopping, whatever …
> to visit friends and shopping … and nearly always went to the News Cinema – that was
> a treat.

In recounting their trips to the news theatres, for example, research participants revealed an enormous amount of detail not only about their personal relationships, but about society more generally. Thus, from the research data, we can situate the formation of newsreel memories within a series of meaningful contexts or frames of meaning.[13]

Newsreel memories of historic events

Within the gathered memories, there were individual newsreels that were remembered with greater clarity. While to refer to them as 'treasured memories' would be misleading, they are examples of historic event memories. At these moments, audiences experienced a distinctive type of cinematic pleasure centred round what we might call the 'spectacle of actuality' (Cowie 1999: 19). The recollections of canonical newsreels of historic or 'marker events' (Teer-Tomaselli 2006), now recalled in newsreel memory, not only provided the basis for participants to remember acts of collective witnessing – as cinema audiences watched the events of history unfolding before them – but provided the foundation on which personal memories were formed, as this recollection from participant Jack Barrie, again remembering the liberation of Bergen-Belsen concentration camp, illustrates: 'There was deathly silence in the audience and everybody went out sort of absolutely shaken.' In addition, in an important imaginative sense, newsreel viewing brought these historic events into existence for cinema audiences. Seventy-three-year-old participant Charlie Hall recalled the wartime newsreels: 'You heard the news but when you saw it actually in black and white you know it really sank in what was happening.'

Further, throughout the research, the recurrence of the same limited number of freely remembered newsreel memories reveals not only the significance of a popular shared memory, but the conflation of personal memory and popular history. The clustering of newsreel memories around a limited number of unusual historic or marker events, and the deeply felt personal emotion with which those memories were expressed, reveals the formative relationship between the historic events recorded by the newsreels and the individual expressions of memory. Such iconic events included Dunkirk (May–June 1940), the Blitz (September 1940–June 1941), the Battle of Britain (1940), the D-Day landings (June 1944), the liberation of Bergen-Belsen concentration camp (April 1945) and Victory in Europe (VE) Day (May 1945).[14]

The research also revealed that memories of particular historic events evoked the specific iconic newsreel images with which they have become synonymous. In this way, newsreel images become etched into both personal and collective memory, not only in terms of their initial exhibition, but also by their frequent reiteration over subsequent decades. Thus the newsreels continue to exert cultural authority because they are taken, for the most part, to be faithful records of major historical events, providing an invaluable empirical record of the past.

While undoubtedly there remains a virtual 'newsreel blackout' in film histories, interest in the newsreels to date has been predominantly as a source of historical evidence or as a filmic 'kite-mark' or guarantee of historic authenticity.[15] As early as 1967, in an article published in *Sight and Sound* magazine, critic Penelope Huston articulated a sense of the uneasy relationship between history and the 'newsfilm'. Referring particularly to the BBC documentary *The Great War* (1964), Huston acknowledged that for most people by the late 1960s, newsreels existed only as the raw material of historical television programmes (2002: 290). In recent years, this situation has only been exacerbated by the emergence of increasing numbers of cable and satellite television channels relying almost entirely on newsreel footage to illustrate history. The peculiar cultural value of the newsreel image as documentary evidence of the real gives rise to a shift in memory, providing newsreels with a renewed, reinvigorated sense of significance. For example, 76-year-old-participant Jean Murray recalled that newsreels contained:

> All the very latest up to the minute news. Like it would have come on the television … as soon as a battle was won or something happened they were at the news theatres. They were all over the country at the news theatres and that was how people, you didn't have to wait for a newspaper the next day you know.

What Jean did not recall was that newsreels were not available to screen on the day they were filmed, and could be weeks late in second-, third- or even fourth-run venues. Thus it appears that because of the popular regard in which the newsreels are held as an example of genuine historical documentation, their historical significance becomes heightened in personal memory.

The repeated recollection of a handful of iconic newsreel images (noted above), remembered throughout the gathered narratives, suggests the existence of a canon of newsreel footage, not only in newsreel memory but in popular cultural memory. Further, the repeated media use of this particular newsreel footage reinforces the canon that, over the years, has become both over-exposed and ultra-familiar. Who and what gets remembered relies partly on the availability of 'memorable enough' newsreel footage and the appropriation of this footage to re-present a version of the past. In this way, cultural memory and history become entangled in the reuse and popular reappropriation of newsreel material. Indeed, the memory of a specific event is often perceived to be located within particular newsreel footage to such a degree that it is impossible to imagine the event in the *absence* of the newsreel footage.

The issue of the evidential status of the newsreel image took the research beyond most cinematic memory studies into an examination of the role of newsreel viewing as a form of secondary witnessing, and thus newsreel memory as a unique example of cultural memory was foregrounded.[16] Precisely because of its basis in a factual cinematographic form, newsreel memory provides an unprecedented insight into the extent of cultural memory's entanglement with cultural production – that is, the way in which newsreel memory is entwined with the use and reuse of the newsreel image within a wide range of popular cultural products. The saturation of popular culture with recollections of World War II and the Holocaust results in memory – and newsreel memory no less so – that is almost impossibly entangled. What came through strongly in reviewing the interviews was the extent to which newsreel memories have been framed by the subsequent use of newsreel material in other contexts and that popular conceptions of newsreels undoubtedly influenced the memories gathered for the project.

The entanglement of newsreel memory

In her excellent interdisciplinary account of the ways in which American culture remembers, memorializes and even re-enacts traumatic events, Marita Sturken (1997) considers how television images of traumatic events not only feed into official histories, but also play an important role in the production of cultural memory. She writes that 'true distinctions between personal memory, cultural memory and history cannot be made' (1997: 6). This contention is borne out by the newsreel memories gathered for the research that have become impossibly entangled with a series of cultural products – particularly, as noted, the over-exposure of newsreel footage in a variety of media forms, including television documentary and historical re-enactment. Thus the gathered newsreel memories were the result of a process of reproduction – that is, they were filtered through a series of cultural products. Sturken refers to these cultural products as 'technologies of memory' (1997: 10): the objects, images and representations through which cultural memory is produced, shared and given meaning. Both personal and cultural memory is articulated through these processes of representation. While memorials are the most traditional example of memory objects, cinematographic memorials increasingly represent a significant site or repository of cultural memory; images of the past, and particularly moving images of the past, are crucial to its survival. Ironically, perhaps, this is no less true for those who actually lived through the events depicted. As Sturken notes, 'cinematic representations of the past have the capacity to entangle with personal and cultural memory' (1997: 10), and as the Tyneside study revealed, time and time again, participants were unable to distinguish between their original encounters with specific newsreels and subsequent encounters on the small screen. When asked to elaborate on his memories of wartime newsreels, participant Steve Whitley explained:

> I'm sorry I can't remember. I do have images in my mind … and I wasn't there so I must have seen it at some stage but whether this was contemporaneous or much later, I'm sorry, I can't remember.

As a result, newsreel memory slides effortlessly between cultural memory, personal memory and history. To this end, we expose the problematic nature of encounters with newsreel images in which formative personal encounters become inextricably bound up with recurrent interactions over subsequent decades, and in which the moment of the original encounter continually slips from view.

Sturken also explores how the shared experience of watching traumatic national events – often broadcast live – represents significant moments in which individuals perceive themselves as part of the nation – or, as she phrases it, 'participants in the nation' (1997: 13). Newsreel memories also reveal how shared experience of the historical or marker events shown in the newsreels tended towards the creation of an imagined nationhood – in this case, Britishness. In the period 1939–45, when Britons listened to, read about and eventually watched events of global significance unfolding before them, they regarded themselves as part of a national audience, regardless of the regional, political, cultural or class differences between them. Nationhood was realized through engagement with a range of media, with the implicit understanding of sharing an historic experience with other users of radio, newspapers and newsreels. Newsreel viewing in particular is remembered as engendering a feeling of communion with others, both those encountered in the cinema itself, and those in other imagined cinemas across the country. Despite dislocation in time (as noted above, audiences in second-, third- and fourth-run venues encountered newsreels that were often weeks late) and space, participants' memories revealed a sense of being part of a shared experience, as this exchange between husband and wife Frank and Marjorie Knaggs illustrates:

> MK And Hitler came on and everybody laughed and jeered.
> FK Yes it was, 'Get out of it, go on'.
> Int So people would shout at the screen?
> MK Oh yes! And Mussolini – he was a figure of fun, used to shout at him as well.

The gathered memories suggest, as Sturken asserts in relation to national television viewing, that 'viewers engage with, whether in agreement or resistance, a concept of nationhood and national meaning' (1997: 24). Of course, World War II threw the definition of British national identity into stark relief, and mobilized the whole country into a nation-building exercise of phenomenal speed and reach. As a result, national identity came to the fore at this time, remade around the idea of Britain at war. What makes the newsreel memories of this wartime generation particularly valuable is that this period has become an integral part of the nation's shared memory or history.

Cultural historian Susannah Radstone argues that memory work's theoretical position and its objects of study are liminal (2000: 12). Indeed the recollections gathered for the Tyneside study suggest that newsreel memory slips into a liminal space between the historical and the autobiographical, the shared and the individual. As we have seen, it is the unique ability of the newsreel image to close the gap between first-hand experience and secondary witnessing that is important to highlight here. What is remarkable about newsreel memory talk is that, unlike most memory talk, participants were invariably not recounting first-hand experiences of the event they were recalling, although they were presented as such. For example, Patricia Charlewood recalled: 'I remember when George V died too. I mean we went to see his funeral.' What she was actually recalling was seeing the newsreel footage of the funeral. The news event, as witnessed in the newsreels and recalled in memory, is already a mediated one – a trace, or even a substitute for the 'real thing' – when the audience first encounters it. One might even suggest that the newsreel itself already represents a memory of an event, a recollection on film of an event witnessed elsewhere and else-when.

One of the distinctive features of newsreel footage, with the exception of planned civic occasions and the like, was the fact that what was actually recorded, more often than not, were the traces left behind in the absence of the event itself.[17] We see the destruction of World War II bombing raids, the results of starvation and torture, the aftermath of violent storms, the wreckage of cars, planes and ships – all producing what we might refer to as a post-event memory. Graphic examples of this post-event memory can be seen in the newsreel coverage of the destruction caused by the night-time bombing raids in both London and Coventry throughout 1940.[18] The newsreel audience witnessed and experienced both the event's absence and the newsreel camera's belatedness. As 77-year-old participant John Charlewood described it:

> The Battle of the River Plate in 1940. You didn't actually see the battle but you saw the British ships coming back into port with great big shell holes in them. So I mean you didn't actually see much of what happened.

While the newsreel derives its significance from its iconic status as witness to history, it simultaneously presents an indexical link to the event; it is thus both presence and absence. Yet, despite the passage of time, the newsreels' depiction of historic events is powerful enough to evoke vivid memories and descriptions, which present themselves as if the participants had witnessed the events of history first hand, and with enough resonance for them to recall the viewing experience over 60 years later. As memories of news events witnessed elsewhere and else-when, newsreel memories present the researcher with a unique set of challenges and opportunities, working towards a better understanding of an important type of cultural memory and an oft-neglected cinema audience.

Conclusion

Understanding newsreel memory requires an acknowledgement that personal memories, within which newsreel memory is embedded, are located between the complex processes of memory construction and the events of history. Thus newsreel memory appears to occupy a liminal space between personal memory and popular history; as a result, it requires analysis that acknowledges its status as *both* personal cinematic memory *and* the memory of the events of history. The evidential status of the newsreel further complicates the process, as the newsreel image is routinely taken to be empirical evidence of the historic event itself. While the term 'cultural memory' suggests a type of memory constructed from other cultural forms, newsreel memory is much more than simply the recollection of a succession of cinematic or televisual encounters. It is, in fact, a complex process of memory formation shaped and structured by numerous mnemonic communities and encounters with newsreel footage in a variety of contexts over many decades. More often than not, newsreel memories are anchored within the personal, as recollections are framed within a familial context and integrated into the routines and rituals of everyday life. This characteristic demands that the researcher situate the formation of newsreel memory within a series of meaningful contexts or frames of meaning. As we have seen, newsreel viewing engendered a unique viewing experience. Undoubtedly, the pleasures afforded by newsreels – offering as they did the spectacle of actuality, as well as a sense of experiential immediacy and imagined communion with other cinema audiences – render newsreel memory as a distinctive form of cultural memory. Further, the newsreels' popularly regarded status as visual confirmation of the news leads to memories that are distinct from, but no less important than, those described by other studies of cinema memory.

Acknowledgements

My thanks go to all those participants who took part in the research.

References

Anderson, L. (2010), 'Else-where and Else-when: The Formation of Newsreel Memory as a Distinctive Type of Popular Cultural Memory', unpublished PhD thesis, Newcastle University.

The Arts Review (1947), 'The News Film', in *The Factual Film: A Survey*. London: Oxford University Press, pp. 136–43.

Apel, D. (2002), *Memory Effects: The Holocaust and the Art of Secondary Witnessing*, New Brunswick, NJ: Rutgers University Press.

Barker, M. and Brooks, K. (1998), *Knowing Audiences: Judge Dredd its Friends, Fans and Foes*, Luton: University of Luton Press.

Box, K. (1946), *The Cinema and the Public: An Inquiry into Cinema Going Habits and Expenditure Made in 1946: The Social Survey*, London: British Film Institute Library.

Box, K. and Moss, L. (1946 [1943]), 'Wartime Social Survey: Statistics of Cinema Attendance', in J.P. Mayer (ed.), *Sociology of Film*, London: Faber and Faber, pp. 251–75.

Breakwell, I. and Hammond, P. (eds) (1990), *Seeing in the Dark; A Compendium of Cinema-going*, London: Serpent's Tail.

Calder, A. (1992), *The Myth of the Blitz*, London: Pimlico.

Cowie, E. (1999), 'The Spectacle of Actuality', in J. Gaines and M. Renov (eds), *Collecting Visible Evidence*, Minneapolis, MN: University of Minnesota Press, pp. 19–45.

Fiske, J. (2000), *Reading the Popular*, London: Routledge.

Frisch, M. (1990), *Shared Authority: Essays on the Craft and Meaning of Oral and Public History*, Albany, NY: State University of New York Press.

Goffman, E. (1997), 'Frame Analysis: An Essay on the Organization of Experience', in C. Lemert and A. Branaman (eds), *The Goffman Reader*, Oxford: Blackwell, pp. 149–66.

Guerin, F. and Hallas, R. (2007), *The Image and The Witness: Trauma, Memory and Visual Culture*, London: Wallflower Press.

Hiley, N. (1998), 'Audiences in the Newsreel Period', in C. Jeavons, J. Mercer and D. Kirchner (eds), 'The Story of the Century!' An International Newsfilm Conference', London: British Universities Film and Video Council, pp. 59–62.

Hirsch, M. (2000), 'Surviving Images', in B. Zelizer (ed.), *Visual Culture and the Holocaust*, Piscataway, NJ: Rutgers University Press, pp. 215–46.

Huggett, N. (2002), 'A Cultural History of Cinema-going in the Illawarra (1900–1950)', unpublished PhD thesis, University of Wollongong.

Huston, P. (2002), 'The Nature of the Evidence', in L. McKernan (ed.), *Yesterday's News: The British Cinema Newsreel Reader*, London: British Universities Film and Video Council, pp. 290–99.

Jancovich, M., Faire, L. and Stubbings, S. (2003), *The Place of the Audience: Cultural Geographies of Film Consumption*, London: British Film Institute.

Kaplan, E.A. (2005), *Trauma Culture: The Politics of Terror and Loss in Media and Literature*, New Brunswick, NJ: Rutgers University Press.

Kuhn, A. (1995), *Family Secrets: Acts of Memory and Imagination*, London: Verso.

——— (2002), *An Everyday Magic: Cinema and Cultural Memory*, London: I.B. Tauris.

Lewis, L. (ed.) (1992), *The Adoring Audience: Fan Culture and Popular Media*, London: Routledge.

Low, R. (1979), 'News Films', in R. Low, *Films of Comment and Persuasion of the 1930s*, London: George Allen & Unwin, pp. 9–59.

Mayer, J.P. (1948), *British Cinemas and their Audiences*, London: Denis Dobson.

Maynes, M.J., Pierce, J. and Laslett, B. (2008), *Telling Stories: The Use of Personal Narratives in the Social Sciences and History*, Ithaca, NY: Cornell University Press.

Miskell, P. (2006), *A Social History of the Cinema in Wales 1918–1951: Pulpits, Coal Pits and Fleapits*, Cardiff: University of Wales Press.

Moseley, R. (2002), *Growing Up with Audrey Hepburn*, Manchester: Manchester University Press.

Myers, D. (1936), 'Newsreels Lack Drama: Interview with A.W.F. Sinclair', *World Film News*, 1: 6, p. 31.

O'Brien, M. and Eyles, A. (eds) (1993), *Enter the Dream House: Memories of Cinemas in South London from the Twenties to the Sixties*, London: British Film Institute.

Passerini, L. (1987), *Fascism in Popular Memory: The Cultural Experience of the Turin Working Class*, Cambridge: Cambridge University Press.

Portelli, A. (1991), *The Death of Luigi Trastulli and Other Stories: Form and Meaning in Oral History*, New York: State University of New York Press.

Pronay, N. (1976), 'The Newsreels: The Illusion of Actuality', in P. Smith (ed.), *The Historian and Film*, Cambridge: Cambridge University Press, pp. 95–119.

—— (2002), 'British Newsreels in the 1930s: 1. Audiences and Producers', in L. McKernan (ed.), *Yesterday's News: The British Cinema Newsreel Reader*, London: British Universities Film and Video Council, pp. 138–47.

—— (2002), 'British Newsreels in the 1930s: 2. Their Policies and Impact', in L. McKernan (ed.), *Yesterday's News: The British Cinema Newsreel Reader*, London: British Universities Film and Video Council, pp. 148–60.

Radstone, S. (ed.) (2000), *Memory and Methodology*, Oxford: Berg.

Richards, H. (2004), '"Something To Look Forward To": Memory Work on the Treasured Memories of Cinema Going in Bridgend, South Wales', *Scope*, http://www.nottingham.ac.uk/film/scopearchives/articles/bridgend.htm Accessed7 November 2010.

Smith, M. (2000), *Britain and 1940: History, Myth and Popular Memory*, London: Routledge.

Sontag, S. (2003), *Regarding the Pain of Others*, Harmondsworth: Penguin.

Stacey, J. (1994), *Star Gazing: Hollywood Cinema and Female Spectatorship*, London: Routledge.

Sturken, M. (1997), *Tangled Memories: The Vietnam War, The Aids Epidemic, and the Politics of Remembering*, Berkeley, CA: University of California Press.

Taylor, H. (1989), *Scarlett's Women: Gone with the Wind and its Female Fans*, London: Virago Press.

Teer-Tomaselli, R. (2006), 'Memory and Markers: Collective Memory and Newsworthiness', in I. Volkmer (ed.), *News and Public Memory: An International Study of Media Memories Across Generations*, New York: Peter Lang, pp. 225–49.

Young, C. (2005), 'The Rise and Fall of the News Theatres', *The Journal of British Cinema & Television*, 2: 2, pp. 227–41.

Zelizer, B. (2000) (ed.), *Visual Culture and Holocaust*, New Brunswick, NJ: Rutgers University Press.

The Mass Observation (Newsreel) File Reports No. 16 (7 January, 1940); 22 (28 January, 1940); 141 (May, 1940); 215 (19 June, 1940); 314 (2 August 1940); 394 (10 September 1940); 444 (7 October 1940); 524 (11 December 1940). All available to download from the British Universities Film and Video Council website, http://bufvc.ac.uk/newsonscreen/learnmore/texts. Accessed 20 December 2012.

All newsreels mentioned can be viewed at either the British Pathé on-line archive, http://www.britishpathe.com or the British Movietone digital archive, http://www.movietone.com. Accessed 20 December 2012.

Notes

1 Newsreels were regularly produced weekly or bi-weekly round-ups of news and topical items screened in cinemas.

2 A total of 77 individuals took part in the research, 48 female and 29 male. The dataset was deliberately limited in keeping with the oral history-based approach and to facilitate detailed analysis of the gathered material. As a regional case study, the Tyneside research builds on and complements both other local cinema memory studies (Janovich et al. 2003; Miskell 2006; Richards 2004) and those national studies conducted by Stacey (1994) and Kuhn (2002).

3 The research formed the basis of my PhD thesis, 'Else-where and Else-when: The Formation of Newsreel Memory' (2010).

4 Some of the most important cinema memory research has been conducted by Stacey (1994), Kuhn (2002) and Moseley (2002).

5 Nicholas Pronay's two short essays 'British Newsreels in the 1930s: 1. Audiences and Producers' (2002) and 'British Newsreels in the 1930s: 2. Their Policies and Impact' (2002), first published in 1971 and 1972 respectively, represent the key texts on the subject of newsreel audiences.

6 The first news theatre opened in New York in 1929. The first news-only screening in Britain was at the Avenue Pavilion on Shaftsbury Avenue in London on 18 August 1930. According to the annual returns of the News and Specialized Theatres Association of Great Britain and Northern Ireland, membership peaked in 1940–41 at 36.

7 Mass Observation produced a number of reports on newsreel audiences during 1940.

8 The report of The Arts Enquiry, *The Factual Film* (1947), listed the five companies producing and distributing British newsreels as the subsidiaries of feature film companies: British Movietone News, Twentieth Century Fox (US); British Paramount News, Paramount Pictures Inc. (US); Gaumont-British News, Gaumont-British Picture Corporation Ltd (British); Pathé News, Associated British and Warner Brothers (British–US); Universal News, British Pictorial Productions Ltd (British). It was the financial relationship between the newsreel subsidiaries and their parent companies that both guaranteed the newsreels' place in the larger cinema circuits and dictated their style and content.

9 In an article from *World Film News* published in September 1936, A.W.F. Sinclair, editor of the *Daily Sketch*, described the newsreels thus: 'You mustn't think of the newsreel as a rival to the newspaper … the paper gives its reader up-to-the-minute news and pictures, and then he [sic.] goes to the cinema to see what he has read about in animated form' (Myers 1936: 31). Sinclair goes on to speak of a, 'triumvirate of technology' (1936: 31) in which radio, the newspaper press, and the newsreels work in harmony to bring the news to the public, each

performing a specific, yet inter-related function, 'the newspaper reflects life, the radio gives it atmosphere, and the newsreel gives it animation' (1936: 31).

10   Some of the participants were well into their nineties at the time of interview.

11   Annette Kuhn (1995) refers to these groups as 'memory communities'.

12   See Angus Calder's careful analysis in *The Myth of the Blitz* (1992), which refuses the simplistic divisions between reality and myth. See also Malcolm Smith, *Britain and 1940: History, Myth and Popular Memory* (2000).

13   The notion of interpretative frames of meaning derives from anthropologist Erving Goffman's frame analysis (1997), in which he identifies 'frames of meaning' to describe the way we chose to interpret our lives (including our past). Goffman suggests that the ways in which we view the past, are generated in the present and usually affirm a collective view of the world, while satisfying our desire to organize our lived experiences into meaningful activities. Goffman's approach insists that individuals will, within their individual frames of meaning, interpret the past in different ways.

14   For examples of newsreel footage of these historic events, see *Pathé Gazette*, 'Evacuation of the BEF (AKA Dunkirk)', 6 June 1940, film ID. 1047.12 (Dunkirk); *British Movietone News*, 2 January 1941, 'City Fire Raid – The Fire of London', story no. 40217 (The Blitz); *British Movietone News* 1940, 'Battle of Britain', story no. 80273A (The Battle of Britain); *Pathé Gazette*, 12 June 1944, 'D-Day, Greatest Combined Operation in World's History', film ID. 1360.03 (D-Day Landings); *British Movietone News*, 30 April 1945, 'Atrocities-The Evidence', story no. 45699 (Liberation of the German Concentration Camps); *Pathé Gazette*, 17 May 1945, 'Fruits of Victory', film ID 1155.01 (Victory in Europe Day).

15   The kite-mark is a UK certificate of product and service quality.

16   For discussion of the notion of secondary witnessing in the context of Holocaust memory study, see Hirsch (2000); Zelizer (2000); Apel (2002); Sontag (2003); Kaplan (2005); Guerin and Hallas (2007).

17   Of course, there were memorable occasions in which the newsreel camera filmed the heart of the action. See in particular the footage from the D-Day landings (above) and *Pathé Gazette*, 27 July 1944, 'Combat Pictures', film ID. 1364.01.

18   See *British Movietone News*, 12 September 1940, 'Battle of London', story no. 39700 and *British Movietone News*, 21 November 1940, 'King in Coventry – The Martyr City', story no. 40012.

Chapter 5

Why are Children the Most Important Audience for Pornography in Australia?

Alan McKee

Who watches pornography in Australia? If you listen to public debates about the genre, the answer is clear: children. Children are accessing pornography on smartphones (Murray and Tin 2011). They are taking 'lewd' photographs of themselves, creating their own pornography (Nelligan and Etheridge 2011). Indigenous Australian children must be protected by banning pornography (*The Age* 2011). Pornographic magazines are placed where children can see them (O'Rourke 2011), and exposure to pornography is damaging children (Sundstrom 2011). The Australian government insists that the Internet must be filtered to protect children from pornography (Collerton 2010). And if indeed any adults are watching pornography in Australia, then it is child pornography they are viewing (MacDonald 2011; Ralston and Howden 2011).

In story after story, public debate about pornography focuses on children as its audience. There is no suggestion that children are numerically the *largest* audience of pornography in Australia. But, emphatically, the suggestion is that children are the *most important* audience to be taken into account when thinking about the genre.

The audiences for pornography

Media audiences do not exist in a simple concrete sense. Unlike individual viewers, you cannot see or touch them:

> In no case is the audience 'real', or external to its discursive construction. There is no 'actual' audience that lies beyond its production as a category, which is merely to say that audiences are only ever encountered *per se* as *representations*. (Hartley 1992: 105)

In his discussions of the way in which television audiences have been imagined, Hartley notes a tendency towards 'paedocratization' – 'the audience is imagined as having childlike qualities and attributes' (1992: 108). By contrast, in Australia in the twenty-first century, the audience for pornography is literally described as children.

What are the effects of such a discursive position? Hartley further notes that representations of audiences serve the purposes of the institutions that create them:

> Audiences are not just constructs; they are the invisible fictions that are produced institutionally in order for various institutions to take charge of the mechanisms of their

own survival. Audiences may be imagined empirically, theoretically or politically, but in all cases the product is a fiction that serves the need of the imagining institution. (1992: 105)

We can see that, in the case of Australia, imagining children as the most important audience for pornography serves a key political purpose: it justifies the intervention of the state in the media consumption, production and communication practices of its citizens.

Adult consumers of pornography

As a point of calibration, we can start by looking at a statistical approach to the audiences of pornography in Australia. The Australian Study of Health and Relationships was a nationally representative survey of the sexual behaviour of 19,307 Australian adults conducted in 2000–03 (Smith et al. 2003). The study found that in the previous year, 'about a quarter of all respondents had watched an X-rated film (37% men, 16% women)' (Richters et al. 2003: 180). The researchers gathered a variety of demographic data and found a number of correlations with the consumption of pornography. For men:

The likelihood of having watched an X-rated video was significantly higher among younger men … men who identified as gay or bisexual … men who had not completed post-secondary education … men living in major cities … men with blue collar or white collar occupations … men who had a non-live-in regular partner … [and] men who had more than one partner … (2003: 186)

Similarly for women, a number of correlations emerged:

The likelihood of having watched an X rated video was significantly higher among younger women … women who spoke English at home … women who identified as bisexual … [and] woman who had more than one sexual partner in the past year. (Richters et al. 2003: 186)

Statistical information is not more 'objective' than other forms of data-gathering (McKee 2003: 2–3). It can provide only a partial picture of a population. The information that is gathered will be limited by the kinds of questions that researchers think are important to ask – some pieces of demographic information were not asked about in this survey, but might have proved important in understanding consumption of pornography. And questions always frame the topic in a particular way – this survey, for example, asked about X-rated videos or films, but what about pornographic magazines? Or non-pornographic images that might be used for sexual excitement – art, perhaps, or *National Geographic*? And it is also important to note that quantitative data doesn't tell us much about *how* people use pornography – if you have been forced to watch pornography by a domineering partner, is that the same as choosing to watch it for your own pleasure?

Nevertheless, I want to use this large-scale statistical survey as a touchstone as we go on to think about how the audiences for pornography are conceptualized in public debates in Australia. This is a representation of the adult audience for pornography in Australia. This makes up about a quarter of adult Australians in 2000–03, including 37 per cent of men. The use of pornography by its audience is linked to a host of social and cultural factors, including age, language spoken at home, class, education level, sexual identity and sexual practices. This is a complex social practice, and there is much to be researched and discussed here.

It is also worth noting that the majority of consumers of pornography report their experiences as positive: in an Australian survey in 2004, 57 per cent of consumers reported that pornography had a positive effect on their attitudes towards sexuality, while only 7 per cent felt it was negative (McKee et al. 2008: 83). The positive effects included making them more 'comfortable and relaxed about sex', more 'open-minded' and more 'tolerant', providing 'sexual arousal and pleasure', educating them and helping them to 'maintai[n] a sex life in a long-term relationship' (2008: 85).

And yet Australian public debates about the audiences for pornography are often about children. These adult consumers and their experiences vanish.

Collectively shouting in the community

A key point in these debates in Australia is the publication in 2006 of the Australia Institute report *Corporate Paedophilia: Sexualisation of Children in Australia* (Rush and La Nauze 2006). This was one of the first formal reports in the English-speaking world to popularize the concept of the 'sexualization of children'. Along with the 2007 release of the first edition of American Psychological Association's *Report of the APA Taskforce on the Sexualisation of Girls* (Zurbriggen et al. 2010), it is still commonly used as a touchstone in governmental and media concerns about pornography. Produced by a left-wing think-tank, the report draws on feminist concerns about the objectification of women in the media and extends them to children. The Australia Institute report reproduces a number of – apparently quite innocuous – photographs of children from the catalogues of department stores and produces shocking interpretations of them. It discusses the clothes worn by the young people, claiming to see a sexualization of the children wearing them:

... bolero cross-over tops and low necklines, both designed to emphasise the breasts of adult women; 'crop tops' which draw attention to the waist and navel area; dangling jewellery from necks, ears or wrists, dangling belts from the hips or waist, and rings on the fingers, again designed to attract attention to sexually differentiated features of adult women, and some styles of dress or skirt, most particularly very short skirts, and dresses held up by thin straps. For boys, examples include suit jackets designed to emphasise the shoulders of adult men ... (Rush and La Nauze 2006: 7)

The report suggests that ideals of physical beauty 'contribut[e] to the development of eating disorders' (Rush and La Nauze 2006: ix). It worries that advertising may encourage girls to behave sexually, and in doing so 'play a role in "grooming" children for paedophiles' (Rush and La Nauze 2006: ix) There is no mention of pornography in the report. So what does all of this have to do with pornography? Nothing – and everything. The report stands as a key text in a messy nexus of concerns around children and sexuality that does not recognize academic concerns about coherent definitions or logical connections. It collapses together a range of topics that academic research would recognize as being quite distinct, about:

- children being targeted as a market by consumer capitalism
- children in twenty-first-century Australia becoming sexual at an earlier age than previous generations
- levels of sexual abuse of children in Australia increasing
- the 'raunchy' sexual behaviour of young adults over the age of consent
- non-explicit sexualized images of adults in the media that might be seen by children
- the fact that post-pubescent adolescents are exploring their sexual identities
- body-image disorders in girls and young women
- the production of sexually explicit images of children (child pornography/child abuse materials)
- children seeing adult pornography (see McKee 2010: 133–34).

Academic research would recognize each of these topics as distinct, and as having a distinct aetiology. But in the Australia Institute report, these topics are collapsed together under the rubric of 'sexualization of children'. They are presented as being porous, so commentators can slip from one to the other as though they were the same thing, with any of them being either a cause or an effect – girls are buying into raunch culture because there is too much sex in the media. Or girls are becoming anorexic because of raunch culture. Or more children are being abused because they are becoming sexual too early. Or children are becoming sexual too early because of too much sex in the media (see McKee 2010: 134). And this vague label of 'sexualization of children' also serves as a powerful cultural trope for addressing the circulation of pornography in Australia.

The image of the 'sexualized child' has become a powerful one for lobby groups such as Collective Shout. This anti-pornography group is led by Melinda Tankard Reist, a right-wing religious lobbyist and former human rights adviser to Senator Brian Harradine (Harradine 2005: 88):

Collective Shout is a new grassroots campaigns movement mobilising and equipping individuals and groups to target corporations, advertisers, marketers and media which objectify women and sexualise girls to sell products and services ... Collective Shout is for anyone concerned about the increasing *pornification of culture* ... Collective Shout builds on work carried out in recent years around the issue of objectification and sexualisation. This includes research like Australia Institute's *Corporate Paedophilia* report. (Collective Shout, n.d., emphasis added)

The key term here is 'pornification of culture'. Pornography is now everywhere, the discourse claims. It is at one and the same time a discrete category from which children must be protected and present everywhere in culture. Everything sexual must be read through the filter of children, and everything to do with children must be read through the filter of sex. Terms are expanded and collapsed together so that discussions of children become discussions of pornography, and vice versa. Publicity for Reist's book *Big Porn Inc* claims that:

> the unprecedented mainstreaming of the global pornography industry is transforming the sexual politics of intimate and public life, popularising new forms of hardcore misogyny, and strongly contributing to the sexualisation of children (Spinifex Press 2011).

Pornography is everywhere, this discourse claims, and children are its most important audience.

Little children are sacred to the Australian government

Such discourses are not only at the heart of community debates about censorship in Australia. They also inform government policy in Australia. In 2008 the Federal Senate asked the Senate Standing Committee on Environment, Communications and the Arts to hold an inquiry and prepare a report on

> the sexualisation of children in the contemporary media environment, including radio and television, children's magazines, other print and advertising material and the Internet (Senate Standing Committee on Environment 2008: 1).

The terms of reference for the inquiry opened with:

> In 2006, the Australia Institute published two discussion papers on the issue of the sexualisation of children in the contemporary media: *Corporate paedophilia: sexualisation of children in the media* and *Letting children be children: stopping the sexualisation of children in Australia* ... (Senate Standing Committee on Environment 2008: 1)

The terms of reference for the report drew explicitly on the language and ideas of the Australia Institute report, with the Committee tasked to 'examine the sources and beneficiaries of premature sexualisation of children in the media' (Senate Standing Committee on

Environment 2008: 1). (Note that there was no requirement to examine whether, or to what extent, premature sexualization of children in the media was in fact taking place.)

This Senate report contributed to the porousness of the term 'sexualization of children'. The Australia Institute report did not explicitly mention children seeing pornography, nor did the report of the Senate Inquiry. Yet it became clear that in the public discussions around the topic, the boundaries between what was pornographic and what was not could easily collapse when children were involved. As the Committee report noted: 'Many writers, either implicitly or explicitly, drew a comparison with, or connection between, contemporary media standards and pornography' (Senate Standing Committee on Environment 2008: 22).

Such confusion can be immensely productive for governments wishing to push through illiberal policies. In 2007, a shocking report was released on the sexual abuse of Indigenous children in remote Australia. The *Little Children are Sacred* report presented an overview of the situation:

> Excessive consumption of alcohol, variously described as the cause or result of poverty, unemployment, lack of education, boredom and overcrowded and inadequate housing. The use of other drugs and petrol sniffing can be added to these. Together they lead to excessive violence. In the worst case scenario it leads to the sexual abuse of children. (Northern Territory Board of Inquiry 2007: 7)

Pornography was not listed as a key factor in this overview. It was mentioned in a later section, but in an ambivalent way. One page says that 'the issue of children's and the community's exposure to pornography was raised regularly in submissions' (2007: 199); on the next page, Indigenous interviewees 'said that they are not aware of pornography being a big problem but they were aware of American movies' (2007: 200). Some Indigenous interviewees said that pornography was a problem, and 'SBS and Austar are probably the main sources' (2007: 199). The report then recommended:

That an education campaign be conducted to inform communities of:

a. the meaning and rationale for film and television show classifications
b. the prohibition contained in the *Criminal Code* making it an offence to intentionally expose a child under the age of 16 years to an indecent object or film ... (Northern Territory Board of Inquiry 2007: 200)

The response of the Howard government (a policy that has been continued by Labor) was to ban X-rated pornography in these communities alongside bans on grog and new attempts to force Indigenous Australians into school and the workforce (Franklin and Rout 2011). By the time this reached public debate, in newspaper stories, the leading paragraph was about 'degrading pornography' in Indigenous communities (Rothwell 2007: 6) – despite the fact that the term 'degrading' was not used by any respondents.

The report did not call for pornography to be banned, and it did not list it as a key problem in its overview of the situation. To the extent that it did identify sexualized material as a problem, SBS and Austar were identified as the culprits. Yet the government did not seek to ban SBS or Austar from these communities. The imagined audience of children exposed to pornography is such a powerful image that lack of evidence is unimportant in the preparation of government policy. Public debate and policy are distracted from more important issues facing young people.

And critics of government policies can be dismissed by the invocation of children. For example, an internet filter proposed by the Labor government in 2007 (a policy that has since been abandoned) benefited from rhetoric around the sexualization of children, with Communications Minister Stephen Conroy insisting that 'if people equate freedom of speech with watching child pornography, then the Rudd Labor Government is going to disagree' (Seymour 2008: 10). Similarly, the Senate Legal and Constitutional Affairs Reference Committee, in its 2011 report on the National Classification Scheme, quoted with approval from the submission of Melinda Tankard Reist's Collective Shout:

> Those who oppose filtering on the grounds of free speech, civil liberties or the alleged rights of adults to see anything they want are best described as sexual assault or child porn libertarians rather than 'civil' libertarians (quoted in Legal and Constitutional Affairs Reference Committee 2011: 108)

The problems with focusing on children as consumers of pornography

I quoted above from John Hartley:

> In no case is the audience 'real', or external to its discursive construction. There is no 'actual' audience that lies beyond its production as a category, which is merely to say that audiences are only ever encountered *per se* as *representations*. (Hartley 1992: 105)

I want to insist that my concerns about the representations of the child audience for pornography in Australian public debates are not that they are simply wrong. There is no single image of 'the porn audience' that is true. As I have suggested above, in public discussions about pornography, the relentless focus on children suggests that they are the most important audience for the genre. This ignores the 25 per cent of adult Australians who are using pornography, and generally finding it a positive experience. But it isn't possible, using logic, to *prove* which of these audiences is more important. As logicians put it, questions of the relative importance of different issues come down to differences in *attitudes* rather than differences about *facts* (McKee 2005: 18). But having said all that, I do worry that the image of the helpless child audience exposed to pornography serves a number of dangerous social and political ends.

The first – and I think the worst – is that the image of the child audience threatened by pornography distracts political and public attention away from the real threats facing young people in Australia. Child sexual abuse may be decreasing (Dunne et al. 2003), but it remains a real problem. Up to 10 per cent of girls and up to 5 per cent of boys in 'high income countries' (Australia, New Zealand, Canada and the United States) experience penetrative sexual abuse during their childhood (Gilbert et al. 2009: 9). The research shows that they are not being sexually abused by strangers, who are turned on by watching adult pornography. They are being sexually abused by members of their own families. Some 55 per cent of child sexual abuse cases in the United States in 2006 were committed by a parent or other relative, and an even higher percentage were committed by an acquaintance or authority figure already known to the child (Gilbert et al. 2009: 8). Importantly, children are not being abused because they have watched pornography and become sexual; in fact, abusers are turned on by the innocence of children – the more innocent they are, the more attractive they are to abusers (Krafchick and Biringen 2002: 59; Sanderson 2004: 55).

Research has identified a number of clear predictors for child sexual abuse. Girls are abused more than boys. Children with disabilities are abused much more than children without disabilities. Children in institutional care have a massively increased chance of being abused (Gilbert et al. 2009: 10, 11). A cluster of problems for parents are related to abusive behaviour, including 'poverty, mental-health problems, low educational achievement, alcohol and drug misuse, and exposure to maltreatment as a child' (Gilbert et al. 2009: 11).

Researchers in the area of child maltreatment prevention have not identified the existence of pornography as a contributing factor to child sexual abuse. But the image of the helpless child who must be protected from pornography is so common and so powerful that it leads to governmental policy forming around it, regardless of the facts, and in the process distracting us from the real issues.

Second, I am concerned that the image of the child audience for pornography obscures adult consumers of the genre. As noted above, a statistical approach suggests that a quarter of all adult Australians – including over a third of adult men – consume pornography. And research suggests that their experiences of the genre are mostly positive. But it is difficult to see this picture when the focus is unrelentingly on children as the most important audience for pornography.

Third, I worry that the image of the child audience is too homogenous to account for the interactions of young people with Sexually Explicit Materials. In debates about children being exposed to pornography, the category 'child' covers everyone from birth to 16 years of age. *The Report of the APA Task Force on the Sexualisation of Girls* features on its cover images of children between about five and 16 years old. This imagined audience is represented as all equally helpless in the face of a sexualized culture. I would suggest, by contrast, that there is an important distinction between pre-pubescents and post-pubescents in relation to pornography. There is little systematic research in this area; nevertheless, what does exist is suggestive on this point. Some interviews with adults who first encountered pornography as pre-pubescent children suggest that they were unlikely to seek out such material. They were not particularly interested in sexually explicit material and at the time they found it (discovering a stash hidden by an older relative, for example), they found it 'meaningless' or 'funny':

> I remember actually in primary school I found a porn book on the way home from school. I had no idea what any of it was about. There were all these graphic descriptions ... And I read it and just thought it was either hysterical – like the bits that I could get I thought were really funny – and the bits – most of it I had no idea what they were talking about, and all these explicit descriptions and I was sitting there thinking I don't even know what that means (laughs). (McKee 2007: 119)

By contrast, it is more likely that post-pubescent adolescents will seek out sexually explicit materials, for information or as a rite or passage (McKee 2007: 119). There exist a number of models in psychology to explain the relationship between young people's sexual development and their media consumption – for example, social cognitive theory (Bandura 1994), cultivation theory (Gerbner et al. 2002) and priming theory (Roskos-Ewoldsen et al. 2002). However, the most valid, in the sense of matching observed everyday behaviour, is the 'media practice' model (Steele 1999). This suggests that: 'Not unlike adults at social functions, teens look for people or situations "like them" in the media. When they find people or story lines that resonate with their lives, they pay attention' (Steele 1999: 335). Those adolescents who are exposed to sexually explicit media tend to be those who are seeking it out for themselves in order to help them make sense of their developing sexuality (Brown 2000: 35).

Finally, the image of children who are the key audience for pornography in Australia isn't fair to children themselves. It is viewed as uncontroversial by experts in children's development that 'the development of sexuality in children in a normal part of their general development' (Sanderson 2004: 57). But the image of the child audience in Australia is of young people who are – and who should be – completely ignorant about sex. In this picture, the ideal child – until they are corrupted by exposure to pornography – knows nothing about their own body, their own development or their own sexuality. Experts insist that children need comprehensive, age-appropriate information about sexuality from a young age (Walsh 2011), and access to such information is consistently demonstrated to have positive outcomes for healthy sexual development (Goldman 2010: 421). Indeed, 'discourses of innocence profoundly endanger children' (Renold, quoted in Goldman 2010: 421). The ways in which we represent children – as naturally innocent, completely asexual, threatened by pornography – are actually dangerous for children in the real world, who are nothing like that.

Conclusion

On 24 June 2011, a Senate Committee Report on the National Classification Scheme was released. The opening sentence of the newspaper coverage: 'Australia censorship system is fundamentally flawed, it fails to protect children from pornography' (Dick 2011: 8). In public discussions about pornography, children keep appearing as the first audience called to mind.

I suspect that the reason for this is not hard to find. As I have argued elsewhere, following John Hartley, children are the last group in western societies to be routinely excluded from suffrage, and thus understood to be helpless and in need of protection (McKee 2010). In previous centuries, women, the working classes and Indigenous people were all understood to be incapable of managing their own best interests, and thus in need of protection (read control) by the state. The political parties currently in power in most western countries pay lip-service to 'liberal' ideals – that citizens should be judged as competent to make their own decisions about their lives. In practice, however, even the most liberal of politicians tend to retain a strong desire to control the behaviour of populations (and in fact it may be right-wing politicians who exhibit this desire most strongly – Thatcher, Reagan, Bush, Howard). But this raises a rhetorical problem: if your political rhetoric is based on government not interfering with the choices of the individual, then how can you effectively mount an argument for such interference?

And here we hit children. Because they have remained outside of citizenship, they constitute the one group who, politically, we can still lay a claim to 'protect'. They are the one group still seen to be helpless. This means that any public argument for government interference in the behaviour of citizens can immediately gain rhetorical force by claiming that we have to interfere in order to protect children (Brennan 2001).

Relentlessly focusing on children as the most important audience for pornography therefore serves well the purposes of politicians who want to retain illiberal policies. The problem with this is not, as I suggest above, one of inaccuracy – there is no single correct image of the audience for pornography. It is rather one of focus. If the helpless child is the only viewer of pornography allowed into the public sphere, then adult viewers watching adult pornography vanish. If we see pornography as the biggest cause of sexual abuse in Australia, then we fail to notice the real causes. If we see children only as helpless innocents who must be protected from information about sexuality, then we don't pay attention to their very real need for comprehensive, age-appropriate information about their own sexual development.

If we want to look seriously at the place of pornography in Australian culture, and if we want to understand the healthy sexual development of young people, then the impossibility of seeing past children as the most important audience of pornography is a problem that we must overcome.

References

The Age (2011), 'Intervention Must Consult if It is to Succeed', The Age, 24 May.
Bandura, A. (1994), 'Social Cognitive Theory of Mass Communication', in J. Bryant and D. Zillmann (eds), Media Effects: Advances in Theory and Research, Hillsdale, NJ: Lawrence Erlbaum, pp. 61–90.

Brennan, M. (2001), 'Child(hood) Abuse: Constructing the Australian Public in Public Service Announcements', *Media International Australia*, 99, pp. 91–104.

Brown, J. (2000), 'Adolescents' Sexual Media Diets', *Journal of Adolescent Health*, 27S: 2, pp. 35–40.

Collective Shout (n.d.), Collective Shout website: About, http://collectiveshout.org/about. Accessed 24 June 2011.

Collerton, S. (2010), 'Labor Steadfast Over Internet Filter', *ABC News*, ABC TV, 10 August.

Dick, T. (2011), 'Call for Porn Laws Overhaul', *The Age*, 24 June.

Dunne, M., Purdie, D, Cook, M., Boyle, F. and Najman, J. (2003), 'Is Child Sexual Abuse Declining? Evidence from a Population-based Survey of Men and Women in Australia', *Child Abuse and Neglect*, 27: 2, pp. 141–52.

Franklin, M. and Rout, M. (2011), 'Gillard Puts Jobs, School and Grog Bans at Heart of New NT Push', *The Australian*, 23 June.

Gerbner, G., Gross, L. Morgan, M., Signorielli, N. and Shanahan, J. (2002), 'Growing Up with Television: Cultivation Processes', in J. Bryant and D. Zillmann (eds), *Media Effects: Advances in Theory and Research*, Mahwah, NJ: Lawrence Erlbaum, pp. 43–67.

Gilbert, R., Spatz-Widom, C., Browne, K., Fergusson, D., Webb, E. and Janson, S. (2009), 'Burden and Consequences of Child Maltreatment in High-income Countries', *The Lancet*, 373: 68–81.

Goldman, J.D.G. (2010), 'Responding to Parental Objections to School Sexuality Education: A Selection of 12 Objections', *Sex Education*, 8: 4, pp. 415–38.

Harradine, B. (2005), Valedictory Speech, Senate, Canberra: Commonwealth of Australia.

Hartley, J. (1992), *Tele-ology: Studies in Television*, London and New York: Routledge.

Krafchick, J. and Biringen, Z. (2002), 'Parents as Sexuality Educators: The Role of Family Therapists in Coaching Parents', *Journal of Feminist Family Therapy*, 14: 3/4, pp. 57–72.

Legal and Constitutional Affairs Reference Committee (2011), *Review of the National Classification Scheme: Achieving the Right Balance*, Canberra: Commonwealth of Australia.

MacDonald, V. (2011), 'Police Bust an Alleged National Child Porn Ring: Corio Man Charged', *Geelong Advertiser*, 16 June.

McKee, A. (2003), *Textual Analysis: A Beginner's Guide*, London: Sage.

——— (2005), *The Public Sphere: an introduction*. Cambridge, UK: Cambridge University Press.

——— (2007), '"Saying You've Been at Dad's Porn Book is Part of Growing Up": Youth, Pornography and Education', *Metro*, 155, pp. 118–22.

——— (2010), 'Everything is Child Abuse', *Media International Australia*, 135, pp. 131–40.

McKee, A., Albury, K. and Lumby, C. (2008), *The Porn Report*, Melbourne: Melbourne University Press.

Murray, D. and Tin, J. (2011), 'Smartphones Spell Trouble for Students', *The Sunday Mail*, 29 May.

Nelligan, W.K. and M. Etheridge (2011), 'Facecrooks', *Weekly Times Messenger*, 25 May.

Northern Territory Board of Inquiry into the Protection of Aboriginal Children from Sexual Abuse (2007), *Ampe Akelyernemane Meke Mekarle: Little Children are Sacred*, Darwin: Northern Territory Government.

O'Rourke, P. (2011), 'Children Pawns in Adults' Cruel Agendas', *Newcastle Herald*, 2 May.

Ralston, N. and Howden, S. (2011), 'More Arrests Tipped in Child Porn Bust', *Sydney Morning Herald*, 16 June.

Richters, J., Grulich, A., de Visser, R.O., Smith, A.M.A. and Rissel, C.E. (2003), 'Autoerotic, Esoteric and Other Sexual Practices Engaged in by a Representative Sample of Adults', *Australian and New Zealand Journal of Public Health*, 27: 2, pp. 180–90.

Roskos-Ewoldsen, D.R., Roskos-Ewoldsen, B. and Carpentier, F.R.D. (2002), 'Media Priming: A Synthesis', in J. Bryant and D. Zillmann (eds), *Media Effects: Advances in Theory and Research*, Mahwah, NJ: Lawrence Erlbaum, pp. 97–120.

Rothwell, N. (2007), 'Nation's Child Abuse Shame', *The Australian*, 16 June.

Rush, E. and La Nauze, A. (2006), *Corporate Paedophilia*, The Australia Institute Discussion Papers, Vol. 90, Sydney: The Australia Institute.

Sanderson, C. (2004), *The Seduction of Children: Empowering Parents and Teachers to Protect Children from Child Sexual Abuse*, London: Jessica Kingsley.

Senate Standing Committee on Environment, Communications and the Arts (2008), *Sexualisation of Children in the Contemporary Media*, Canberra: Commonwealth of Australia.

Seymour, J. (2008), 'Wrong Way, Go Back: Conroy Takes Poor Approach to Filtering Porn', *Sydney Morning Herald*, 1 January.

Smith, A.M.A., Rissel, C.E., Richters, J. Grulich, A. and de Visser, R.O. (2003), 'The Rationale and Methods of the Australian Study of Health and Relationships', *Australian and New Zealand Journal of Public Health*, 27: 2, pp. 106–17.

Spinifex Press (2011), *Big Porn Inc* publicity blurb, http://www.spinifexpress.com.au/Bookstore/book/id=217. Accessed 20 February 2012.

Steele, J.R. (1999), 'Teenage Sexuality and Media Practice: Factoring in the Influences of Family, Friends and School', *The Journal of Sex Research*, 36: 4, pp. 331–41.

Sundstrom, K. (2011), 'Porn Exposure Damaging Kids', *Sunshine Coast Daily*, 5 March.

Walsh, J. (2011), *Talk Soon. Talk Often. A Guide to Parents Talking to Their Kids About Sex*, Perth: Department of Health, Government of Western Australia/La Trobe University.

Zurbriggen, E.L., Collins, R.L., Lamb, S., Roberts, T.-A., Tolman, D.L., Ward, L.M. and Blake, J. (2010), *Report of the APA Task Force on the Sexualization of Girls*, Washington: American Psychological Association.

PART II

The Film Industry - Systems and Practices

Chapter 6

Local Promotion of a 'Picture Personality': A Case Study of the Vitagraph Girl

Kathryn Fuller-Seeley

This case study explores the historical context in which an unusually elaborate American film promotional event unfolded in June 1911, in an unlikely rural setting. It occurred at an early moment in the nationwide marketing of 'picture personalities' – as Richard deCordova has termed the first film stars – during the transitional era of American film-making, when most aspects of film production, distribution, exhibition and advertising were in flux (deCordova 1990; see also Keil and Stamp 2004). Individual theatre managers at this time played a pivotal but under-examined role in the development of film advertising and marketing practices, and in creating a solid foothold for cinema in entertainment culture across the United States in the early 1910s.

On Monday evening, 17 July 1911, Vitagraph company actress Florence Turner, touted by her studio as 'The Vitagraph Girl', appeared in person at the Star Theater; this was a 150-seat nickelodeon located on the third floor of a 60-year-old opera house in the isolated upstate agricultural village of Cooperstown, New York, a long eight hours by train from the Vitagraph studio in Brooklyn. The delighted audience viewed a program of Vitagraph films featuring Turner, then joined local children in serenading her with a rendition of the waltz tune 'The Vitagraph Girl', while the accompanying illustrated song slides (featuring hand-coloured photographic images of Florence) were projected on to the screen. 'Vitagraph Boy' Ken Casey, Jean the 'Vitagraph Dog' and film director Larry Trimble were also among the honoured guests. Previously that day, the actors, director and a cameraman had shot footage for a hastily scripted one-reel domestic comedy about a sickly boy's adventures escaping from his overly protective mother's care, which utilized the village's lakeside setting, health-promoting outdoor activities and some Boy Scouts conveniently camping nearby. Many Cooperstown residents were on hand to gawk at the film-makers. The Vitagraph troupe, consulting with Star Theater owner George Carley, made plans to return and film a big-budget, multiple-reel film adaptation of local literary legend James Fenimore Cooper's novel *The Deerslayer*. Tiny Cooperstown, New York (pop. 2500) was poised to become world famous as a modern, media-savvy community and a tourist destination – or so George Carley crowed in the columns of his weekly newspaper, the Cooperstown *Freeman's Journal*, and its summer offshoot, *The Daily Glimmerglass*, throughout the summer and fall of 1911 ('Big Vitagraph Night' 1911).

I first encountered newspaper coverage of this extraordinary local promotion in 1991 while undertaking dissertation research on the history of film exhibition in the US hinterlands. I had discovered that Cooperstown's historical archives possessed not only extensive records of an itinerant film exhibitor from the late 1890s to 1915, but also a local newspaper that contained richly detailed coverage of local film exhibition throughout the silent film era (Fuller 2001). In the pre-Internet age of archival research, I had no guides to which other small towns might have had their movie-going cultures as thoroughly documented, and could only gather additional examples by reading discussions of local newspaper coverage in the film trade journals, and by trawling through countless rolls of microfilm.

Today, the increasing availability on the internet of digitized historical American newspapers, in databases created by the Library of Congress, state and local historical societies, entrepreneurial archivists and commercial websites from Google to Proquest and newspaperarchives.com, enables researchers using the techniques and research questions of what Kate Bowles and Richard Maltby term 'the new cinema history' (Bowles et al. 2011) to delve much more deeply than before into primary source documentation of local cinema promotions and movie-going history. Richard Abel, Paul Moore, Robert Allen and others are investigating the complex relationships in local communities between motion picture exhibitors, movie-goers and newspapers in building an information system that encouraged widespread interest in movies and built local movie fan culture (Bowles et al. 2011; Maltby 2011; Fuller-Seeley 2008; Abel 2006; Moore 2010; Allen 2008). Accessing these research databases, I sought to revisit my search to uncover the extent to which the 1911 events in Cooperstown were a unique promotion or a quotidian event, and to explore how exhibitors across America used newspaper advertisements and articles to spread knowledge to their communities about the earliest 'picture personalities'.

In this nascent era of cinema marketing, film producers (both General Film Company-affiliated studios and the new independent producers) were just beginning to employ the advanced tactics being developed in other sectors of the economy by advertising agencies to establish product brand identity, increase sales and spread consumer culture across America. Between 1909 and 1911, several US film studios made tentative efforts to promote their studio brands and top performers (whom they labeled the Vitagraph Girl, the Imp Girl, the Kalem Girl, etc.), to advertise their major film releases and to expand their audiences by publishing the first specialty fan publications.

Janet Staiger, Moya Luckett and I have documented various aspects of American film producers' reticence to recognize the importance of advertising its films to the public. They provided very limited numbers of posters, press materials or other advertising aids to exhibitors (see Luckett 1999; Staiger 1990; Fuller-Seeley 2012). Staiger has argued that the competition between film producers in this early period was not carried out through product differentiation and marketing (as would occur with many other consumer products), but through litigation and patent rights wrangling. The rapid spread of nickel theatres across the United States in the period 1907–10 also meant that demand for films significantly outpaced the supply. For film producers, it was a seller's market. Edison and his colleagues worried far more about dominating the means of production than marketing their products – and indeed they sold all their films, both good and bad, at standard prices per foot (Staiger 1984; Mahar 2007).

In 1910, the majority of American film companies remained reluctant to spend money on marketing – Biograph, for example, was adamantly against promoting individual performers or investing in longer feature-length film releases. Even innovative producers were organizationally incapable of carrying out extensive campaigns. The scope of their promotional efforts was limited to advertisements and press notices at the national level in exhibitor trade journals. It was entirely up to entrepreneurial local exhibitors to take this marketing information and apply it in their theatres, local newspapers and communities. The nature of film shows in the nickelodeon era, with programs made up of four to six different single-reel film subjects that changed nightly, made it challenging for exhibitors to promote particular film subjects. Some displayed stock posters depicting the genre of the main films being featured, while others provided written lists of titles. Many instead promoted the amenities of the theatre and the pleasures of the movie-going experience. Familiarizing the American movie-going public with the first 'picture personality' performers could only have been accomplished through the efforts of thousands of individual film exhibitors across the country in their own communities.

Searching digitized newspaper databases uncovers the impressive circulation and geographical spread of early local cinema promotions. Often these practices were more extensively documented outside major urban centers than in the cities – advertisements for nickelodeon film programs appear more often in the newspapers of smaller cities, towns and even villages in some parts of the United States. As Moore (2010) and Abel (2006) argue, newspaper publicity was both impractical and unaffordable for nickelodeons in big cities, as it was expensive to advertise in urban newspapers and their film programs changed daily. At least some entrepreneurial showmen in small towns had friendlier relationships with daily or weekly small town newspapers, which offered lower rates, more publicity space for regular advertisers and had been promoting theatrical entertainments in their communities for decades. Information about cinema and picture personalities also circulated among newspaper editors across the nation in multiple ways: through syndication, through retyping articles taken from distant big city newspapers that eventually arrived in the mail, and through trade journal articles or publicity materials acquired from film production companies and distributors by exhibitors.

My research into digitized historic newspapers between 1909 and 1911 found that those local exhibitors who *did* make the effort to spread the film studios' promotional materials did not simply take the information and apply it unthinkingly or without modification. Instead, they often linked promotional information about movie stars to their own community audiences, to other information of a local nature or to promotions of their particular theatre. They also personalized the company-provided information by adding local film reviews, photos, discussions or creative twists of their own to the boilerplate public relations texts. They inserted themselves and their own local voices into the producer-provided material.

Promoting IMP's Florence Lawrence at the local level

I began my nationwide newspaper database research by looking for the IMP Girl. Entrepreneurial film producer Carl Laemmle is considered by film historians to have done a brilliant job of conceiving and orchestrating a publicity campaign centred around Florence Lawrence, the first prominent film actor contracted to his Independent Motion Picture Company (IMP). DeCordova called this 1909–10 campaign 'the most masterful, and probably the most significant, early promotion' (1990: 57). Lawrence's face was already familiar to audiences across the United States through her previous appearances in Biograph films, in the Jones Family comedy series, and in romantic comedies and dramas. (We shall see how local exhibitors continued to call her the original 'Biograph Girl' in their promotions long after Laemmle would have liked.) In late 1909, Laemmle signed Florence Lawrence to perform at IMP, and he immediately began to flaunt her identity and skills in advertisements taken out in the national theatrical trade journals *Moving Picture World (MPW)*, *Billboard* and *New York Dramatic Mirror,* such as 'She's an IMP!' (IMP advertisement 1909; Abel 2006: 232–33, 341; deCordova 1990; Brown 2007). DeCordova and Brown located the month-long campaign of feature articles, photographs and promotions surrounding the build-up to Florence Lawrence's personal appearance in St Louis from 22–28 March 1910 in the *St Louis Post-Dispatch* and *St Louis Times,* while deCordova located several letters from individual fans among Lawrence's personal papers – evidence, he claimed, of 'specific publicity dissemination about Lawrence, probably through local papers or local exhibitors'. But to what extent did this publicity reach exhibitors and audiences elsewhere across the United States? Searching newspaper databases provides another kind of evidence for this circulation of knowledge (deCordova 1990: 57). Local exhibitors used the opportunity of promoting Lawrence to integrate information about their own theatres into IMP-provided text and to add their own editorial flourishes, input and opinions.

The Princess Theater in Hamilton, Ohio was one of the first theatres I could document that jumped on to the IMP promotional bandwagon. On 14 February 1910, the Princess advertised its current feature with the slogan 'Don't fail to see the pretty IMP Girl in this picture' (Hamilton Ohio *Republican-News,* 14 February 1910: 8). The Armory Theater in Massillon Ohio also announced film appearances by Lawrence the former Biograph Girl in their February ads (Massillon Ohio *Independent,* 17 February 1910: 1).

Laemmle's publicity campaign began in earnest in mid-February 1910, with news stories printed in New York City and St Louis papers about Florence Lawrence's demise (although no evidence of these newspaper articles has yet surfaced). Some news reports claimed that Lawrence was killed in New York, others claim it occurred in St Louis (deCordova 1990: 58–59), and there is confusion among them about whether she was run down by a street car or killed by a speeding auto while filming in the streets (Brown 2007: 52, n. 12, quoting from the Louisville *Courier-Journal*). DeCordova notes: 'There is not much respect for consistency in these articles, much less truth.' (See also discussion on Lawrence's publicity circus in Mahar 2007: 53–55.) Florence Lawrence herself recalled seeing an article about her death in a New York City paper, accompanied by a photograph (Brown 2007: 52, n. 6). In early March 1910, Laemmle began trumpeting a denial of the rumours, in a notice printed in *MPW* and articles in the trade journal *Billboard*, and the St Louis papers. Then the story began to circulate more widely as individual film exhibitors began to promote reprints of the article in their local newspapers, adding embellishments of their own.

On 8 March 1910, the *Iowa City Daily Press* featured a quarter-page article, 'Rumor Hands a Hot One: Florence Lawrence has the exquisite if rare privilege of testing the love and loyalty of her friends; Incidentally Carl Laemmle excited.' (*Iowa City Daily Press*, 8 March 1910: 8). The Iowa City film exhibitor who provided the article to the newspaper noted that it had been reprinted from *Billboard*, embellished it with three photographs of Lawrence, and then – to cement a local connection – added: 'This wonderful Pantomimist appears exclusively in the IMP films. To be seen twice a week at the Arcade Picture Theatre.'

During the week Florence Lawrence appeared in person in St Louis, publicity about her surfaced in *The Washington Post*, *Chicago Tribune* and *Louisville Courier-Journal*, with a half-page article, 'Here's the Girl of a Thousand Faces; Miss Florence Lawrence, widely known as the Maude Adams of Moving Pictures'. It featured nine photo portraits of Lawrence portraying various emotions, along with boxed text announcing: 'This 20 year old girl – Learns 300 different roles per year. – Is said to be the highest salaried moving picture actress – Is the storm center of a national moving picture war' – Is known to thousands as "the IMP Girl"' (*Washington Post*, 20 March 1910: 4; *Chicago Tribune*, 20 March 1910: G7).

In early April, a smaller article on Lawrence – 'You've Seen Her Face So Often! Now You Know Who This Girl Is' – appeared in newspapers in towns across the nation as varied as Tacoma, Washington and Logansport, Indiana (*Tacoma Times*, 4 April 1910: 3; Logansport, Indiana *Daily Reporter*, 7 April 1910: 5).

Local exhibitors subsequently created their own Lawrence publicity events. On 30 May 1910, the Queen Theater in Marion, Ohio trumpeted the fact that it was showing both a Biograph film (an older reissue especially dug up from the vaults of the exchange for the occasion) with Florence Lawrence and King Baggott, and an IMP feature with the two, noting that now they worked for IMP:

> The Queen is the only picture show in the United states that has ever run a Biograph and an IMP the same night, showing the same leading actor in both pictures … The Queen is equipped as well as any New York or Chicago theater, it is only at the Queen that you can see every kind of picture made, Independent or licensed. If they are good the Queen shows them. (Marion *Daily Mirror*, 30 May 1910: 12; see also 21 May, 30 May and 17 June 1910)

On 23 June, The *Seattle Star* ran a half-page feature article, 'Travel Not Necessary', which promoted local film exhibitor James Clemmer, the amenities of his Dream Theater and the ability of motion pictures to show audiences the world's splendours in equal measure to the photos and text of its discussion of Miss Lawrence and her acting talents (*Seattle Star*, 23 June 1910: 7; 'A Famous IMP Picture' 1910; 'Acted by Miss Lawrence' 1910).

On 12 August, the Princess Theatre in Victoria, Texas enthused about the 'Big Doings' currently happening at the theatre in a brief news story:

> Up to about the first of this year, the Biograph was recognized as the best film made, but since then the moving picture lovers have been clamoring for the Imp productions. Why? Because up to the first of the year the Biograph Company had Miss Florence Lawrence for its leading lady and as leading man Mr. Moore. These two people are generally recognized as the leading actors in the moving picture profession today, and at the time Miss Lawrence left the Biograph people and joined the Imps it was reported that she had been killed in an accident. The report is false. See the wonderful Imp pictures. We have two a week.

The article also detailed a current contest draw for prizes in the window of a local jewellery store, and the display in the lobby of 'two monster Japanese lizards' who were 'very vicious and poisonous and eat only once in ten days' ('Big Doings at the Princess Theatre' 1910).

Mentions of Florence Lawrence in local nickelodeon advertisements continued through the summer of 1910 in Midwestern towns like Xenia, Ohio and Janesville, Wisconsin, but then abruptly ceased. Florence Lawrence and IMP had acrimoniously parted company in September 1910, and she was off screen until she joined the Lubin Company in early 1911.[1] In Butte, Montana, the *Anaconda Standard* announced her return in February 1911:

> Miss Lawrence comes back to the Orpheum; Miss Florence Lawrence, who was a favorite with the Orpheum patrons so long and was lovingly called the 'Biograph Girl' and was best known in the Jones comedies, has come back to the fold and will be seen in *His Bogus Uncle*. The mere fact that this popular little lady is cast in a comedy is sufficient guarantee of its merit.

Similar newspaper notices appeared in smaller towns as diverse as Lawrence, Kansas; Monessen and Titusville, Pennsylvania; Hudson, New York; Greenville, Mississippi; and Hamilton, Ohio – from the same theatre that had one year earlier enthusiastically promoted her as the IMP Girl.[2]

Finding Vitagraph's Florence Turner at the local level

I then turned to searching newspaper databases for the Vitagraph Girl. A film historian perusing only the national theatrical trade papers would note that the *New York Dramatic Mirror* contained brief notices in April 1910 that Florence Turner made a personal appearance at the Saratoga Park Theater in Brooklyn, when the theatre presented an all Vitagraph film bill and the audience serenaded her with the illustrated song 'The Vitagraph Girl' (*New York Dramatic Mirror*, 23 April 1910: 20). Research into digitized newspaper databases, however, uncovers evidence that the origins of some form of promotion for Florence Turner extended back more than a year earlier. In January 1909, a full-page feature article, 'The Strange Adventures of a Moving Picture Heroine', was first published in *The World* (probably the *New York Evening World*). The lengthy article detailed Turner's early theatrical endeavours, her career with Vitagraph and her adventures in making adaptations of literary classics and her near-drowning and physical and emotional pluck in shooting daring water rescues in Long Island Sound off Brighton Beach. Several large photograph stills taken from Vitagraph film scenes accompanied the article. Despite the reluctance that the Vitagraph and the other General Film Trust companies may have expressed towards identifying its players, this major article does not shy away from focusing on Turner by name.

Such newspaper articles were not only available to metropolitan New York City readers, but could be also read by people in other towns whose newspapers reprinted the feature story in whole or in part. This article on Turner resurfaced in my database search as a heavily illustrated feature story in another major city, in the *Cleveland Plain Dealer* on 10 January 1909 and – somewhat improbably – in the *Dawson City* (Yukon Territory) *Daily News* on 24 February 1909. The newspaper editor in the isolated gold-mining territory condensed the article to a third of a page, removed identification of the Vitagraph studio by name and did not reproduce the photos ('The Strange Adventures' 1909; 'Dashing Heroine' 1909). Nevertheless, that a newspaper in a gold rush settlement 4000 miles (6500 kilometres) from New York would publish an article on a 'picture personality' (on a page shared with an advertisement for the arrival at local stores of a shipment of fresh eggs) demonstrates the rapid and geographically wide diffusion of interest in motion pictures and popular culture.

In late 1909, the Vitagraph company commissioned publication of the song 'The Vitagraph Girl' from the music publisher Havilland and the production of accompanying illustrated song slides from the prominent firm of Scott and Van Altena. In Spring 1910, Vitagraph slipped publicity notices into the trade press (*Variety*, *MPW*) about Florence Turner's appearance at several New York City-area theatres in connection with song-and-film performances. With little further promotion at the national level, however, it was up to individual entrepreneurial film exhibitors across the nation to put this publicity into action. On 12 April 1910, the *Ogden (Utah) Daily Standard*'s advertisement for the Globe Theater announced: 'The song *The Vitagraph Girl* at the Globe is a very pretty little song and is immediately followed by the Vitagraph picture *Mystery of the Temple Court* in which this pretty girl is in the leading role.' Theatres in Xenia, Ohio and Billings, Montana followed suit.[3]

In the summer of 1910, Florence Turner was mentioned by name in scores of newspapers (in both small and larger towns) in connection with her co-starring appearance in a Vitagraph film with boxer Jim Corbett, titled *How Championships are Won and Lost* (*NY Dramatic Mirror*, 25 June 1910: 21; *NY Dramatic Mirror*, 13 August 1910: 30; 'Vitagraph Night' 1910). The purpose of the film was to exploit Corbett's celebrity, but Turner's renown is acknowledged as Corbett is introduced to her, laughs with and playfully spars with her on screen. Vitagraph trade journal notices announce the availability of posters and souvenir leaflets that exhibitors can order to promote the (anonymous) Vitagraph Girl in connection with the film. However, in their own local advertising in places as diverse as Prescott, Arizona; Meriden and New London, Connecticut; Silverton, Colorado; Sheridan, Wyoming; Jonesboro, Arkansas; and Seattle, Washington, most exhibitors identified Turner by name rather than just by her studio sobriquet.

Local exhibitors began to add their own comments on Turner's performances into their advertisements, such as the Alhambra Theater in Washington, DC, which held Vitagraph Nights every Friday. The theatre advised with regard to one film, *The Sage, the Cherub and the Widow*: 'If you miss this one you will be sorry. Miss Turner's in it –That's enough to say, its good … Get acquainted with the daintiest girl of them all, Miss Florence Turner. You'll like her' (Alhambra Theatre, 1910). On 5 December, the New Lyric Theater in Palestine, Texas offered the film *A Modern Knight Errant*, which the manager described as:

One of those high art Vitagraph pictures featuring Miss Florence Turner, the most popular lady in motion photoplays, will be the feature film. This picture has a hunch on the dramatic end of the business. It is full of the red blood of human nature. We cannot help feeling glad that we are real men and women when we see such pictures as this. (Palestine, Texas *Daily Herald*, 5 December 1910: 4)

Individual film exhibitors were not just reprinting Vitagraph advertising lines; they added their own personal comments on Turner and her performances that connected this picture personality to their audiences, and used her celebrity to build up the value of their local theatre.

In 1911, local newspaper promotions of Turner and Lawrence were buttressed by film producers' expansion of 'picture personality' film publicity at the national level. The studios stepped up their publicity efforts through greater production of movie posters and a few more promotional aids, and with the founding in February 1911 of *Motion Picture Story Magazine*, which featured novelizations of Trust Company films, illustrations of film scenes and eventually articles about their performers. Richard Abel (2006: 233) notes that at least one of the major New York newspapers, the *New York Morning Telegraph*, began publishing photographs of film actors on its Motion Picture page in February 1911. *Photoplay Magazine*, sponsored by the independent film production studios, also began publishing in September 1911 (2006: 236).

Across the hinterlands, a growing number of nickelodeons promoted the names of 'picture personalities' who appeared on local screens. Richard Abel found more theaters (such as those in northern Ohio cities) willing to promote actor names to satisfy audience desires to see their favorites (2006: 236). In searching one large digitized newspaper database for 1911, Lawrence received mention in 25 newspapers, ranging from several medium-sized cities (Oakland, California; Fort Wayne, Indiana and others in Texas, Wisconsin and Massachusetts) to small towns in Pennsylvania, Utah, Iowa, Ohio, Oklahoma, Texas, Nevada, Mississippi and Montana. In the same database, Florence Turner of Vitagraph garnered mention in 19 papers during 1911, of which 16 of the newspapers (85 per cent) had also promoted Lawrence. This suggests that individual film exhibitors now regularly advertised film performers from many of the producers whose films they showed, not just one, and also spurred on their local competition to promote stars, as their audiences in their communities apparently responded well to this interest in the actresses.

Cooperstown, New York: 'the Vitagraphers are here!'

My research into digitized newspapers thus far has uncovered no film promotional campaign as elaborate and as well documented in newspapers as George Carley's Vitagraph events held in Cooperstown, New York in the summer of 1911. Carley's simultaneous positions as nickelodeon owner and newspaper editor may have opened his eyes to the possibilities of novel forms of publicity, and his stance as a booster of Cooperstown's local commerce and literary fame may have compelled him turn a keen eye to opportunities to promote the community as well as his business. Carley connected film star celebrity and film production to wider publicity possibilities of film for enhancing tourism and a town's economic health. Carley schemed in order that both local interests and the film producers would benefit – that the movies and supporting publicity campaigns would advertise the beauty and historic literary heritage of Cooperstown (the setting of popular nineteenth-century novelist James Fenimore Cooper's *Leatherstocking Tales*) to the world and bring tourism to the small town. Carley's promotional campaign could have served as a model for innovative marketing of cinema and its performers in America in 1911, if only the fates had not conspired against him. Carley's marketing ideas were a bit too far ahead of their time.

George Carley was relatively young, in his thirties, and educated; he was a great booster of local commerce and culture, active in fraternal lodge activities and village cultural events. Unlike the much more conservative civic leaders of the neighbouring health resort community of Richfield Springs, 10 miles north of Cooperstown, he was also accepting of new modes of entertainment culture. Since assuming editorship of the Cooperstown *Freeman's Journal* newspaper in 1903, Carley had featured advertising from itinerant film exhibitors such as Cook and Harris and Lyman Howe, and had published generous reviews of their performances. His weekly paper regularly included articles that shed favourable light on the movies, especially stories that detailed film's potential for Progressive education, reform and uplift. In 1908, soon after the village's first stationary nickelodeon opened on the third floor of the Iron Clad Building above his newspaper office, Carley purchased a half-interest in the moving picture show, which he renamed the Star Theater. Carley was an enthusiastic early proponent of movie star culture – for example, mentioning in a summer 1910 Star Theater ad that the theatre was showing a Biograph film, *Ramona*, 'featuring little Alice Sterling, the Biograph Girl'. Here, Carley gamely invented a name for the film actress for whom Biograph had mandated anonymity (in this case, Mary Pickford) (*Glimmerglass*, ? August 1910: n.p.; see discussions of Cooperstown in Fuller 1997 and in Fuller-Seeley 2011)

In early 1911, Carley took the initiative to begin conversations with Vitagraph company officials downstate in Brooklyn about filming on location in Cooperstown. In mid-March, he began frequently promoting Vitagraph performers Florence Turner, Ken Casey and Jean the Vitagraph Dog in his local news columns (Cooperstown New York *Freemans Journal*, 17 May 1911: 4). By late May, Carley's persistent inquiries were getting results, and he could report in the newspaper that 'Vitagraph Company May Visit Cooperstown', reprinting a letter from the studio's head scenario editor, Mrs Beta Breuil, who wrote that the company had taken note of his proposition and thought favourably of it ('Vitagraph Company May Visit' 1911; *Moving Picture World*, 3 June 1911: 1261). Carley's public relations plans truly began to gel when Vitagraph director Larry Trimble visited Cooperstown on 2 July while on a scouting trip by automobile across upstate New York, looking for suitable scenic locations for film-making ('Otsego Lake' 1911).

Carley's entreaties dovetailed with Vitagraph's own goals: to attract larger numbers of middle-class viewers by producing movies that had closer ties to 'high culture'. A Vitagraph company executive interviewed in 1911 by the *New York Times* pointed to a schedule of the studio's upcoming productions, which included adaptations of such literary classics as *Uncle Tom's Cabin*, Scott's *Kenilworth*, Cooper's *Leatherstocking Tales*, *Macbeth*, *Richard III*, *Julius Caesar*, *The Merchant of Venice* and others. The Vitagraph official asserted that location shooting added to the authenticity and legitimacy of turning classic theatrical productions into the more modern art ('Is the Moving Picture' 1911: SM 8–9).

Carley had made his Cooperstown readers knowledgeable about the Vitagraph company brand name and its actors. His extended newspaper coverage of the Vitagraphers' visit to Cooperstown would significantly increase local public awareness of the new movie stars and involve them much more deeply in this new expanded world of motion picture promotion (Fuller 1997; deCordova 1990; 'Scouts in Moving Pictures' 1911; 'Dr. Cooke's Story' 1911).

On Monday, 17 July, Carley's summertime news sheet, the *Glimmerglass Daily*, prominently featured the 'picture personalities' on its front page with a headline, 'Vitagraph Visitors: Who they are and what they are doing in Cooperstown', just as if a famous general, politician or industrialist had arrived in the village. Carley lavished paragraphs on descriptions of the celebrity and prominence of these upstart movie company visitors, and emphasized the film-makers' star personae:

Miss Turner is the popular Vitagraph girl, who is one of the best-known actresses in the world. She had a successful career upon the regular stage before she entered the moving picture field. It is stated that her audience now comprises a million and a half of people every day. Her versatility is wonderful. She has appeared in almost every imaginable role in the moving pictures from princess to slave. In the *Uncle Tom's Cabin* pictures she was Topsy; she has appeared in several boy roles and once in a moving picture did a boxing turn with James J. Corbett. She is as charming to know personally as she is upon the screen …

Larry Trimble is a scenario director and writer. He directs the taking of the Cooperstown pictures, and has directed some of the greatest productions that have been done by the Vitagraph Company, his masterpiece being 'The Battle Hymn of the Republic' which has not yet been seen here. Mr. Trimble is charmed by the beauty of Cooperstown and Otsego Lake, and it was upon his judgment after a visit to this locality two weeks ago that the decision was made by the Vitagraph Company to take a series of Indian pictures here. Mr. Trimble will have charge of all the pictures to be taken in this locality. ('Vitagraph Visitors' 1911; 'A Cinch' 1911; 'Joke on Village Cop' 1911).

After the company arrived and spent the day filming on Otsego Lake at the foot of the village, Cooperstown residents were treated to a visit of the actors to the Star Theater. 'Everyone is going to the moving pictures tonight,' Carley crowed in the 'Cooperstown Happenings' column in the *Glimmerglass* ('Cooperstown Happenings' 1911; 'Tonight' 1911) Florence Turner's appearance at the special Vitagraph Night on 17 July was the most successful night in the Star Theater's history, Carley ecstatically reported the following day ('Big Vitagraph Night' 1911; 'A Vitagraph Showing Miss Tuner' 1911).

That the visit of the Vitagraph Company is appreciated by the people of Cooperstown was proved by the large crowd that came out to see them at the Star Theater last evening. For the first show the house was packed to standing room. And was well filled for the second performance. The pictures presented upon the screen were *Jean Goes Foraging, A Dixie Mother*, and *The Misses Finch and Billy*. Miss Turner appeared in all three pictures, Jean in the first and Kenneth Casey as 'Billy' in the last. After the pictures, Mr. Larry Trimble of the Vitagraph Company introduced separately Jean, Kenneth and Miss Turner, each of whom did a little turn. Needless to say the audience went wild with enthusiasm.

As a little surprise to Miss Turner, the Tanner twins [local boys Muir and Murray] sang 'The Vitagraph Girl' a popular illustrated song, with Miss Turner in the slides. When the twins responded to the encore, Miss Turner popped out from behind the screen and embraced them, then, standing between the twins, bowed and smiled as only the Vitagraph Girl can. ('Vitagraph Girl' song c. 1910)

The Vitagraphers decamped the next morning to journey towards their next filming location. They returned to Cooperstown in early September 1911 to film a two-reel adaptation of Cooper's *The Deerslayer*, with another wave of publicity by Carley published in the *Freeman's Journal*. Unfortunately, from a promotional standpoint, the company was held up from shooting for several weeks in building substantial wooden water-borne Muskrat Castle and Ark sets and authentic-looking canoes on the lake. Local Cooperstown photographer 'Putt' Telfer spent several days on the *Deerslayer* sets shooting photographs of the actors and director at work. He published them as a set of 54 real-photo postcards to sell at his shop to Cooperstown movie fans, an extraordinary record of shooting on location in 1911 (NYSHA website Telfer Collection 1859–1954). However, steady rainfall further continually delayed the filming week after week, while 16 Vitagraph actors and crew members shivered in rental cottages located up the lake at Hyde Bay ('Vitagraph Folks are Here' 1911; *LA Times*, 15 July 1911: 17; 'Pantomime Actors Arrive' 1911; *Freemans Journal*,

20 September 1911: 5). Six weeks later, on 11 October, the film company was forced to decamp back to the Brooklyn studio, having only shot about three-quarters of the script and still missing the climactic scenes of the burning of Muskrat Castle and the big fight between Indians, soldiers and pioneers. The Vitagraphers left, but the rival village newspaper, *The Otsego Farmer* (which gave the filming almost no coverage), reminded locals that they were not forgotten – 'persons having bills against the Vitagraph company may leave them with George H. Carley who will forward them to the treasurer of the company for payment' (*Otsego Farmer*, 13 October 1911: 2).

At the end of October 1911, the short comedy filmed in Cooperstown was released; it was now called *The Wig Wag* (a scouting term for sending Morse Code messages by waving signal flags) (*Freemans Journal*, 27 September 1911: 2). But lack of interest and coordination at the regional film exchange kept Carley from even being able to show the film in Cooperstown until several weeks later. The *Freeman's Journal* gamely reported the film's local success: 'After the seats were filled for the first evening show, Policeman Southworth was called upon the keep the crowd back and the stairway clear. The house was also well-filled for the second show. Scenes on the lake and in the village are the background for the picture and the faces of Cooperstown people are easily recognized' (*Freemans Journal*, 1 November 1911: 5). The filmed version of *The Wig Wag*, unfortunately, was not quite the public relations bonanza that Carley had sought – the specific mentions of Cooperstown had been edited out of the final film ('Cooperstown Boy Scouts' 1911; '*Wig Wag*' 1911).

Even more devastating to George Carley's promotional hopes, the two-reel *Deerslayer* project also turned out to be a fiasco. While the *Freeman's Journal* quoted director Larry Trimble announcing that the film would be released in January 1912, accompanied by a feature spread in the February issue of *Motion Picture Story Magazine*, the story appeared, but no film. An unfortunate series of events, from Florence Turner's extended serious illness (pneumonia caught on location in Cooperstown) to Turner's and Trimble's departure from Vitagraph to form their own production company, left the unfinished *Deerslayer* in limbo, as longer five- and six-reel feature films became increasingly desirable to movie audiences across the nation (*Freemans Journal*, 29 November 1911: 4). After a delay of 18 months, a hastily cobbled-together two-reel *Deerslayer* that featured a departed star that Vitagraph was uninterested in promoting was finally released in May 1913 (*Freemans Journal*, 9 April: 5). Carley staged a successful local premiere in Cooperstown, but the film quickly sank out of sight, as did his hopes of promotional success in motion pictures (*Freemans Journal*, 30 April 1911; *Otsego Farmer*, 9 May 1913: 5).

Conclusion

The moviegoers of Cooperstown, New York who viewed the *Deerslayer* in May, 1913 were by this point very knowledgeable consumers of movie star culture – through the pages of the *Freeman's Journal* and the fan magazines, they knew that Florence Turner (accompanied by

Larry Trimble) had left Vitagraph to form their own film production company in England. They knew (courtesy of George Carley's regular news stories) who were the winners of movie actor popularity polls, and the advertisements for the Star Theater were dominated by the names of the picture personalities appearing in the films they saw each week. (They probably also suspected that this two-year-old version of the *Deerslayer* was brief and old-fashioned compared with the five- and six-reel spectacular feature-length films they now frequently saw at the movies.) Carley's campaign to promote interest in cinema in his community had succeeded, even if his ambitious efforts to promote the village had come to nought.

As this example of 'new cinema history' research has demonstrated, the spread of movie star culture and moviegoing as an everyday activity since 1909 had been widespread across the United States from the pages of national film industry trade journals to small villages like Cooperstown, to towns and cities in various locations. Nevertheless, the diffusion of information in newspapers had a hit-or-miss quality, with some communities reading many articles and advertisements about picture personalities being promoted at local theatres, and others receiving no printed information at all. The spread of film promotion in newspapers was largely due to the efforts of on-the-ball theatre managers who took the raw materials of picture personality promotions from the film producers and distributors with whom they did business, and from the trade journals they read and the fan publications they sold, and put them into action in thousands of local communities across the nation.

Newspaper links with motion pictures as complementary systems of cinema information would grow rapidly in the next several years to come, as more urban newspapers created dedicated movie pages for moviegoers and fans, as more theaters advertised feature films and personalities. And then with the creation of film serials like *What Happened to Mary*, *The Adventures of Kathlyn* and *Our Mutual Girl*, motion pictures and newspapers would become intertwined (see Staiger 1990; Luckett 1999; Mahar 2007; Wilinsky 2000; Bean 2001; Singer 2001). Continued research into databases of historic local newspapers will undoubtedly provide even more evidence of the creative and unusual ways in which individual theatre managers and newspaper editors educated community audiences about the earliest film celebrities.

As competition between film producers became more mature and film companies larger after 1911, and as the systems of feature film production and distribution became more solid, film producers began to take more responsibility for film and movie star promotions. Staiger notes that:

Predictable distribution procedures meant not only that exhibitors knew when they would receive new films but they also had advance notice of possible selling points such as genre, plot, stars, spectacle, and realism. Additionally, feature films that constituted at least one-half of the program's length could justifiably become the focal point of the exhibitor's publicity. (1990: 6)

Studios created more elaborate posters (as I have discussed elsewhere) and advertising aids like campaign books, ready-made advertisements and articles for individual exhibitors to insert in local newspapers, and the studios placed more advertisements in national magazines and large urban newspapers (Fuller-Seeley 2012). Local exhibitors would still play a vital role as conduits of information about Hollywood films and actors to their community audiences, but as the film industry coalesced, local theatre managers made use of the promotional tools provided to them, instead of having to create so much of their own.

References

Abel, R. (2006), *Americanizing the Movies and 'Movie-Mad' Audiences 1910–1914*, Berkeley, CA: University of California Press.

'Acted by Miss Lawrence, Formerly the Biograph Girl', advertisement, Moberly, Missouri *Daily Monitor*, 28 June.

'Alhambra Theater in Washington DC' (1910), *Herald*, 9 October 9, second part, p. 7.

Allen, R.C. (2008), 'Going to the Show: What is a Venue?', http://docsouth.unc.edu/gtts/about-venue.html. Accessed 20 December 2011.

Bean, J.M. (2001), 'Technologies of Early Stardom and the Extraordinary Body', *Camera Obscura* 48, 16: 3, pp. 8–57.

'Big Doings at the Princess Theatre' (1910), Victoria, Texas *Daily Advocate*, n.d., p. 3.

'Big Vitagraph Night' (1911), *Glimmerglass*, 18 July, p. 1.

Bowles, K., Maltby, R., Verhoeven, D. and Walsh, M. (2011), *The New Cinema History: A Guide*, New York: Wiley-Blackwell.

Brown, K. (2007), *Florence Lawrence, the Biograph Girl: America's First Movie Star*, New York: McFarland.

'A Cinch' (1911), *Glimmerglass*, 17 July, p. 2.

'Cooperstown Boy Scouts in Moving Pictures' (1911), *Otsego Farmer*, 20 October, p. 4.

'Cooperstown Happenings' (1911), *Glimmerglass*, 17 July, p. 2.

'Dashing Heroine of the Moving Picture', *Dawson City Daily News*, 24 February, p. 3.

deCordova, R. (1990), *Picture Personalities: The Emergence of the Star System in America*, Champaign-Urbana, IL: University of Illinois Press.

'Dr. Cooke's Story: Along the Blazed Trail' (1911), *Glimmerglass Daily*, 15 July, p. 2.

'A Famous IMP Picture with Miss Florence Lawrence the Beautiful Biograph Girl' (1910), Ada Oklahoma [newspaper name not known], 24 June.

Fuller, K. (2001), *At the Picture Show: Small Town Audiences and the Creation of Movie Fan Culture*, Charlottesville, VA: University Press of Virginia.

Fuller-Seeley, K. (ed.) (2008), *Hollywood in the Neighborhood*, Berkeley, CA: University of California Press.

—— (2011), 'Modernity for Small Town Tastes: Movies at the 1907 Cooperstown, New York, Centennial', in R. Maltby and R. Allen (eds), *Explorations in New Cinema History: Approaches and Case Studies*, New York: Blackwell, pp. 280–94.

——— (2012), 'Storefront Theater Advertising and the Evolution of the Film Poster', in A. Gaudreault, N. Dulac and S. Hildalgo (eds), *A Companion to Early Cinema*, New York: Wiley, pp. 398–419.

'Imp Advertisement' (1909), *MPW*, 18 December.

'Is the Moving Picture to Be the Play of the Future?' (1911), *New York Times*, 20 August, pp. SM 8–9.

'Joke on Village Cop' (1911), *Glimmerglass*, 19 July, p. 4.

Keil, C. and Stamp, S. (2004), *American Cinema's Transitional Era: Audiences, Institutions, Practices*, Berkeley, CA: University of California Press.

Luckett, M. (1999), 'Advertising and Femininity: The Case of Our Mutual Girl', *Screen*, Winter, pp. 363–83.

Mahar, K.W. (2007), *Women Film-makers in Early Hollywood*, Baltimore, MD: Johns Hopkins University Press.

Maltby, R. (2011), 'New Cinema Histories', in R. Maltby, D. Biltereyst and P. Meers (eds), *Explorations in New Cinema History: Approaches and Case Studies*, New York: Wiley-Blackwell, pp. 3–40.

Moore, P. (2010), *Now Playing: Early Moviegoing and the Regulation of Fun*, Albany, NY: SUNY Press.

'Otsego Lake the World Over! Vitagraph Company of America to Take Moving Pictures of Cooper Tales Here' (1911), *Freeman's Journal*, 5 July, p. 4.

'Pantomime Actors Arrive; Make Moving Pictures' (1911), *Otsego Farmer*, 15 September, p. 5.

'Scouts in Moving Pictures: The Vitagraph Actors will Arrive This Week' (1911), *Glimmerglass Daily*, 10 July, p. 1.

Singer, B. (2001), *Melodrama and Modernity: Early Sensational Cinema and Its Contexts*, New York: Columbia University Press.

Staiger, J. (1984), 'Combination and Litigation: Structures of U.S. Film Distribution, 1896–1917', *Cinema Journal*, 23: 2, pp. 41–72.

——— (1990), 'Announcing Wares, Winning Patrons, Voicing Ideals: Thinking About the History and Theory of Film Advertising', *Cinema Journal*, 29: 3, pp. 3–31.

'The Strange Adventures of a Moving Picture Heroine' (1909), *Cleveland Plain Dealer*, 10 January 1909, p. 45.

'The Vitagraph Girl' song (c. 1910), Haviland Music, words by J.A. Leggett, music by Henry Frantzen.

'Tonight' (1911), *Glimmerglass*, 17 July, p. 1.

'Vitagraph Company May Visit' (1911), Cooperstown New York *Otsego Farmer*, 2 June 2, p. 4.

'Vitagraph Folks are Here' (1911), *Freemans Journal*, 6 September, p. 1.

'Vitagraph Night at Bay Ridge NY Airdome' (1910), *NY Dramatic Mirror*, 5 October, p. 33.

'A Vitagraph Showing Miss Tuner and Kenneth Casey' (2011), *Glimmerglass*, 18 July, p. 4.

'Vitagraph Visitors' (1911), *Glimmerglass*, 17 July, p. 1.

'Wig Wag' (1911), *Moving Picture World*, 21 October, p. 228.

Wilinsky, B. (2000), 'Flirting with Kathlyn: Creating the Mass Audience', in D. Desser and G. Jowett (eds), *Hollywood Goes Shopping*, Minnesota, MN: University of Minnesota Press, pp. 34–56.

Notes

1 Xenia Ohio Dreamland Theater, 22 August 1910; Janesville, Wisconsin, 'The IMP Girl', 30 September 1910 and 5 October 1910.

2 Butte, Montana, *the Anaconda Standard*, noted 10 February 1911, p. 12; Lawrence, KS, *Daily Journal*, 10 February 1011, p. 6; Monessen, PA, 28 February 1911; Hamilton, OH *Evening Journal*, 17 March 1911. Hudson, NY *Evening Register*, April 20, 1911 p. 8 – 'Pictures at Hudson Theater', 'You will see Arthur Johnson and Florence Lawrence in this Lubin Picture tonight, who we used to see so much of in the Biograph'. The Titusville, PA *Herald* (20 March 1911) calls her 'original Biograph Heroine Florence Lawrence'; Greenville, MS *Daily Democrat*, 19 May 1911, p. 5.

3 Ad for Oracle, Globe, Isis and Joie Theaters, Ogden UT; Billings Montana *Daily Gazette*, 3 July 1910 p. 5; Xenia, OH *Gazette*: 'Orpheum Theater is Playing the Illustrated Song', 27 July 1910, p. 12.

Chapter 7

'Calamity Howling': The Advent of Television and Australian Cinema Exhibition

Mike Walsh

When Twentieth Century-Fox executive Emanuel Silverstone arrived in Australia at the end of 1949, television was the subject on everyone's lips. Silverstone was at pains to quiet the fears of Australian exhibitors about the effects of the new technology. 'Television will no more put picture theatres out of business than home cooking has put restaurants out of business,' was his reassuring (albeit chronologically confused) analogy headlined by trade paper *Film Weekly* ('Emanuel Silverstone Here' 1950).

There has been considerable analysis of the coming of television to Australia. Most of it has foregrounded the politics that delivered Australia a mixed system of state-run and commercial television, with the latter owned predominantly by dominant newspaper interests sympathetic to the Menzies Liberal government (Arrow 2008; Curthoys 1986; Hazelhurst 1982–83; Walter 1994). Cameron Hazlehurst sees two groups who opposed the introduction of television: those who thought that the post-war economy could not afford it and those who thought that its cultural impact would be negative (1982–83: 67). He neglects to mention a third group: those who feared and opposed television because the new medium stood to decimate their businesses.

The Australian cinema industry fell squarely within this third group. This chapter reviews the discussions about television that appeared in the leading Australian cinema trade paper, *Film Weekly* (henceforth *FW*), during the decade 1950–59. I hope to give some sense of the range of attitudes and strategies deployed in the face of this new medium. Given that *FW*'s readership consisted mainly of people involved in the distribution and exhibition sectors, it is instructive to track the rhetorical shifts of the paper as the rapidly changing nature of the Australian mediascape brought out major tensions within the motion picture industry – what *FW* called the MPI.

This acronym is one that is purely of *FW*'s invention, as no trade body bearing that name existed in Australia. Each state had its own Motion Picture Exhibitors' Association and the major distributors had a nationwide Motion Picture Distributors' Association of Australia (MPDAA). Elsewhere, I have concluded that the introduction of synchronized sound to Australia needs to be read in terms of the contesting interests between the distribution and exhibition sectors (Walsh 1999). One of the primary assumptions of this study is that the introduction of a new technology typically places strains on the uneasy and informal alliances that underlie everyday business practices in the film industry. Television would expose the tensions that were always present within the Australian cinema industry: industrial tensions between distribution and exhibition, national tensions between

America and Australian interests and intra-national tensions between different tiers of the exhibition sector.

I would suggest that now is an excellent time to revisit the story of television. With the continuing decline of theatrical box office as an element in the overall revenue stream, we have come to regard theatrical exhibition as occupying a place alongside, or in front of, other ancillary revenue streams – most of which lead to consumption on television screens. Taking this long view, the introduction of television now looks like a massive success in expanding the consumption of films. But try telling that to the readers of *FW* in 1950.

The storm clouds loom, the heat rises in the kitchen …

The advent of television is usually positioned as a bad news story in cinema histories, being linked to the decline in the number of cinemas. Diane Collins (1987) begins her analysis of television's introduction by likening television to that other technology of the post-war era, the atomic bomb. She switches metaphors to declare that 'television dealt a knockout blow to moving pictures' (1987: 214). Shirley and Adams note 'the severe erosion of cinema attendance by television' (1989: 221). Pike and Cooper claim that the distribution and exhibition sectors in Australia 'fell into deep pessimism as they confronted competition from television' (1998: 201).

Even if we accept these metaphors of disaster, we are in need of a more fine-grained time scale to describe the process. Television did not appear throughout Australia at a single moment, and theatres did not suddenly vanish overnight. Table 7.1 shows a steady decline in cinema admissions for the immediate post-war period up until 1950, but then a recovery. The number of cinema tickets sold – which had dipped from its wartime high of 151 million to as low as 129 million in 1949–50 – recovered to around 140 million by the 1952–53 financial year. It seems to have stabilized at the point where the Commonwealth government's entertainment tax was rescinded and reliable nationwide statistics ceased. At the start of 1956, the first year of regular broadcasting in Sydney and Melbourne, the number of cinemas in Australia was still rising – a rise that continued until a peak of over 1800 in 1959.

By the beginning of the 1970s, the number of cinemas in Australia had dropped to 735, a decline of around 60 per cent, even as Australia's population grew by 25 per cent. The number of seats in hardtop 35mm cinemas similarly decreased by over 60 per cent. What happened? It has become something of an international orthodoxy to dispute the adequacy of ascribing the decline in cinemas and cinema-going simply to television (Balio 1990). Post-war suburbanization, the baby boom, the explosion of hire-purchase commitments that ate into disposable income and the attraction of other leisure activities are a few competing candidates.

However, in the minds of *FW*'s editorial staff, there was no doubt that television was the main game. Although hire purchase, state Entertainment Taxes, economic contraction – even the introduction of parking meters – are occasionally invoked, the themes harped upon the pages of *FW* are that television is coming, that it will be bad for cinemas and that what

Table 7.1: Cinema admissions, 1944–45 to 1971*

Year	Theatres	Admissions	Seats
1944–45		151,144,831	
1945–46		142,970,672	
1946–47		136,889,246	
1947–48		133,151,865	
1948–49	1674	129,871,525	
1949–50	1676	129,028,000	
1950–51	1656	133,959,000	1,164,035
1951–52	1650	133,959,000	1,150,139
1952–53	1663	140,085,000	1,181,785
1953–54	1730		1,188,941
1954–55	1728	137,861,000	1,186,719
1955–56	1731		1,198,896
1956–57	1765		1,192,235
1957–58	1774		1,195,143
1958–59	1822		1,263,458
1960–61	1579		1,032,064
1961–62	1512		947,169
1962–63	1317		860,641
1963–64	1124		679,421
1964–65	1205		769,849
1965–66	990		641,998
1966–67	963		641,998
1968–69	786		496,928
1969–70	744		471,488
1971	735		478,402

Source: Figures from *FW Directory* summaries. Admission figures based on Commonwealth Entertainment Tax. Seats refer to 35mm hardtop cinemas only.

* Data for 1967–68 is not available

FW calls the MPI had better be prepared. An editorial in 1952 begins: 'That small black cloud, television, which has been hovering on the Australian horizon for so long, is rapidly growing. In the not too distant future, the storm will break.' ('Consolidate, While There's Yet Time!' 1952)

Regular television broadcasting did not arrive in Australia until relatively late by the standards of major western societies. The Australian cinema industry had a lot of time to contemplate its arrival. Prior to 1956, the question posed to every overseas visitor or returning traveller was about what sort of a challenge television constituted. The United States was looked to as the laboratory for media experimentation. *FW* carries an ongoing commentary drawn from the US press and from interviews with those returning from US visits. In the first part of the 1950s, these forecasts acknowledged the potential threat of television, but generally put a reassuring face on things.

The decline in the American box office was an undeniable fact, though not everyone saw it as permanent or attributed it to television. Those prioritizing wider social factors were split between narratives that blamed the poor state of the consumer economy (the rising cost of living meant that consumers had less disposable cash for movies) and those who pointed to the booming nature of the economy. In this latter narrative, economic expansion produced an explosion of hire purchase which ate into disposable income.

Clyde Waterman, the general manager of the Hoyts Ozone circuit and head of the South Australian Motion Picture Exhibitors' Association, is typical of early attempts to downplay television. In 1950 he returned from a trip to the United States and assured *FW* that television would be no threat, citing the continued building of cinemas there. He described a rosy situation in which there was increased leisure time so that the two media could happily coexist. He assumed that motion pictures would be the big brother in the relationship, with television acting as a minor league developer of new talent for the movies ('Waterman Intends to Operate Drive-ins' 1950).

An analogy with radio was constantly evoked during this pre-television period ('Busy Time for Daff' 1953). According to this analogy, film had accommodated the introduction of one new entertainment medium, and it would do so again. Television might even help the cinema by providing another means of building star popularity, which could then be exploited on the bigger screen. Television could also provide another weapon with which the Australian showman could 'ballyhoo' his film attractions. For Norman Rydge, chairman of Greater Union, 'theatres offer an exclusivity of entertainment that could not be obtained on the television set' and hence, like film and radio, 'they will exist side by side, each fulfilling an individual role in the entertainment of our people' ('Rydge says GUT Set' 1950). Ernest Turnbull, managing director of Hoyts, was equally upbeat – though not so sure that the two media were necessarily complementary. Television would, he claimed, 'take its place in the community, and our task is to see that it doesn't take *our* place' ('Turnbull Feted' 1950).

Those who inclined to dismiss the threat of television did so on the basis of one of two broad grounds: the film medium or consumer behaviour. The former position cited either economic or textual reasons why television could not sustain its challenge. Economic explanations suggested that television's content was too cheap, that its producers could not command the resources to make films that would compete against big-budget Hollywood productions. Textual explanations abstracted out the formal qualities of the image from any context of consumption. The television image was dismissed as small and grey in comparison to the technologies of spectacle Hollywood was unleashing. An RCA executive in 1951 proclaimed: 'It is not possible for TV to provide entertainment equal to the scope of the movies with their immensely superior technique' ('Optimistic Forecast' 1951). While television's content was too cheap, as a consumer medium television could be claimed to be too expensive. A new set cost over £200 as opposed to 3 shillings for a movie ticket.

Consumer-based arguments continually stressed that television's novelty appeal to consumers was likely to wear off quickly, and that people would always want to go out (presumably the logic that Silverstone saw as saving restaurants after the invention of home cooking). Through the middle of the 1950s, the dominant assumption of the optimists was that television's appeal would be transient and could be fought through. Wolfe Cohen, the head of Warner Bros' international distribution division, visited Australia in 1951 and stated: 'Television is a big opposition, but it is not that permanent exhibition that it was expected to be' ('TV Not the Bogey' 1951). Eric Johnston, the head of the MPDAA, suggested that television's impact would be a 20 per cent drop in box office lasting between 12 and 15 months before a recovery ('TV Causes 20% b.o. Drop' 1954). Television, like the Axis powers during the war, had stolen a march but motion pictures were now fighting back and stemming the tide. Australian-born Universal executive Al Daff went so far as to suggest that investors in Australian television would lose their shirts and Universal wanted nothing to do with it ('Please Install Wide Screens!' 1954). This seemed to be the company line at Universal, echoed by long-time manager Herc McIntyre, on the basis that television programmers would not be able to maintain a supply of good material ('Sell 'em Harder' 1955).

Another optimistic position in the first part of the 1950s was the possibility that, rather than challenging cinema, television might be co-opted by it through the implementation of technologies by the major US studios, such as large-screen theatre television (White 1990). In 1950, Clay Hake, the new head of Paramount's Australian subsidiary, invoked this alliance of interests to claim that 'to protect exhibitors throughout the world, we [Paramount] are trying to harness television for the theatres' ('Hake Talks on TV' 1950). Fox's investment in Eidophor theatre television was widely touted in *FW*'s pages (especially as Fox controlled Hoyts cinemas, and Ernest Turnbull served as both the chair of Fox's Australian subsidiary and the managing director of Hoyts). *FW* was heavily invested in the mythology of an MPI that would get through the crisis cooperatively. This was why theatre television was so important for *FW* to highlight. Here was a technology (like synchronized sound) developed by a global distribution sector headquartered in the United States, for use by local exhibitors.

The years 1953 and 1954 were a time of wonder for *FW*, a period when US studios produced a myriad of these new technologies aimed at securing the advantage of cinema consumption. These included 3D, widescreen systems such as CinemaScope, larger negative formats including VistaVision, Todd AO and CinemaScope55, and enhanced sound systems. Even here, though, we can see the consensus of MPI interests being put to the test, as there was an element of division between the large exhibition circuits and the smaller exhibitors. CinemaScope was pushed strongly by Hoyts, which was controlled by Fox, holder of patents for CinemaScope. A week after the average cost of conversion to CinemaScope was reported as £6300 to £4500, Hoyts announced that it would spend £1.5 million installing widescreen technologies at its major cinemas, with an average cost of £20,000 per theatre ('Hoyts to

Spend £1½m' 1953). Diane Collins claims that only one-third of Australian cinemas adapted for widescreen in the first 18 months of its availability in Australia (1987: 219). Two years after the introduction of CinemaScope, Hoyts' Ernest Turnbull acknowledged that the technology had been divisive, and that 90 per cent of Australian exhibitors had hoped for the failure of CinemaScope so that they would not have to bear the cost of installing it ('Nonsense to Minimise' 1956). The diffusion of new technologies always involves relations of economic power and contains industrial tensions that reverberate throughout the marketing chain. Survival might turn out to be the survival of the fittest.

While *FW* always champions Hollywood production and the US distribution subsidiaries in Australia, tensions are sometimes evident. The 18 December 1952 issue reprints a United Press article by Marquis Childs (1952), by-lined from Hollywood. He explains that Hollywood studios were cushioning the effects of decreasing foreign revenues by cooperating with their domestic television sector though pay television and making telefilms. *FW* appends an editorial comment, pointing out 'the ominous overtones' of the article before pulling back to safer ground by praising Hollywood studios for having the courage to make 'really big, really seat-selling product'. What is ominous is the threat that Hollywood might cut its own deal with television and desert the local exhibition sector. That prospect was too terrible to contemplate; it was much better to look on the bright side and concentrate on the way that Hollywood could supply better weapons for the exhibitor.

The bitter edge of the relation between Hollywood supply and Australian marketing arose occasionally. An article about market research cites a common, sceptical objection found by researchers: 'We in Australia can't change the type of pictures we get from overseas, so what's the use of finding out what people want?' (Mooney 1953). Turnbull tried to put a positive spin on this dependency when he wrote that: 'Unquestionably, when television reaches its peak, our surest defence will be Hollywood's awareness of its responsibility to the motion picture industry' (Turnbull 1956).

Prior to 1957, when television was a prospect rather than a reality, *FW* was committed to a guardedly optimistic position based on the agency of individual participants acting within an assumed model of cooperation between distribution and exhibition, rather than any structural analysis of the future directions of the media. So *FW*'s solution to the looming storm clouds of television was two-pronged: distribution must supply good films and exhibitors must persevere with good showmanship. In October 1952, *FW* gave its front page over to Greater Union's Norman Rydge, who labelled television 'virulent competition' but went on to reassure the industry that 'good pictures answer any challenge' ('Good Pictures Answer' 1952). A September 1952 editorial predicting that television's 'impact will be terrific here' then suggests that 'the need today is for greater and greater showmanship drive … this does not necessarily mean increased expenditure. But it does mean greater personal effort' ('Consolidate While There's Yet Time!' 1952)

Within the Australian trade press, showmanship was always a particularly powerful term. It served as the form of local agency within a system where product innovation always took place offshore. It was also general enough to serve as the basis for the myth that distribution and exhibition did essentially the same thing: distribution subsidiaries aggressively sold films to exhibitors, and exhibitors continued this process by pitching the films to audiences. What unites and drives the whole process is willpower and energy rather than any wider economic explanation. John Davis, managing director of the J. Arthur Rank Organisation, typically exhorted Australian exhibitors that courage and hard work were the solution to television ('Courage, Hard Work' 1955).

The dangers were also painted in terms that were personal rather than industrial. The danger was constantly seen as fear and inaction rather than television itself. Daff warned in early 1953 against hanging black crepe in Australian cinemas ('Daff's "Bunk!"' 1953). *FW* followed up later that year with a front-page story suggesting that apathy was 'white-anting the virile structure of the industry' ('Apathy Can White-ant' 1953). Even when critical, *FW* could never bring itself to be critical of specific individuals or companies. The roles with which it was most comfortable were boosterism and consensus-building.

Occasional pessimistic voices emerged from the exhibition sector, which was the one most vulnerable to television. Dick Stephens, of the Queensland Motion Picture Exhibitors Association, labelled television 'a grave menace' at his organization's 1951 convention. Citing the precedent of the United States, he forecast a 25 per cent drop in box office. Stephens drew an early line in the sand, setting out several of the tensions that would build as television became an established part of the revenue chain. He declared that the 'Future of the motion picture industry depends on keeping our films and our stars [by which he meant Hollywood films and stars] away from the TV stations' ('QMPEA Defers Moves' 1951). He forecast that smaller cinemas would be particularly vulnerable, and that 50 per cent of Australia's cinemas could close within three years of television's introduction ('TV Could Close Theatres' 1951).

Stephens also had ideas about how this threat could best be blunted: 'Government control of TV could be one of the theatre owners' best safeguards,' he said, coming down on the Labor Party's side in the debate over whether Australia should follow the US or British model for granting television licences ('TV Could Close Theatres' 1951). The managing director of the Snider and Dean exhibition circuit concurred with Stephens, noting that 'as long as television shall be government controlled in this country, the picture business will have little to fear' ('Sees Govt Control' 1951). One of the directors of the Savoy art cinema circuit agreed that the British model of state control was preferable since, 'as long as it was not operated by commercial interests, television offered no serious menace to film exhibition' (Dawson 1952). Even visiting Fox president Spyros Skouras agreed that 'television would be a serious threat only if operated by private enterprise' (Realistic Warning on TV' 1952). While it was perverse to see conservative capitalists supporting Labor in opposition to the entrepreneurialism of the Liberal government, the threat of television made for strange bedfellows.

When the 1955 Royal Commission rubber-stamped the government's decision to allow commercial television licences, divisions opened up as it became clear that factions within *FW*'s MPI – both Australian and American, in distribution and in exhibition – wanted a piece of the action. In 1954, in the same month that Universal's Al Daff was rallying *FW* support with his disparagement of television, Al Hollander of the Paramount-owned

Dumont television arrived in Australia to advise Turnbull on Hoyts' television licence application ('TV experts in Sydney' 1954). As early as 1952, Turnbull had said that if the government decided on granting commercial licences, Hoyts 'plans to be represented in this field' ('Turnbull Recommends' 1952). Paramount was part of the successful consortium that bid for the licence for TCN9 in Sydney. Despite Norman Rydge labelling television 'virulent competition' in 1952, Greater Union, in partnership with Hoyts, had a minority shareholding in the company that founded GTV9 in Melbourne.

In the course of these debates, there were also some interesting asides on the MPI's ideas about its consumers. Most explanations of consumer behaviour were spun out of the nuclear family: father (who worked), mother (who was in the home all day) and children. Women were several times invoked as the potential saviours of cinema-going. In 1953, columnist Percy L. Curtis wrote that:

> The housewife, as relief from her monotonous daily routine of chores, will always have that feeling of 'Let's get out of the house for a night and go and see a bright show.' She will want to be surrounded by the glamour of the theatre and in the company of hundreds of others of her ilk similarly seeking the same freedom and relaxation which can only really be achieved by getting out of the house (Curtis 1953).

Spyros Skouras similarly described 'the natural desire of women everywhere to have a regular night out, accompanied by their husbands, and perhaps other members of the family' ('Quality and Quantity' 1957).

Others focused on children as a market segment that needed to be defended. One Brisbane exhibitor labelled television's attraction for children as 'the most dangerous aspect' of the new medium. He saw Saturday matinees as a habit learned in childhood, which would result in regular customers who would attend cinemas up to three nights per week (Palmer 1954). An American survey, however, suggested the opposite demographic analysis. It showed that the primary decline in attendance post-television was by older people, and that the 10–19 years age group was now the leading demographic for continued cinema attendance ('Effect of TV Set Ownership' 1955). Norman Rydge echoed this when, in previewing prospects for 1956, he cited government statistics showing that there were now 1,721,000 boys and girls in the five to 15 demographic 'who may rightly be regarded as the potential for our matinee trade' ('1956 Forecast' 1955).

Slowly, cracks start to open up in the rhetoric of the urban nuclear family. By 1957, Rydge had drawn lessons from the breakout popularity of *Rock Around the Clock* and was beginning to shift his demographic markers. The key group he picked out for emphasis was now teenagers in the 16–18 years age group. *FW* concludes:

> Research report gives unqualified praise to the 'commercial cinema' for its unequalled power and fascination over the minds of a vast majority of young people, which has never been truly appreciated or harnessed. ('Statistics Forecast MPI Future' 1957)

The defence of this 'commercial cinema' – that is, a consensus around the status quo, with its reliance on Hollywood product, and the assumption that the new audience would behave in essentially the same ways as the old audience – was a dangerous lesson to draw.

During 1955, Australia officially registered its millionth post-war immigrant, and both Rydge and Universal's Herc McIntyre pointed to this as a source of optimism. Migration meant the expansion of the pool of potential cinema-goers. Rydge put it as a straightforward process: 'the greater the population the greater the demand for entertainment of all kinds, and the greater the opportunity for the cinema to win new patronage' ('Sell 'em Harder' 1955; '1956 Forecast' 1955). Turnbull similarly rejoiced in the possibilities of immigration, writing: 'Statistics remain just so many figures until we transform each cipher into a human being – a wage earner with money to spend on food, clothes, entertainment. In fact, a potential picture-goer' (Turnbull 1956).

However, both Rydge and Turnbull both failed to account for the possibility that new migrants displayed distinctively different linguistic and cultural preferences, for which Australian 'commercial cinema' – with its long-standing reliance on Hollywood production – could never cater. Turnbull's insistence on turning immigrants from ciphers into human beings ended by transforming them into another type of cipher: a consumer with no difference from existing consumers. This kind of blinkered vision was far from an aberration. One exhibitor put it succinctly: 'We'll leave the sociological and moral worries to the sociologists and moralists. They won't worry about box office for us.' (Palmer 1954)

In 1954, Norman Rydge stated that 'our business is supported largely by 25% of metropolitan populations', and saw this as the basis of an expansion of the audience base ('Rydge Sees "Enormous Scope"' 1954). While there are many anecdotal mentions of rural exhibitors in *FW*, there is very little discussion of rural exhibition. As television rolls out unevenly across Australia, an atmosphere of alarm stems from the situation in Sydney, and especially Melbourne. This might invite ideas on just how narrowly constituted is the base of *FW*'s MPI.

The limbs are lopped, and if you can't stand the heat …

Regular television broadcasting began in Sydney and Melbourne in the latter part of 1956 (Moran 1991). Initially, the spectre of television could usefully be tied to other political agendas by those in the MPI. When the Victorian government increased its Entertainment Tax in 1956, Norman Rydge invoked cinema's 'gravest era from competition with television' ('Australian MPI' 1956). Rydge was quick to turn away from his previous optimism and cite figures to show that British attendances had dropped by 450 million a year since 1946. A visiting executive of Republic International claimed *FW*'s front page by saying that US attendances had plunged from 90 million per week in 1944 to 37 million in 1955 ('Rep. Topper Sees Huge Potential' 1956).

However, this short period of alarmism (perhaps mixed with alarm) seems to have passed. In March 1957, *FW* claimed that television was not having much effect on box office ('TV Not Yet Affecting' 1957). At this point, only 30,000 television licences had been taken out (20,000 of them in Victoria, with the quicker uptake explained by the Melbourne Olympic Games). *FW*'s line on television fluctuated considerably throughout the first half of 1957, but disturbing signs were beginning to appear. Al Daff, who had previously proclaimed that Universal would have nothing to do with television, was now talking of 'a marriage between television and motion pictures'. Ominously, he went on to say that the motion picture industry had 'got fat and sloppy as a result of the prosperity we enjoyed without having to exert any particular effort' ('Daff Sees a Magnificent Future' 1957). Suddenly the pre-television period was recast in a new light, as a time of ease. This retrospective view of the previous decade was to become an enduring part of *FW*'s accepted view of its clients' recent history.

Once television began to take root, the fallback position of many was to acknowledge that some cinemas would need to close, but to suggest that the victims would be expendable because they deserved their fate. Daff stated that although 5000 US cinemas had closed, 'the theatres that closed, deserved to close ... most of them were dirty, old-fashioned and badly-run' ('Daff Sees a Magnificent Future' 1957). Daff tied this to the familiar model of consumer behaviour, which suggested that 'people want to go out, and go out in glamorous circumstances'. There is an implication here that exhibitors who could not afford to supply consumers with the trappings of glamour would quickly find themselves damned among the dirty and badly run cinemas of which he had washed his hands.

Hoyts' Ernest Turnbull wrote that television had transformed 'from a vague threat into a vicious competitor' ('Turnbull urges MPI Overhaul' 1957). He followed up Daff's rhetoric, saying that the elimination of 'old theatres in over-seated areas' would be good for the industry as a whole. The large circuits such as Hoyts and Greater Union were better placed, as they had the capital to introduce new technology as well as the ability to transfer resources between different components of their exhibition businesses, which included both first-run and suburban houses. Their dominance of first-run cinemas allowed them to long run the new wave of blockbusters from *The Robe* (CinemaScope) to *South Pacific* (Todd-AO), which provided the cinema-friendly part of Hollywood's response to television.

However, Turnbull drew the opposite lesson to Daff, claiming that exhibition needed to cut costs in response to television. Instead of Daff's emphasis on 'trappings of glamour', Turnbull was pondering whether 'the industry has involved itself too deeply in lush commitments' during the period now defined as one of easy prosperity and posed the question 'are we operating on too grand a scale?' ('Turnbull urges MPI Overhaul' 1957). Presumably, these lush commitments would not include the expensive CinemaScope installations that Turnbull had so proudly championed.

By October 1957, a striking change had taken place in *FW*'s understanding of the impact of television, and it is evident that the bravado about the MPI's resilience could no longer be sustained. The Melbourne box office was described as suffering 'a dramatic falling off in trading during the latter portion of 1957' ('"Lift" Evidenced' 1958). *FW* published a front-page editorial that brought together many of the motifs established thus far. The lead paragraph reads: 'The Australian motion picture industry must close its ranks, linking distribution and exhibition in vigorous showmanship.' Two weeks later, the first cinema closures were reported in Melbourne, accompanied by reports that attendances were down 16 per cent year on year ('Tax, TV Closing' 1957).

Although this was within the parameters of what had been discussed in *FW* during the previous six years, the alarming thing was that only 14 per cent of Melbourne homes and 11 per cent of Sydney homes had acquired a television set thus far. The rate at which television licences were being issued was increasing (a development followed closely by *FW*, which printed licence figures every two weeks as they were released). In January 1958, *FW* published an alarming US survey claiming that movie attendance fell by 77 per cent in homes where a television set had been bought ('US Report Details Television Activity' 1958). By November 1958, a director of Greater Union was putting the decline in attendance at 40 per cent ('TV May Close 200 More Theatres' 1958). Perhaps the most interesting statistics came from Jack Graham, chief executive of Victoria's Cinematograph Exhibitors' Association (Graham 1959). Graham gave Victorian admissions figures as:

- 1956/57: 34 million
- 1957/58: 28.5 million – (16 per cent decline over 1956/57) – 95,000 TV licences
- 1958/59: 21.5 million – (37 per cent decline over 1956/57) – 209,000 TV licences
- 1959/60 (forecast): 17.5 million (48 per cent decline over 1956/57).

The most significant thing about these figures was Graham's claim that the decline was in direct correlation to the increase in the number of television licences. In 1957/58, attendances had declined at a rate of 58 for every television licence and in 1958/59, the equivalent figure was 60.

FW's columnists, such as Bill Beecham, continued to isolate film's textual elements. He wondered that anyone would want to watch a 21-inch black and white screen when they could be watching CinemaScope instead (Beecham 1959). *FW* printed stories of exhibitors who set up televisions in their foyers—not to attract patrons, but to demonstrate the inferiority of the television image. This isolated films from the context of consumption (the home) as well as ignoring the exponential increase in scale of consumption enabled by the new medium. The average viewing time for those with televisions was initially reported at 30.2 hours per week ('TV Survey' 1958). For the previous 30 years, distributors had employed block-booking more or less successfully on the basis that scale of supply mattered to their customers. However, the scale of demand had now expanded enormously. If the average Australian had previously visited cinemas 15 times per year, it meant the consumption of roughly 45 hours of screen material per year. That had now blown out with the potential of over 1500 hours of consumption per year per consumer. Motion pictures might offer a larger screen, but if supply and demand factors are considered, television was set to dwarf cinema consumption.

Throughout 1958, an air of panic hung over *FW*. Every week brought a vague yet urgent call for an 'all-industry' front by the MPI. We have seen that Australian exhibitors had long constructed their business on the basis that product would be made and distributed by the US majors. Television represented a threat not only to take away their customers, but also to take away their supply if Hollywood cut its own deals with the new technology and left cinema exhibition out in the cold. The initial form of this threat was that US studios, following the example of Columbia's Screen Gems subsidiary, might convert their operations to produce telefilms.

Later in the decade, another and more dangerous threat emerged. In 1957, *FW* reported that many people were now under the impression that television screenings of major films would follow quickly after theatrical release ('Sindlinger Report' 1957). The imminent sale of post-1948 film libraries to television was a blow that *FW* countenanced with undisguised hostility. The emerging core of *FW*'s call for a united front was the demand for Australian subsidiaries of US distributors not to license their libraries for television broadcast.

These demands could only be approached indirectly by *FW* through transferring the debate offshore. Acting on the basis that the best ideas came from British and American cinema industries, there was a stream of reports on the efforts of exhibitors' associations to raise money to keep feature films off television. Repeated stories during 1958 centred on the efforts of British exhibitors to institute a £500,000 fund, financed by a levy on ticket sales, to buy and cancel British television rights. Throughout 1959, *FW* reported approvingly on trade associations such as the UK Film Industry Defence Organisation (FIDO) and the American Congress of Exhibitors (ACE) in their efforts to keep feature films off television. *FW* reported on the fighting funds started by local state-based Motion Picture Exhibitors' Associations, though these raised relatively small amounts.

Yet, despite the apparently cataclysmic situation being faced by the MPI, *FW* came up with few new ideas. In May 1958, the paper lead with the headline: 'Local MPI Should Learn US Lessons' – a headline that might have appeared at any time in its previous existence ('Local MPI Should Learn' 1958). The United States was the model for all business practices, so long as you concentrated on that section of the United States that demonstrated the point you wanted to make. The lessons drawn in this story (and many others) are, unsurprisingly, the need for distribution and exhibition to work together, with the prime example of this cooperation being the refusal to sell post-1948 libraries. *FW* summed it up in this way:

> The industry must make immediate steps to close its ranks with distribution and exhibition interests working more closely together for the common good. Certainly, one cannot prosper without the other. ('Local MPI Should Learn' 1958)

The problem was that it was becoming increasingly possible for distribution to prosper in ways that did not entail cinema exhibition on the scale of the past. Within a week, *FW* was announcing (in a small paragraph) that United Artists had licensed 65 post-1948 features to American television, right beneath a much larger piece on Spyros Skouris's criticisms of the sale of television rights ('UA Post-48 Pix' 1958).

In August 1958, a speech given by Ernest Turnbull was *FW*'s lead story under the sensational headline '"Calamity Howling" Hits MPI' ('Calamity Howling' 1958). It is an astonishing headline, given that there is no mention of calamity until the final paragraph, tucked away on page 3, in which Turnbull says: 'I feel quite certain that "calamity howling" will not only not provide a solution but will do irreparable damage.' Turnbull acknowledges that the sale of television rights is 'an accomplished fact which has to be faced'.

It is doubtful that Turnbull and Hoyts had any interest in the all-industry front proposed by *FW*. In 1959, *FW* reported a speech given by Turnbull in which he once again castigated 'calamity howlers.' He acknowledged that television had been 'more devastating' than anticipated, but after the usual exhortations to show some Anglo-Saxon (so much for the new migrant audience) guts, he got to the main point of his strategy: 'I would be grateful now if we were not so numerically strong.' He signalled that Hoyts would start to contract, closing some of the 178 cinemas it controlled. His metaphors were now horticultural: Hoyts would prune dead wood, allowing space for fresh growth at an appropriate time in the future (Turnbull 1959).

Although Hoyts did not endorse *FW*'s all-industry campaigns, it started it own publicity campaign to get people back to cinemas (especially Hoyts cinemas). In January 1959, the company took out display ads in the women's pages of daily newspapers in Sydney and Melbourne. The ads returned to the theme of women within the nuclear family driving cinema attendance by urging their husbands to deliver them from their domestic monotony. 'There's nothing so good for a walled-in wife as a night at the pictures,' reads the ad directed at husbands, while the other demands of women, 'Isn't it about time we house-bound wives did something about it!' ('Unique ads in Hoyts' 1959). The idea seems to have returned with a vengeance, as the head of United Artists' Australian subsidiary was soon talking of the need 'to stimulate the housewives' natural desire to get out of the house' (Michaels 1959).

The ads urge housewives and their husbands to act on their natural urges by attending Hoyts cinemas, where long-running blockbusters deploying new technologies developed in the United States await them: *South Pacific, Around the World in 80 Days* and *This is Cinerama*. These were not the films that would be the salvation of suburban or rural cinemas. In a curious sense, they were small films rather than big ones. They entailed the kind of contraction of cinema exhibition advocated by Turnbull. New technologies (synchronized sound, widescreen, 70mm, digital 3D) always act in the interests of sections of the film industry. Turnbull, in his joint roles representing both Hoyts and Fox, was presiding over a movement in which first-run, downtown exhibition would gain market share, while suburban, neighbourhood exhibition retreated.

The reason there was no united front within the MPI was that the divisions between distribution and exhibition, and within exhibition, continued throughout the decade and were plainly visible in *FW*'s summaries for 1959. In South Australia and Western Australia, television was just beginning by the end of the decade, and exhibitors previously had congratulated themselves on the additional time they had to prepare for television. However, reports from these states contain prominent complaints by exhibitors against the higher percentage terms being charged by distributors for the technology-driven blockbusters that constituted such an important element of their response to television. Bill Beecham commented that in Western Australia, 'exhibitors who, having some "beef" against a distributor will refuse to join any organisation which has been founded for the good of the industry as a whole, wholly and solely on this particular ground' (Beecham 1959).

Without the possibility of taking sides, *FW* settled into its familiar pattern of ascribing problems to individual rather than industrial causes – failures of will and courage. Dave Joel, of the Snider and Dean circuit, received page one headlines for saying that 'not one section of the MPI had yet begun to fight' ('Joel Calls for MPI' 1958). The final irony – and one that might amuse Emanuel Silverstone – was Joel's claim that restaurateurs were now realizing that they too were victims of television, as it was becoming increasingly difficult to draw people out of their homes.

Conclusion

This trip through *Film Weekly* has spanned the decade from 1950 to 1959. It is a relatively arbitrary place to stop. At the end of 1959, television in Australia was only just beginning to spread outside of its beach-heads in Sydney and Melbourne. There were 738,000 viewing licences in Australia – a figure that would more than quadruple in the next 14 years (figures sourced from *Commonwealth Year Books* from 1958 to 1973). This period through the 1960s was one of contraction for *FW*'s conception of an MPI centred on cinema exhibition. Alternately, it can be read as a period of enormous expansion for the nexus of production, distribution and exhibition industries that comprised the film industry, and whose point of consumption increasingly became the television set. Jeffrey C. Ulin (2010) has written recently of 'living room convergence', where 'TV remains the Holy Grail' among release platforms. Media technologies are not simple in their effects, in part because media industries are rarely the unified entities that exist in the imaginations of trade journals such as *Film Weekly*.

The overwhelming concentration of film historians in Australia has been on restricting themselves to questions of local production and dismissing everything else as the tyranny of Hollywood. I hope this chapter has shown that Australian cinema history is full of rich and complex narratives structured by the kinds of internal divisions I have tried to sketch out here. The introduction of television is a period when these tensions rose to the surface, and where unities such as *FW*'s imaginary MPI can be interrogated for the multiple and uneven sets of interests and priorities that continue to percolate through the Australian media.

Acknowledgements

I would like to thank Olympia Szilagyi of the AFI Research Library in Melbourne for sourcing material for this chapter.

References

Arrow, M. (2008), '16 September, 1956. "It's Here At Last!" The Introduction of Television in Australia', in M. Crotty and D. Roberts (eds), *Turning Points in Australian History*, Sydney: UNSW Press, pp. 143–78.

Balio, T. (ed.) (1990), *Hollywood in the Age of Television*, Boston: Unwin Hyman.

Beecham, B. (1958), 'Film Tracks', *Film Weekly*, 13 February, p. 3.

Beecham, B. Sr (1959), 'The Past Year has Been a Disturbing One in WA', *Film Weekly*, 17 December, p. 40.

Childs, M. (1952), 'The Foreign Market, TV, Things to Come', *Film Weekly*, 18 December, p. 35.

Collins, D. (1987), *Hollywood Down Under*, Sydney: Angus & Robertson.

Commonwealth Year Books (1958 to 1973), Canberra: Commonwealth of Australia.

Curthoys, A. (1986), 'The Getting of Television: Dilemmas in Ownership, Control and Culture, 1941–56', in A. Curthoys and J. Merritt (eds), *Better Dead Than Red: Australia's First Cold War: 1945–59, Volume 2*, Sydney: Allen & Unwin, pp. 123–54.

Curtis, P.L. (1953), 'Wanted Urgently: More of Al Daff's Enthusiasm', *Film Weekly*, 23 April, p. 3.

Dawson, P. (1952), 'Who's Afraid of TV (BBC-style Anyway)?', *Film Weekly*, 23 October, p. 3.

Graham, J. (1959), 'Association Leaders', *Film Weekly*, 17 December, p. 39.

Hazlehurst, C. (1982–83), 'The Advent of Commercial Television', *Australian Cultural History*, 2, pp. 104–19.

Michaels, R. (1959), 'Talk, but No Deeds from MPI', *Film Weekly*, 7 May 1959, p. 1.

Mooney, R. (1953), 'There's No "Hit-or-miss" About Market Research', *Film Weekly*, 13 March, p. 3.

Moran, A. (1991), 'Some Beginnings for Australian Television: The First Governor-General', *Continuum*, 4, 2, http://www.mcc.murdoch.edu.au/ReadingRoom/4.2/Moran.html. Accessed 16 June 2011.

Palmer, M. (1954), 'Learn to Combat Television Before It Cuts into b.o.!', *Film Weekly*, 30 December, n.p.

Pike, A. and Cooper, R. (1998), *Australian Film, 1900–1977*, rev edn, Melbourne: Oxford University Press.

Shirley, G. and Adams, B. (1989), *Australian Cinema: The First Eighty Years*, rev edn, Sydney: Currency Press.

Turnbull, E. (1956), 'Immigrants will Aid MPI Prosperity', *Film Weekly*, 20 December, p. 5.

—— (1959), 'No Reason for Pessimistic Down-beat Thinking', *Film Weekly*, 26 March, p. 3; 'Can't Win TV Fight by Running Away', *Film Weekly*, 2 April, p. 1.

Ulin, J.C. (2010), *The Business of Media Distribution*, Oxford: Focal Press.

Walsh, M. (1999), 'The Years of Living Dangerously', in D. Verhoeven (ed.), *Twin Peeks: Australian and New Zealand Feature Films*, Melbourne: Damned Publishing, pp. 69–84.

Walter, J. (1994), 'Controlling the Technology of Popular Culture: The Introduction of Television in Australia', in I. Craven (ed.), *Australian Popular Culture*, Cambridge: Cambridge University Press, pp. 66–78.

White, T.R. (1990), 'Hollywood's Attempt at Appropriating Television: The Case of Paramount Pictures', in T. Balio (ed.), *Hollywood in the Age of Television*, Boston: Unwin Hyman, pp. 145–60.

Film Weekly articles with no author cited

'1956 Forecast: Year of Even Bigger Trade' (1955), *Film Weekly*, 22 December, p. 24.

'Apathy Can White-ant Pic Biz' (1953), *Film Weekly*, 6 August, p. 1.

'Australian MPI Faces Grave Threat' (1956), *Film Weekly*, 20 September, p. 1.

'Busy Time for Daff on Home Town Visit' (1953), *Film Weekly*, 8 January, p. 6.

'"Calamity Howling" Hits MPI' (1958), *Film Weekly*, 21 August, p. 1.

'Consolidate, While There's Yet Time!' (1952), *Film Weekly*, 18 September, p. 5.

'Courage, Hard Work to Beat Video: John Davis' Formula' (1955), *Film Weekly*, 3 February, p. 14.

'Daff Sees a Magnificent Future' (1957), *Film Weekly*, 7 March, p. 1.

'Daff's "Bunk!" to Black Crepe' (1953), *Film Weekly*, 15 January, p. 1.

'Effect of TV Set Ownership on b.o.' (1955), *Film Weekly*, 10 November, p. 14.

'Emanuel Silverstone Here on First Visit' (1950), *Film Weekly*, 5 January, p. 1.

'Good Pictures Answer Any Challenge' (1952), *Film Weekly*, 2 October, p. 1.

'Hake Talks on TV, Drive-ins' (1950), *Film Weekly*, 3 August, p. 5.

'Hoyts to Spend £1½m on C'scope £20,000 per Theatre' (1953), *Film Weekly*, 22 October, p. 1.

'Joel Calls for MPI to Fight' (1958), *Film Weekly*, 10 July, p. 1.

'"Lift" Evidenced in Melbourne Trade' (1958), *Film Weekly*, 16 January, p. 12.

'Local MPI Should Learn US Lessons' (1958), *Film Weekly*, 8 May, p. 1.

'Nonsense to Minimise TV Threat' (1956), *Film Weekly*, 2 February, p. 1.

'Optimistic Forecast on Large-screen TV' (1951), *Film Weekly*, 15 February, p. 5.

'"Please Install Wide Screens!" Al Daff's Plea' (1954), *Film Weekly*, 23 December, p. 12.

'QMPEA Defers Moves on Price Rise, Tax' (1951), *Film Weekly*, 2 August, p. 5.

'Quality and Quantity will Top TV' (1957), *Film Weekly*, 2 May, p. 1.

'Realistic Warning on TV' (1952), *Film Weekly*, 13 November, p. 3.

'Rep. Topper Sees Huge Potential (But TV Hits US biz' (1956), *Film Weekly*, 24 May, p. 1.

'Rydge Says GUT Set to Meet TV's Advent' (1950), *Film Weekly*, 17 August, p. 5.

'Rydge Sees "Enormous Scope for Expansion"' (1954), *Film Weekly*, 30 September, p. 3.

'Sees Govt Control of TV OK for Pix' (1951), *Film Weekly*, 6 December, p. 1.

'Sell 'em Harder, Urges McIntyre' (1955), *Film Weekly*, 22 December, n.p.

'Sindlinger Report Slates Movie–Television Marriage' (1957), *Film Weekly*, 19 December, p. 12.

'Solid Front Necessary to Win Fight' (1957), *Film Weekly*, 17 October, p. 1.

'Statistics Forecast MPI Future' (1957), *Film Weekly*, 15 August, p. 1.

'Tax, TV Closing Two Vic. Houses' (1957), *Film Weekly*, 31 October, p. 1.

'Turnbull Feted' (1950), *Film Weekly*, 29 July, p. 17.

'Turnbull Recommends Govt. Inquiry on Video' (1952), *Film Weekly*, 4 December.

'Turnbull Urges MPI Overhaul' (1957), *Film Weekly*, 4 April, p. 1.

'TV Causes 20% b.o. Drop – Temporarily' (1954), *Film Weekly*, 18 November, p. 6.

'TV Could Close Theatres, Says Veteran Exhibitor' (1951), *Film Weekly*, 19 July, p. 19.

'TV Experts in Sydney' (1954), *Film Weekly*, 16 December, p. 1.

'TV May Close 200 More Theatres: Evans' (1958), *Film Weekly*, 20 November, p. 1.

'TV Not the Bogey It was Feared – Cohen' (1951), *Film Weekly*, 22 March, p. 1.
'TV Not Yet Affecting Box Office' (1957), *Film Weekly*, 28 March, p. 1.
'TV Survey Sees NSW Topping Vic.' (1958), *Film Weekly*, 20 March, p. 1.
'UA Post-48 Pix for Television' (1958), *Film Weekly*, 15 May, p. 1.
'Unique Ads in Hoyts National Back to Pictures Campaign' (1959), *Film Weekly*, 15 January, p. 6.
'US Reports Details Television Activity' (1958), *Film Weekly*, 16 January, p. 9.
'Waterman Intends to Operate Drive-ins in South Australia' (1950), *Film Weekly*, 20 July, p. 5.

Chapter 8

A Nation of Film-goers: Audiences, Exhibition and Distribution in New Zealand

Geoff Lealand

We New Zealanders are a nation of film fans.

(Gordon Mirams, New Zealand Film Censor, 1945)

There has been much written about film in New Zealand in terms of its history, as a series of 'fits and starts' (Gerstner and Greenlees 2000). More recently, there have been explanations as to how this small South Pacific nation became a site for global film-making on an unprecedented scale (Lealand 2011). As with other countries, there is abundant information on cinema audiences through sites such as http://www.boxofficemojo.com, providing box office data on the performance of local and imported film titles in New Zealand, together with lists ranking films from the most popular to the least popular.

But such information constructs the film audience as an abstraction, or as aggregated figures of fee-paying customers. It tells us very little about who these film-goers are, in terms of their age, gender, ethnicity, taste preferences and motivations. Never has there been so much known about the film audience, and yet so little. Even those commercial enterprises (such as the UK media company Screen Digest) that specialize in selling audience information to clients provide little beyond bare figures, in many cases based on secondary data. This is the case with New Zealand; knowledge is scarce in respect of the motivations, preferences and responses of a film-going population of little more than four million, in a country where film has long been – and remains – a primary entertainment activity, with New Zealanders in 2010 numbering third in the world in terms of cinema attendance per capita, behind Iceland and the United States, according to one online source (Nationmaster 2011).

Indeed the very first New Zealand Cinema Census took place in March 2011 – 115 years after the first public film screening in New Zealand, in Auckland on 13 October 1896 (New Zealand Film Archive 2011). More on this 2011 Census shortly, but for most of the history of film-going in New Zealand, we have had to depend on scraps of information – box office data, memoirs and biography (such as the Gordon Mirams quote above), local and national histories of film distribution and exhibition (of which Wayne Brittenden's 2008 *The Celluloid Circus: The Heyday of the New Zealand Picture Theatre* is the best) and the occasional piece of scholarship. One rare example of research that approached the audience from a *qualitative* rather than *quantitative* perspective is a 1994 report *Understanding the New Zealand Film Market: The Audience's Perspective*, conducted on behalf of the New Zealand Film Commission by Heylen Research Centre (Heylen Research Centre 1994). Although primarily approaching the film audience as a commodity, this research did explore motivations for watching films (including factors of 'energizing', 'fantasizing' and 'thinking'), and it could be argued that such reasons still provide the motivation for New Zealanders to go out to the movies.

There is also an element of audience feedback in another New Zealand Film Commission-sponsored publication, in respect of online opinions on New Zealand-made films, which is incorporated in Petrie and Stuart (2008), *A Coming of Age: Thirty Years of New Zealand Film*. On occasion, the Film Commission has also sought early audience feedback for locally produced fare, through its Test Screening Programme.

All this information is partial and conditional, and does not constitute a full or necessarily convincing body of knowledge on the New Zealand film audience. Knowledge of real or potential audiences is also a persistent problem in film generally (for funders, producers, distributors and directors) and in the main, the film audience is constructed from a mix of past experiences, current box office performance of similar films and a large dash of hope. In the largest markets, such as the United States, more formal strategies such as concept testing or pre-release focus group testing are used to obtain early audience feedback.

The field of film studies generally has done little to increase our understanding of the film audience, with a prevailing neglect of the role of the audience in a discipline dominated by explorations of the text and, to a lesser extent, the political economy of production and distribution.

Obviously, shaping audience anticipation, matching audience expectations and creating perfect conditions for the exchange of cash for cinema tickets (or DVD copies) is the *raison d'être* of contemporary cinema. Even in those circumstances where films flourishes through forms of subsidy (state or institutional funding, preferential distribution or exhibition), the primary imperative is to cover the cost of production and, ideally, recover above-the-line costs. The role of the audience is central to this process, and an increasingly large proportion of any film budget is now spent on publicity and marketing (Wasko 2003), persuading and cajoling potential audience members to make the 'right' choice in a very cluttered marketplace, winning their good favour and, most importantly, generating good word of mouth. The last – largely uncontrollable – factor has become increasingly important in a media environment in which opinion – both bad and good – flourishes and proliferates through networks of Facebook, Twitter and mobile media.

Considerable energy is now expended on using such social media in advance of a film's release, through teasers posted on the Web or through tit-bits fed to fan-sites. This was a strategy adopted by New Line Cinema to build hype in New Zealand and internationally in advance of the release of the first film in the Peter Jackson-directed *The Lord on the Rings* trilogy (2001–03), at a time when other film studios were threatening legal injunctions against film fan-sites. The New Line experience was shown to be highly successful, so most studios now regard the web as a friend rather than a foe in terms of audience–film relationships.

Even though there are new ways of reaching massive numbers of potential film-goers, the days of marketing films to very large, homogenous audiences have largely gone. The web enables audience targeting to both primary and niche audiences, and audiences are fragmented and segmented in terms of their demonstrated value at the box office, allocated by http:///www.filmprofit.com to demographic categories such as the following:

Gen Y Audiences. Approximately 28 percent of American society aged 14 to 26, and of primary interest to traditional movie marketers.

Gen X Audiences. Baby Busters – now tagged Generation X, approximately 18 per cent of American society, aged 26 to 42. Strong audience for independent films, goes their own way, seeks out the unknown and undiscovered.

Boomer Audiences. The strong new audience segment, approximately 32 per cent of American society, 43 to 56 years old, empty-nesters with time and money and strong appetites for interesting films. (Wasko 2003: 192)

Despite the propensity for such market research to force very large and unruly populations into tidy categories (as well as bending the rules of grammar in the process), such visions or versions of the audience tend to prevail, both in North America and globally. Just as Hollywood has long exported its product to the world and dominated global screens, it has also exported constructions of the film audience. There are, for example, alternative ways of describing the above demographic groups. Gen Y could also be described as 'The Y-Pay? Generation', in that it includes the largest number of computer-savvy, downloading individuals who are posing a new threat to traditional methods of film distribution and exhibition, but in a very broad sense, such groupings do represent contemporary film audiences, in terms of their size and significance – both globally and locally.

The audience response to two films screening in New Zealand in late April 2011 illustrates this audience segmentation. The Academy Award-winning, art-house drama *The King's Speech* (Tom Hooper 2010) was in its thirteenth week of release and had earned a very respectable NZ$5.075 million at the box office. With little ongoing formal marketing, but excellent word of mouth and audiences dominated by older film-goers, it continued to appear on 41 screens around the country. On the Easter weekend in April, following three months of a significant slump (28 per cent) at the New Zealand box office, *The Fast and Furious 5* (Justin Lin 2011), the fifth version of this franchise, arrived in New Zealand with the year's highest grossing opening week, earning NZ$1.13 million, as against the opening weekend of NZ$680,000 for *The King's Speech* (http://www.flicks.co.nz, accessed 20 February 2012). One Facebook contributor, commenting about this news, declared: 'Like I've always said, homies and boy racers are among our biggest spenders at the cinema. The forgotten demographic.' (Rajneel, 27 April 2011)

These two films well illustrate the divergent nature of the film audience in New Zealand in 2011, as well as advantages and constraints permitted to various sectors of the film audience. Audiences, exhibitors and distributors coexist in a state of interdependency, and the New Zealand film audience both shapes and is shaped by what films get released in the country, and where they screen.

Film exhibition

Rather than being the 'forgotten demographic' (above), it can be argued that the young and male audience for films such as *The Fast and Furious 5* constitutes the audience sector best provided for in New Zealand. In terms of film screening options, the Val Morgan Cinema Network, the dominant company in cinema advertising in New Zealand, lists 90 operating cinema complexes encompassing 366 screens, with one-third (126) clustered in the largest population region of Auckland, ranging from the 12-screen Event complex in Queen Street, to the historic single screen Capitol in the inner-city suburb of Balmoral.

Even though New Zealand has been following international trends in locating multiplexes within large retail-oriented shopping malls on the outskirts of larger cities and towns (such Sylvia Park in South Auckland or The Base on the northern boundaries of Hamilton), numerous cinemas remain in the central business district, closely associated with urban night life. Some of these are twin-screen or multiplex conversions of older, single-screen movie theatres. Others are purpose-built multiplexes within downtown shopping malls and/or food-halls. But there are also remnants of an older and grander style of urban film-going. The Embassy Theatre in Wellington and The Civic in Auckland are examples of urban film palaces with a unique architectural presence.

The Embassy, with the largest cinema screen in the Southern Hemisphere, hosted red-carpet premieres of the Peter Jackson trilogy *The Lord of the Rings* and The Civic hosts silent features with full orchestra, as part of the annual International Film Festival. Indeed, The Civic (which also host overseas music acts) is listed as a leading example of cinema restoration, with the unique glory of this purpose-built, 3500-seat picture palace (opened in 1929) still on display – including plaster elephants and tigers, blue-eyed panthers under a drifting high ceiling of twinkling stars and flying clouds. Indeed, http://www.sharingtravelexperiences.com cites it as one of the 'Best Places in the World to Watch a Film' (accessed 20 February 2012).

Other city or small-town cinemas retain signs of their glory days, even though foyers have been modified for a new clientele and projection boxes altered for different screening ratios. The SBS St James Theatre, established in 1936 in the South Island farming town of Gore (population 9970), continues to service a catchment audience of 12,000. The cinema retains its sweeping staircase and cavernous foyer, but offers two screens (258 seats and 80 seats), with modern projection and a schedule of recent releases. It also illustrates the reality of ensuring the financial viability of cinemas still surviving in the small towns of New Zealand, in that it is dependent on some corporate sponsorship (the Southland Building Society, in this case). Other small-town cinemas find support through community trusts, or through the dedication of particular individuals.

In terms of mainstream fare, however, the patterns of ownership, distribution and exhibition in 2011 closely follow those that prevailed through the twentieth century. As Brittenden points out in his excellent 2008 history, film distribution and exhibition in

New Zealand have long been monopolized and centrally controlled by a small group of interests, who carved out fiefdoms of screening venues:

> By the late 1940s Kerridge-Odeon and Amalgamated were pretty much in control of the cinema business in New Zealand. At their peak, Kerridge-Odeon had 133 theatres and Amalgamated sixty-eight. (Brittenden 2008: 31)

The owners of these two chains (Robert Kerridge and Mike Moodabe, respectively) exerted extraordinary influence over film-going in New Zealand throughout the twentieth century, and wielded considerable political power, halting plans to introduce drive-in movies in the early 1950s, and closing provincial theatres by mutual consent. They are the closest New Zealand has ever got to locally produced movie moguls (Peter Jackson might be considered a more recent example); displaying a mixture of benign dictatorship and hard-boiled commercialism, as well as filtering the films locals got to see, through their own set of prejudices and preferences. In the early 1970s, according to Brittenden (2008: 38), the deeply conservative Robert Kerridge turned down distribution of *Woodstock: The Movie* (Michael Wadleigh 1970) in favour of the jingoistic John Wayne-directed *The Green Berets* (1968).

The control over film distribution and exhibition in New Zealand wielded by these two men declined by the later decades of the twentieth century, to be replaced by corporate ownership of chains – primarily overseas owned. Into the twentieth century, the major control resided with major Australian-based chains such as Village Roadshow, which decided what would be released in New Zealand cinemas, how long films stayed in circulation and who profited from the box office.

Village Roadshow has withdrawn from the New Zealand market (its interests were purchased by the New Zealand casino company SkyCity Entertainment in 2001). However, ownership returned to Australian hands in November 2009 when Amalgamated Holdings (Australia's biggest cinema exhibitor) acquired holdings of 113 screens in New Zealand and Fiji. When ownership was passed from SkyCity to Amalgamated, these screens were earning up to 65 per cent of Auckland cinema revenue and 38.5 per cent of national cinema revenue (Drinnan 2009). This purchase made Amalgamated Holdings the world's fifth-largest cinema exhibitor, with 561 screens in Australia, New Zealand, Germany and the Middle East (Drinnan 2010).

In July 2010, SkyCity Cinemas were re-branded as Event Cinemas, and the company continues to dominate the multiplex audience in the North Island cities of Auckland, Hamilton, Lower Hutt, Whangarei and New Plymouth, with a commitment to equip all its 14 New Zealand multiplexes with 3D capacity by 2012, along with technological upgrades that enable same-day releases of Hollywood movies.

The two other major players in New Zealand film exhibition are Hoyts Corporation (Australia) and Reading Cinemas (USA). Hoyts operates 55 cinemas in Australia and New Zealand, and increased its share of the New Zealand market in March 2010 through its acquisition of the last locally owned independent Berkeley Cinemas chain (21 screens in four venues in the Auckland region), and now owns 11 multiplexes in the North and South Islands, with 70 screens in total. Hoyts also owns Val Morgan Cinema Advertising, the largest cinema advertising company in Australia and New Zealand and Hoyts Distribution, a major player in independent film distribution in both countries.

In December 2011, two of Hoyts' Christchurch locations (the Regent on Worcester and Hoyts Moorhouse) remained closed, due to serious damage sustained in the February 2011 Christchurch earthquake. However, new cinemas are being built, with Hoyts opening a six-screen, fully digital venue at The Base, a large shopping complex on the northern outskirts of Hamilton, in August 2011, and Rialto opening a five-screen multiplex in Howick (East Auckland) in September.

Reading Cinemas in New Zealand, American-owned but controlled from Australia, is part of a chain of 30 locations across Australia and New Zealand. It owns a prime site in the entertainment precinct of Wellington – Courtenay Central, with ten screens – as well as multiplexes in provincial cities such as Napier, Hastings, Invercargill and Rotorua. It has little presence in the prime market of Auckland, apart from its shared partnership (with Event Cinemas) of Rialto Cinemas, the New Zealand art-house film circuit. The latter has locations in Newmarket (Auckland), Palmerston North, Dunedin and Christchurch (as with the Hoyts cinemas in the city, currently closed).

Film distribution

As with film exhibition, film distribution in New Zealand is a matrix of interlocking relationships and arrangements. It is also dominated by Australian interests, through Australian-owned distribution companies (such as Hopscotch and Madman) or through Australian-based subsidiaries of American media corporates (such as Paramount, Universal, Twentieth Century Fox and Disney). Deals for the release date, number and circulation of prints, and the duration of particular films in New Zealand cinemas are largely made in Australia, with particular cinema chains having exclusive (but sometimes shared) arrangement with particular distributors. There is obviously a degree of competition for prized titles, but also a degree of cooperation in a small market, through the Motion Picture Distributors Association of New Zealand (MPDA).

Film distribution in New Zealand in the twenty-first century is a more complex situation than the heyday of the Kerridge Odeon/Amalgamated duopoly, when both had exclusive deals with rival American majors and divided the New Zealand film audience between their two chains. The film audience is now more diverse and dispersed, and film distributors now tend to cater for targeted audience segments, rather than a single, undifferentiated New Zealand audience. Such audiences include the young and male-dominated mainstream multiplex audience, the older and affluent art-house audience, the film festival aficionados, the school holidays audience (children and caregivers), and targeted audience segments such as the Asian Cinema slot provided in several city theatres.

This segmentation of the New Zealand film audience and resultant scheduling of films is based on prior experience. But it is also based on international models of film distribution and revenue-sharing, which have been filtered through a largely Australian experience. In addition, distributors have had to adjust to changing economic times, as New Zealander Michael Eldred observed in a 2010 seminar discussion about film distribution:

> Competition for cinema real estate is intense and expensive. Over 300 films are released in New Zealand every year. That's a lot of noise in the papers and over the internet for the movies and what's coming up. Tighter profit margins have caused a shift in exhibition focus to mainstream and slightly art house films. Others may go straight to Festivals or DVD. (Script to Screen seminar 2010)

At the same seminar, New Zealand Film Commission head Graeme Mason stressed the critical role of distribution for locally made movies, and the need for writers and film-makers to understand its role in the dynamics of film:

> The majority of films coming into New Zealand appeal to a market and have a distributor [and] to secure funding from the NZFC, projects must have a distributor who will guarantee to release the film and provide funds upfront and a market validation clearly describing the audience who will pay to see the finished product. (2010)

Many films imported into New Zealand via Australian-based distributors have already passed one critical test, for they have been market-tested in other, larger territories, as well as being filtered through Australian perceptions of New Zealand needs. New Zealand-made features (films and documentaries) have to face additional barriers, in that they receive little preferential treatment in their release patterns, with minimal print and advertising (P&A) budgets. Indeed, as Andrew Cornwell (general manager of Sony Pictures NZ) points out:

> I don't need to release any New Zealand movies because it's not in my brief but I do so because I enjoy it. I don't look for a particular genre – I look for something a bit different that can earn back its P&A. It's really about whether the film will work with the audience. (Script to Screen seminar 2010)

Nevertheless, local films can be advantaged by the attention they receive from local media (press stories and interviews, television news items); however, such attention is usually dispersed and uneven. There is also support provided by the New Zealand Film Commission, through its Domestic Distribution Policy, which provides a P&A grant for qualifying New Zealand theatrical releases. This grant pays for the production of film prints, which are rented to a distributor for New Zealand theatrical release. The Film Commission retains ownership of the prints, which currently cost NZ$500 per print. They also provide a 25 per cent subsidy of publicity and advertising for New Zealand features, offering one dollar for every three dollars spent by distributors (New Zealand Film Commission 2011).

The levels of unsolicited publicity New Zealand films receive cannot compete with the scale of print release, and the integrated marketing campaigns that precede the opening of imported films – coordinated and well-funded campaigns using billboards, banners, extensive media advertising, preview screenings, cinema trailers, and cross-media promotions (such as radio contests).

As film distribution in New Zealand is further concentrated in the hands of the dominant players, some producers of New Zealand features and documentaries (especially low-budget features) are turning to new means of distribution and publicity. They are utilizing social networking through Facebook and Twitter to find screening venues and reach potential audiences, as co-producer of the 2010 Oscar-nominated New Zealand documentary *This Way of Life*, Sumner Burstyn, explains:

> Just as digital technologies [have] revolutionized and democratized film production over the last 10 years, the same is starting to happen with distribution. We as film-makers and audience are beginning to take back the screens. All across New Zealand, there are small, boutique, community focused cinemas opening up – all digital. (Burstyn 2011)

In addition to more accessible technologies of production and distribution, Burstyn also points to the changing demographics of the New Zealand film audience:

> Part of the story is a boomer one, of course. As we age, we don't want to see *Pirates of the Caribbean* but we do want to see a great little doco on what the bees are telling us (*Queen of the Sun*, in theatres right now), or a look at the life of our most wonderful poet Sam Hunt (*Purple Balloon*). Both are distributed by us using these new methods. (Burstyn 2011)

This is the optimistic view of the prospects for locally made, digitally based cinema, in a small marketplace where there is proliferation of short films, low-budget (often self-financed) local features, larger-budget New Zealand Film Commission-funded features or co-productions such as the UK Film Council/NZ Film Commission production *The Tracker* (Ian Sharp 2011), together with an unrelenting flow of imported titles clamouring for attention.

The independent/art-house sector

Within the potential film-going audience in New Zealand of 4.406 million citizens, with a median age in the population of 36.8 years (Statistics New Zealand, June 2011), it is possible to identify two major audience strands: the mainstream, multiplex audience described above; and an older, primarily middle class who favour independent or art-house cinemas. The latter are identified from their independence from the dominant exhibition chains (though not necessarily independent in respect of distribution systems), and they number at least 100 different venues, with slightly more in the North Island than the South Island (a closer count will result from research underway by the author, which is centred on the development of a website http://cinemasofnz.info). Such venues are distinguished by their location, scale and architecture: they are usually single-storey, stand-alone venues in city centres, up-market suburbs and resort towns, and are seldom associated with shopping malls or large commercial destinations; they are also places where popcorn is conspicuous by its absence. They can also be identified by their names, which evoke a different kind of cinema experience than that at the branded Event, Reading, Hoyts or Berkeley cinemas: The Penthouse, Cinema Paradiso, Dorothy Brown's Arrowtown Cinema, Waiheke Island Community Cinema and The Lido. A recent addition to the list is The Roxy, a lavishly restored, art-house cinema in Miramar, Wellington, situated close to the Park Road production facilities of Sir Peter Jackson, and financed and designed by a consortium that includes Sir Richard Taylor and Jamie Selkirk of Weta Workshop and *The Lord of the Rings* fame.

One exemplary example of the independent cinema experience in New Zealand was the Crooked Mile Talking Pictures theatre (closed in April 2012 due to rising insurance costs), in the West Coast, South Island town of Hokitika (population 3400); a former gold-mining and forestry now dependent on the passing tourist trade. As one of the two operating cinemas in Hokitika (The Regent, a single-screen independent is the other), the Crooked Mile, which specialized in New Zealand and art-house films, was housed in an impressive old former bank building and was owned and operated by a sole proprietor who acted as ticket seller, bartender and projectionist. In direct contrast to the expensive operation of multiplex facilities, bottom-line costs were minimal, according to an admiring article in *The Globe and Mail*, the leading Canadian newspaper:

> He needed only four customers to make a go of it each evening. Digital is the cost-cutting key. A former projectionist, now he just slips in a DVD (Jenkins 2008).

Digital projection might well be considered the critical element in the financial viability and future of other small enterprises, where staff costs are kept low, and the operation and maintenance of complex projection equipment is not needed.

Russ Collins, cinema owner and a leader of the Art House Convergence in the United States, expresses similar optimism:

> Instead of seeing digital cinema as a harbinger of Art House doom, I see it as an exciting opportunity. Digital conversion and the preservation of celluloid exhibition formats are, to me, do-able issues that will be most effectively addressed by 'new model' community-based, mission-driven Art House cinemas. Digital cinema can provide wider, quicker access to both historic and contemporary cinema repertoire and is much more accommodating to local film-makers. (Collins 2011)

Multiplexes in Australia and New Zealand are following international trends towards installing 3D projection. By May 2011, more than one-third of cinema screens in the United Kingdom were 3D-capable, but few independents in New Zealand are following suit – partly due to conversion costs but also because 3D production and projection add little to the kinds of films they screen (low-budget New Zealand films, documentaries, world cinema titles and English-language films characterized by complex narratives and character studies). Hollywood is gambling its future on such technology, but independent cinemas have other imperatives. Their objective is to provide different film fare, but also a film-going experience markedly different from the more generic, multiplex experience, as an enthusiastic posting on the http://www.emigratenz.org website writes about the Cinema Paradiso venue in the South Island resort town of Wanaka:

> Wanaka is well known for its lake and stunning mountain backdrop. But it's getting more and more well-known for its cinema … Wanaka doesn't have an everyday, run-of-the-mill cinema. Oh no! Wanaka has a cinema unlike any other you've probably been in before. Instead of the regulation big screen complex, Cinema Paradiso has comfy old sofas, armchairs you can sink into, airline seats. A lazyboy and even three seats inside an old yellow Morris Minor. (posting by benlia, 19 September 2010)

This enthusiastic film-goer goes on to wax lyrical about the food and beverage options available. Indeed, one of the most important differences between the multiplex and the art-house experience is the 'refreshment' factor: while the former offers standard fare of popcorn, soft drinks and candy bars, the latter offers coffee or alcohol and fashionable food items, to meet the expectations of its 'adult' clientele as a primary income source for the theatre.

The economics of film distribution and exhibition in the Western world determine that theatres derive their primary income not from ticket sales, but from the 'extras' for which film-goers pay, as another contributor to http://www.emigratenz.org comments:

> It's not widely appreciated, but for atypical movie house, the only profit in running the place is that generated by the concessionaires, especially popcorn, and drinks out of the fizzy drink machines ('post-mix'). Most of the admission price for first-run movies (as much as 90% in the first week) goes to the distributors, and what's left barely pays the rent and staff. Think of a cinema as a lousy restaurant that happens to put on movies, and you won't be far wrong! (posting by DB, 24 September 2010)

This explanation of film distribution/exhibition economics, as prevalent in New Zealand as in other Western economies, tends to be supported by more scholarly investigations, such as economist Richard B. McKenzie's *Why Popcorn Costs So Much at the Movies and Other Pricing Puzzles*, but it is certainly a factor that has to be added to any considered investigation of film-going in New Zealand.

Future directions for the New Zealand film audience

The results of The New Zealand Cinema Census (released May 2011) provide new and interesting insights into the local film audience. Initiated by the online film site http://www.flicks.co.nz and film impresario Ant Timpson, this census attracted nearly 4000 participants, with near-even gender balance (51 per cent males; 49 per cent females) but dominated by younger respondents (82 per cent aged between 15 and 35 years). They responded to questions about their film-going habits, film choices, attitudes to the multiplex experience, use of online movie sites, home entertainment use and attitudes to New Zealand films.

It can be argued that the domination by younger film-goers, with only 16 per cent of respondents aged 46 years or older, could be expected from this kind of online survey, and it does shape the overall conclusions. For example, the great majority of respondents (89 per cent) turned to online sources for movie information, rather than the more traditional media sources of newspapers or magazines. The type/genre of a movie was also the primary determining factor in film choices for most, rather than director or cast details.

Overall, those in the census tended to go to the cinema more frequently than the general population (53 per cent of respondents went at least once a month), and generally favoured the multiplex over art-house venues. Both ticket prices and candy bar prices were regarded as excessive by the great majority (74 per cent for the former, 92 per cent for the latter). This may be a significant factor in the finding that watching movies on DVD, or Blu-Ray, viewing them on pay TV or downloading or watching online (in 87 per cent of cases, *not* from a pay service) was generally favoured over going out to see a movie, with the 'big screen and sound system experience' being nominated as the major inducement to do so.

In respect of attitudes to New Zealand film, responses were lukewarm, with only 16 per cent requiring New Zealand-funded movies to tell 'specifically New Zealand stories'. Perceived reasons why some New Zealand films failed at the box office included 'story doesn't seem interesting' (41 per cent), 'looks low budget' (23 per cent') and 'a feeling that New Zealand movies are generally bad' (21 per cent). Great word of mouth and local media attention were seen to help local cinema, and there was a strong desire (83 per cent) to see New Zealand short films screen prior to some movies in cinemas.

A 2010 research exercise with 524 Media Studies and English students, aged between 15 and 19, in New Zealand and conducted on behalf of the Office of Film and Literature Classification, also suggested that out-of-cinema film viewing was increasingly the norm. Only 61 per cent of students reported going to the cinema at least once every two to three months, while 73 per cent indicated that they watched films on DVD at least once a week (Office of Film and Literature Classification 2010: 6). Such findings add fuel to a general belief in the film industry that the traditional audience base is slipping away, or shifting to other formats (both legal and illegal), and that new film-going audiences have to be found. Thus the emphasis on technological 'solutions' (3D in particular, with its ability to earn extra revenue from premium ticket prices), and the targeting of potentially lucrative audience sectors, with family movies or releases geared towards older filmgoers as Screen Engine CEO Kevin Goetz (2010) argues: 'Older people have a history, a habit and nostalgia for going to the movies, and the young don't have that relationship' (McNary 2010).

Even though understanding or predicting the behaviour of film audiences remains a difficult – perhaps wilful – enterprise, some understanding can be gained from examining the experience of a small country like New Zealand. Here, film-going has long been important and the structures of distribution, exhibition and audience response are more visible than in much larger markets. It is hoped that this chapter has provided a base for further inquiry and understanding.

References

The 2011 New Zealand Cinema Census, www.flicks.co.nz/features/the-2011-new-zealand-cinema-census/nzfilm, accessed 10 May 2011.

Brittenden, W. (2008), *The Celluloid Circus: The Heyday of the New Zealand Picture Theatre*, Auckland: Random House.

Burstyn, S. (2011), personal communication, 22 May.

Collins, R. (2011), 'Digital Projection WILL NOT Convert Art Houses Right Out of Existence!', http://iradeutchman.com/indiefilm/digital-projection-will-not-convert-art-houses-right-out-of-existence, accessed 3 May 2011.

Drinnan, J. (2009), 'Skycity May Return to Movies – Chief', *New Zealand Herald*, 26 November, p. B1.

——— (2010), 'Cinema Chain Vows Big Changes', *New Zealand Herald*, 1 June, p. B1.

Flicks.co.nz (2011), http://www.flicks.co.nz/news/fast-and-furious-5-highest-box-office-opening-for-2011.html. Accessed 29 April 20-11.

Gerstner, D. and Greenlees, S. (2000), 'Cinema by Fits and Starts: New Zealand Film Practices in the Twentieth Century', *CineAction*, February, p. 1.

Heylen Research Centre (1994), *Understanding the New Zealand Film Market: The Audience's Perspective* (1994), Report for the New Zealand Film Commission by The Heylen Research Centre, Wellington: NZFC.

Jenkins, A. (2008), 'Saved by the Movie Man in the Velvet Coat', *The Globe and Mail*, 26 January, http://www.theglobeandmail.com/life/saved-by-the-movie-man-in-the-velvet-coat/article664011/email. Accessed 2 June 2011.

Lealand, G. (2011), 'The Jackson Effect: The Late 1990s to 2005', in L. McDonald, F. Stark and D. Pivac (eds), *New Zealand Film: An Illustrated History*, Wellington: Te Papa Press, pp. 264–82.

McKenzie, R.B. (2008), *Why Popcorn Costs So Much at the Movies and Other Pricing Puzzles*, London: Springer.

McNary, D. (2010), 'Studios Now Targeting Older Auds', http://www.variety.com/article/VR1118027986. Accessed 3 May 2011.

Mirams, G. (1945), *Speaking Candidly: Films and People in New Zealand*, Hamilton: Paul's Book Arcade.

Nationmaster (2011), http://www.nationmaster.com. Accessed 20 April 2011.

New Zealand Film Archive (2011), 'The First Picture Show', http://www.filmarchive.org.nz/archive_presents/boerwar?firstpicturesghow.html. Accessed 8 May 2011.

New Zealand Film Commission (2011), 'Domestic Distribution Policy', http://www.nzfilm.co.nz/SalesandMarketing/DomesticDistributionPolicy.aspx. Accessed 25 May 2011.

Office of Film and Literature Classification (2010), *Young People's Use of Entertainment Mediums – 2010*, Wellington: OFLC, p. 6.

Petrie, D. and Stuart, D. (2008), *A Coming of Age: Thirty Years of New Zealand Film*, Auckland: Random House.

Script to Screen seminar (2010), 'Setting Ourselves Up for Box Office Success … or Failure', Auckland, 23 February, http://www.script-to-screen.co.nz/2010/12/setting-ourselves-up-for-box-office-success…or failure. Accessed 19 May 2011.

Sharing Travel Experiences (2011), http://www.sharingtravelexperiences.com. Accessed 5 May 2011.

Statistics New Zealand (2011), 'Estimated Resident Population of New Zealand', http://www.stats.govt.nz/tools_and_services/tools/population_clock.aspx. Accessed 10 June 2011.

Wasko, J. (2003), *How Hollywood Works*, London: Sage.

Chapter 9

The Critical Reception of *Certified Copy*: Original Art or Copy of a Rom-com?

Eylem Atakav

The critical reception of a film is not independent of its mode of introduction to the cinema going public. Marketers and advertisers tend to use a limited set of categories, which are prone to be disjunctive and thereby intrinsically unsuited to any film that crosses genre boundaries as defined by the industry. This can lead directly to a situation of critical reception in which a film is misunderstood through being promoted into one or another disjunctive category or genre and then adversely criticized for being neither one nor the other. Whether the effects of such transgressions are long term or not depends on other factors, including a film's reception by the public and word-of-mouth opinion. This can, of course, be undermined at the outset by the categories employed in marketing and advertising campaigns. As David Bordwell and Kristin Thompson appositely argue, 'a genre is easier to recognize than to define', and there are no 'strictly logical distinctions [that] can capture the variety of factors that create the genres we have' (2004 [1979]): 108–09). This is further complicated by the fact that genre is a fairly broad term, one that encompasses many different films within any single category. For this reason, some films may be perceived as straddling multiple genre classifications.

This chapter examines Abbas Kiarostami's 2010 film *Certified Copy* in the context of its marketing and critical reception. While this film conforms to many of the conventions of an art film, the promotional material and reviews that accompanied its release tended to position it as a romantic comedy. This apparent disconnection provides the focus of the investigation, which takes up several key questions. What discursive, conceptual and commercial structures underpin the classification of a film with serious art film credentials as a comparatively light romantic comedy (rom-com)? How does the critical reception of *Certified Copy* complicate and/or transgress the boundaries of the romantic comedy genre? By opting for or accepting the rom-com categorization, what criteria might film reviewers be setting for what is (or what is not) considered a European art film? Finally, from a marketing perspective, does the rom-com positioning represent a contrived attempt to broaden the audience for the film and thereby enhance its prospects for commercial success? Before turning to the critical reception of *Certified Copy* and these underlying questions, it is necessary to provide some background on the film and the film-maker.

Certified Copy – the film

Certified Copy is a full-length film in English, French and Italian, a co-production of France, Italy and Belgium. It was directed by Kiarostami, one of the most distinctive contemporary Iranian film-makers, whose work has been acclaimed at international film festivals. The influences on his work range from Ozu's minimalist approach through to Italian neo-realist cinema. He has a highly developed, individual style that is distinguished by techniques of long-take cinematography and working with non-professional casts, illustrating his minimalist approach. His expertise as a poet and a photographer is easily recognizable in his films' narratives. *Certified Copy* was his first full-length feature film shot outside his native Iran, although he had already worked overseas before on such projects as *A.B.C. Africa* (2001), *Tickets* (2004) and *Five* (*2003*). In any case, Kiarostami was already well known, with the critical success of *Taste of Cherry* (1997) and *The Wind will Carry Us* (1999) helping to give him a distinct auteur status.

As the review by Peter Bradshaw points out, *Certified Copy* 'has resemblances to other Kiarostami films: there are extended dialogue scenes in cars, and business with mobile phones indicating a breakdown in communication' (2010). Geoff Andrew in *Sight and Sound* notes that:

> While *Certified Copy* maybe unprecedentedly high-profile addition to Kiarostami's ouvre, it's still as quirkily personal, playful, artisanal and attentive to small, intriguing details as anything he's made. Indeed, for all the talk of 'a rom-com with a difference' that greeted its Cannes premiere, it's the difference from other people's work rather than from his own that should probably be stressed. (2010: 36)

Certified Copy is set in Tuscany, and tells the story of a day in the life of a French art dealer and an English author, who is in Italy to give a talk on his book on the concepts of original and copy in art. James Miller (William Shimell), a British art historian, comes to give a talk on his recently published book *Certified Copy*, which focuses on originals and copies of artworks. The film's opening scene presents a roomful of people waiting to listen to his lecture. But Miller is late for this event. So is 'She', a woman figure played by actor Juliette Binoche who is never given a particular name during the course of the film, a strategy that suggests that the story told in the film can in fact happen to anyone and everyone.

She arrives after the talk starts, entering the room with a smile on her face. She walks straight to the front row and sits next to the organizer of the talk. As Miller, the art historian, talks, the woman listens to him in admiration. The woman's young son stands in one corner of the room and looks annoyed at her because he wishes to leave. She leaves a note with Miller's translator and departs. She is a gallery owner in Tuscany, the birthplace of Renaissance and hence a place with direct associations with art. The next segment of the film is set in an antique shop owned by the woman. Miller enters but it is not clear whether the two know each other from a previous time. They talk briefly about art and she offers to show him around the local area. They drive to a nearby village, walk in the streets, go to museums and drop into a cafe where they are mistaken as a couple. They end up in a hotel room remembering their – possibly non-existent – past. The presentation of the two figures is deliberately altered throughout the film. At times, the man and woman can be understood as a married couple who are separated; at other times, they seem only to be friends; at yet other times they appear to be a couple on the verge of a break-up. Neither of the lead characters' actions or conversation confirm or discount any of these possibilities. Have they been, are they or will they be a couple? The story teases the audience about the answer to these questions.

As this account has implied, *Certified Copy* does not have a linear narrative. Miller and the woman discuss art, life, love and relationships, yet the film leaves the audience questioning whether this is a representation of a real relationship or a copy of many relationships between men and women. Are the two play-acting or are they really an estranged husband and wife? We never find out – it is left to our imagination, and as audience we are offered the opportunity of interpretation. As the two lead characters drive to a village nearby to witness a wedding and visit museums, they talk about art, originals and copies of artworks, children, men and women. The film's 'action' revolves around a series of philosophical conversations concerning relationships between men and women, mothers and sons, art and aesthetics. Through this interplay of characters and settings, the audience is invited to question issues around aesthetics and to consider the concepts of originality and reproduction. Indeed, *Certified Copy*, as Geoff Andrew aptly puts it, 'covers a range of Kiarostami's concerns to do with the male–female relationships and art, presence and absence, reality and representation, while its deceptively naturalistic native is built on a typically meticulous *mise-en-scène* that includes a long conversation in a car, much mischief, reflections and frames within frames, and some sly play with perspective' (2010: 36).

The film can be (and has been) construed as a romantic comedy – a characterization that is not inappropriate but is certainly inadequate. At the same time, its art film credentials have been downplayed almost entirely by marketers and critical reviewers. This suggests that the rom-com positioning may be a deliberate attempt to promote the film against the concept of art film in order to help assure its commercial success, even at the risk of creating confusion among audiences over its appropriate designation. In order to shed light into the language created on the film around the genre of romantic comedy, this chapter analyzes a range of reviews of the film published after its initial screening at the Cannes Film Festival in 2010, as well as the film's trailer and press kit. Overall, it argues that although these sources position the film squarely within the romantic comedy genre, such a singular association seriously misreads it.

Given the terms used in the critical reception of *Certified Copy*, it is worth revisiting the rom-com genre in the context of art films. Love and romance may be recurring themes, but romantic comedy is not a genre commonly associated with European art films. Writing about the emergence of art cinema in Hollywood, Bordwell argues that art cinema may be regarded as a genre that foregrounds the author 'as a structure in the film's system', where realism meets authorial expressivity (1985: 374). Applying Bordwell's point to *Certified Copy*, it is possible to conceive of the film as straddling two genre classifications: art film and rom-com. On the one hand, as the review in *The Independent* (2010) argues, *Certified Copy* comes across 'a little too neatly like a handsome, high- to middle-brow bourgeois European art film … it looks and feels entirely like Kiarostami'. On the other, as Peter Bradshaw writes in his review, it is 'influenced by Woody Allen and Diane Keaton's initial squabble in *Manhattan*'. In an interview for *Sight and Sound*, Kiarostami was asked about the exact status of the ambiguous relationship between the man and the woman in the film, and whether he could provide background on the couple's history. He answered:

> I still don't know. Truth is a possibility – what the reality is does not really matter so much. What matters here is that they are possibly a couple. In the film Shimell's character does say 'We make a good couple, don't we?' And as long as the cafe proprietor regards them as a couple, then in a sense their being a couple is true, regardless of whether they are in reality. (Andrew 2010: 39)

This explicitly ambiguous nature of the relationship between the two characters seems to evidence, at least in part, its art film credentials by not giving the audience neat answers – thereby fitting in with the conventions of art film.

Bob Tourtellotte (2010), writing for *The Daily Star* (Lebanon), also takes up the concept of representation and reality and the play between original and copy. He argues that the film is 'an enigmatic tale', and that it challenges audiences to decide whether their marital status – be it real or a reproduction of reality – is even important in terms of how we judge them as people. Tourtellotte goes on to refer to Kiarostami's own words, which state that 'the value of a human being depends very much on how you look at it'. This play between representation and reality, and the power of interpretation, is also further articulated in the part of the press kit of the film, which was written by Juliette Binoche. She discusses the pre-production phase of the film and the initial conversations she had with Kiarostami. She shares an anecdote that is highly relevant to the dichotomy around the real and the unreal:

> Once upon a time, I went to Iran to meet Abbas … One night he told me the story we shot together this summer. He told me every detail: the bra, the restaurant, the hotel. In short, he told me that the story had happened to him. At the end, after talking for 45 minutes in perfect English, he said, 'Do you believe me?' I said, 'Yes.' And he said, 'It's not true!' I burst out laughing so hard, and I think that may have been what made him want to do the film! Reality and fiction have always made me laugh because I truly believe that anything is possible. To this day, I'm sure he lived this story. Just as I'm sure that he didn't. (*Certified Copy* Press Kit 2010)

As this quote demonstrates, the interplay between fiction and reality, original and copy and the represented and the real is not only inherent in the film's narrative, but is also apparent within the pre-production stage. Binoche's interpretation of the comedic elements of the film is also thought-provoking. Her take on the ambiguity of the film is further highlighted in an interview, during which she defines the narrative as a 'comedy': 'It is more of a comedy than tragedy. It is tragic at the end … This film puts a lot of questions together and doesn't give answers.' (Binoche 2011). What Binoche articulates here is a different kind of comedy to the one we might expect from a rom-com film. It is a more uncertain type of humour inherent in the roots of the relationship between men and women as well as the relationship between the real and the fictional.

The trailer for *Certified Copy* similarly emphasizes romance over other elements of the narrative: 'He … a writer in search of meaning. She … an art dealer in search of originality.' Deborah Young, a reviewer from *The Hollywood Reporter*, is also quoted: 'A delicate, bittersweet comedy set in romantic Italy.' The trailer brings scenes where He and She are seen together, and clearly assembled in a way that suggests a romantic relationship. This results in a mismatch between the trailer and the film itself, for in the latter the focus is not just on the romance – nor is there much comedy. Indeed, *Certified Copy* seems to be missing many of the rom-com conventions identified by Deborah Jermyn and Stacey Abbott (2009). They argue that 'the perception of [rom-]comedy per se as inherently frivolous and anti-intellectual has resulted in its critical and cultural marginalization, where it is presumed that eliciting laughs from the audience is antithetical to "serious" reflection' (2009: 2). *Sight and Sound* (2010) wrote about the film under the title of 'restoration comedy', announcing it as 'both a romantic comedy and a vehicle for Juliette Binoche'. Lee Marshall (2010) read it as a 'mature romantic comedy', and called it an 'intellectual rom-com with Allen-esque overtones'. In *The Hollywood Reporter*, Deborah Young writes:

> After years of working on photography, poetry and more experimental films, Kiarostami makes an engaging return to narrative cinema in a delicate, bittersweet comedy set in romantic Italy. *Certified Copy* slyly explores the ins and outs of marriage and the many ways men and women fail to think alike. Juliette Binoche will give the film a leg up in Europe, though wide international audiences are probably not in the cards for such an off-beat item. (2010)

These reviews allow us to see two issues related to the critical reception of the film and its positioning specifically as a romantic comedy. The first issue is that the film appears to fit within the genre of a rom-com – it is set in a romantic setting and somewhat light-heartedly explores the relationship between men and women. On one level, it is indeed a girl-meets-boy story. However, the narrative structure complicates this relationship. While girl meets boy, the audience is expected to think more about this meeting, rather than to expect a 'they lived happily ever after/marriage' ending. The second issue is that analysis of the film's narrative and tone highlights a number of 'art film' conventions, which are largely ignored by most reviewers in favour of the 'rom-com' classification.

The reviews surveyed above also illustrate the problem of defining comedy and the parameters of the rom-com genre. These become more apparent as further reviews are taken into consideration. *The Radio Times* (2009) downplays the comedic elements of the film, asserting *Certified Copy* is 'an unconventional love story. Kiarostami's film touches on love, marriage and art, feeling at times like a dry seminar.' *The Telegraph*'s review is concerned about the film for the same reason: it argues that it 'is likely to appear almost entirely academic' (Sandhu 2010). Moreover, according to Peter Bradshaw:

> In its very strangeness, and unworldliness, and utter unreality' the film has a species of charm. It is an intensely choreographed film in its way, unmistakably an example of Kiarostami's compositional technique, though not a successful example. It may go down as the strangest 'meet cute' in the history of cinema. (2010)

In contrast, Mike McCahill (2010) refers to the film as an 'upscale romance', while David Jenkins (2010) sees it as 'a droll coffee-table rom-com' and 'an intellectual hide and seek'. Andrew O'Heir calls it a 'romantic fable of two strangers in Tuscany' (2010). One reviewer on salon.com refers to the film as 'a psychological drama, a slow dissecting of the human psyche as we watch the interplay of our two protagonists. The action is subtle. The nuances are delicate' (NB 2010).

The two people who make up the 'couple' in the film discuss Jasper Johns and Andy Warhol, and how context can shift the meaning of an object by throwing the focus on the observer. So, as in the film, the review in *New Statesman* argues (Gilbey 2009): 'The easy harmony between two intelligent and reasonable strangers keeps threatening to break down' throughout their discussions on art and throughout the film. For that reason, it is no coincidence that Edward Lawrenson sees *Certified Copy* as 'a talky drama about a couple who may or may not be pretending to be lovers', and argues that the film 'sees the Iranian director swap his usual nimble intelligence for plodding observations about the nature of artifice and deception' (2010: 56). It is interesting to see from these reviews that the critical approaches to film reflect upon the philosophical nature of the narrative. In other words, the reviews themselves read as philosophical texts due to the film's highly sophisticated attitude towards relationships and art. In addition, Colin MacCabe writes about the film as one that 'scored high marks for pretentiousness but low marks for insight':

> The Iranian master seems to have been reading a lot of out-of-date European theory and much of the dialogue is taken up with well-rehearsed riffs on the relation between original and copy. If this wasn't bad enough, his account of a mature woman meeting a visiting lecturer (or is it in fact not an original meeting but yet another copy in an overlong relationship?) stars Juliette Binoche in her most irritating vein, never using one simper when three will do. (2010: 59)

This negative review, which does not refer to the film as a rom-com, shrewdly sums up the storyline: there is not much romance in the film, nor is there much comedy inherent in this potentially pretend 'relationship'. This takes me back to the question I posed at the outset: how and why does a film which has almost nothing to do with romance or comedy come to be referred to as rom-com? Does this attempt to situate the film within rom-com signify a shift in the boundaries of the genre? Or is this all a cunning strategy to market a 'European art film', full of dialogues on aesthetics as two people walk around the historical assets of Tuscany, that otherwise might not sell?

Marketing

The press kit for *Certified Copy* very clearly introduces the film as 'a story of love and romance' (2010). This immediately creates a disconnect between the actual theme of the film's narrative and the language used to introduce and market the film. The press kit presents the story as follows:

> How can one tell yet another story about love in Tuscany? *Certified Copy*: by playing around with the clichés. With the usual settings, the small love-nest hotels, the cups of coffee cooling as the lovers drink each other in, the narrow streets where they go astray, hurt themselves, find themselves, their heels clattering on the cobblestones … The love affair of a single day that opens onto life: this is a film neither of phantoms not regrets, and where all illusions are not lost.

The image used in the press kit is taken from the scene in which She and He are sitting on the stairs in front of a building. Binoche's head is on Shimell's shoulder as she smiles, and Shimell's head is leaning towards her. This image is intended to highlight the romantic relationship between the protagonists. The press kit chooses this scene to help establish the film as a romantic comedy, and to enhance its prospects for commercial success – even at the risk of creating confusion over its appropriate designation.

It may be argued, then, that *Certified Copy* represents an attempt to market an art film as a romantic comedy. The positioning of the film is an expedient marketing strategy rather than an art film's excursion to the rom-com genre. *Certified Copy* reminds the audience of the famous balcony scene in *Annie Hall*, which uses subtitles to reveal the real feelings of the characters as they talk about art and aesthetics on their 'first' date. In that scene, Annie Hall and Alvy Singer, who met on the day, are talking to each other about their likes, dislikes and tastes. The conversation sounds highly intellectual, yet the subtitles are used to translate the intellectual talk to the characters' real thoughts and feelings towards each other. The use of subtitles here is part of the comedy element inherent in the film. *Certified Copy* engages in a similar philosophical discussion to that of Annie and Alvy, but proceeds to extend this to the entire film. The conversations that He and She have are highly sophisticated, philosophical and intellectual – even when they are about relationships. For instance, as they start their conversation while travelling in Her car, He says: 'The purpose of life, the whole meaning of existence is to have fun, to have pleasure.' In another scene, as they walk in the streets, She cries as she complains: 'My family lives their own life and I live my own. What kind of philosophy is that!?' These type of conceptual statements are embedded in the dialogue throughout the film. As Jermyn and Abbot aptly put it:

> While rom-coms in recent years often struggled to be taken seriously – to win awards or critical enthusiasm or academic attention – they have remained beloved of fans and a virtually constant presence in popular cinema in some shape or form since the 1930s. Allen's *Manhattan*, like its 'nervous romance' predecessor *Annie Hall* (1977), succeeded in attracting all these forms of attention precisely because it was seen in many ways at this time as reinventing a tired and predictable genre ... To win critical approbation within the broad arena of the rom-com by the late 1970s, it seemed, one had to undo the popular image of it. (2009: 2)

Certified Copy as an art film?

Certified Copy may have appropriated the rom-com genre in a deliberate attempt to sell a 'European' art film. At the same time, however, it also won critical praise for being exhibited within the context of international festival circuits and UK art-house cinemas. It is worth exploring how Jermyn and Abbott identify the rom-com's place in contemporary cinema, as this helps to critically reflect upon *Certified Copy*'s rather questionable generic positioning. Their discussion continues as follows:

> Firstly, [rom-com's] audience is enduringly presumed to be predominantly female and 'chick flicks' in all their incarnations are frequently critically constructed as inherently trite or lightweight. Second, romantic fiction generally is thought to be essentially calculating in its execution, cynically manipulating an emotional and sentimental response from the viewer... The genre is widely depicted as slavishly formulaic, adhering to well-worn and obvious conventions (boy meets girl; boy and girl face obstacles to their romantic union; boy and girl conquer obstacles to find true love). (2009: 2)

Certified Copy is indeed different from traditional rom-coms, in the sense that it does not remain 'slavishly formulaic'. In fact, the film challenges many of the genre's conventions. For example, the ending is intentionally left vague and the audience is left looking at the church bell ringing from within the hotel room where the two characters are located. The audience knows that they are there, but they are not visible. Whether the image of the church bells ringing signifies a wedding or not is left open. By not suggesting a clear ending, and by not offering a 'they-lived-happily-ever-after' ending through a wedding scene, the film strives to be different to other films that tell love stories at locations of romance.

Finally, raising further questions about the boundaries and conventions we place around films, it is worth noting that *Certified Copy* is banned in Iran. *Variety* has written about the film under the title of 'Iran Scraps Local "Copy": Iranian Authorities Crack Down on Kiarostami Pic':

> According to the Iranian media, the official reason for the ban is the attire of Binoche in the film. 'If Juliette Binoche were better clad it could have been screened but due to her attire there will not be a general screening of the film,' Deputy Culture Minister Javad Shamaqdari was quoted saying by local newspapers. He said, however, that the film could be shown 'in some private circles and universities.' Shamaqdari, who attended the film festival, went on, however, to describe *Certified Copy* as 'not a bad film', though he doubted it would in any case appeal to Iranian audiences. (2010)

The refusal to screen Kiarostami's film in his native Iran is perhaps not entirely surprising. Perhaps more perplexing is the decision by the London Iranian Film Festival (2011) not to exhibit the film, stating: 'We would not choose to screen *Certified Copy* as we feel it does not include the Iranian cultural elements consistent with our programming.' Was this judgement based on the fact the film was perceived as not serious enough to be considered an Iranian film, or was it because it was shot outside Iran? Is the storyline too controversial, as it does not conform to patriarchal ideology? It would indeed be interesting to explore in a further study the production of rom-coms in Iran, and how a national cinema defines generic conventions.

Conclusion

As this chapter has demonstrated, the critical reviewers of *Certified Copy* accept – up to a point – the conscious attempts to position the film as a romantic comedy. Their reviews refer to the film as rom-com in both title and content. Similarly, the spin put on the marketing of the film deliberately highlights the rom-com elements. The latter is perhaps designed to assure the commercial success of what may be more appropriately classified as an art film, but there is more at stake here than simply marketing expediencies. While many of the critics accepted the rom-com positioning, they also demonstrated awareness of and interest in the 'art film' aspects of the film – its unconventional aesthetics, the complexity of the relationship between a man and a woman in its philosophical context, the storyline and the director's cinematic background. This raises some important questions about the 'fixed' nature of the categorizations that are placed around certain types of film. Jermyn and Abbott argue that 'while the rom-com frequently maintains certain of its traditions and conventions it is nevertheless a living genre' (2009: 2). Genres grow and develop, not least by incorporating elements from other genres. There is an obvious process of negotiation involved. Within this perspective, we need to give greater consideration to the role that art films such as *Certified*

Copy might play in shifting the boundaries and expanding the definitional parameters of romantic comedy.

References

Allen, W. (1977) *Annie Hall*, United States: MGM.

Andrew, G. (2010), 'Restoration Comedy', *Sight and Sound*, 20: 9, pp. 36–39.

Binoche, J. (2011). Interview about *Certified Copy*, http://www.youtube.com/watch?v=KXr_qMsTzqI. Accessed 21 September 2011.

Bordwell, D. and Thompson, K. (2004 [1979]), *Film Art: An Introduction*, New York: McGraw Hill.

Bordwell, D., Staiger, J. and Thompson, K. (1985), *The Classical Hollywood Cinema*, New York: Columbia University Press.

Bradshaw, P. (2010), 'Film Review: *Certified Copy*', *The Guardian*, 2 September.

Certified Copy Press Kit (2010).

Gilbey, R. (2010), '*Certified Copy*', *New Statesman*, 1 September.

Iran Scraps Local "Copy": Iranian Authorities Crack Down on Kiarostami Pic', *Variety*, 29 May.

Jenkins, D. (2010), '*Certified Copy*', *TimeOut London*, 14 September.

Jermyn, D. and Abbott, S. (eds) (2009), *Falling in Love Again: Romantic Comedy in Contemporary Cinema*, New York: I.B. Tauris.

Kiarostami, A. (1997), *Taste of Cherry*, Iran: Abbas Kiarostami Productions.

——— (1999), *The Wind Will Carry Us*, Iran: MK2 Productions.

——— (2001), *A.B.C. Africa*, Iran: IFAD.

——— (2003), *Five*, Iran: Behnegar, NHK, MK2 Productions.

——— (2004), *Tickets*, Italy: Fandango, Medusa Produzione, Sixteen Films.

——— (2010), *Certified Copy*, United States: MK2 Productions and BiBi Film.

Lawrenson, E. (2010), 'Cannes Notebook: Job Well Done', *Film Quarterly*, 64: 1, pp. 56–58.

MacCabe, C. (2010), 'Cannes Notebook: An Amorous Catfish', *Film Quarterly*, 64: 1, pp. 59–61.

Marshall, L. (2010), '*Certified Copy*', *Screen Daily*, 18 May.

McCahill, M. (2010), '*Certified Copy* review (Seven Magazine Review)', *The Telegraph*, 2 September.

NB, 'Movie Review: *Certified Copy*', http://www.//open.salon.com/blog/wqbelle/2011/05/22/movie_review_certified_copy. Accessed 19 June 2011.

O'Heir, A. (2011), 'Best of Cannes: Kiarostami, Binoche Make a "*Certified Copy*"', http://www.salon.com/2010/05/21/certified_copy/, 22/05/2010. Accessed 21 September 2011.

Romney, J. (2010), '*Certified Copy*', *The Independent*, 5 September.

Sandhu, S. (2010), '*Certified Copy* Review', *The Telegraph*, 2 September.

Tourtellotte, B. (2010), 'Copie Conforme: Kiarostami Speaks Out on Behalf of Detained Colleague', *The Daily Star* (Lebanon), 20 May.

Young, D. (2010), 'Film Review: *Certified Copy*', *The Hollywood Reporter*, 14 October.

PART III

Movie Theatres - From Picture Palace to the Multiplex

Chapter 10

Movie-going in the Shenandoah Valley of Virginia: A Case Study of Place, Transportation, Audiences, Racism, Censorship and Sunday Showings

Douglas Gomery

Movie-going in the United States has for too long simply been examined where the profits and crowds lay – in urban America. But in terms of social impact, we should not ignore the rural United States. Here we have scattered evidence that for rural viewers, going to the movies was an important part of their daily lives. We wish we had diaries of movie-going, but in the case of the Valley of Virginia we almost have one. Because a poor female movie-goer, Virginia Hensley, became country music star Patsy Cline, we know a great deal of her movie-going habits. A rural female, Virginia's neighbours, relatives and school mates speak to her passion for movie-going.

Indeed, her considerable singing talents were first displayed publicly when at age 16 she began consistently winning amateur talent contests held in Winchester's Palace Theatre. Virginia Hensley sold hot dogs in a tiny 'hole in the wall' up the street. Before the talent contest was about to start, the manager of the Palace sent someone to tell her to take a ten-minute break. She rushed down the block and belted out Al Jolson songs such as 'Rock-a-bye Your Baby with a Dixie Melody' – and usually won some sort of prize (Gomery 2011). During the late 1940s, amateur contests were held every Saturday afternoon at the Palace. These talent shows gave the cinema an edge over its only central city rival, the Warner Bros-owned Capitol, and two new drive-ins on the edge of town.

We know of Patsy Cline's true obsession with Hollywood movies because she named her first child after a character in Cecil B. DeMille's *Samson and Delilah* – eight years after she saw it at the Capitol. On either 8 or 9 July 1950 – or both – she was stunned by DeMille's latest Technicolor spectacle – nationally released on 21 October 1949 by Paramount. 'Semadar' – played by Angela Lansbury – was listed third in the credits behind Samson (Victor Mature) and Delilah (Hedy Lamarr). On 25 August 1958, she named her first child Julie Simador Dick, approximating the spelling of the name based on a still vivid motion picture impression. Such was the power of the movies in rural America in general, and in the Valley of Virginia in particular (Ringgold and Bodeen 1969: 341–50).

To better understand the culture that led to this inspiration, I shall analyse the historical conditions of movie-going in Virginia's north-western flank, in the Valley between the gentle Blue Ridge and Appalachian highlands. This was rural America, dotted with farms of fertile limestone soils and rolling pastures. The Valley of Virginia is a portion of the chain of valleys that parallels the Appalachian Mountains at the west, but for this chapter I shall take up only a three-county portion of this Valley, starting in the north in Frederick county (county seat Winchester), moving south to rural Shenandoah county (county seat Woodstock) and ceasing with Rockingham county (county seat Harrisonburg). Here is a manageable region, book-ended by two towns of similar small size, and was purely rural in-between (Salmon and Campbell 1994: 3–10).

This Valley remained rural, but was connected by one of the first highways in the United States – The Valley Pike. This common route ran though Winchester, south through a series of small towns including Woodstock, and into the heart of Harrisonburg. Farms surrounded these communities, and rural movie-goers supported movie houses in town through the first two-thirds of the twentieth century. In all three counties, Winchester, Woodstock and Harrisonburg prospered as county seats, hubs of business and shopping. Yet only Winchester topped 10,000 in population by 1950 (Rouse 1995; Wayland 1967: 1–39).

From Winchester to Harrisonburg along The Valley Pike, the settlement pattern meant towns were dotted about every 7 miles. Surrounding these communities were farms of about 125 acres. Some industry was attracted to Harrisonburg and Winchester, but not as much as in the north, as Virginia remained a staunch non-union state. The Valley Pike was key. Helped by the power of state political boss Harry Flood Byrd of Winchester, it went directly through all towns, defined Main Streets, and so provided the link among communities. It was part of life's rural routine that farmers weekly went to town on Saturdays (Hamilton Suter 1999).

In sum, the Valley offers a unified region of the upper South, where elites dominated, but could not stop the innovation of the movies. Movie-going trends were set in Winchester, the Valley's biggest city, by 1910, and then generally followed in Harrisonburg and the smaller communities along The Valley Pike. After 1928, Warner Bros also owned the two largest Valley cinemas – the Capitol in Winchester and the Virginia in Harrisonburg. Valley movie-goers saw the best of the 400–500 films Hollywood produced each year, but months after citizens of the big cities to the north. This backlog meant frequent – sometimes daily – programming changes. This history ends with the coming of Interstate 81, shopping malls and multiplexes (Dabney 1971: 442–43).

The political machine of Harry Flood Byrd tried to manage this movie invasion. Byrd organized white males to run the Commonwealth from the 1920s through the 1960s. Byrd owned the monopoly newspapers both in Winchester and Harrisonburg, and directly benefited from and participated in the rise of the cinema and its paid advertising. Of all the states, Virginia was the most thoroughly controlled by an elite oligarchy. Byrd subverted democratic institutions, and deprived most Virginians – all poor whites and all Blacks – of a voice in government. Between 1925 and 1945, a smaller portion of the population voted – about 10 per cent – than in any other state (Hawkes 1974).

By the mid-1920s, the elite had grown so suspicious of the movies that they stepped in and created laws constraining and defining movie-going. Whites and Blacks could not legally sit together, so every cinema had a 'restricted' balcony; a state censor board in Richmond examined, approved, sometimes cut and sometimes denied access to controversial Hollywood movies; and a Commonwealth law denied for much of the first half of the twentieth century the ability to see any films on Sundays (Key 1950: 19–36).

Winchester – the trendsetter

The Valley of Virginia has long been dominated by trends set in its biggest town, Winchester. Movies first came during the week of 5–12 March 1897 at the city's opera house – with reserved seats for 25 cents and general admission at 15 cents. In 1900, a new city hall opened, with its second floor billed as the 'new city Auditorium'. Holding up to 800 persons, the Auditorium became the new center of the town's entertainment world. Managed successfully by Fred and Herman Hable, the Auditorium had a balcony for African Americans, and was only used in the evening so as not to disrupt city operations. Still, the Hables could get in two shows a night (Pickeral and Fogg 1930).

The Hables were outsiders, Jews in a Christian community. Their father, Solomon Hable from Germany, had come to Winchester in 1872 to open a men's clothing store, and prospered. Hable's sons booked both live shows and movies in the Auditorium. Their success inspired a wave of nickelodeons, all located in storefronts on Winchester's Main Street. Into the 1910s, the Dixie, Casino, Bijou Dream, Grand, Strand, Hippodrome, Movieland and Wonderland did their best to compete with the Auditorium a block away ('Another House' 1912; 'Auditorium Theater Flourished' 1954; 'Casino Theater' 1981; 'In Old Kentucky' 1909; 'Herman Hable' 1913).

On Christmas Day 1913, Winchester entered a new era when the 1000-seat Empire Theatre opened across from the courthouse. Here was the first grand Vaudeville and movie palace, bigger than the Auditorium, designed by a professional architect and built by the William E. Frazer construction company, also of Baltimore. Co-owner Henkel Henry (former nickelodeon operator) managed; partner William H. Baker, a member of the town elite as proprietor of the Baker Chocolate Company, backed Henkel Henry ('New Empire Theatre Will Open' 1913; 'The New Empire Opens' 1913; 'Mayer Opens' 1913).

Henry and Baker also used the Empire to solidify their political connections. So when native son Harry Flood Byrd climaxed his campaign for Governor on 3 August 1925, his final rally before the Democratic primary was an appearance on the stage of the Empire. (In Virginia, being nominated by the Democrats meant assured election.) Byrd's newspaper, *The Evening Star*, located several hundred feet from the Empire, urged supporters to crowd the theatre to 'Welcome Harry Home'. Some 300 extra seats were placed on the stage to accommodate the crowd. Byrd would go on to win, become Governor in February 1925, and define his state's politics for 40 years.

In 1927, Baker sold out to Hollywood's Universal studio, which in turn sold the Empire to Warner Bros two years later. Warner installed sound, and renamed the theatre 'the Capitol'.

Every Saturday, farmers poured into town. By dusk, a solid line of cars was cruising the block past the Capitol. All parking was taken; people sat in the cars and became part of the show. And the Capitol was filled with fans watching all their Hollywood favourites. The Capitol's manager, assistant manager, four ushers, 'candy girl' and doorman handled the crowds. A highlight came during the week of Lincoln's Birthday in February 1940, when the Capitol displayed flags of the Confederacy as it was showing *Gone with the Wind*.

During the late 1920s, and into the 1930s, Warner Bros had Winchester to itself. Then, on 15 October 1931, independent Herman Hable opened the Palace. Designed as an atmospheric cinema, with projected stars and clouds, glowing over a Spanish courtyard, the Palace had a 200-seat balcony for Blacks and 500 seats in its main auditorium for whites. Herman Hable erected large lighted sign that spanned Loudoun Street, which Main Street had been renamed, that blinked 'P-A-L-A-C-E', with each letter following the last. Hable was on the city council when the necessary special ordinance was passed – to help business downtown during the Great Depression (*Manufacturers Record*, 2 July 1931: 56; 'The Palace Theater' 1994).

Yet Warner Bros did not want to allow Hable to book any recent major studio pictures. Hable constantly struggled until he and Warner Bros created an informal split: Hable got Fox pictures, and those of all the minor studios, while the Capitol played Paramount, RKO, MGM and Warner Bros films. To differentiate his product, Hable pushed live country shows, booking the likes of Wally Fowler & His Oak Ridge Quartet, Grandpa Jones and His Grandchildren, and Cowboy Copas.

He began Saturday afternoon amateur shows in 1949 – with Jack Fretwell as master of ceremonies and Kenny Windell as piano player accompanist – to attract fans away from the Capitol, and the shows proved a hit with rural folks in town on Saturdays. The crowds were so large that Hable kept order with a corps of ushers wearing scarlet, double-breasted suit jackets with brass buttons, clip-on bow ties and blue pants with gold piping running along the sides. It was these conditions that began Patsy Cline's career (Advertisements, *The Winchester Star*, 21 September 1945: 12, 4 January 1950: 10).

Harrisonburg and gender

Harrisonburg's movie-going history offers an almost mirror image of that of Winchester. This is not unexpected. Harrisonburg was the next regional central place down The Valley Pike – some 68 miles south of Winchester. As in Winchester, movies were shown first in a public facility – the Assembly Hall on the second floor of the Rockingham County Courthouse. Likewise, all nickelodeons failed. In 1913 came the Virginia theatre, Harrisonburg's equivalent of Winchester's Empire, a 1000-seat live and motion picture venue. Through a complex deal, Warner Bros acquired the Virginia, and continued its run from the late 1920s to the early 1950s as the top theatre in town (*Film Daily Year Book* [subsequently FDYB] 1926: 589–759; 1928: 668; 1929: 724; 1931: 813; 1937: 995).

It would take outsiders, the Roth family, to expand Harrisonburg's movie-going opportunities. On 13 September 1934, the Roths opened the 650-seat State Theatre; four years later came the Strand, across the street. Jewish immigrant Morris Roth had started as a travelling show operator, going from town to town, renting high school gyms or local opera houses, to show his package of one-reelers, before he settled in Harrisonburg.

But Roth had a different audience – the presence of female college students from Madison College. So Harrisonburg could support three theatres between 1939 and 1949, when larger Winchester could support only two. Here was the gender difference as the all-female teachers college expanded movie-going options (FDYB 1952: 1137; 1949: 1013; 1970: 398).

In March 1908, the legislature of Virginia located a second all-female teacher training school in Harrisonburg. In 1913 the Virginia movie theatre took over these functions. To see films, the female students needed special written permission go downtown, but rarely got it. By 1920, films were being presented on campus, selected by the faculty. With the advent of talkies, more permissions were granted to go downtown. Through the 1930s, the college enrolment of females passed 1000 – no wonder the Roths opened their cinemas downtown (Dingledine 1959: 222–39).

In May 1941, a student revolt came to the newly named Madison College – pushing to further liberalize rules. Following agreement from college leaders, attendance at movies downtown increased dramatically. Students could go downtown on dates or in groups of three or four to the movies simply by signing out. The Virginia, State and Strand were packed. The audience of an extra 1300 female students of prime cinema-going age made Harrisonburg more of a cinema-going town than Winchester.

The Dalkes and small-town cinemas

There were six towns with populations of about 1000 along The Valley Pike between Harrisonburg and Winchester. All were more rural in cinema culture than Winchester or Harrisonburg, and all saw their first visit to the movies around the turn of the twentieth century from travelling show operators – with a projector showing outside in the summer and space rented in the colder months. Only after the nickelodeon era was over did Strasburg, Woodstock, Edinburg, Mt. Jackson, and New Market gain permanent cinemas. And, unlike the two bigger Valley towns, one local chain – Dalke's Valley Theatres – dominated all these small towns. Based in Woodstock, midway between Harrisonburg and Winchester, founder William Dalke and his son, William Jr, did not want to fight Warner Bros, and so chose not to invade Harrisonburg or Winchester (MGM Pictures 1945: 164).

Each of these towns was a fifth the size of Winchester or Harrisonburg, and they were located in a string of small towns all on The Valley Pike. Farming remained the dominant activity, with a mix of orchards, poultry houses, dairy herds and feed grain fields. Farmers never accounted for many people – fewer and fewer as mechanization replaced labour-intensive activities – but they stood at the core of county activities, and their towns functioned as trading centres.

Dalke's Valley Theatres territory started in Strasburg, 17 miles south of Winchester, and ended in New Market, 17 miles north of Harrisonburg. Dalke chose Woodstock as its headquarters because it was nearly in the middle between the two 'big towns'. In order down The Valley Pike, they had cinemas in Strasburg (1901 population in 1940), Woodstock (population 1552), Edinburg (500), Mount Jackson (600) and New Market (650). With populations so small, the bulk of their audiences came from rural folks living within driving distance of each community (Dalke 1996: 3).

Dalke built a nickelodeon on Main Street – the 350-seat Woodstock theatre. His wife Nora, from Mount Jackson, was the pianist; they settled in a house next door to the Woodstock, and made so much money that in 1925 they rented space located in the Holtzman Hotel, and constructed the 500-seat 'New' Theatre. The two theatres, located in a town with a population of 1580 (1930 Census), survived both the coming of sound and the Great Depression. It was not until the Valley began to recover that Dalke, in late 1937, decided to tear down the primitive Woodstock and build a new theatre on the same site. The Community opened on 22 September 1938, and the 'New' became the Uptown – surviving until a 1949 fire. At 650 seats, the Community was state of the art in cinema building – air-conditioned and designed for sound, not adapted to it (FDYB 1926: 589, 759; 1929: 724; 1931: 813; 1937: 995).

With a thriving cinema business in Woodstock, Dalke branched out: first to the north – to Strasburg, some 18 miles south of Winchester and 12 miles north of Woodstock. In 1921, he opened the Strand. His father-in-law lived upstairs and managed the 260-seat theatre at the centre of a town of just 650 people. In 1949, Dalke closed the Strand and replaced it with the ultra-modern 600-seat Home Theatre. During the early 1930s, they accepted script instead of money. They knew their audience – fellow Germans (Hageman 1986: 236; FDYB 1926: 589; 1929: 724; 1931: 813; 1937: 995; 1949: 974, 1138; 1960: 1082).

After expanding north, William Dalke Snr next moved south (towards Harrisonburg) to Mount Jackson, a classic small town of 600 people. In 1923, Dalke bought a small hall located next to his father-in-law's grain and feed store and turned it into the 275-seat New Theatre. Thus Dalke had defined his geographic space of dominance. By 1925, the Dalkes had theatres in Woodstock, Strasburg and Mt. Jackson. Thereafter, they would fill in – covering all small towns in Shenandoah County. Edinburg is but five and half miles south of Woodstock, and in 1926 Dalke took over the existing Pearl White theatre in a town of fewer than 600 people. In New Market, the final outpost of Dalke's Valley empire, they opened the 200-seat New Theatre in 1926. Later renamed the Hiway, this was Dalke's smallest cinema, managed by Anna Cornell, one of William Dalke Snr's sisters-in-law. Anna Cornell lived in an apartment above the theatre, and was one of a handful of female cinema managers in the Commonwealth of Virginia (Writer's Program 1940: 422; FDYB 1926: 589; 1931: 812; 1937: 994–95; 1949: 1138).

But from the mid-1920s through the 1950s, the Dalke theatres defined cinema culture in Shenandoah County. And since all had stages, they hosted live shows, beauty pageants, high school plays and graduations, and town meetings. The centrally located Community in Woodstock even hosted the likes of Gene Autry and Lash LaRue, plus professional country music shows, and the other events that required an auditorium, as none of the country's high schools had a permanent stage (Schwab 2003; Jenkins 2002).

Race, Virginia and the Valley

Because of relatively small populations of African Americans in the Valley, there never came to be any separate theatres for 'Negroes', as there were in all major Virginian cities. Yet racism was never far from Valley life. Winchester and Harrisonburg both relied upon African

Americans to perform menial labour as cooks, labourers, servants and maids. All towns and counties had separate churches, cemeteries, clubs and schools. With its German influence, the Valley had long been less extreme on race, but still followed the laws set by the elite leaders and politicians centred in Richmond. The Constitution of Virginia – rewritten in 1902 – saw Black Virginians (and poor whites) legally disenfranchised from voting, and from attending school together (Dailey 2000: 32–33).

From the beginning, the informal solution for movie theatres was segregation to the balcony – even in 250-seat movie houses. A former usher who worked at Winchester's Palace matter-of-factly stated:

[T]hey [African Americans] knew where they were supposed to sit when they came in. When folks from up North would come in, then we'd have some problems. Most of the time African Americans paid at the same box-office, and then climbed to what was called a 'crow's nest. (Noble 1997: B1)

Over time, this custom proved inadequate for the elite, so they mandated a legal solution. But this would not come until 1926. Harry Flood Byrd and his allies walked a fine line between custom and 'race laws'. Douglas Freeman, the editor of the *Richmond News Leader*, typified the racial attitudes held by most of Virginia's elite, arguing for the rightness of segregation, but in a gentle form. Freeman and Byrd preferred what they called 'separation by consent', an arrangement by which blacks and white would agree to lead separate lives as long as whites provided more equitable treatment than could be expected in the Deep South. Consistent with his philosophy, Byrd and Freeman denounced Klu Klux Klan extremists who threatened to undermine their visions of a 'gentile white supremacy' ('Separation by Consent' 1930).

However, in the 1920s the elite grew scared, and so more than in any other state in the United States Byrd passed laws to make sure the proper lines were legally drawn – cresting with two laws. In 1924 the legislature passed the *Racial Purity Act*, which classified Virginia citizens with even a drop of 'Negro' blood as not white. During the spring of 1926, legal racism crested when the Public Assemblages Bill was passed – requiring that at any gathering, including movie-going, the races must be separated. On 5 February 1926, the Bill passed the Virginia House of Delegates 63–3; on 9 March 1926 it passed the Virginia Senate 30–5; Governor Harry Flood Byrd permitted it to become law on 22 March 1926. Failure to enforce separate seating became a misdemeanour punishable by a fine for both operators and patrons. Operators could be fined $100 to $500, while patrons would be ejected from the theatre, not have their money returned and fined $10-$25 (Sherman 1988).

Significantly, Governor Harry Flood Byrd did not sign the law – preferring the separation to be handled by custom – but was unwilling to buck such overwhelming legislative votes. Here he reflected his Valley roots – he may have been a racist, but he was always a pragmatist. In the end, he sought to maintain his political machine, so did not buck the wishes of the elite. By keeping a relatively restrictive poll tax, Byrd and his elite supporters ruled as they saw fit from the 1920s to the 1960s. This was just another example of Byrd's vision. On one hand, he sponsored Virginia's anti-lynching law of 1928; on the other, he gave in to the forces that pushed to separate the races. In the end, he calculated how best to maintain his power – and it worked. Political scientist V.O. Key concluded at the middle of the twentieth century that, compared with Virginia, 'Mississippi, by contrast, [was] a hotbed of democracy' (Key 1950: 19–36).

Why the need for such a law? The push for legal separation in movie houses – the only such law ever passed in the United States – began innocently enough. On 21 February 1925, Grace B. Copeland arrived late for a dance recital at stately Ogden Hall of Hampton Institute, a Black-only state college. Copeland, white and the spouse of the owner/editor of the *Daily Press of Newport News*, was shown to a seat next to black patrons. Mixed seating was not uncommon at such schools – indeed, the faculty was by and large white. Through the performance she seethed, but as a member of the Virginia elite she did not make a fuss. However, Walter Copeland soon did, when he wrote and published on his editorial page:

> Here in this old Virginia community, rich in history and tradition, here where the first permanent white man's settlement was made, there is an institution which teaches and practices social equality between the white and Negro races.

He went on to warn that: 'Amalgamation would mean the destruction of the Anglo-Saxon race in America.' And he offered the initial call for a law separating the races in all places of public entertainment. His campaign would take just a year (Smith 1993: 13–65).

From the outset, Copeland and his allies defined themselves in opposition to the Klu Klux Klan, and asserted their intention to achieve their goals 'in the spirit of good sportsmanship and fair play on which rests all decency in personal relationships'. Copeland scored a coup when his proposal for a law to separate the races at all public assemblages was supported by the powerful newspaper, *The Richmond Times-Dispatch*. Virginia's Anglo-Saxon Clubs supported the proposal, and gave it a gentlemanly air. Both allied the elite in the push towards making the Act seem respectable. Delegate George Massenburg, a Democrat representing the portion of the Commonwealth within Copeland's sphere of newspaper influence, introduced the law as a personal favour ('The Chief and the Klan' 1921; 'White Ministers' 1921; *The Winchester Star* Advertisements, 8 July 1950: 12. 'Post No. 1' 1923).

Copeland found allies. One was Dr Walter A. Plecker, the long-time head of the state's Bureau of Vital Statistics, whose job it was to classify the state's population by race; he defended the Massenburg Bill in scientific terms. With Eugenics at its peak, he offered high-minded 'proof'. Noted concert pianist and Virginian John Powell was also an adherent of the Eugenics movement, which held that society and humankind's future could be improved by 'proper' breeding. In the North, this legislation was seen as an embarrassment. However, the Shenandoah Valley elite – led by Harry Flood Byrd – ignored the drive, and remained indifferent (Dorr 2000).

This proved the high point of the Eugenics movement in Virginia. The elite of the Valley simply went along. To theatre owners, the new law simply made custom a legal matter. The *Public Assemblages Act* seemed no radical step in 1926 in Virginia law, which in part stated:

> It shall be the duty of any person, firm, or institution conducting any public hall, theatre, motion picture show, or any place of public entertainment or assemblage which is attended by both white and colored persons, to separate the white race and the colored race …

The Byrd machine 'gentlemanly' avoided comment. Overt Southern white racists openly proclaimed that there were not enough troops in the US Army to force Virginians to admit African Americans into its theatres (Cooper and Morris 1976: 58; Guild 1936).

For 37 years, Virginia was the only state in the United States where it was illegal for whites and African-Americans to sit together in a movie theatre. Only in June 1963 was the law declared unconstitutional. Theatre after theatre in the Valley quickly and quietly desegregated. The Dalkes, for example, simply closed their balconies. Here the Valley was different (Sherman 1987; Greenberg 1959: 9).

Selection by the elite: state censorship

If segregation was imposed on Valley theatres, so were censored versions of films they could watch. Here again, the Valley elite seemed indifferent, but state leaders pushed for Virginia Censorship Board (later called Division), which commenced in 1922 and lasted until 1966. For 44 years, the Commonwealth of Virginia maintained a three-person Broad of Censors, who by law were required to approve all films shown. While in the 1910s, urban America – led New York City and Chicago – led the way to legal prior restraint, Virginia was among the last to climb aboard (*Mutual Film Corporation v Industrial Commission of Ohio*; MacGregor 1926: 168).

The genesis in Virginia came from religious leaders, following in the wake of the US Supreme Court's 1915 approval of a state's right to censor movies. In Virginia, the first censorship Bill was introduced in the legislature in 1918. Supporters blamed a rise in juvenile crime, an increase in alcohol consumption and other criminal activities on the negative effects of the movies. They saw students draw away from their studies to the movie show, and argued that all this 'proof' demanded a state censor board. The initial proposal failed, and was brought up again – and again. By 1922, Virginia's Episcopalians – the church of the elite – argued for 'cleaner' movies. Methodists were outraged by the moral decay, and decline portrayed by Hollywood. These powerful religious organizations brought enough pressure so the legislature and governor went along. Valley religious leaders proved indifferent to the issue. German Lutherans, particularly in rural Shenandoah county, did not see what all the fuss was about. Mennonites and United Brethren sects did not care, as they simply prohibited their members from going to any movie – state approved or not (Shepherd 2001: 127–28; *Richmond Times-Dispatch*, 28 February 1922: 1).

The Virginia Censorship Board came into being on 1 August 1922. Eight years later, as Harry Flood Byrd was ending his term as Governor, the board became a formal division under the Attorney-General. Through its history, its three members were appointed by the Byrd political machine, and paid modest salaries to watch and judge all movies produced, including newsreels. The Board could also censor printed movie advertising, and movie trailers as well (educational films were exempt). The exhibitor paid a fee of $2 per reel, which amounted to thousands of dollars of revenue for the Commonwealth per year. Fines for violation ranged from $25 to $100. Since nearby Maryland and Pennsylvania also had Boards, Valley movie-goers sometimes saw three seals – in about ten seconds – at the beginning of each Hollywood distributed feature and short (Virginia State Board of Censors 1923).

The politics was one of appeasement by the Democratic political machine headed by Harry Flood Byrd. While he would become famous for his streamlining of state government, and elimination of dozens of agencies, in this rare case he stated in his inaugural address: 'I construe my election [as Governor] as a mandate to me as a businessman to institute the best methods of efficiency and economy in State affairs … Useless offices must be abolished …' But not a Censor Board (Hawkes 1974).

Indeed, the Board was so well accepted that it was not until 15 years after its passage that a test case was brought. On 26 February 1940, the Virginia Supreme Court ruled state law trumped any local decision. Since a state Censorship Board existed, and had approved the film in question, a local authority could not step in and stop its presentation. The test case involved *The Birth of a Baby*, a 1938 film that documented the human experience, but outraged the citizens of Lynchburg, Virginia. The film was produced not by Hollywood, but by the American Committee for Maternal Welfare, and financed by Mead, Johnson, a maker of baby food. The American Medical Association, the American Hospital Association and the US Public Health Service endorsed this 72-minute educational film. Yet the city manager of Lynchburg, a crossing site of the James River – not in the Valley – and about 100 miles south-east of Harrisonburg, declared it obscene, and sued to stop its showing. He lost since the state Board approved it (*City of Lynchburg v Dominion Theaters*; Heinemann 1996: 32–36).

The original three censors included Evan Chesterman, chair with Mrs Emma Speed Sampson and R.C.L. Moncure. All were white elite Democrats.

By its final decade, the Board was wholly composed of widowed wealthy noblesse oblige Democrat females. Many stayed on for several four-year terms, always rotating the chair. This was a minor pay-off for loyal members of the Byrd machine. They worked closely with the Hays Office, and so increasingly saw themselves as a buffer between Hollywood's industrial self-regulation and the particular values – especially on race – of Virginia. The Board objected to any depiction of interracial contact, any negative portrayal of whites in favour of blacks, and any images that they deemed showed the potential for interracial violence ('Films Rejected' 1922; *International Motion Picture Almanac* 1937–38: 1030; 1940–41: 789; 1945–46: 741; 1950–51: 697; 1955: 934; 1959: 722).

Valley residents missed many of Hollywood's greatest films. For example, a dust-up of complaints in the early 1930s came about over gangster films. Since, for example, Warner Bros was a major producer of these, such as *Little Caesar* and *Public Enemy*, the versions Valley residents saw and heard – at Winchester's Capitol and Harrisonburg's Virginia theatre surely – were not even close to the originals, but sanitized prints. In its 44 years, the Board viewed nearly 53,000 films, requiring about 2400 eliminations and just under 160 out-right rejections. Valley residents would have to await film preservation to see whole versions of movies that had been sanitized by outsiders (*Variety*, 19 January 1966: 24; 9 March 1966: 13).

Religion and movie-going

On Saturday, 6 September 1947, the headline on page 1 of Harry Flood Byrd's own *Winchester Star* newspaper blared: 'Sunday Movies Promised, Beginning September 28'. Based upon state court decisions, and faced with two TV stations beaming in from Washington, DC – with a third promised for October – Winchester picture palaces – Warner's Capitol and Hable's Palace – decided to present movies on Sundays for the first time. Management accommodated religious leaders by first offering afternoon screenings, then 'going dark' so people could attend evening services, and then reopening for a 9.00 p.m. screening. The state law permitting only 'necessary' activities to be performed on Sunday had become, in the words of one town official, 'antiquated'. Indeed, Warner Bros officials declared Sunday screenings a 'public service', noting that for a long time 'everybody has demanded them'. The leading ministers stated their regrets, but went along – almost surprised that it had taken so long. Here Winchester (and Harrisonburg) did not set the trend ('Sunday Movies Promised' 1947; 'Ministerial Assn. Regrets' 1947).

In contrast, ministerial pressure was not strong in Shenandoah County. William Dalke sensed that realities brought about by the Great Depression would lead even the most devout of his fellow Lutherans not to object to evening Sunday movie shows. So, beginning during the Christmas season of 1938, Dalke staged Sunday benefit movie screenings in his small-town cinemas. Sunday showings were common through World War II, as folks worked longer hours because the 'boys' were overseas. Lutherans did not possess an anti-movie-going belief, and this made all the difference. A Lutheran elite did not control Winchester, and so it took longer there. In contrast, Woodstock – where Dalke lived – had just one small Roman Catholic church, with no political connections like his, and even smaller fundamentalist Christian sects that opposed movies as 'evil' – no matter what day of the week it was. In the Valley, where the Lutheran Church was king, church leaders followed what was stated in the official *Lutheran Encyclopedia*:

The church should under all circumstances seek to make use of its right [in the USA] to cooperate with the motion picture industry.... [As part of pastoral care] Lutheran ministers [are] urged to counsel movie choices, but not dictate them.'

Lutherans went along with the Hays Code, and the Dalkes knew of Virginia's Board of Censors so business proved good – Sunday was the best day after Saturday (Bodensieck 1959: 850–81; Wust 1969: 77–249).

Other religious sects found a degree of comfort in the Hays Code and the Virginia Censorship Board, yet simply would not buck centuries-old Blue Laws that restricted activities on the Christian Sabbath. At first they opposed the automobile as 'the devil's wagon', but soon realized the Model-T Ford made 'going to town' easier – both on Saturday to shop and attend a show, and on Sunday to attend services. Strident Christian pastors quoted the Fourth Commandment: 'Remember the Sabbath day, to keep it holy'. Yet as the twentieth century progressed, even the strictest ministers agreed that 'works of necessity' – to quote the Virginia Blue Law – should be allowed, but fought modernism in a slow retreat. The Great Depression surely signalled that they were fighting a losing battle, as more and more folks who needed the work – as in the case of the Dalkes – or simply wanted to see a show and relax were willing to ignore the 'old-fashioned' Blue Laws (Hill 1984: 163–229).

Cinemas did not want the bad publicity of an arrest, so sensitive owners such as William Dalke advertised screenings as 'Sunday benefits'. Martin Quigley's *Motion Picture Almanac* of 1936–37 recognized that changes were afoot when in this edition it offered its first summary – state by state – of Sunday show legislation and court decisions. In 1931, the Arkansas legislature passed 'local option' legalization, nearby Maryland opened cinemas in Baltimore, Montgomery, Prince George's, Cecil, and St Mary's counties by vote of their residents, and Texas, New Jersey and New York repealed their Blue Laws for movie shows. Two years later, North Dakota and Wisconsin followed suit; two years after that Pennsylvania legalized Sunday shows. In states like Mississippi and West Virginia, Sunday screenings remained illegal, but exhibitors ran shows any way, and paid their fines as a 'cost of doing business' (*International Motion Picture Almanac* 1936–37: 1316–17; Dilloff 1980: 695–97).

Virginians tested their law. In 1935, a Norfolk court held that motion pictures were 'works of necessity', and thus not prevented. A year later, a Richmond court permitted Sunday shows so long as the monies collected were contributed to charity, and a jury in Charlottesville failed to convict a theatre operator. In 1939, a court declared that Sunday screenings were legal in Arlington county. Then, in 1942, came *Williams v Commonwealth*, where the Supreme Court of Virginia approved Sunday shows if the monies went to charity. Three members of the court dissented, arguing there should be no restrictions at all as 'movies were work of necessity as was required by the law'. Still, as in the case of Winchester, it would take local negotiation to determine that no bad publicity would result (*Williams v Commonwealth*; Virginia Advisory Legislative Council 1963: 10–20; *Motion Picture Herald*, 31 October 1936: 18; 10 October 1942: 47; *International Motion Picture Almanac* 1937–38: 937–38; 1940–41: 792).

World War II had pushed the issue to its limits, as workers laboured around the clock. One report from Richmond from October 1942 noted that Sunday was the biggest day of the week for the movie business, as war workers had plenty of money to spend. With a

2.00 p.m. opening, movie houses did such good business on Sundays that all tickets for the rest of the day were sold before the first show ended at 4.00 p.m. Sunday afternoons were particularly crowded because of the servicemen on leave, coming from several army camps located nearby. It seemed unreasonable not to open the door to movies as a 'necessity' of modern life. It was surprising that such a breakthrough took so long in Winchester, but Harry Flood Byrd had by then turned to protecting the past rather than operating government like a modern business (*Motion Picture Herald*, 24 October 1942: 46; *Film Daily Yearbook* 1949: 935).

Theatre owners had long resented that radio listeners could tune in any day of the week – and indeed Sunday night broadcasts were the most popular of the week. They lived with that. But the coming of television seemed unfair. As Valley farmers raised TV antennae in 1947 to pick up Washington, DC signals, movie theatre owners' resentment boiled over. It was no wonder that Winchester theatre owners washed aside their self-imposed Sunday screening prohibition in October 1947, the beginning of the first true television season, with three stations airing from the nation's capital into the Valley. In this particular case, TV really did matter (*Mandell v Hadden*; *Malibu Auto Parts v Virginia*; Laband and Heinbuch 1987: 131–33).

Learning from regional movie-going

Movie-going in the Valley of Virginia was typified by thousands of fans like Virginia Hensley. Farm families and their small town cousins patronized the movies in equal numbers across class lines – save Harry Flood Byrd's elite. These fans are not celebrated in the histories of Virginia, but Warner Bros and its competitors from the 1920s through the 1950s offered them the whole of the Hollywood corpus as sanitized by the Censorship Board. While the major studios provided all the films, the bulk of the theatres in the Valley were owned and operated as independents – by Herman Hable, the Roths and the Dalkes. Hable and the Roths were true outsiders – Jews drawn to opportunities denied in other professions by rapid anti-Semitism of the day. In the more rural Shenandoah county, the Lutheran Dalkes personified the status quo, and reflected the values of their neighbours – again save the restrictions imposed by segregation and Blue Laws.

The uniting variable was The Valley Pike, which enabled prosperous and poor farmers alike to be able to drive to town to see a show. One 1946 study by Leo Handel indicated that they would drive up to 10 miles on average to go to the movies. This was approximately the average distance between towns along The Valley Pike. Historians have long argued that the break in this movie-going continuity came with the introduction of television, yet Valley residents only slowed their rate of movie attendance, even as they could get three stations as early as the fall of 1947. The opening of a TV station in Harrisonburg in 1953 simply meant less listening to radio and more watching of TV. Movie attendance remained relatively strong so long as the ritual of going to town on Saturday persisted.

Yet the Valley was invaded by more than television. Different in many fundamental ways from the rest of its Commonwealth, Richmond imposed a state Censorship Board and legal segregation. There was no movement in the Valley for these measures; the Byrd machine forced them upon the area. The Byrd machine gave in reluctantly to Sunday screenings, even as dominant Lutheran doctrine embraced the new medium. Thus the Byrd political machine meant much more than building roads and streamlining government. It also meant severe constraints on movie-going – the most severe found in the United States during this period. Byrd reached out and imposed restrictions on rural lifestyles as much as did any religious doctrine. Still, our best evidence indicates that Valley residents saw movies about as early as people in the cities; they had mini-picture palaces, and saw all Hollywood produced. An image of rural isolation needs to be abandoned because The Valley Pike offered such a powerful social and cultural connective tissue.

However, that ended in the 1960s when Interstate-81 replaced The Valley Pike. The new highway did NOT go through downtowns past existing theatres, but paralleled The Valley Pike to the east. In time, shopping malls – including multiplexes – came where I-81 crossed the main road into town. By the late 1960s, there was no reason to go downtown to shop, and the weekly Saturday ritual was ruptured as one could easily drive to the mall in less time. In the Valley in the 1960s, the Interstate altered the society and culture just as paving of The Valley Pike and the coming of the automobile had done half a century earlier. And this radical break created a movie culture just as it did in suburbanized America.

References

Bodensieck, J. (ed) (1959), *The Encyclopedia of the Lutheran Church* Minneapolis, MN: Augburg Publishing House.

'The Chief and the Klan', *The Norfolk Virginian-Pilot*, 18 September 1921, p. 6.

City of Lynchburg v Dominion Theaters 175 Va. 35 or 7 S.E.2d 157 (1940).

Cooper, W. and Morris, T.R. (1976), *Virginia Government and Politics*, Charlottesville, VA: University Press of Virginia.

Dabney, V. (1971), *Virginia: The New Dominion*, Charlottesville, VA: University Press of Virginia.

Dailey, J. (2000), *Before Jim Crow: The Politics of Post-emancipation Virginia*, Chapel Hill, NC: University of North Carolina Press.

Dalke, A. (1996), 'The History of Dalke's Theatres, Inc', unpublished manuscript.

Dilloff, N.J. (1980), 'Never on Sunday: The Blue Laws Controversy', *Maryland Law Review*, 39: 4, pp. 695–97.

Dingledine, R.C. Jr (1959), *Madison College: The First Fifty Years*, Harrisonburg, VA: Madison College.

Dorr, G.M. (2000), 'Assuring America's Place in the Sun: Ivey Foremen Lewis and the Teaching of Eugenics at the University of Virginia, 1915–1953', *The Journal of Southern History*, 46: 2, pp. 257–95.

Gomery, D. (2011), *Patsy Cline: The Making of an Icon*, Bloomington, IN: Trafford.

Greenberg, J. (1959), *Race Relations and the Law*, New York: Columbia University Press, 1959.

Guild, J.P. (1936), Black Laws of Virginia: A Summary of the Legislative acts of Virginia Concerning Negroes, New York: Whittet & Shepperson.

Hagemann, J. (1986), The *Heritage of Virginia*, Norfolk, VA: The Donning Company.

Hamilton Suter, S. (1999), *Shenandoah Valley Folklife*, Jackson, MS: University Press of Mississippi.

Hatch, A. (1969), *The Byrds of Virginia*, New York: Holt.

Handel, L. (1950), *Hollywood Looks at Its Audience*, Urbana, IL: University of Illinois Press.

Hawkes, R.T. (1974), 'The Emergence of a Leader: Harry Flood Byrd, Governor of Virginia, 1926–1930', *The Virginia Magazine of History and Biography*, 82: 3, pp. 259–81.

Heinemann, R.L. (1996), *Harry Byrd of Virginia*, Charlottesville, VA: University Press of Virginia.

Hill, S.S. (ed.) (1984), *Encyclopedia of Religion in the South*, Mercer, GA: Mercer University Press.

Jenkins, B. (2002), 'Family Affair', *The Winchester Star*, 3 April, p. A3.

Key, V.O. Jr (1950), *Southern Politics in State and Nation*, New York: Knopf.

Laband, D.N. and Hendry Heinbuch, D. (1987), *Blue Laws: The History, Economics, and Politics of Sunday-Closing Laws*, Lexington, MA: Lexington Books.

Malibu Auto Parts v Virginia 218 Va. 453 (1977).

Mandell v Hadden 202 Va. 979 (1961).

'Ministerial Assn. Regrets Opening of Sunday Movies' (1947), *The Winchester Star*, 11 September, p. 1.

MGM Pictures (1945), *Motion Picture Showmen: A Compilation of Biographies*, privately published.

MacGregor, F.H. (1926) 'Official Censorship Legislation', *The Annals of the American Academy of Political and Social Science*, 28, p. 168.

Mutual Film Corporation v Industrial Commission of Ohio 236 U.S. 230.

Noble, S. (1997), 'The Palace's Reel Life', *The Winchester Star*, 22 November, p. B1.

Pickeral, J.J. and Fogg, G. (1930), 'An Economic and Social Survey of Frederick County', *University of Virginia Record Extension Series*, 15: 2, pp. 9–18.

'Post No. 1, Anglo-Saxon Clubs, Has 400 Members' (1923), *The Richmond News Leader*, 5 June, p. 18.

Ramsaye, T. (ed.) (1933), *International Motion Picture Almanac*, New York: Quigley.

Ringgold, G. and Bodeen, D. (1969), *The Films of Cecil B. DeMille*, New York: Citadel Press.

Rouse, P. Jr (1995), *The Great Wagon Road*, Richmond, VA: The Dietz Press.

Salmon, E.J. and Campbell E.D.C. Jr (1994), *The Hornbook of Virginia History*, Charlottesville, VA: University Press of Virginia.

Schwab, T. (2002), '90th Anniversary', *Northern Virginia Daily*, 30 April, p. A8.

'Separation by Consent', *The Richmond News Leader*, 20 May, p. 8.

Shepherd, S.C. Jr (2001), *Avenues of Faith: Shaping the Urban Religious Culture of Richmond, Virginia, 1900–1929*, Tuscaloosa: University of Alabama Press, 2001.

Sherman, R.B. (1987), 'The "Teachings at Hampton Institute": Social Equality, Racial Integrity, and the Virginia Public Assemblage Act of 1926', *The Virginia Magazine of History and Biography*, 95: 1, pp. 275–300.

—— (1988), '"The Last Stand": The Fight for Racial Integrity in Virginia in the 1920s', *The Journal of Southern History*, 54: 1, pp. 69–92.

Smith, J.D. (1993), *The Eugenic Assault on America*, Fairfax, VA: George Mason University Press.

'Sunday Movies Promised, Beginning September 28' (1947), *The Winchester Star*, 11 September, p. 1.

Virginia Advisory Legislative Council (1963), *The Virginia Laws Relating to Working or Transacting Business on Sunday: Report to the Governor and the General Assembly*, Richmond, VA: Commonwealth of Virginia, Department of Purchases and Supply.

Virginia State Board of Censors (1923), '1923 Censorship Law and Rules and Regulations' (Richmond, 1923), p. 3, copy located in folder entitled 'Motion Picture Censorship', Box 44, Executive Papers, Harry F. Byrd, 1926–30, Library of Virginia.

Wayland, J.W. (1967), *The Valley Turnpike*, Winchester, VA: The Historical Society.

'White Ministers Would Not Help Check Ku Klux' (1921), *The Norfolk Journal and Guide*, 7 May, p. 1.

Williams v Commonwealth 179 Va. 741 (1942).

Writer's Program of the Works Projects Administration in the State of Virginia, Virginia (1940), *A Guide to the Old Dominion*, New York: Oxford University Press.

Wust, K. (1969), *The Virginia Germans*, Charlottesville, VA: University Press of Virginia.

Chapter 11

From Mom-and-Pop to Paramount-Publix: Selling the Community on the Benefits of National Theatre Chains

Jeffrey Klenotic

Advertising is selling. This selling, as far as it applies to the theatre, exerts its influence in activities which are practically countless.(Sam Katz, President of Publix Theatres 1929, in Gomery 2002: 131).

By the late 1920s, Hollywood's major studios – including Paramount, Warner Bros, Fox, MGM and RKO – held broad national holdings of first- and second-run theatres in large urban markets. Historical research on the economics of these theatres foregrounds the centrally managed, chain-store business strategies that were used to rationalize and integrate previously local or regional spheres of exhibition (Gomery 1992: 34–82; see also Gomery 1978, 1979a, 1979b, 1985, 2002). This chapter reframes economic accounts of the rise of national theatre chains within a cultural studies paradigm that considers not only the viewpoint of production and industry but also that of reception and community (Allen 2006; Hall 1981, 1993; Hoggart 1957; Jancovich et al. 2003; Johnson 1986–87; Klenotic 1996a, 1996b, 2007; Maltby 2006; Thompson 1963). To illustrate this approach, a study of the 1929 grand opening of the Paramount Theatre in Springfield, Massachusetts is presented.

In 1928, influential film exhibitor and managerial consultant Harold Franklin observed: 'The motion picture theatre is the most representative building in many communities and probably entertains within its walls more persons than repair to any other' (Franklin 2002: 123). When the Paramount Theatre opened in Springfield a year later, it lent credence to Franklin's statement by immediately becoming one of the city's landmark buildings: a deluxe movie palace with 3200 seats built at a cost of US$1.1 million ('New Paramount Theatre' 1929: 2G). But while the theatre did represent the community, it was not locally owned. Instead, it was owned by Publix Corporation, an affiliate of Paramount Studios. Publix was the largest of the studio chains and, as Douglas Gomery (2002) has shown, the company 'took the localism out of movie exhibition. Gone was the power of the local manager. Under Publix control they became glorified janitors. Power would forever go to the national office' (2002: 134). How, then, was this transfer of social, cultural and economic power discursively articulated? How were the delocalizing effects of this process made sense of and legitimized, both in the main office and on the ground? To explicate the cultural politics of community consent to studio-integrated theatres, the homogenizing strategies of chain store operations must be placed in the context of what Maltby (2007, 2011) and Bowles et al. (2011) call a 'cinema history', as opposed to a 'film history', perspective that explores the tactical meanings these theatres held for audiences and other groups within the community. In Springfield, such an analysis reveals that the reception of the Paramount had as much to do with property values, taxes, job-creation, debates over the built environment and problems coping with urban modernization as it did with the attractions of famous players in famous plays.

The economics of chains

It was via the chain-store strategy of exhibition that the film industry merged 'into the mainstream of mass-retailing, big-business practice' sweeping the United States after World War I (Gomery 1985: 219). Inspired by grocery chains and department stores, film studios guided the distribution and marketing of movies in line with other commodities. Movies were circulated as disposable consumer goods, and movie palaces afforded luxurious settings for packaging and presenting these goods to buyers. Palaces also offered hospitality services – plush seating, air conditioning, attentive ushers, doormen, smoking lounges, nursing care, children's rooms – that supported and enhanced the consumer's purchasing decision (Franklin 2002; Gomery 2002). Major studios sought to brand their goods and services in distinctive ways that consumers could recognize and differentiate. Soon, the film business 'resembled typical American industries – its production, distribution, and exhibition branches corresponded to the manufacturing, wholesaling, and retailing activities of other firms' (Balio 1985: 122). Hollywood's push for vertical integration also reflected larger trends in industry, which was developing along oligopolistic and monopolistic lines, with fewer companies garnering a larger share of overall business and profits (Huettig 1944; Porter 2006).

Economic studies of exhibition bring exemplary sophistication and elegance to our understanding of the strategies driving studio expansion into theatre ownership. Yet the clarity of such accounts depends upon a top-down approach to the problem of explaining how control over urban film exhibition shifted from localism to centralized planning and national standardization. For the most part, this shift is seen to have occurred without public engagement or even discursive mediation from the resident population. Major studios simply imposed their power over exhibition because they realized that such expansion was in their best economic interests.

But where is the community in this process? Usually the community is reduced to the audience, and the audience is reduced to the large crowds that rushed to movie palaces signalling increased demand for this type of venue. From the industry's perspective, lumping individual ticket sales into an aggregate measure of demand makes sense because one ticket ostensibly equals one satisfied customer, and the theatre that sells the most tickets is judged the most popular and successful in the community. Viewed from the bottom up, however, there is little reason to believe the myriad experiences of several thousand people who purchased tickets to access a theatre's amenities, attractions and films (or simply as an excuse to get out of the house) all amounted to the same thing. A significant problem with box office as a measure of satisfaction is that movie tickets – like most purchases – are paid for before goods and services are delivered but, unlike other retailers, cinemas offer no guarantees as to the quality of their wares. Dislike a movie and you may be told there is no accounting for taste. Dislike a seat and you may be granted a new one but not refunded your money. With the exception of the film projector breaking down completely, the show must and will go on. A ticket therefore represents a pre-test expression of consumer *interest* rather than a post-test measure of satisfaction, and consumer interest forms from a range of social, cultural, economic and geographic factors (Schudson 1984) that have little to do with the merits of a film or theatre. Indeed, historical case studies of movie-going, exhibition and reception find wide diversity in motivations for cinema attendance and meanings of cinema experiences (Stokes and Maltby 1999, 2004; Maltby et al. 2007; Fuller-Seeley 2008; Maltby et al. 2011).

The problem that emerges here is central to any attempt to explain how Hollywood came to dominate local, regional and national cultures in the United States. In most economic analyses, the community's role in the rise of studio-owned theatre chains is considered only by proxy of a film's box office and length of run (Hanssen 2010). Audiences are viewed as rational consumers in the film market, rather than as grounded inhabitants of local geography who have social, emotional and economic investments in their senses of place and space (Tuan 1977), inhabitants who might be concerned (or at least aware) when the power to control an important local institution has been transferred from mom-and-pop down the street into the hands of distant Hollywood monopolists.

It was just such concern about the loss of local control that inspired widespread popular and legislative revolts against chain stores in general. Daniel Scroop, for instance, finds that:

> [T]he idea that punitive taxation was required to protect local communities from the pernicious influence of the chains was far from being novel. In fact, chain store taxes were the most concrete achievement of the great wave of anti-chain store protest that swept through the United States in the 1920s and 1930s. (2008: 925)

For Scroop, the anti-chain store movement was founded upon 'a political-economic perspective deeply indebted to the antimonopoly tradition, which was based on hostility toward large aggregations of economic and political power' (2008: 927).[1] Godfrey Lebhar, editor of *Chain Store Age*, similarly concluded that 'in the second decade of the century, chain-store expansion in all lines had been so active that by the early '20s the movement was being widely discussed as a menace to the existing order' (1952: 112). For Lebhar, the main criticism against chain stores had to do with 'price-cutting' facilitated by economies of scale that made local retailers unable to compete on price. While Lebhar found no evidence that chains killed independent retail – in fact, he was adamant that chains helped local retailers grow stronger[2] – he did believe that concerns about price-cutting intensified fears that chains were driving mom-and-pop stores out of business, which was seen as detrimental to the quality of residents' cultural life. Transient chain store managers shipped in from out of town may have 'the same abilities of leadership and the same community spirit that the former local leaders had' but 'generally speaking … and through no fault of their own, they do not have the same vital personal interest in the affairs of the community' (1952: 293).

To what extent did broader controversies about chain stores apply to national cinema chains? Simply put, we don't yet know – a lack of studies on the reception of movie palaces makes it difficult to answer this question with authority. However, on the issue of price-cutting, the film industry did stand in contrast to other chain retailers. As Gomery explains, with 'the run-zone-clearance system setting fixed prices, ever lower as one awaited the next run, the Publix promotion staff could not herald what most chain stores did: lower prices. Instead they sought to induce the potential patron to pay top dollar' (2002: 131). Because of this, national theatre chains may have received less public hostility than other chains when it came to fears about mom-and-pop being driven out of business. Nonetheless, within those mom-and-pop theatres themselves, and within the US government as well, vigorous antipathy was building against Hollywood's monopolistic tendencies (Dale 1939: 253).

Hollywood addressed its critics through the Motion Picture Producers and Distributors of America (MPPDA), which used public relations to 'neutralize public opinion' by channelling MPPDA power through a vast network of women's clubs (Dale 1939: 255–57). Women's clubs were among the industry's most vocal critics. They expressed particular concern about the questionable selection of movies in neighbourhood theatres frequented by children (Klenotic 2001). In response, the managers of these theatres complained that studio booking practices forced them to take blocks of morally objectionable pictures under the terms required to obtain 'better' films. Amidst these concerns about Hollywood's pernicious influence on local culture, the MPPDA sought to focus community fears and hostilities on films rather than theatres. Since the source of Hollywood's wealth lay not in films but in real estate (Huettig 1944), public perception of theatres – especially studio-run palaces – had to be protected at all costs. As Paul Moore (2008) puts it, studios 'held generous amounts of real estate in all major cities ... incredibly valuable because much of it was downtown. The city was, in a sense, being shaped and changed by moving picture theatres, not the other way around' (2008: 110). In light of the shifting balance between local and national influence, and with the powerful anti-chain store movement ever looming, national cinema chains were never more than a hair's breadth from being lumped in with local concerns over 'immoral' film content and block-booking.

While it is reasonable to interpret audience attendance as a sign of tacit support for a theatre's presence in the community, using box office as the lone indicator of the community as a whole obscures knowledge about the nature of that support. Without exploring the 'structures of feeling' (Williams 1977: 128–35) in a given place and time, we have little hope of understanding *why* communities bought into an exhibition system dominated by national corporations, and *how* residents made sense of absentee-owned movie palaces as features of the local landscape.

Springfield's Paramount Theatre

A case study of one studio's expansion into an urban setting can illuminate the complex discursive structures through which shifts in social, cultural and economic power were articulated across local, regional and national layers of experience and influence. On 28 September 1929 in Springfield, Massachusetts, Publix Corporation opened what at that time became the city's largest theatre and New England's newest deluxe movie palace.[3] The opening of the 3200-seat Paramount Theatre was met with great fanfare and no discernible protests. Advertising copy heralded the tremendous public reception:

> They came, they saw, and they went away shouting. Thousands of people stormed the doors of the Springfield Paramount Theatre yesterday and saw the greatest show they had ever seen!! Shouting the praises of the magnificent palace of amusement. (Publix 1929b: 7F)

Publix's interest in Springfield reflected the Corporation's rise to dominance on the regional, national and international levels. Publix was formed in 1925 when Famous Players-Lasky merged its chain of nearly 500 theatres with Chicago's Balaban and Katz chain (Gomery 2002: 128). The new entity, now called Paramount-Publix, launched a furious process of accumulation and consolidation of holdings. This process peaked in September 1929, when plans of a merger between Paramount-Publix and Warner Bros were announced. The new company was to be named Paramount-Vitaphone, and would include 'over 1700 theatres, six motion picture studios, CBS, the Columbia Phonograph Company, and Warner's vast holdings in music publishing' (Gomery 1979a: 37). Threatened by President Herbert Hoover's administration with anti-trust action, the merger never closed, though Paramount did acquire a 50 per cent stake in the CBS radio network (Gomery 2002: 130). Even without Warner Bros, Paramount's Publix Theatres remained the 'largest, most profitable, and most powerful motion picture circuit in cinema history', and by May 1930 held '1200 theatres, dominating the southern United States, New England, and the states of Michigan, Illinois, Minnesota, Iowa, Nebraska, and the Dakotas. Through Famous Players Canadian, Publix extended its hegemony to Canada' (Gomery 1985: 225–26). Springfield's Paramount Theatre was the final screw in the company's tightening control over the New England region. Edward Cuddy, Publix's District Manager for Springfield, put a positive spin on these developments when he appealed to a perceived desire of Springfield residents for national status:

> The Publix Theatres Corporation, which also operates the Broadway here, now has 110 theatres in New England and 1100 in the entire country. The Springfield theatres will be a link in a chain that includes the Paramount in New York City and the Metropolitan in Boston, two of the leading theatres in the country. ('Paramount to Open' 1929)

Because its power relied on popular consent, and because its rapid expansion roused anti-trust concerns within federal government, Publix spent much effort devising a publicity and advertising discourse that framed monopolistic practices within the context of local service and the 'publix' well-being. This discourse articulated the benefits of big business for cultural uplift, social assimilation and democratic egalitarianism. These linkages were made in many ways, but often they took the form of a pledge. A ten-page section of the local newspaper devoted to the opening of Springfield's Paramount contained the following 'Publix Pledge to the People of New England' from J.J. Fitzgibbons, Director of Theatre Operations, New England Division:

> PUBLIX, in all of its theatres, pledges entertainment that is the best obtainable. This high standard can be maintained because of our dominating position in the film industry. Always a good clean show.
>
> PUBLIX has but one standard for relations with its patrons – the height of courtesy. The comfort, well-being and safety of those who attend our theatres is our first thought. (Fitzgibbons 1929)

The first half of the pledge posited a causal relation between monopoly power ('our dominating position in the film industry') and the 'high standard' of entertainment. Smaller companies, it was implied, lacked the resources to produce uplifting shows that were consistently inoffensive to local citizens. The second half of the pledge then shifted from production to exhibition, justifying monopoly power because of its capacity to ensure the safety of movie palaces as sites for interclass and inter-ethnic mixing – sites designed, as Lary May puts it, for 'merging low life with high life' (1980: 152). If Paramount movies and shows were to reflect the highest standards of refined culture, then Publix theatres had to provide safe, comfortable environments where genteel audiences would not feel threatened by those matriculating from below. It was only through the integration of exhibition and production, the integration of local culture into a national standard, that all this uplift could be achieved.

Another pledge stated in stronger terms the link Publix sought to establish between reaching out to all classes and ethnic groups on the one hand, and upholding genteel norms of civility as the standard to which all aspired on the other:

> Publix … is the realization of future hope for an industry that progressed from a disreputable gypsy origin into an honored and civilized force that is felt and appreciated from the tiniest crossroads hamlet theatre to the splendor-castles of the mightiest metropolis. (Publix 1929c)

Publix here turned itself into a metaphor for the civilizing rise of mass culture by stereotyping and disowning its own 'gypsy' heritage. This disavowal of the old days of 'disreputable' nickelodeons and low-brow films spoke to several classes of patrons. To the immigrant working classes, Publix presented itself as a model of assimilation, framing stubborn adherence to ethnic traditions and past ways of life as blocking the path to success, acceptance and civility. To the emergent middle and established upper classes, Publix made a pledge of allegiance, a promise to behave, to respect and propagate polite society's codes of conduct and consciousness as universal ideals.

As these pledges suggest, Publix justified its monopolistic growth by virtue of an enhanced ability to effect an egalitarian dispersal of cultural capital on a national scale. Distinctions between urban high-class culture and rural low-class culture were dissolved, as 'the tiniest hamlet theatre' was raised by studio integration to a standard on par with the 'splendor-castles of the mightiest metropolis'. However, rather than raising all boats equally, such discursive efforts to flatten culture into one universal standard achieved the exact opposite result of increasing the distinction between metropolitan and all other forms of movie-going. As Kathy Fuller puts it:

> The local Bijou on Main Street was increasingly an insufficient outlet for consumer-culture-driven fantasies; as one Iowa exhibitor reported, people in small towns wanted the standards of movie presentation found in the big cities. Even setting their sights higher did not help, for no matter how elegant the large town and small city's mini-palaces strove to be, they were continually outclassed by the ever more huge and overblown big-city palaces. (Fuller 1996: 112)

For Springfield, which in population had become a 'big city' but by measure of cultural distinction was still considered provincial in its tastes, Publix emphasized how its new deluxe movie palace brought the city closer to the refinement and status of New York and Chicago. Accordingly, the entertainment presented for the grand opening appealed to Springfield's metropolitan ambitions and national aspirations (see Figure 11.1). The program included a filmed performance by the New York Symphony Orchestra and live music from Joe Alexander, a nationally known personality organist who had played at Balaban & Katz Theatres in Chicago and was 'a featured organist at many of the deluxe houses in the Publix chain' ('Joe Alexander, Featured Organist' 1929). The first feature screened at the Paramount was *The Dance of Life* (Cromwell and Sutherland 1929), starring Nancy Carroll and Hal Skelly. Advertising stressed the film's status as an adaptation of 'the sensational stage success *Burlesque*', and predicted patrons would 'gasp in surprise at the gorgeous Broadway review' (Publix 1929a). Billed as 'the greatest story of show business ever screened', *The Dance of Life* exemplified the backstage musical genre, which used 'show-world settings … to reproduce or mimic established performances and to foreground 'Broadwayness' as a major part of appeal to urban consumers' (Jenkins 1990: 37).

   In addition to promoting the high status of its entertainment, Publix highlighted features of the theatre itself that brought Springfield into line with other 'modern' cities. Organist Joe Alexander, for instance, worked his musical magic from a spotlighted platform that rose as he played from a location below the orchestra floor to a position of suspended elevation, where he could be viewed without obstruction from every seat in the house. Studio publicity commented that this 'big city innovation' ('Organ Player will be Lifted' 1929) was 'new to Springfield but quite the vogue in large New York and Chicago theatres' ('New to Springfield' 1929). Much was also made of the Paramount's $100,000 'scientific' air-conditioning system, described as the most 'modern type' and the first 'to be installed in Western Massachusetts on plans developed over a period of 10 years following experiments first made in Chicago' ('Air-Cooling Plant' 1929). Being newly constructed in 1929, the Paramount was fully equipped for talking pictures. Publicists pointed out the distinct advantages of this newness, heralding that 'countless theatres, including the largest and costliest in the country, have

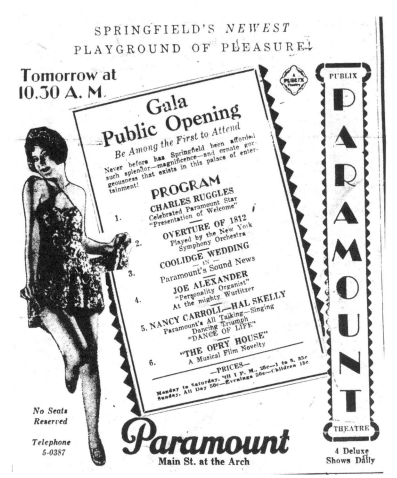

SPRINGFIELD'S *NEWEST*
PLAYGROUND OF PLEASURE!

**Tomorrow at
10.30 A. M.**

Gala
Public Opening
Be Among the First to Attend

Never before has Springfield been afforded
such splendor—magnificence—and ornate gor-
geousness that exists in this palace of entertainment!

PROGRAM

1. CHARLES RUGGLES
Celebrated Paramount Star
"Presentation of Welcome"

2. OVERTURE OF 1812
Played by the New York
Symphony Orchestra

3. COOLIDGE WEDDING
—IN—
Paramount's Sound News

4. JOE ALEXANDER
"Personality Organist"
At the mighty Wurlitzer

5. NANCY CARROLL—HAL SKELLY
Paramount's All Talking—Singing
Dancing Triumph
"DANCE OF LIFE"

6. "THE OPRY HOUSE"
A Musical Film Novelty

—PRICES—
Monday to Saturday, 'till 1 P. M., 25c—1 to 5, 85c
Sunday, All Day 50c—Evenings 50c—Children 15c

*No Seats
Reserved*

*Telephone
5-0387*

Paramount
Main St. at the Arch

PUBLIX

PARAMOUNT

THEATRE

4 Deluxe
Shows Daily

Figure 11.1: The public opening at the Paramount Theatre appealed to Springfield's metropolitan ambitions and national aspirations – advertisement from *The Springfield Daily Republican*.

been remodeled to meet the demand for sound pictures, but the Paramount is one of the first and one of the largest to be planned from the beginning as a sound picture theatre'; moreover, 'anticipation of the new developments which are to come in the next few years in theatre entertainment, has led builders to provide for magna film, third dimension, or depth, Technicolor and, in the future, television' ('New Paramount Theatre Largest' 1929).

While only a sampling, these rhetorical appeals were part of a larger discourse of the 'modern' and the 'new'. Through pledges and proclamations, Publix sold the vision of a momentous, egalitarian social revolution that enabled Springfield to leap ahead of its regional competitors to stand with the largest, most urbane and most advanced cities in the United States. In this respect, Publix's promotional discourse was little different from advertising practice in general during the 1920s. In fact, this discourse of egalitarianism fits comfortably within what Roland Marchand (1985) calls 'the most pervasive of all advertising tableaux of the 1920s – the parable of the Democracy of Goods. According to this parable, the wonders of modern mass production and distribution enabled every person to enjoy the society's most significant pleasure, convenience, or benefit' (1985: 217–18). Marchand points out, however, that this was not a matter of social ideology being foisted upon unsuspecting citizens. Rather, advertisers employed the egalitarian vision of the parable of the Democracy of Goods 'primarily as a narrow, non-ideological merchandising tactic':

> Advertisers did not have to impose the parable of the Democracy of Goods on a contrary-minded public. Theirs was the easier task of subtly substituting this vision of equality, which was certainly satisfying *as a vision* (emphasis in original), for broader and more traditional hopes and expectations of an equality of self-sufficiency, personal independence, and social interaction. (1985: 220–21)

Publix suggested that all one need do to partake of this vision was to buy it – literally by purchasing a ticket to Springfield's new 'wonder' theatre, and figuratively by defining this experience as the tangible form of an egalitarian revolution. In this discursive context, the Paramount Theatre became both the product and the promise of national social progress fuelled by science, technology and industrial consolidation.

Publix's vision of progress and social equality was founded on big business, mass culture and consumerism, but the company recognized that such a vision could produce alienating side-effects on the local level, precisely because, as Marchand (1985) notes, this view of society substituted itself for 'more traditional hopes and expectations of an equality of self-sufficiency, personal independence, and social interaction'. Publix was therefore extremely careful to appear responsive to concerns about community disinvestment and loss of economic independence:

> The Publix Corporation believes in the policy of spending money where it is earned. Statistics on file at the local Publix offices show that nearly 50 cents of every dollar taken in at Publix theatres remains in the community where the theatre is located. So far as possible, local labor and local contractors are employed in the building of the Publix theatres. ('Publix to Spend More Money' 1929)

In the manner of 'scientific management', the Paramount Theatre's entire managerial staff was brought in from out of town by the national office. However, service staff and labourers were found locally. Construction of the theatre itself was contracted to local firms, with 391 labourers employed, all of whom were Springfield residents, 'except for a few foremen'. The theatre took six months to build at a total cost of $1,118,000, of which $300,000 was paid to local employees. Upon completion, the theatre was staffed by 90 personnel hired from 1000 local applicants ('Local Labor' 1929). Publix's investment in the local economy was commended by Springfield Mayor Fordis C. Parker, who praised the amount paid to resident wage-earners and further noted how 'Springfield benefits materially because $1,000,000 is added to the city's taxable property' ('Coolidge Wedding Film' 1929).

This comment about property taxes hints at local discourses, entwined with studio promotional discourses, that shaped the theatre's meaning for residents. City planning documents provide fuller context for the mayor's statement, and suggest that the new theatre had as much a place in the city's own plans for growth and urban renewal as it did in Paramount-Publix's strategy for corporate expansion.

The city's interest in the theatre centred around its northerly location on Main Street at the corner of Railroad Street, just south of an elevated railroad arch that had been constructed to deliver trains to a new passenger station and freight-yard on the east side of Main Street (Figure 11.2). Built by Boston and Albany (B&A) Railroad in 1890, the arch was controversial from the start. According to Donald D'Amato, critics charged that the arch 'created a psychological barrier between two once-united neighbourhoods' – namely, the north end and downtown (1985: 139).

Before 1890, the north end – which began on Liberty Street – was closely tied to downtown and was considered a prestigious residential area, though several light manufacturing companies were mixed in among the houses (see Figure 11.3a). Members of the city's middle and upper classes lived there alongside workers employed at neighbourhood industries (D'Amato 1985: 142). Upon completion of the arch, many north-enders felt isolated from downtown, and those who could afford to move out did so. The outward flow of middle- and upper-class residents was accelerated by Springfield's trolley system, which by 1905 had

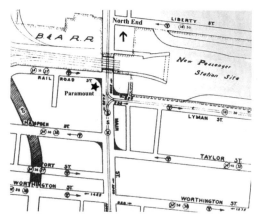

Figure 11.2: The Paramount Theatre was located adjacent to an elevated railroad arch built to deliver passengers to a new station on the east side of Main Street – detail from city planning map.
Source: Springfield Planning Board (1923: 103).

No. 6 Old Grade Crossing, Springfield, Mass. Abolished 1890.

Figure 11.3a: Corner of Main and Railroad Streets prior to the arch; view looking north at the open border that joined downtown Springfield to the once vibrant and prestigious north end – photo from pre-1907 postcard.

No. 2. Railroad Arch, Main Street, Springfield, Mass.

Figure 11.3b: Corner of Main and Railroad Streets after the arch; view looking north at the new boundary separating north end from downtown. The arch solved one traffic problem but created new ones – photo from pre-1907 postcard.

94 miles of track that enabled convenient travel between downtown and suburban areas (Johnson 1972).

Newly available north-end real estate was purchased primarily by industry, and the district quickly developed into an insular, multi-ethnic, working-class area marked by overcrowded tenements and 'nuisance industries' such as soap factories, abattoirs and asphalt manufacturing – all of which contributed odours and noise to the environment. Springfield was not averse to industrial development, which added to the city's tax base, but there was concern that heavy industrialization in the north end endangered Springfield's reputation as a genteel 'City of Homes' (D'Amato 1985: 142; 'Vigilance Keeps Us' 1929). In addition to triggering the rapid demise of the north end as a prestigious residential district, the arch also increased downtown traffic congestion. Originally intended to alleviate traffic, the arch proved too narrow and low (Figure 11.3b) to accommodate the glut of pedestrians, trolleys, horse-drawn buggies, jitneys and automobiles navigating Main Street (D'Amato 1985: 139).

The arch was not solely responsible for changing demographics in the north end, but it was perceived as a blight on the landscape and a malign symbol of Springfield's problems coping with modernization. The arch was not initially built from the desire of Springfield residents for a new train station. The old station, in fact, was a popular local landmark. Instead, the arch resulted from B&A's largely unilateral decision in 1890 to remove its existing station on the west side of Main Street and build a new one across the street on the east side. The new station fronted Lyman Street on the south side of the arch, and vehicles travelling to and from the station created blockages that often congested traffic for

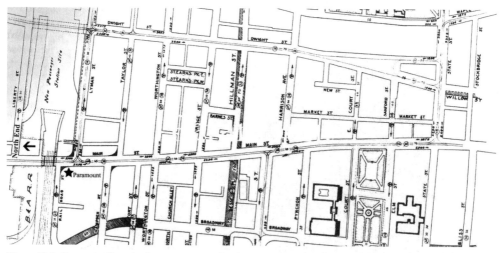

Figure 11.4: To ease traffic and raise property tax valuations near the railroad, Springfield rebuilt the Boston and Albany passenger station so that it fronted Liberty Street rather than Lyman Street. Paramount's new theatre near the railroad arch was taken as a sign that the plan had worked – detail from city planning map.
Source: Springfield Planning Board (1923: 103).

nine blocks south down Main Street all the way to State Street (Figure 11.4) (Springfield Planning Board 1923: 50). This condition troubled citizens on a personal level, but it also concerned the city government because of the resulting drop in tax values for properties surrounding the station:

> An abrupt drop of values takes place at Stockbridge Street toward the south and at the Boston and Albany railroad crossing to the north. The northern drop is due to the railroad and conditions created by the railroad. A similar condition appears when values along Dwight Street are considered. Dwight Street property is assessed at about $9.50 near State Street, about $20.00 in the vicinity of Worthington Street, and only $5.00 near Lyman Street and the railroad (Springfield Planning Board 1923: 50).

While citizens and government recognized the problems associated with the arch and B&A station, they could not deny that the railroad was key to the city's growth, with over 100 trains passing daily through Springfield during the 1920s (D'Amato 1985: 140). The solution was not to restrict the railroad, but to effectively manage the city. In 1923, the Springfield Planning Board produced a plan to remedy traffic congestion caused by the railroad. The plan recommended that another new B&A station be built on the existing site, but fronting Liberty Street north of the arch rather than Lyman Street to the south (Figure 11.4). Though the station built by B&A in 1890 was barely 30 years old, the city budgeted $1 million to demolish it and construct an entirely new station. This budget came from projected increases in property taxes that Springfield would receive from property owners in the business district surrounding the arch and new station (Springfield Planning Board 1923: 50–51). The city was banking that the $1 million to build the station would be offset by future increases to tax revenues resulting from the improved station itself. If the station succeeded, it would lift the value of nearby commercial properties, which would attract new business and real estate investment, and all of this would bring more tax money into the city's coffers. If it failed, homeowners would get the tab and see their own tax rates go up. It was a gamble by Springfield's political leaders, but the plan was implemented in 1926. The new B&A station, also known as Union Station, was built and in operation by year's end (D'Amato 1985: 171).

Viewed in context of Springfield's city plan, the Paramount Theatre can be read as possessing multiple meanings for various segments of the population. When Mayor Parker lauded the new theatre by stating that 'Springfield benefits materially because $1,000,000 is added to the city's taxable property', perhaps what he was saying was: 'We have just laid the foundation to pay for your new train station. Paramount-Publix will pay the taxes so you don't have to.' National corporations like Paramount gained local political leverage because the presence of their theatres in central business districts helped elected officials solve financial problems related to modernizing and maintaining urban infrastructures. In this case, a new form of visual transportation (cinema) helped to subsidize an old form of physical transportation (rail).

But the meaning of the theatre wasn't only about taxes. It was also about Springfield's development from provincial big city to major metropolitan area:

> There is a distinct metropolitan atmosphere to the Paramount and its appointments are far superior to anything hitherto seen in this city. It is comparable only to the better type of theatre in cities such as New York or Boston. ('City Leaders Among 3000' 1929)

Hailed as a 'tremendous asset for Springfield' ('City Leaders Among 3000' 1929), the Paramount signalled that the city's hopes for rejuvenating the border between north end and downtown through managed growth were being realized, because a nationally powerful and prestigious corporation had chosen to invest heavily in an area once synonymous with traffic congestion and encroaching 'nuisance industries'. Indeed, Paramount's advertising regularly featured the proud phrase 'Main Street at the Arch', which located the theatre for patrons and granted redemption to the arch – that formerly notorious landmark and symbol of the city's past problems coping with modernization.

Any lustre the Paramount added to Springfield would also have had meaning for the city's social elites and genteel classes, who perhaps found in the theatre's luxurious interior design and rococo architecture ample reason for optimism that the fruits of urban progress and national mass culture could improve public taste and promote uplift. For workers and immigrants in the north end, the theatre may have offered a similar sense of possibility – a feeling that personal success and upward mobility were, like the Paramount itself, just up the street and across the railroad tracks. The egalitarian vision embedded in the theatre's architecture and in Publix's promotional discourse, however, remained mostly an attractive ideal, as class segregation in the city remained strongly intact (Douglass 1926: 261–78, 404–18).

Conclusion

Many patrons were no doubt thrilled when they visited the gleaming Paramount for the first time and experienced its pleasures. The community at large, however, gave the theatre a more complex reception. The new 'palace' was mediated through structures of thought and feeling that sought to map out the implications of studio-branded real estate for the perception, meaning and value of Springfield's geography. To examine national theatre chains in this way – from the viewpoint of cultural studies – is not to discount Hollywood's strategic interest in selling a centralized, standardized and delocalized system of exhibition. Rather, excavating community meanings for studio-owned movie theatres unearths these sites as locations where struggles for social and political effectivity took place. In Springfield, studio promotional campaigns were launched in the context of many other discourses into which the Paramount Theatre might have been inserted, and off which its meanings might have been read.

This was not simply a case in which discourses existed side by side, each to its own and each equal to the other; rather, it was marked by the emergence of a discourse that became dominant – in this case, an egalitarian vision of national social progress spurred by big business, mass culture and consumerism – by creeping into and intersecting other discourses – discourses about taxes and property valuations, job creation and economic development, the attractiveness of the urban landscape and its landmarks, and the prospects for uplift, modernization and regional advancement. If locals bought the Paramount Theatre as a sign of progress, this was not purely an abstract exchange, but one grounded in concrete conditions and plans for Springfield in the 1920s.

The rise of national cinema chains was a process of negotiation over the meaning of space and place, an attempt to secure legitimacy for a set of discursive articulations that constituted a layering of cultural space that shaped the experiences and meanings that accrued to a given place. This legitimacy, however, was not total or permanent. When Wall Street crashed in October 1929, structures of feeling in the city began to change. As the Great Depression unfolded, downward mobility created exigencies that produced new discourses that questioned the vision of endless social progress and national economic expansion that only recently had seemed so natural. In 1933, Paramount-Publix went into receivership, bankrupted by unmet mortgage payments on its vast real estate holdings as well as by debts incurred rigging all those theatres for talkies. In 1935, the company reorganized as Paramount Pictures. This process subtracted Publix from the official corporate name, and resulted in the city's largest movie venue ending up in the hands of two long-time Springfield residents, Samuel and Nathan Goldstein. This was not the end of Paramount's national theatre chain as a whole, but it did mean that community understandings of the 'Paramount Theatre on Main Street at the Arch' underwent a sea change. Meanings for this once proud symbol of national aspiration were renegotiated and relocalized, with Publix's once powerful discursive presence greatly weakened – albeit still preserved in the sediment of a rich but rapidly receding layer of the theatre's and city's archaeological history.

References

'Air-Cooling Plant of Modern Type' (1929), *The Springfield Sunday Union and Republican*, 29 September, p. 2G.

Allen, R.C. (2006), 'Relocating American Film History: The "Problem" of the Empirical', *Cultural Studies* 20: 1, pp. 48–88.

Balio, T. (1985), 'Struggles for Control, 1908–1930', in T. Balio (ed.), *The American Film Industry*, Madison, WI: University of Wisconsin Press, pp. 103–31.

Bowles, K. Maltby, R. Verhoeven, D. and Walsh, M. (2013), *The New Cinema History: A Guide*, Oxford: Wiley-Blackwell.

'City Leaders Among 3000 at Opening of Paramount' (1929), *The Springfield Union*, 28 September, p. 1.

'Coolidge Wedding Film for Opening' (1929), *The Springfield Daily Republican*, 26 September, p. 6.

Dale, E. (1939), 'The Motion Picture Industry and Public Relations', *The Public Opinion Quarterly*, 3: 2, pp. 251–62.

D'Amato, D. (1985), *Springfield – 350 Years: A Pictorial History*, Norfolk, VA: The Donning Company.

Douglass, H.P. (1926), *The Springfield Church Survey*, New York: George H. Doran.

Fitzgibbons, J.J. (1929), 'Publix Pledge to the People of New England', *The Springfield Sunday Union and Republican*, 29 September, p. 3G.

Franklin, H.B. (2002 [1928]), 'Motion Picture Theatre Management', in G. Waller (ed.), *Movie-going in America: A Sourcebook in the History of Film Exhibition*, Malden, MA: Blackwell, pp. 116–23.

Fuller, K.H. (1996), *At the Picture Show: Small-Town Audiences and the Creation of Movie Fan Culture*, Washington, DC: Smithsonian Institution Press.

Fuller-Seeley, K.H. (ed.) (2008), *Hollywood in the Neighborhood: Historical Case Studies of Local Movie-going*, Berkeley, CA: University of California Press.

Gomery, D. (1978), 'The Picture Palace: Economic Sense or Hollywood Nonsense?', *Quarterly Review of Film Studies*, 3: 1, pp. 23–36.

—— (1979a), 'The Movies Become Big Business: Publix Theatres and the Chain Store Strategy', *Cinema Journal*, 18: 2, pp. 26–40.

—— (1979b), 'The Growth of Movie Monopolies: The Case of Balaban & Katz', *Wide Angle*, 3: 1, pp. 54–63.

—— (1985), 'U.S. Film Exhibition: The Formation of a Big Business', in T. Balio (ed.), *The American Film Industry*, Madison, WI: University of Wisconsin Press, pp. 218–28.

—— (1992), *Shared Pleasures: A History of Movie Presentation in the United States*, Madison, WI: University of Wisconsin Press.

—— (2002), 'Fashioning an Exhibition Empire: Promotion, Publicity, and the Rise of Publix Theatres', in G. Waller (ed.), *Movie-going in America: A Sourcebook in the History of Film Exhibition*, Malden, MA: Blackwell, pp. 124–36.

Hall, S. (1981), 'Notes On Deconstructing the Popular', in R. Samuel (ed.), *People's History and Socialist Theory*, London: Routledge & Kegan Paul, pp. 227–40.

—— (1993), 'Encoding, Decoding', in S. During (ed.), *The Cultural Studies Reader*, New York: Routledge, pp. 90–103.

Hanssen, F.A. (2010), 'Vertical Integration During the Hollywood Studio Era', *Journal of Law and Economics*, 53: 3, pp. 519–43.

Hoggart, R. (1957), *The Uses of Literacy*, London: Chatto and Windus.

Huettig, M. (1944), *Economic Control of the Motion Picture Industry*, Philadelphia, PA: University of Pennsylvania Press.

Jancovich, M., Faire, L. and Stubbings, S. (2003), *The Place of the Audience: Cultural Geographies of Film Consumption*, London: British Film Institute.

Jenkins, H. (1990), "Shall We Make It for New York or for Distribution?': Eddie Cantor, *Whoopee*, and Regional Resistance to the Talkies', *Cinema Journal*, 29: 2, pp. 32–53.

'Joe Alexander, Featured Organist at Console in Paramount Theatre' (1929), *The Springfield Sunday Union and Republican*, 29 September, p. 9G.

Johnson, R. (1986–87), 'What is Cultural Studies Anyway?', *Social Text*, 16, pp. 38–80.

Johnson, S.R. (1972), 'The Trolley Car as a Social Factor: Springfield, Massachusetts', *Historical Journal of Western Massachusetts*, 1: 2, pp. 5–17.

Klenotic, J. (1996a), 'A Cultural Studies Approach to the Social History of Film', PhD thesis, University of Massachusetts – Amherst.

―――― (1996b), 'Class Markers in the Mass Movie Audience: A Case Study in the Cultural Geography of Movie-going, 1926–1932', *The Communication Review*, 2: 4, pp. 461–95.

―――― (2001), '"Like Nickels in a Slot": Children of the American Working Classes at the Neighborhood Movie House', *The Velvet Light Trap*, 48, pp. 20–33.

―――― (2007), '"Four Hours of Hootin' and Hollerin'": Movie-going and Everyday Life Outside the Movie Palace', in R. Maltby, M. Stokes and R.C. Allen (eds), *Going to the Movies: Hollywood and the Social Experience of Cinema*, Exeter: University of Exeter Press, pp. 130–54.

Lebhar, G.M. (1932), *The Chain Store – Boon or Bane?* New York: Harper and Brothers.

―――― (1952), *Chain Stores in America: 1859–1950*, Clinton, MA: Colonial Press.

'Local Labor Had Important Part in Building Theatre', *The Springfield Sunday Union and Republican*, 29 September, p. 2G.

Maltby, R. (2006), 'On the Prospect of Writing Cinema History From Below', *Tijdschrift voor Mediageschiedenis*, 9: 2, pp. 74–96.

―――― (2007), 'How Can Cinema History Matter More?', *Screening the Past*, 22, http://www.latrobe.edu.au/screeningthepast/22/board-richard-maltby.html. Accessed 10 June 2011.

―――― (2011), 'New Cinema Histories', in R. Maltby, D. Biltereyst and P. Meers (eds.), *Explorations in New Cinema History: Approaches and Case Studies*, Oxford: Wiley-Blackwell, pp. 3–40.

Maltby, R., Biltereyst, D. and Meers, P. (eds) (2011), *Explorations in New Cinema History: Approaches and Case Studies*, Oxford: Wiley-Blackwell.

Maltby, R., Stokes, M. and Allen, R.C. (eds) (2007), *Going to the Movies: Hollywood and the Social Experience of Cinema*, Exeter: University of Exeter Press.

Marchand, R. (1985), *Advertising the American Dream: Making Way for Modernity 1920–1940*, Berkeley, CA: University of California Press.

May, L. (1983), *Screening Out the Past: The Birth of Mass Culture and the Motion Picture Industry*, Chicago: University of Chicago Press.

Moore, P. (2008), *Now Playing: Early Movie-going and the Regulation of Fun*, Albany, NY: State University of New York Press.

'New Paramount Theatre Largest, Most Modern in Western Massachusetts' (1929), *The Springfield Sunday Union and Republican*, 29 September, p. 2G.

'New to Springfield' (1929), *The Springfield Daily Republican*, 27 September, p. 9.

'Organ Player will be Lifted Amid Floodlights' (1929), *The Springfield Sunday Union and Republican*, 29 September, p. 6G.

'Paramount to Open Later in Month' (1929), *The Springfield Sunday Union and Republican*, 8 September, p. 8F.

Porter, G. (2006), *The Rise of Big Business, 1860–1920*, 3rd edn, Arlington Heights, IL: Harlan Davidson.

Publix (1929a), Advertisement, *The Springfield Daily Republican*, 28 September, p. 3.

―――― (1929b), Advertisement, *The Springfield Sunday Union and Republican*, 29 September, p. 7F.

―――― (1929c), 'A Publix Theatre', *The Springfield Sunday Union and Republican*, 29 September, p. 1G.

'Publix to Spend More Money Here' (1929), *The Springfield Sunday Union and Republican*, 29 September, p. 5G.

Schudson, M. (1984), *Advertising, The Uneasy Persuasion*, New York: Basic Books.

Scroop, D. (2008), 'The Anti-Chain Store Movement and the Politics of Consumption', *American Quarterly*, 60: 4, pp. 925–49.

Springfield Planning Board (1923), *A City Plan for Springfield, Massachusetts*, Springfield, MA: Springfield Printing and Binding Company.

Stokes, M. and Maltby, R. (eds) (1999), *American Movie Audiences: From the Turn of the Century to the Early Sound Era*, London: British Film Institute.

—— (eds) (2004), *Hollywood Abroad: Audiences and Cultural Exchange*, London: British Film Institute.

Thompson, E.P. (1963), *The Making of the English Working Class*, London: Victor Gollancz.

Tuan, Y.F. (1977), *Space and Place: The Perspective of Experience*, Minneapolis, MN: University of Minnesota Press.

'Vigilance Keeps Us a City Of Homes' (1929), *The Springfield Sunday Union and Republican*, 8 September, p. 2E.

Williams, R. (1977), *Marxism and Literature*, Oxford: Oxford University Press.

Notes

1 For Scroop (2008: 927), the anti-chain store movement continues to inform contemporary efforts to resist and reform 'big-box' retailers like Wal-Mart.

2 Evidence from Springfield lends some support to Lebhar's claim. Between 1926 and 1932, when Fox, Paramount and Warner Bros all entered the city's exhibition market, the number of locally owned theatres increased from eight to 11, though the percentage of the city's total seating capacity owned by local theatres dropped from 53 per cent to 44 per cent during this period (Klenotic 2007: 134–37).

3 There was also a private opening by invitation only on 27 September. In 1929, Springfield had a population of approximately 160,000, making it the third largest city in Massachusetts behind Boston (780,000) and Worcester (195,000).

Chapter 12

A Progressive City and Its Cinemas: Technology, Modernity and the Spectacle of Abundance

Mark Jancovich and Lucy Faire with Sarah Stubbings

According to Maggie Valentine, the Depression hit the film industry hard in the United States, and studios 'could ill afford to spend money on building' new cinemas (1990: 90). As a result, cinema construction declined during the 1930s, and those cinemas that were built 'were much smaller and simpler in scale than those of the previous decade' (1990: 91). In Britain, however, the story was somewhat different. First, while the United States was building huge, lavish movie palaces in the 1910s and 1920s, the cinemas built in Nottingham during this same period were far smaller and, despite being lavish, there was no comparison with their counterparts in the United States. Second, while the number of cinemas built declined in the United States during the 1930s, this same period saw a boom in cinema building in Britain and the construction of the large 'supers' – exotically designed cinemas with huge seating capacities that were comparable to the cinemas built in the United States during the 1910s and 1920s.

Size was a major feature of these new theatres. According to the 1921 edition of the *Kinematograph Year Book*, there were some 4000 cinemas in the United Kingdom, 'not far short of the maximum number ever to operate in Britain, 4900 in 1949'. However, the average seating capacity in 1921 'was around 600, much smaller than the 2000- and 3000-seater cinemas built during the heyday of the late 1920s and throughout the 1930s' (Gray 1996: 35). But it was not size alone that distinguished the cinemas of this period. As Sharp comments, the '"super" cinema was a direct result of the attempt of exhibitors and designers to provide the cinema-goer with greater "illusion", elegance and comfort in their buildings' (1969: 104). Furthermore, as Atwell notes, this was the period that saw 'the first influx of American style atmospherics' (1980: 88) – large cinemas that did not just signify luxury and extravagance, but created the 'illusion' of exotic fantasy worlds in their design and décor. It was during this period that cinemas started to be designed not to resemble up-market theatres, but rather Moorish palaces, Egyptian temples and Gothic cathedrals (1980).

For Atwell, these cinemas were 'built in Britain to cope with the new phenomenon' of the 'talkies' (1980: 87). However, the 'talkies' do not explain this building boom. For a start, no such boom followed the arrival of talking pictures in the United States. And, while it is certainly true that a limited number of cinemas could not be satisfactorily converted to sound, and were therefore closed down, this was not a common practice. For example, in Nottingham, only four cinemas closed between 1928 and 1932, and most cinemas made the transition to sound without many problems. However, Gray's explanation for the boom is no more convincing:

> there had been a moratorium on inessential building construction during the First World War, and it had taken exhibitors most of the decade after the end of the war to realise that it was possible to regularly fill a large cinema of 2000- or 3000-seat capacity. (1996: 54)

Not only did the moratorium fail to prevent continued cinema building in the late 1910s and 1920s, but also there is no explanation for this oversight on the part of exhibitors. American practices were familiar to British exhibitors, and it is difficult to see why they would have missed the presence of such a large demand if, in fact, it had been present.

The answer may therefore lie elsewhere, in developments within British society and culture more generally. As Peter Hall (1996) argues, the nineteenth-century city came to be seen as a place of squalor and corruption, and this situation prompted a widespread concern with the reform of the city in the late nineteenth and early twentieth centuries. One particularly prominent exponent of reform was William Booth, the founder of the Salvation Army, who was born in Sneinton, Nottingham, and later claimed that he had been motivated by 'the degradation and helpless misery of the poor stockingers of my native town wandering gaunt and hunger stricken through the streets' (Booth, quoted in Beckett with Brand 1997: 35; see also Booth 1890).

The pressure for reform was therefore particularly acute in Nottingham, which had been transformed during the nineteenth century from a 'garden town [to] an urban slum' (Beckett with Brand 1997: 35). Even by 'the early years of the nineteenth century, visitors no longer went into raptures about Nottingham, and nor is it surprising: population had tripled in sixty years without any appreciable expansion of the built-up area. The result was congestion.' (Beckett with Brand 1997: 35). Part of the problem was that Nottingham was unable to expand beyond its medieval boundaries until after 1845. However, the problems only intensified as the century progressed, and by 1919, 'nearly 9000 houses were considered unhealthy' (Beckett with Brand 1997: 79).

Matters came to a head, however, when these problems were used as 'one reason why the application by the Nottingham Corporation (town council) in 1920 for a further boundary extension was turned down by central government' (Beckett with Brand 1997: 79) The refusal was a blow to the Corporation and severely compromised the image of Nottingham that it had fought so hard to develop. It therefore prompted the corporation to start 'a massive modernisation programme' (1997: 79). In the years between the two wars, the corporation built 17,461 houses, which 'represented 65.5 per cent of the total addition to stock' (1997: 79); this needs to be compared with a city such as Leicester – Nottingham's nearest rival – in which the corporation was only responsible for 35 per cent of the new housing stock (Hayes 2000).

Urban redevelopment and cinema construction

This modernization programme created two immediate outcomes. On the one hand, it involved extensive redevelopment of the town centre in which the Old Market Square was redeveloped and a huge new council house was built. On the other, it led to a massive expansion of new suburban estates. The first of these processes was a highly contested one, involving the removal of both the market and Goose Fair from the Old Market Square and the building of a monumental neo-baroque council house. This redevelopment was a conscious attempt to transform the identity of the city. The old exchange building was deemed no longer 'worthy of a progressive city' (*Nottingham Daily Guardian*, 20 March 1926), and its demolition was therefore part of a process through which the Corporation 'came to identify civic pride and identity with big, sometimes grandiose municipal gestures' (Chambers 1956: 44). This process was therefore contested on two grounds.

First, it was criticized along the same lines as the City Beautiful Movement described by Hall, which was attacked by the likes of Lewis Mumford as a 'municipal cosmetic' (Mumford, quoted in Hall 1996: 182), which he would later compare with the 'planning exercises of totalitarian regimes' (1996: 182). In short, the City Beautiful Movement and its monuments were attacked for 'ignoring housing, schools, and sanitation' (1996: 182) Similarly, there was a public outcry over the money spent on the council house – money that, it was argued, should have gone into the housing programme in which the Corporation was also engaged.

However, the link with totalitarianism did not end there. Not only were these developments attacked for their arrogant neglect of the material conditions under which most people in the city lived, but they were also attacked as exclusionary. These developments mirror – almost too neatly – the processes described by Stallybrass and White (1986), through which bourgeois respectability was constructed through the expulsion of the market, fair and carnival, as well as the imposition of classical order. It was a process through which the square was appropriated by the Corporation, which literally excluded the world of popular leisure in an attempt to redefine the area as one of high-income consumption. It was therefore unsurprising that so many felt excluded from the square. After all, the process was clearly one in which the square was being redefined as a place that was literally 'not for the likes of them'. But these matters were made still worse by the Corporation's decision to ban the public from the council building itself, shortly after its opening, on the pretext that it needed to be protected from vandalism.

As should be clear, however, this 'modernization' of the town centre was directly related to the redefinition of the types of consumption appropriate to it. As Don Slater (1997) argues, the 1920s 'promoted a powerful link between everyday consumption and modernization. From the 1920s, the world was to be modernized partly *through* consumption' (1997: 12). Of course, not all forms of consumption were appropriate. It is therefore interesting that, alongside the new places of consumption that flourished in the square, a new 'super' cinema also emerged: The Ritz. Indeed, it was not only permitted within this area but was actively encouraged. As we have argued elsewhere, cinema had been seen as inappropriate to places of high-income consumption in the early teens, when the Long Row Picture House was proposed (Jancovich and Faire with Stubbings 2003), but by the late 1920s and 1930s, cinema was actively encouraged within such places. However, while The Ritz was built in a position almost directly opposite the new council house, from the start its image was directly opposed to that of the council house for many sections of the population. While the council house came to stand for the arrogance and authoritarianism of the Corporation, the new cinema became an emblem of democracy and classlessness.

The Ritz, however, was also tied to the second process of urban redevelopment in the 1930s: the Corporation's slum-clearance programmes and the construction of new suburban estates, and it was this second process that largely was responsible for the dramatic boom in cinema building during the late 1920s and 1930s. Of the 21 cinemas that opened in Nottingham during this period, 19 were in the suburbs. Thus, while suburbanization has often been seen as the cause of cinema's decline, it might be more accurate to see it as the reason for the phenomenal boom in cinema-going from the late 1920s onwards – a period that saw the high point in cinema attendance, and that therefore has often been referred to as the 'age of the dream palace' (It is for this reason that Jeffrey Richards' book on British Film Culture in the 1930s takes this as its title: Richards, 1984).

One crucial problem with the new suburban estates was the lack of facilities and centres for communal leisure, and while the move to the suburbs has often been seen as a retreat from public life into the private sphere of the domestic home, there was still a strongly felt need for 'getting out' – especially among those women who were not employed outside the home. However, the local influence of temperance organizations effectively blocked licences for public houses within these housing developments, and in this vacuum the cinema was virtually the only form of local public entertainment and leisure available. In these communities, the 'local' therefore came to refer to the cinema rather than, as was traditional, the public house. As Richards puts it: 'The neighbourhood cinema had come to assume a place in the life of the community analogous to those other prime foci of leisure time activities, the church and the pub' (1984: 18). Indeed, in most suburban estates the cinema was usually there either before, or even in place of, these other two foci.

Selling cinema

As cinemas became bigger and more spectacular, individual cinemas became objects of consumption as much as the films that they showed, and the cinema advertisements of the period made this quite clear.[1] Certainly many cinemas advertised the films that they showed, but in all cases the cinema itself was foregrounded as a major attraction, and in many cases it was presented as *the* major attraction. Even though the city-centre cinemas almost exclusively attracted the first-run films, which were not shown in the suburbs until up to a year later, it is significant that there was little reference to this asset in the advertising of the period. Advertisements were far more concerned to distinguish cinemas from one another through their use of the full programme. Most cinemas in the period featured a double bill, but they also showed cartoons, newsreels, trailers and sometimes a serial. The Ritz, for example, made the best promotional use of its full programme, and its policy was to regularly present details of the entire programme – it was a policy that made the cinema programme appear far more substantial than its competition, but also appealed to a wide number of different potential audiences. As Thomas Doherty points out, one of the key points about the full programme was that the different parts were meant to appeal to different sections of the audience so that there would be 'something for everybody' (Doherty 1999). The following example from a 1937 advertisement for The Ritz is typical: 'Sydney Howard in *Chuck*, also Eddie Quillan and Chic Sale in *The Gentleman from Louisiana*, Jack Heyler radio organist and *Three Blind Mouseketeers*, silly symphony' (*Nottingham Daily Guardian*, 3 April 1937).

Furthermore, as the decade wore on, an increasing number of cinemas advertised their newsreels, which had become a standard feature of the cinema once sound was introduced. No doubt this was due partly to growing concern about international affairs and crises in the build-up to World War II,[2] but it was also that these newsreels provided a sense of event and spectacle. For example, the King died in 1936 and, while the royal funeral was covered by the local papers, the Hippodrome offered 'special pictures of the Royal Funeral' (*Nottingham Evening News*, 31 January 1936) and the New Empress went one better by announcing that it had the 'Royal Funeral Official Film' (*Nottingham Evening News*, 1 February 1936). Newsreel footage of sporting events also featured in the advertisements for some cinemas.

However, while these aspects of the advertisements emphasized the films shown, the advertisements also highlighted other features of the cinemas themselves, and some adverts made no reference to the programme. These other features can be divided into three main areas of promotion: technology, facilities, and location. Obviously one of the most important aspects of technology in the period was the presence of a sound apparatus, although some cinemas also made a point of advertising themselves as 'The Silent House'. Others silent cinemas also tried alternative methods of attracting customers, such as the Victoria Picture House, which highlighted the presence of a 'brilliant musical interlude by the Victorians' as part of its programme (*Nottingham Evening News*, 1 July 1930).

The appeals of sound were not, however, advertised in a uniform way, and cinemas used the presence of sound not only to distinguish themselves from silent houses, but also from other houses with sound. The first advertisements, of course, simply advertised the novelty of sound, with The Hippodrome announcing an 'all talking, all singing, all dancing' programme (*Nottingham Daily Guardian*, 7 January 1930) and The Elite referring to *Careers and Love's Test* as 'all talking, all drama' (*Nottingham Daily Guardian*, 1 March 1930). However, as talking pictures became more established, the refinements in sound technology came into play. For example, The Tudor promoted itself as 'the house with sound system supreme' (*Nottingham Evening Post*, 25 February 1932) and the New Empress claimed that it was 'the house with perfect sound' (*Nottingham Evening News*, 5 July 1930).

A cinema's facilities also represented another means of differentiation in the advertisements. In the early 1930s, advertisements for The Elite regularly mentioned its restaurants and cafes, and even referred to the availability of particular menus. An advertisement in the *Nottingham Daily Guardian* (2 March 1931) even promoted businessmen's lunches, which also served to advertise the high-class, successful clientele that The Elite supposedly attracted. However, these advertisements were not just aimed at these sections of the population, but also those who aspired to the sense of class and grandeur that this clientele implied. As a result, The Elite described itself as 'the most elegant public building in the town', which featured 'a French menu in true French style', and it also claimed that 'nothing differs between our presentations and that of the London theatres' (*Nottingham Journal*, 2 December 1926). Here, décor and facilities become the markers of class, but also the markers of a truly metropolitan experience rather than a mere provincial one.

When it opened in 1933, The Ritz soon superseded The Elite's role as Nottingham's leading cinema, and it too emphasized its restaurant and décor. However, The Ritz had a further attraction that distinguished it from the rest of Nottingham's cinemas: a monumental organ played by the well-respected organist Jack Heyler. Indeed, Heyler was such a local cinema phenomenon that his name is still being used today for his association with the cinema. A recently released video of Nottingham's cinema history not only mentions him during the video, but uses his name on the cover as a selling point (*Nottingham at the Cinema* 1999). However, in his day he was also a major selling point, as is clear from the following advertising copy: 'Jack Heyler at the console of the Ritz wonder organ. Hear the latest and most marvellous addition to the Ritz organ' (*Nottingham Evening News*, 2 April 1934). His significance is also underlined by the advertisements that not only listed the times of the films but also the times of his performances. The coverage accorded to Helyer in the Nottingham Archives also provides further evidence of his significance. As radio ownership in the decade increased from 1 per cent of English households in 1922 to 71 per cent in 1939 (McKibbin 1988: 457), Heyler came to be promoted as a 'radio organist' who was not only a local celebrity but one that appeared on national radio (*Nottingham Daily Guardian*, 1 April 1937). In other words, he was seen as a figure of national renown. He 'was never a superstar, but to Nottingham and to wireless listeners further afield, he was a household name' – one who put Nottingham on the map by 'frequently broadcasting for the BBC from the cinema' (*Nottingham Evening Post*, 16 October 2000).

Furnishings, décor and design were used to advertise a cinema's luxuriousness. As we have already seen, this was particularly true of the new suburban cinemas, of which the following claims are representative: 'Nothing has been spared to ensure complete comfort.' (*Nottingham Daily Guardian*, 8 November 1935); 'a luxury cinema … with artistic green and gold interior decorations and furnishings' (*Nottingham Daily Guardian*, 1 December 1932); and 'there is little doubt that the patron will be sensitive to a feeling of modern liner luxury' (*Nottingham Journal*, 17 October 1936). The last quote also demonstrates the ways in which luxury and modernity were seen as almost interchangeable terms in the period, and many of the cinemas sought to claim that they were 'the most up-to-date in every respect' (*Nottingham Daily Guardian*, 8 November 1935).

For example, from the mid-1930s onwards, certain cinemas began to include a phone number in their advertisements, along with an invitation to book seats by phone. However, as few people had access to a phone at this time, the management was probably less concerned to advertise the convenience that this technology supposedly offered than to suggest an association with a wealthy upper-class lifestyle to which others might aspire. The same is also true of the many cinemas that advertised the availability of car parking. Car owners were a small minority in 1930s Britain, yet all the suburban cinemas advertised their parking facilities.[3] The parking facilities at these cinemas were derisory by present-day standards – parking for 200 cars was normal at a cinema seating between 1000 and 1500 – but even in terms of their parking facilities, cinemas sought to distinguish themselves from one another. The Astoria, for example, promised a 'large, floodlit car park' for its patrons' use (*Nottingham Evening News*, 28 November 1936).

On a more down-to-earth note, other forms of transport were also prominent in cinema advertising. Many suburban cinemas included advertisements for bicycle sheds, which clearly had a considerable resonance – in the mid-1930s, one and half million bikes were sold each year (McKibbin 1988: 379). Advertisements also included details of bus numbers and their departure points from the city. The implication was that some people would travel some considerable distance – possibly on two buses – to visit these cinemas. Location and transport were not so heavily promoted by the city centre cinemas, which were well established and could rely on the fact that most residents of the city would already know of their location and how to travel to them. The New Empress did take out a large box advertisement, separate from the main cinema listings, to announce that it was 'near the new market and central bus station' (*Nottingham Evening News*, 5 July 1930). However, this was designed to draw attention to the cinema's place within the new layout of the town centre after the redevelopment of the market square, and its resulting impact on the area within which the cinema was located.

Mediating modernity: cinema buildings and the local press

Many of these concerns were also evident in the newspaper articles that announced the openings of the new cinemas during this period; however, as has already been claimed, these articles tended to concentrate on the modernity of these building and convey a powerful sense of optimism and confidence in the 'progress' that these cinemas were supposed to represent. In a report of the opening of The Ritz, for example, special mention is made of 'a singularly happy speech' that 'referred to the wonderful age in which we live, and mentioned the momentous consequence that that followed the first flight, 30 years ago, by the American inventor Orville Wright'. In other words, both the speech and the newspaper's account of it directly associated the opening of the cinema with a narrative of human progress (*Nottingham Journal*, 5 December 1933). Similarly, the Astoria Cinema in Lenton Abbey opened in 1936, and the report of its opening in the *Nottingham Evening Post* presents its supposed modernity as being its main attraction, rather than the films that it would show. Noting its 'many novel features', the article uses these to support the claim that 'it is the most up-to-date [cinema] in the country', stressing that the cinema had, to its advantage, harnessed the latest techniques and technologies: 'For the first time in any cinema in the kingdom plastic mural photography has been introduced into the decorations', and a constant temperature was ensured by the use of 'robot-fed boilers'. In this account, modernity is equated with a positively presented progress, which supposedly creates an environment that is comfortable, secure and well regulated. Extractor fans 'draw off foul air' and an automatic battery back-up meant that the cinema would never be entirely dark, even in the event of a power failure (*Nottingham Evening Post*, 8 June 1936).

This positive representation of modernity is also reproduced in most, if not all, accounts of the cinema openings in this period, and it extends to aspects of architecture, design and technology. The report of the opening of The Savoy in 1935, for example, claims that it 'demonstrated how really beautiful modern architecture can be' (*Nottingham Daily Guardian*, 11 November 1935), while the account of The Curzon's opening in Carrington is especially effusive in its welcoming of modernity to the city. This 'modern stream-lined cinema' is an 'outstanding demonstration of progress' that benefits from 'modern furnishings' and 'up-to-date technical equipment'. It features 'the latest hygienic silent action seats', and even its brickwork is of 'the most modern type' (*Nottingham Daily Guardian*, 1 August 1935). Similarly, the souvenir programme of the opening of The Ritz makes special mention of the use of electricity, and the cinema, it claims, 'functions almost entirely on this mysterious agency', which powers all the elements that 'are necessary to run the theatre efficiently' (*Souvenir Programme* 1933). As a result, this modernity was praised for its supposed ability to create order, harmony and balance – an assumption that was crucial to the accounts of the architecture and design of these cinemas. In the construction of The Ritz's café, it was claimed, every 'detail has been considered to give the atmosphere of harmony and rest' (*Souvenir Programme* 1933), and an account of The Aspley's opening in 1932 comments on its 'dignified and elegant structure' (*Nottingham Journal* 1936), while The Roxy is praised for its 'Plain, simple lines which blend harmoniously with its surroundings' (*Nottingham Daily Guardian*, 12 December 1937).

Indeed, a sense of balance was continually emphasized. For example, several accounts of suburban cinemas allay worries by stressing that this modernity and streamlined design does not go 'too far'. It was therefore claimed that the Dale Cinema in Sneinton had been built 'on the most modern lines', but 'without embarking on futuristic design'. Here, homeliness and modernity had been harmonized so that 'cosiness has been achieved without cramping design' (*Nottingham Daily Guardian*, 27 December 1932). Similarly, the Plaza Cinema, Trent Bridge was designed in 'the Continental modernistic style', but also gives 'an impression of warmth and cosiness' (*Nottingham Evening Post*, 13 May 1932). These suburban cinemas therefore had to balance their claims to modernity with the reassurance that they were in keeping with both the existing low-rise architecture and the culture of domestic comfort within which they were located. Their success in doing so was also highly significant. Many of the articles present these cinemas as valuable contributions to the sense of pride and identity of the communities within which they were located. The Ritz was even claimed to have made a major contribution to the history of the city.[4] Slightly more modestly, it was claimed of The Curzon that it 'adds to the appearance of the neighbourhood' (*Nottingham Daily Guardian*, 1 August 1935), while The Majestic was supposed to have 'provided Mapperley with one of its finest buildings' (*Nottingham Journal*, 12 June 1929). In this way, these reports suggest a strong sense that each suburb should have its own sense of identity, and that cinemas were an intrinsic element in the production of that sense of identity.

However, while this careful balance of modernity and cosiness is evident in the articles on the suburban cinemas, in the city centre it was the most up-to-date look that was valued. The Ritz did make special mention of the comfort offered by the cinema: the lighting provided a 'comfortable glow' and the auditorium had 'just the amount of light for your comfort'. Similarly, the café had 'plenty of room for the comfort of taking meals', and employed 'Rayred heating panels [to] maintain an even temperature designed to add to the comfort of patrons' (*Souvenir Programme* 1933). Nonetheless, on 4 December 1933 – the day of its opening – the Ritz received a full page of editorial and advertising in the *Nottingham Daily Guardian*, the city's most up-market newspaper, which was aimed at the business and professional class, and it concentrates almost exclusively on issues of strength, steel and destruction. The article states unequivocally that 'it is difficult to acquire a site for a theatre capable of holding an audience of 2,500 in a commanding position in the centre of an ancient, commercial and industrial city like Nottingham, and this has only been possible by the ruthless demolition of existing property' (*Nottingham Daily Guardian*, 4 December 1933). However, this 'ruthless demolition' is not presented negatively, but rather as necessary for the creation of a modern, progressive building. Furthermore, alongside the editorial are advertisements by the various contractors who worked on the project, including Hawley Brothers, the demolition contractors, who state with pride that they 'removed 150,000 cubic feet of earth' (*Nottingham Daily Guardian*, 4 December 1933).

The article also concentrates on the structure of the building and the engineering skills that were required in its construction. In the process, there it makes an abundance of references to steel: we learn that the whole of the shell of the theatre is made of steel; that both the auditorium and the stage are completely steel-framed; and that the construction as a whole involving the use of 650 tons of steel. A couple of days later, the *Nottingham Journal* also carried a short article exclusively on the steelwork of the Ritz, which was apparently the work of the builders of the Sydney Harbour Bridge, a fact that was seen as 'sufficient evidence of the strength of the structure in every part' (*Nottingham Journal*, 6 December 1933).

The scale of the enterprise was therefore a key feature in its promotion, and this extended into other areas. For example, it was claimed that 'no question of expense has been considered but everything possible has been done to ensure perfect reproduction' in both sound and picture quality (*Souvenir Program* 1933). However, it is probably the Conacher organ that is most often used to signify scale: the *Nottingham Daily Guardian* claimed that it was 'one of the largest cinema organs in the country' (4 December 1933), while the *Nottingham Journal* went so far as to maintain that it was 'the second largest in Europe' (5 December 1933). More recently, in 2000, a letter to the *Nottingham Evening Post* on the closure of the cinema claimed that he could 'recall being struck by the sheer width of the Ritz stage and the height of the proscenium' (Rippon 2000).

However, despite the focus on luxury and distinction within these reports, the grandeur and spectacle of these cinemas was continually presented as anti-elitist. Many cinemas associated themselves with a life of leisured luxury, but they also presented themselves as places where all could, at least for a time, enjoy such a life. For example, Rita Dove remembers that, when she worked at The Ritz, the door commissionaires 'always had to wear white gloves no matter what' and that 'Barbara Mason used to be in the foyer to greet the customers … always dressed in a black evening gown' (Dove 2000). Similarly, the *Nottingham Daily Guardian* claimed: 'Reminiscent of the first night at the opera would perhaps be a fitting description of last night's opening ceremony of Nottingham's super-cinema, the Ritz in Angel Row' (*Nottingham Daily Guardian*, 5 December 1933). However, despite its high-class associations, the music played at the cinema clearly identified its intended audience. At the opening ceremony, a full band 'gave a selection of popular music', and Jack Heyler organ performances would later include an eclectic mix of styles, which 'always included ten minutes of jazz and classics, a waltz and – to finish – something light' (*Nottingham Evening Post*, 27 January 2001). Furthermore, while these cinemas stressed the luxury that they offered, they especially mentioned the fact that their prices were 'extremely modest' (*Souvenir Programme* 1933). In other words, it was implied that luxury was available to all without distinctions of class. All benefited, for example, in a place where 'the system of no tipping is in vogue' (*Nottingham Evening Post* 1936), and where 'Every part of the theatre now affords a comfortable seat' (*Nottingham Daily Guardian*, 8 November 1927). This was also the period, as we have seen, when benches were removed from many cinemas in order to remove the class distinction that they signified, even though classes still tended to be distinguished geographically between cinemas and spatially within them. As a result, these cinemas represented a modernity that brought security, comfort and luxury to all. Cinemas such as The Aspley provided a spectacle of abundance, but at 'a low price' (*Nottingham Daily Guardian*, 1 December 1932), and so promised a world in which progress would obliterate class distinction and provide affluence for all – a life beyond the demands of necessity.

The irony was, of course, that luxury was often signified through the service provided. While these places announced their anti-elitism, they offered their clientele the opportunity to experience the ministrations of a servant class; the opportunity to be the recipient of service rather than a servant themselves.[5] In this way, these cinemas presented themselves as places of fantasy in which the social relations of the outside world were momentarily neutralized or inverted. They presented themselves as places in which a 'dream [can] come true' and, in the *Nottingham Journal* report on the opening of The Ritz, the newspaper even went so far as to suggest that the construction of the cinema itself was the realization of an impossible fantasy:

> A few years ago a Nottingham man, Mr S.W. Gibbons, had a vision, a vision of a super cinema. Everyone thought he would never succeed. The difficulties were too great … But what was a dream 25 weeks ago was an accomplished fact today. (*Nottingham Journal*, 5 December 1933)

Cinemas were not just places to show films they were celebrated as spectacles of consumption in themselves and, as a result, *The Kinematograph Year Book* of 1932 commented on 'the advance made in this country in what has been termed "the architecture of pleasure"' (*Kinematograph Year Book* 1932: 209).[6]

Acknowledgement

This article is an abridged version of material published as Mark Jancovich and Lucy Faire with Sarah Stubbings, *The Place of the Audience: Cultural Geographies of Film Consumption* (London: British Film Institute, 2003).

References

Atwell, D. (1980), *Cathedrals of the Movies: A History of British Cinemas and their Audiences*, London: Architectural Press.

Beckett, J. with Brand, K. (1997), *Nottingham: An Illustrated History*, Manchester: Manchester University Press.

Booth, W. (1890), *In Darkest England and the Way Out*, London: Salvation Army.

Chambers, J.D. (1956), *Modern Nottingham in the Making*, Nottingham: Nottingham Journal.

Doherty, T. (1999), 'This is Where We Came In: The Audible Screen and the Voluble Audience of Early Sound Cinema', in M. Stokes and R. Maltby (eds), *American Movie Audiences*, London: British Film Institute, pp. 143–63.

Dove, R. (2000), Letter to the *Nottingham Evening Post*, 30 October.

Gray, R. (1996), *Cinemas in Britain: One Hundred Years of Cinema Architecture*, London: Lund Humphries.

Hall, P. (1996), *Cities of Tomorrow: An Intellectual History of Urban Planning and Design in the Twentieth Century*, London: Blackwell.

Hayes, N. (2000), 'Civic Perception, Decision-Making and Non-Traditional Housing in Leicester and Nottingham in the 1920s', paper presented to Urban History Seminar, 24 March.

Jancovich, M. and Faire, L. with Stubbings, S. (2003), *The Place of the Audience: Cultural Geographies of Film Consumption*, London: British Film Institute.

McKibbin, R. (1988), *Classes and Cultures: England 1918–1951*, Oxford: Oxford University Press.

Nottingham at the Cinema 1999, Viewpoint Video.

Richards, J. (1984), *The Age of the Dream Palace: Cinema and Society in Britain 1930–1939*, London: Routledge.

Rippon, D. (2000), Letter to the *Nottingham Evening Post*, 4 November.

Sharp, D. (1969), *The Picture Palace and Other Buildings for the Movies*, London: Hugh Evelyn.

Slater, D. (1997), *Consumer Culture and Modernity*, Cambridge: Polity Press.

Souvenir Programme, The Opening of the Ritz (1933).

Stallybrass, P. and White, A. (1986), *The Politics and Poetics of Transgression*, London: Methuen.

The Kinematograph Year Book, 1932: 209.

Valentine, Maggie, (1994), The Show Starts on the Sidewalk: An Architectural History of the Movie Theatre, New Haven: Yale University Press.

Notes

1   Of course, it should be remembered that not all cinemas advertised in the press, and it was rare for the 'flea pits' to do so. The audiences to which a cinema wanted to appeal would not only determine whether they advertised or not, but also in which local papers they placed their advertisements if they did decide to advertise.

2   Filmed records of major events had been an attraction from the very earliest days of film and, even in the early 1920s, advertisements for the Long Row Picture House claimed that the programme included the 'latest news in pictures'.

3   By our calculations, about 2 per cent of the total population had a car, although this does not account for those who were too young to drive. In 1930, there were 1,050,000 registered cars for a population of 46,040,000 (1931 census). If the average family size at the time was about four, then 9 per cent of families had a car – assuming, of course, that each family only owned one car, which would have been unlikely.

4   The souvenir programme opens with a two-page history of Nottingham that tries to establish both its national and international significance, after which is added the following: 'Today, December 4th, 1933, the Ritz Theatre ... opens its doors, girded by the hopes of its sponsors that they will have given to the City a building, and with it entertainment, worthy of the fair fame and traditions of the City of Nottingham' (*Souvenir Programme* 1933). The cinema is therefore seen as the fulfilment of Nottingham's history, and as a major contribution to its identity as a modern, progressive city.

5   The *Souvenir Programme* from the opening of the Ritz devotes a special section to the service on offer in the cinema and states that any suggestions 'from patrons as to any manner in which their comfort and convenience can be studied still further, will be welcomed by the Management and, if found to be practicable, will be put into operation' (1933).

6   This is taken from a discussion of S.L. Rothafel's visit to England. Rothafel, or Roxy, was then 'chief of 'Radio City', the proposed huge amusement centre in New York.

Chapter 13

'They Don't Need Me in Heaven ... There are No Cinemas There, Ye Know': Cinema Culture in Antwerp (Belgium) and the Empire of Georges Heylen, 1945-75

Kathleen Lotze and Philippe Meers

Introduction

On 16 December 1944, during the screening of *Buffalo Bill*, a V2 rocket hit one of Antwerp's most prestigious cinemas at that time, the Rex. What was once a glorious cinema palace had turned into wrack and ruin. The bomb killed and wounded hundreds of people inside and outside the cinema. Amongst the casualties were staff members of the Rex and other Antwerp cinemas, who had gathered for a meeting in the same building. One of this meeting's few survivors was Georges Heylen (1912–95),[1] director of the Rex and son-in-law of the cinema's owner (who was one of the casualties). Less than three years later, Heylen would reopen the Rex and soon become the most influential cinema entrepreneur in Belgian cinema history.

Within Flanders, the northern, Dutch-speaking part of Belgium, the medium-sized sea port city of Antwerp played a vital role in film distribution and exhibition. At the end of World War I, Antwerp had 39 cinemas and by the 1950s the number had risen to 50.[2] The high concentration of screens was mirrored by high admission figures. In 1951, for instance, average admission figures in Antwerp's inner-city and working-class neighbourhoods were four times higher than average admission figures in the whole of Flanders.[3] Cultural life was most vibrant in the Station Quarter, the neighbourhood near Antwerp's Central Station and along both sides of the sumptuous Avenue De Keyserlei. Some rather chauvinistically called the Avenue De Keyserlei Antwerp's Champs-Elysées (Lauwers 1998: 4, 9). It was here that the city's most prestigious cinemas – including the Rex – were located, and where Heylen would start building his cinema empire.

Within two decades after the reopening of the Rex in 1947, Heylen had taken over one cinema after the other until, in the 1960s, he practically had a monopoly position in Antwerp's inner city: the only cinemas not belonging to Heylen's cinema empire were niche cinemas in the sense that they showed so-called 'forbidden films' – that is, more sexually explicit material. An exemplary part of his success was the way he confronted a boycott of cinemas by Hollywood's major distributors in the late 1960s and early 1970s. Heylen had grown from a local exhibitor to an internationally renowned player in film exhibition and distribution. He ruled his empire with a grip of steel and was merciless towards his competitors. At the same time, among cinema audiences he had the reputation of having the most beautiful cinemas where people could see the best films and were treated like kings and queens.

In this chapter, we propose a multimethod approach to the study of Antwerp's cinema culture during the rise and flourishing period of the Rex cinema group of Georges Heylen. We draw on two related research projects, the 'Enlightened City' project on screen culture and film consumption in Flanders (1895–2004) and the 'Antwerp Cinema City' project on the evolution of film exhibition and reception in Antwerp (1945–95), with a focus on Heylen's Rex cinema group.[4] Both are inspired by new cinema history approaches (Maltby et al. 2011; Biltereyst et al. 2012). By triangulating cinema infrastructure, film programming and cinema-going memories, we can link institutional history to individual experiences of cinema-going and draw a multi-layered picture of a local cinema culture – all informed by the broader context of socio-political and cultural transitions in the 1950s and 1960s, and more particularly the (political-)economic changes in the film industry and the rapid decline of cinema attendance from the 1950s onwards.

The *Antwerp Cinema City* project as a 'new cinema history' inspired multimethod investigation into local cinema culture

New cinema history focuses on the concrete (everyday life) contexts of films' production, distribution, exhibition and consumption. These contexts can be social, cultural, political or economic. Cinemas are considered 'sites of social and cultural significance' shaped by 'patterns of employment, urban development, transport systems and leisure practices' (Maltby 2011: 9). The viewer plays an active role as an agent, instead of being merely a constructed, passive object with neither name nor background. Where traditional film history focuses primarily on evolutions on the macro scale, new cinema history combines quantitative and qualitative approaches and links macro- and micro-history (Maltby 2006: 91).

More concretely, this brings us to the combination of methods and insights from social geography, economy, economic history and oral history. Succeeding the Enlightened City project, the Antwerp Cinema City project investigates the three facets of local cinema culture outlined in the introduction on three separate research levels. While the first facet – cinema-infrastructure – addresses questions of cultural geography (How were different types of cinemas distributed across a city or within a region?) and economy (According to which economic models did the individual cinemas operate?), the second facet – film programming – investigates potential patterns of media consumption (Which types of films were screened, where and how successful where they?). The third facet, cinema-going memories, is concerned with how cinemas and films are actually remembered by their social audiences, and what role cinema played in their everyday lives.

A historical dimension is added by investigating all three facets for three specific moments in time (1952, 1962 and 1972), spanning the period of the rise and flourishing of the Rex cinema group of George Heylen.[5] Based on three corresponding databases – the cinema infrastructure database, the programming database and the cinema memory database – we analyse the three aspects of Antwerp's cinema culture synchronically and diachronically.

In this chapter we focus on the period stretching from the late 1940s to the mid-1970s. This roughly covers the first three decades of the Rex cinema group up until its heyday. This timespan is also interesting because of the dramatic changes that occurred in the film industry during these years. The demise of the Hollywood studio system and an ongoing worldwide recession in the film industry from the 1950s onwards went hand in hand with a rapid decline in cinema attendance. The fight over cinema patrons manifested itself, among other things, in the introductin of protectionist measures in a number of Western European countries, which were designed to counter the flood of the so-called backlog of films from Hollywood and boost national film industries. On a socio-cultural level, the post-war period also witnessed changed patterns of leisure activities due to increased wealth and mobility.

Cinema infrastructure: from a highly fragmented market to a quasi-monopoly

By cinema infrastructure, we mean the geographical diffusion of cinemas across a particular place as well as individual features of the cinemas themselves. Dependent on access to historical sources, examined features are architectural (size, capacity of a theatre), economic (ownership) and/or ideological (e.g. Catholic, socialist, liberal). For our investigation of Antwerp's cinema infrastructure, we made use of an extensive database set up within the framework of the Enlightened City project.[6] The database contains information about all exhibition venues in – among many other places – the city of Antwerp, including their locations (addresses), capacities (number of seats), opening and closing dates, personnel and organizations involved (names of exhibitors) and, if applicable, their ideological affiliations. Subsequently, the locations of all cinemas in the city of Antwerp were marked on a map for our three sample years: 1952, 1962, 1972 (Figure 13.1).

Throughout the period under examination, Antwerp's cinema landscape was characterized by a great variety in terms of seating capacity. Single-screen cinemas of all shapes and sizes were scattered across the city, ranging from small cinemas with fewer than 200 seats up to picture palaces with 2000 seats. Middle-sized theatres (500–1000 seats) were predominant (Figure 13.2). It is remarkable that their proportional shares remained approximately the same in all three examined years. This leads us to conclude that – at least up until the 1970s – the size of the cinemas was not the most decisive criterion for closing down cinemas. In other words, it were not necessarily the smallest or largest cinemas that closed down first. Rather, their geographical position was more important.

In Figure 13.1 we see a high concentration of cinemas in Antwerp's Station Quarter. From the late nineteenth century until the mid-1980s, the Station Quarter was the place where Antwerp's cultural life was most vibrant. This was where Antwerp's first permanent cinema would open in 1907, and where cinema mogul Georges Heylen would establish a quasimonopoly position. The map also reveals that there were quite a few cinemas that vanished between 1952 and 1972 (these cinemas are marked with a circle instead of a

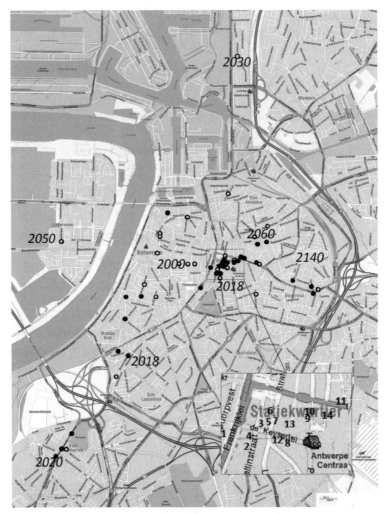

Figure 13.1: Cinemas in the city of Antwerp (post codes 2000–2060 & 2140) in 1952, 1962 en 1972. Cinemas that had vanished by 1972 are marked o. Detail: Cinemas in Antwerp´s Station Quarter in 1972. 1 – Odeon (600 seats), 2 – Quellin (640), 3 – Rex (1120), 4 – Pathé (1170), 5 – Metro (1650), 6 – Ambassades (450), 7 – Vendôme (240), 8 – Capitole (1000), 9 – Astrid (520), 10 – Savoy (540), 11 – Rubens (1070), 12 – Paris (300), Plaza (525), 14 – Royal (300). (Numbers 1–11 represent cinemas owned, exploited and/or programmed by Heylen.)

solid dot). Nearly all districts and neighbourhoods of Antwerp faced a massive closing down of cinemas from the 1960s onwards. This process of downscaling was not a local phenomenon, but occured worldwide, and was one of the consequences of the dramatic decline in cinema attendance (e.g. for Britain, see Hanson 2007: 92ff). Increased wealth, changed patterns of leisure activities (including spending time watching television) and

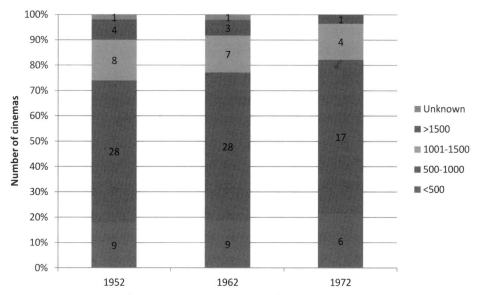

Figure 13.2: Seating capacities of Antwerp cinemas in 1952, 1962 and 1972.

increased mobility (greater access to automobiles) were predominant factors leading to a continuing decline in cinema attendance – and the film industry's earnings – from the 1950s onwards. In particular, neighbourhood and peripheral cinemas suffered from these developments. Their functions as social meeting places and extensions of home had become obsolete. Antwerp's Station Quarter was about the only place in town where most cinemas survived.

In addition to the geographical (central) position, ownership was a decisive criterion for a cinema's chance of survival. Antwerp's post-war cinema landscape was characterized by a highly fragmented market. It was dominated by mostly private exhibitors exploiting just a few cinemas – usually one or two.[7] In 1952, Heylen exploited three cinemas in the Station Quarter. Most of Heylen's competitors disappeared from Antwerp's cinema landscape during the following decades. By the 1970s, the once highly fragmented cinema sector of Antwerp had become a quasi-monopoly under the control of Georges Heylen (Figure 13.3). Only three independent cinemas were still active in the Station Quarter in 1972, and none of them was programming regular films, but specialized in the 'forbidden films'.

Two major distinctions emerge from our analyses of cinema infrastructure. The first is the classical distinction between neighbourhood cinemas and cinemas in the centre of the city. Second, we can distinguish cinemas belonging to the city's most dominant theatre chain, the Rex cinema group, from cinemas operating independently from it. Cinemas in all categories differed less in size or architecture, and rather in ticket prices and film programming, as well as comfort and service, as we shall see below.

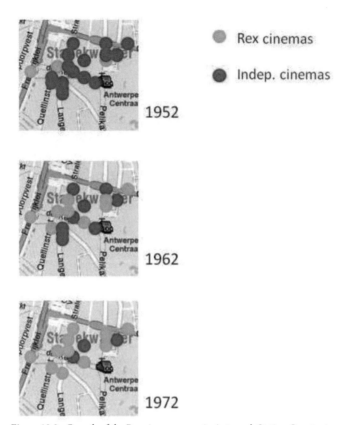

Figure 13.3: Growth of the Rex cinema group in Antwerp's Station Quarter in 1952, 1962 and 1972.

Film programming and cinema profiles

The supply of films at cinemas is a good indication of its potential audiences. A number of studies have concentrated on the import of films (e.g. see Thompson 1986). However, this does not tell us much about what actually screened at cinemas and for how long. As Joseph Garncarz has demonstrated, when looking at the demand for films rather than the supply (import), Hollywood films only became consistently popular with German audiences in the 1980s (Garncarz 1994: 95; 2002: 1). Taking the interest in demand even further, Karel Dibbets suggests that: 'Duration introduces time into measurement of success and popularity, a dimension lost in the archives of box office data' (2010: 341). In order to get a good grasp on what people could actually see at Antwerp cinemas, and to find out which films were the most popular ones in terms of duration, an extensive programming database was set up within the Enlightened City project. The database includes information about the screenings (film title as it was distributed in Flanders, date and location of the screening) and the films' main features (original film title, country of origin, year of production, director, main actors, genre, distributor and censorship rating) for our three sample years (1952, 1962 and 1972), each spanning 52 weeks. Information about the particular screenings was gathered from daily newspapers as well as from the original programming books of the Rex cinema group, and complemented with information from the Internet Movie Database on the films themselves.

The programming database yields a vast amount of data and allows for countless possibilities in terms of analysis. We will focus on three particular findings here, resulting from our programming analysis. First, based on a synchronic programming analysis, we present findings relating to the trajectory of films throughout the city. As we shall see, these findings question clear-cut models of the classic distribution system of run zone clearances. Second, we offer results from a diachronic analysis of the competition within a local cinema market and look at its impact on film programming. Third, we present findings concerning the relationship between film distribution and exhibition, adding nuances to the discourse of unchallenged dominance of Hollywood within local cinema markets. All three analyses are closely linked to each other. They perfectly illustrate the dynamics within a local cinema landscape – whether between exhibitors of neighbourhood cinemas versus centre cinemas, or Heylen versus his competitors. Importantly, they also demonstrate the usefulness of a programming analysis as a bottom-up approach to film supply in cinemas.

Trajectory of films throughout Antwerp in 1952

For 1952, we compared the programming of centre cinemas in the Station Quarter and cinemas in the adjacent neighbourhoods of Stuivenberg and Borgerhout. Both neighbourhoods are situated north-east and east at walking distance from Antwerp's Central Station. These neighbourhood cinemas differed clearly from the centre cinemas with regard to programming as well as ticket prices. Films at neighbourhood cinemas usually changed on a weekly basis, whereas most centre cinemas would program films for longer periods, ranging from several weeks up to several months. In addition, neighbourhood cinemas programmed far more films from the United States than centre cinemas. In two neighbourhood cinemas in our sample, the share of US productions exceeded 90 per cent of the total supply of films at these cinemas.[8] Neighbourhood cinemas were also more likely to screen older films from the year before or even the past decade than centre cinemas. It is here that the hierarchy between neighbourhood and centre cinemas surfaces most clearly: a film falls in value when it travels through space and time. Since there was usually only one copy available per film, and films would play in the centre of the city first and later travel to neighbourhood and suburban cinemas, films in subsequent-run cinemas were often more damaged. The poorer quality of the films and the delay in screening dates were partly compensated for by these cinemas by selling tickets for lower prices and by programming double bills – effectively offering more for less money.

A study of the 28 most popular films in terms of duration at examined theatres shows that films would always travel from the picture palaces in Antwerp's centre to the

231

neighbourhood cinemas. This finding is not new, and can be attributed to the distribution system of run-zone clearance: films premiere for high ticket prices at prestigious first-run cinemas in major cities and subsequently travel to neighbourhood cinemas, where they are shown for less expensive ticket prices. Finally they would move to cinemas in peripheral and more rural areas. However, the classification of first-, second- and subsequent-run cinemas deserves some shading. First, we saw that the hierarchy of cinemas according to runs was not fixed, but subject to change: while for one film a particular cinema would function as first-run cinema, for another the same cinema would function as second-run cinema (Table 13.1).

Table 13.1: Classification of cinemas in 1952 according to frequency of runs of 28 films with longest duration and/or frequent changes of cinemas

	1st run	2nd run	3rd run	4th run	5th run	6th run
Rex (Heylen)	7					
Roxy (+ other cinemas)	4					
Pathé	3					
Anvers P.	2					
Astrid (+ Rex) (Heylen)	1					
Capitole	1					
Empire	1					
Odeon (Heylen)	4	1*				
Ambassades	3	1*				
Metro	4	1*	1*			1*
Coliseum	2	1	2	1*		
Kursaal	1		1			
Astrid (Heylen)		6				
Eden		1				
Astra (Heylen)		5	2			
Rubens		2	1			
Festa (Heylen)		1	4			
Century (Heylen)		1	3			
Majestic		4		1		
Plaza		2	2	1		
Crosly		2		1		
Roma (Heylen)			6	5		
Luxor (Heylen)			4		4	
National (Heylen)			3	3	3	
Dixi (Heylen)			2	5	2	
Victory (Heylen)				1		
TOTAL NUMBER OF FILMS**	33	28	32	18	9	1

Notes: Numbers in columns represent the number of films per run per cinema. Cinemas in bold = cinemas located in Station Quarter; cinemas in italics = cinemas located near Station Quarter and not in neighbourhoods of Stuivenberg and Borgerhout; plain = neighbourhood cinemas in Stuivenberg and Borgerhout

* Films of which the subsequent run was at the same cinema as the first run.

** Multiple counts of one individual film possible, dependent on its trajectory through Antwerp cinemas.

The results of our programming analysis showed that the further down the hierarchy of runs the cinema was, the less fixed its position would be. Although we detected that one particular neighbourhood cinema in Stuivenberg (Dixi) would usually be the last in line to screen a particular film, there would hardly be a fixed hierarchy between other neighbourhood cinemas. Historical economist John Sedgwick came to a similar conclusion upon examination of patterns in first-run and suburban filmgoing in Sydney in the mid-1930s. He attributed the suburban cinemas' instable positions within the sequence of exhibition runs to the accelerated turnover of films due to the screenings of double bills and more frequent programme changes (Sedgwick 2011: 142). In a way, this confirms oral accounts of a former Rex programmer that cinemas would have certain profiles due to specific audiences, but that the programming of films would depend principally on the available timeslots in cinemas' various programmes at a given moment (Corluy 2008). It is here that Heylen's powerful position within Antwerp's cinema market proved highly advantageous for the programming in his own cinemas. According to several historical key players from within his cinema group, as well as among his competitors, Heylen had acquired priority rights for screening films in his cinemas. This implied that he was privileged to screen films (from contracted distributors) first and keep them for as long as they remained above a certain minimum earning treshold. Since Heylen owned premiere theatres as well as subsequent-run cinemas outside of the city centre, this meant competing exhibitors usually had to wait until the film was cleared for distribution in remaining cinemas. Regarding the trajectory of films through Antwerp, this meant that it *could* happen that a succesful film returned to a (competing) centre cinema after it had earned sufficient revenues in all of Heylen's cinemas (including his neighbourhood cinemas).

Second, we detected at least two distinct types of premiere theatre. There were premiere theatres that would launch a film quickly and the film would move on to other cinemas after a maximum of two weeks. Here, the latest releases of films of a broad sprectrum of origin and genres would premiere. Heylen's flagship cinema, the Rex, and later the Metro (after Heylen's takeover) are examples. Then there were premiere theatres where a film would be launched and stay for a substantial period of time, usually exceeding one month. As opposed to the first type the latter had a distinct programming profile. Cinema Odeon, for example, screened preferably French and French-Italian dramas, with no admission for for children under 16. A clean-cut classification of first-, second- and third-run theatres does not account for these nuances, while it might well have an impact on the economics of distribution. Nor does it allow for a consideration of hierarchies between various exhibitors, which we found were important for the circulation of films within a local cinema market.

Competition and its impact on film programming in Antwerp theatres, 1952–62

In our programming analysis of the sample years 1952 and 1962 – the time before Heylen had acquired a quasi-monopoly position – we saw clear differences in the programming of cinemas belonging to Heylen's Rex empire and competing cinemas. Two important

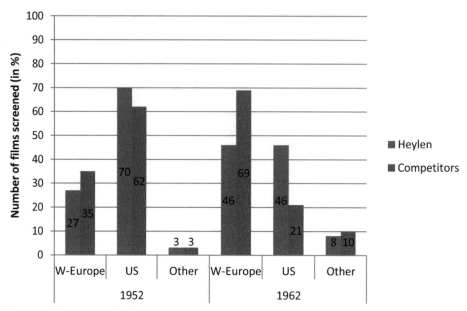

Figure 13.4: Screenings in Heylen's and competing centre cinemas in 1952 and 1962 according to region of origin.

differences concerned the country of origin of the films and – related to it – distributors. In both sample years, on average, Heylen's cinemas showed more films from the United States than cinemas from other exhibitors. In other words, productions from Western European countries dominated in competing cinemas (Figure 13.4) – a difference that became even more pronounced in 1962. For this year, we see an incredible overall increase of (co-) productions from Western European countries, especially France and Italy. This is an increase that can be explained in terms of long-term outcomes from these countries' protectionist film policies and recovering film industries (De Grazia 1998: 26).

The substantial supply of US productions in Heylen's cinemas had to do with his relationship with the major American distributors. Due to restricted sources, we cannot compare all distributors supplying films for Heylen's cinemas and his competitors in 1952. However, we can derive some indications of the dynamics within Antwerp's cinema sector from the data available to us for 1952. Cinema Metro – exploited by MGM between 1947 and 1961 – exclusively screened its own films. It was a clear case of vertical integration of the company's different business sectors. Vertical integration was banned by the Paramount Decree in the United States in 1948, but was obviously still practised abroad. An examination of the exchange of films between Cinema Metro and other cinemas shows that Heylen acquired far more pictures from MGM than his competitors did. Apparently, as soon as Heylen had rented the film from MGM, he had it play in several of his cinemas. This not only prolonged the films' life-cycles but, even more importantly, it blocked them for other exhibitors in Antwerp. The close link between Heylen and MGM might be seen as heralding Heylen's takeover of the Metro less than a decade later. Within a year of his takeover, Heylen had made The Metro his second prestigious premiere theatre (after the Rex). Our programming results from 1962 show that by then The Metro was already screening more films distributed by other majors (Fox, United Artists, UIP) and the Belgian distributor Discibel than films from MGM.

By 1962, the link between Heylen and the major American distributors had become even stronger. By then, eight out of ten of Heylen's cinemas predominantly screened films distributed by the majors. With the exception of the Pathé cinema (it was owned by one of Antwerp's most long-standing cinema groups Tyck/Gommers), none of the competing cinemas predominantly showed films distributed by American majors. Competing cinemas either rented the majority of their films from a Belgian or French distributor or displayed no clear preference. Heylen's power within Antwerp's cinema market serves as one explanation for this situation. As indicated above, Heylen's ability to screen films first (from contracted distributors) meant either that competing exhibitors had to wait until the film was cleared or that they had to look for films elsewhere – usually smaller, independent distributors. In the long run, however, Heylen's powerful position would result in a profound conflict, especially with American distributors in the late 1960s and early 1970s – an incident that turned Antwerp's cinema world upside down.

The conflict between Georges Heylen and the American major distributors: late 1960s–1973

With regard to Heylen's cinemas, we observed a dramatic decline in the number of films distributed by American majors in Heylen's theatres, such as Twentieth Century Fox, Warner Bros and Paramount, in the examined period. While in 1952 the share of films distributed by all American majors amounted to 75 per cent, in 1962 it had fallen to 50 per cent, and by 1972 the majors' share was only 10 per cent. In addition, in 1972 we see the arrival of one extremely powerful player: Heylen's own distribution company, Excelsior. Only a year after it was officially founded, Excelsior's share exceeded that of any other individual distributor in any of our samples. What had happened?

As indicated earlier, by the 1960s Heylen's power over Antwerp's lucrative cinema market had grown so much that he would start dictating prices and rental conditions for films. This, of course, clashed with the interests of distributors who, in the face of the ongoing recession in the film industry, tried to keep their risks low and earnings high. When Heylen refused to give in to the demands, the American majors – supported by the Motion Picture Export Association (MPEA) – evoked a distribution stop for all of Heylen's cinemas. Yet, instead of giving in to their demands, Heylen filled the sudden gap of films and increased business with smaller (national) distributors. He also officially launched his own distribution company, Excelsior. Within a decade, it had grown to become one of the most important distribution companies in the country. A combination of steady investment in good publicity for the films and for a good instinct for choosing prizewinning films paid off in higher revenues as well as the trust of producers (Zeguers, cited in Magiels and De Hert 2004: 69; Corluy 2008). The conflict between Heylen and the American majors not only affected the programming in his cinemas, but also turned out to be favorable for his competitors – if only for a few months. In the midst of the conflict, a number of competing (and less prestigious) neighbourhood cinemas in Antwerp and peripheral districts united against Heylen. Contracts with the Americans procured them hitherto unknown large audiences. The conflict thus had produced a serious break with traditional distribution patterns: no longer did big box office hits premiere in (Heylen's) luxurious centre cinemas, but in the less prestigious neighbourhood cinemas.

The consequences of the lockout were severe for both parties – Heylen as well as the majors. While Heylen had to struggle to fill his film programmes during the lockout, the majors quickly realized that they would never earn the money with independent cinemas as they did with Heylen.[9] In the meantime, plans for the opening of a new cinema complex were realized, in an attempt to break Heylen's quasi-monopoly in the Station Quarter. With the help of the majors, the successful Dutch cinema entrepreneur Piet Meerburg, who (co-)owned around 20 cinemas in the Netherlands at that time, opened the cinema triplex Calypso in 1973 at the heart of the Station Quarter, right across Heylen's flagship cinema Rex (Dibbets 1980: 82). Heylen, Meerburg and the American major distributors had come to an agreement, and eventually the conflict was coming to an end. All in all, Heylen had retained the upper hand in the conflict with the majors, and in the long run also regarding the competition with Meerburg.

The programming trends described here can be explained by developments and occurrences on macro and micro levels, as well as by the interaction of macro and micro forces. The Antwerp case offers a detailed view into the struggles and opportunities of local exhibitors against local as well as global players of the film industry – all facing an ongoing recession after the gradual downfall of the Hollywood studio system from the 1950s onwards. Due to the two world wars, Europe's film industry was also severely damaged. Furthermore, at the end of World War II, European countries were flooded with the so-called backlog films from the United States. In order to counter the flood of these films and boost national film (co-)production(s), protectionist measures were taken by Western European countries such as France, Italy, Spain and Germany.

On the one hand, our programming results mirror the enormous output of national and co-productions from Western Europe from the 1950s onwards. Comparing the years 1952 and 1962, we saw an enormous increase of films from those countries. However, evaluating Heylen's cinemas against those of his competitors, the number of US productions screened by Heylen remained relatively high.[10] Our research has shown that in the constant struggle between Hollywood and Europe, the preference for films by exhibitors did not only depend solely on box office results or audience tastes, but also on the dynamics within local cinema markets. It explains the domination of Hollywood films in Heylen's cinemas in the 1950s and 1960s, as well as their absence in the early 1970s.

In conclusion, we argue that the distinction between different sorts of cinemas in Antwerp – neighbourhood versus centre cinemas, Heylen's cinemas versus his competitors– is equally visible in film programming. A comparison between Heylen's cinemas and those operating independently reveals that, with one exception (Pathé), independent cinemas offered more sexually explicit dramas, mainly from France and Italy, while Heylen would program more light entertainment from the United States and German-speaking countries. As suggested by Dibbets, different cinema exhibitors in one city are able to soften competition by maintaining a certain degree of product differentiation – in other words, by specializing in certain genres or films from certain countries (1980: 108). However, considering the fact that Heylen's programming policies were also extremely varied – with, on the one hand, profile premiere theatres like The Odeon and The Astrid specializing in certain types of films and, on the other, quick-launch premiere theatres and neighbourhood cinemas offering a broad spectrum of films, Heylen's programming strategy virtually rendered all competitors unnecessary.

Cinema-going memories

As discussed previously, Heylen succeeded in gaining maximum profits from rented films by investing in different types of cinemas in Antwerp's Station Quarter, as well as in particular neighbourhoods, and by having films travel from centre to second-run to neighbourhood cinemas. He profited from two different objectives of film exploitation suggested by John Sedwick: while first-run cinemas aimed at attracting 'as large an audience as possible to pay the highest prices possible to watch a single attraction' for as long as possible, subsequent-run cinemas compensated for the disadvantages of older films (often of poorer quality) with lower ticket prices, frequent changes of program and offering double bills (Sedgwick 2011: 156). Yet was the public aware of these differences?

We now move away from the implied spectator-in-the-text towards social audiences. Inspired by Annette Kuhn's (2002) pioneering work on memories of cinema-going in the 1930s, a large-scale oral history study was set up within the framework of the Enlightened City project, offering us a diverse range of perspectives on Antwerp's cinema culture for much of the twentieth century. For Antwerp, a total of 155 in-depth interviews was conducted with Antwerp residents of 50 years and older. The respondents were found in residential homes for elderly people or within the circle of family, friends and acquaintances of the interviewers.[11] The sample of respondents was constituted in ways that would achieve as much variation as possible regarding age, class, sex and political and/or ideological convictions. The degree of film consumption also varied widely, from avid cinema-goers to those who hardly ever went to see a movie. The interviews explored who preferred which kinds of films (according to age, gender, political/ideological conviction), what cinemas in which parts of the city the participants attended, their motives for cinema-going, and rituals connected to particular forms of cinema-going and as everyday practice.

Kuhn observes that cinemagoing memories are structured geographically (2002: 17). For our Antwerp respondents, we also observed a strong tendency towards what Kuhn calls 'topographical memory talk' (2002: 17). Frequently, respondents began their recollections of familiar movie houses in the neighbourhoods where they grew up. Similarily, our respondents' recollections of earliest cinema-going were launched by efforts to remember names of the cinemas as well as their exact locations. Respondents went to great lengths to recall the right names of cinemas and streets, and frequently gave descriptions of nearby buildings or other neighbourhood landmarks. Eddy is only one example of many clearly illustrating this and other facets. He recounted the cinemas of his childhood, all located in the neighbourhood where he grew up (Kiel):

> That was the Moderne on Abdijstraat. At the corner of Alfons de Cockstraat and that was called … I can't come up with the name just now, something with Cross … And then there was the Nova. Just across the Abdijstraat … Next to the Tier, I don't know if you are familiar with Kiel, but that was next to the Tier. Centra was the other one … Centra yes …

The cinemas that Eddy could not recall by name were located geographically by naming the street in which the cinema was located. This locating of cinemas using street names or other landmarks (such as particular shops, restaurants or even the local bakery) was a recurrent phenomenon in our respondents' memory talks. Here, we see the discursive function of cinemas for cultural memory: cinema memories contribute to establishing the mental maps of our (cultural) pasts, while at the same time our (historical) street maps help to trigger cinema memories. They are in constant interplay with each other. In addition, memories like these stress the proximity of the cinemas to the respondents' homes: 'the picture house down the road or on the street corner is sited in memory within that spatial nexus taken for granted as part of one's territory, sometimes even figuring as an extension of home' (Kuhn 2002: 42). In addition, these memories point to the omnipresence of the cinema in the past: 'Take the situation in Antwerp in 1950, for example … there was a cinema in practically every street' (Hugo).

In their walks through the past, respondents moved on from early childhood memories of regular attending neighbourhood cinemas to memories of adolescence and adult life connected to the more luxurious cinemas in Antwerp's inner city. After he displayed the places he had been to as a child, Eddy from Kiel took us further into the city's centre, where his high school was located:

> During that period, I was already, let's say 14, 15 years … I went to school in Antwerp, right. So I lived in Kiel, but I went to school in Antwerp, the Antwerp Atheneum. And when you go there, you have to take the tram, which stopped at the De Keyserlei and I'd always pass cinema Rex, pass cinema Metro, and then to my school.

One particular type of topographical memory talk Kuhn identifies in her study is what she calls 'memory maps' (2002: 18). According to Kuhn, memory maps 'lay out a *mise-en-scène* for the recollections which follow', with the cinemas functioning as stopping-off places (2002: 18). Eddy relived his regular schooldays by taking us by tram, getting off at the De Keyserlei and passing Antwerp's most prestigious picture palaces, the Rex and the Metro. The closer Eddy came to the period of his cinema heyday as an adolescent, the more detailed his walks became (see detail in Figure 1):

> There, there was the big one right … The Rex, the Metro, Ambassades. Across the street, there was this small cinema … [unintelligible]. Pathé was right across the Rex. Later it was called the Sinjoor. The Sinjoor, the Odeon.

We see that, in contrast to the cinemas of his childhood located in Kiel, here Eddy recalls correctly and almost without hesitation the names of almost all cinemas. And even though 'the small cinema' across the Metro and the Ambassades is intelligible to the interviewer, from our research on Antwerp's cinema infrastructure we know that theatre's name, size, ownership and programming profile.

A second type of topographical memory talk identified by Kuhn is the 'guided tour' (Kuhn 2002: 20). Whereas memory maps function as establishing shots, providing an overview of the cinematic landscape of a place at a certain point in time, in the case of guided tours respondents decorate their walks through the past and give their cinema memories more detail and colour. Here, the 'memory landscape is not so much joined up by lines on a mental map … as constructed around a series of anecdotes prompted by remembered places' (Kuhn 2002: 21). When it comes to Antwerp's Rex cinema, for instance, our oldest respondents vividly remembered the day the V2-rocket hit that cinema:

> That one time … when the war was over, you'd have those flying bombs here in Antwerp, the V1 and V2. I was a paramedic at the Red Cross. And I saw how a V2 bomb fell on cinema Rex. That there were 700 casualties. And I worked there in the rubbel for days and nights to save people's lives. And I saved a five year old child, took it on my lap and brought her to her mother who was waiting outside, screaming. Apart from that all cinemas were empty. (Andre)

Apart from this tragic incident, the Rex was the cinema that was remembered most frequently and always positively. In fact, most of Heylen's cinemas were remembered for being the most beautiful and most luxurious ones showing the best films, whether or not respondents knew whether one particular cinema belonged to a certain exhibitor:

> The Rex was, if I remember correctly, the most beautiful cinema of Antwerp. The Rex, that's where we'd go to … that was a colossal cinema with a colossal amphitheatre with a hall and little shops. It was what we found most beautiful. And there they'd also premiere the best films. (André)

It was not only Heylen's cinemas that were remembered as being special, but the whole spectacle that came with them:

> Publicity for big films, that happened at the Century Hotel. That was a big hotel at De Keyserlei, not far from Central Station. It was there that you could see the film stars, who would come to Antwerp to promote their films. All those famous American films or so many famous American film stars came to Antwerp for two or three days to promote their films. Then masses of people came to De Keyserlei to welcome and applaude the film stars, who were actually some kinds of demigods. It was quite some event for many Antwerp citizens. (Leon)

Heylen was known for organizing the most spectacular publicity stunts, often including international film stars who would be present at the premieres of their films. These accounts fit with the status the Station Quarter once had of being Antwerp's cultural hot-spot. In this light, it is not coincidental that the dilapidation of the Station Quarter from the 1980s onwards was paralleled by a dramatic decline of the cinema sector in this area. It culminated in Heylen's bankruptcy in 1993 and the closing down of nearly all cinemas in the Station Quarter.

Figure 13.5: Crowds at De Keyserlei to see international film stars (Photograph by courtesy of Paul Corluy).

Our respondents' memory maps and guided tours along memory lane breathe life into our reconstruction of Antwerp's cinema landscape of the past. We can see that, when choosing a cinema, more forces are at work than simply the kinds of film playing there. The choice of cinema also depends on more personal factors, including accessibility – in geographical as well as in social and moral terms. For some of the respondents, cinema-going was framed by the cinemas' geographical proximity to their homes, while others had to overcome social and/or moral barriers like age or class status. More interestingly, access was different for different people at different stages of their lives. While geographical proximity played a greater role for older respondents, and especially during their childhood years, moral and social status shaped cinema-going during adolescence. Kuhn's (2002) 'topographical memory talk' closely interacts with what could be called *biographical memory talk*: different stages of life are characterized by different topographies of cinema-going. In addition to these two kinds of memory talk, for the Antwerp case, we demonstrated that a third layer shaped the cinema memories of our respondents: the (perceived) hierarchies between the individual cinemas they frequented – cinemas belonging to Heylen's Rex cinema group and those operating independently from him.

Conclusion

The multi-method approach offered here provides a rich and multi-layered picture of Antwerp's cinematic past. At least two hierarchies surfaced that structured Antwerp's cinema culture in different ways and on all three levels (cinema-infrastructure, film programming and cinema memories): on the one hand, the hierarchy between neighbourhood and centre cinemas, and on the other, the hierarchy between cinemas belonging to the Rex cinema group and cinemas operating independently from it. The combination of insights from all three aspects of Antwerp's cinema culture sheds light on the workings of cinema culture on a micro level. The finding that neighbourhood cinemas screened so many more films for children under 16, for instance, is understandable when we know that for many cinema-going started here. Next to that, without the testimonies of 'real flesh and blood human beings' (Kuhn 2002: 47), we tend to forget that, apart from offering daydreams into the glamorous glittery world of famous film stars, cinema was also an ordinary practice in people's everyday lives and hard business for exhibitors. The multi-level approach also helps us to better understand and communicate the workings of media industries on a more global level. For example, detailed knowledge of the distribution conflict between the American majors and Heylen, and the ways in which it was resolved, relativizes and extends existing theories of Hollywood's dominance in Europe.

It is clear that the three aspects of local cinema culture examined here are merely a beginning – the building blocks on which future investigations into cinema history can build. All three aspects need further elaboration. Cinema cultures, for instance, are shaped by other economic and political forces, such as local authorities whose influence has a considerable impact on the local cultural infrastructure and who could make or break a local cinema chain. Our multi-level analysis demonstrates how micro-histories of cinema cultures can feed and enrich our understanding of processes on a macro scale, and can constitute a necessary step towards a broader picture – especially when combined with other national and international case studies. Hopefully, scholars applying similar conceptual and methodological frameworks will join forces to contribute to a patchwork of local studies and draw a map of the functioning of local and global film markets and the lived experiences of millions of cinema-goers.

References

Anon (various editions) *Jaarboek van de Belgische film*, Brussels: Koninklijk Belgisch Filmarchief.
Anon (various editions) Programming books of the Rex cinema group.
Biltereyst, D., Maltby, R. and Meers, P. (eds) (2012), *Cinema, Audiences and Modernity: New Perspectives on European Cinema History*, London: Routledge.
Corluy, P. (2008), Interviews with Kathleen Lotze and Philippe Meers, Antwerp, 25 June and 22 July.
De Grazia, V. (1998), 'European Cinema and the Idea of Europe, 1925–95', in G. Nowell-Smith and S. Ricci (eds), *Hollywood and Europe: Economics, Culture, National Identity, 1945–95*, London: British Film Institute, pp. 19–33.
Dibbets, K. (1980), 'Bioscoopketens in Nederland: Ekonomiese koncentratie en geografiese spreiding van een bedrijfstak, 1928–1977', MA thesis, Universiteit van Amsterdam.
——— (2010), 'Cinema Context and the Genes of Film History', *New Review of Film and Television Studies*, 8, pp. 331–42.
Frederix, B. (1995), 'De bioscoopexploitatie in België en de bioscoop in Antwerpen: Een case study', MA thesis, Vrije Universiteit Brussel.
Garncarz, J. (1994), 'Hollywood in Germany: The Role of American Films in Germany', in: D.W. Ellwood and R. Kroes (eds), *Hollywood in Europe*, Amsterdam: Amsterdam University Press.
——— (2002), 'Germany Goes Global: Challenging the Theory of Hollywood's Dominance on International Markets', paper presented to Media in Transition: Globalization and Convergence conference, MIT, Cambridge, MA, 10–12 May.
Hanson, S. (2007), *From Silent Screen to Multi-screen: A History of Cinema Exhibition in Britain Since 1896*, Manchester: Manchester University Press.
Hollants, J. and Christeyns, M.-L. (2011), Interview with Kathleen Lotze and Philippe Meers, Zwijndrecht, 25 November.
Kloeck, E. (2011), Interview with Kathleen Lotze and Philippe Meers, Antwerp, 25 November.
Kuhn, A. (2002), *An Everyday Magic: Cinema and Cultural Memory*, New York: I.B. Tauris.
L'Epoque, E. (ed.) (various editions) *Annuaire Général du Spectacle en Belgique*, Brussels.
Lauwers, F. (1998), *De Keyserlei 125 jaar*, Antwerpen: New Work Cy.
Magiels, W. (2008), Interview with Kathleen Lotze and Philippe Meers, Antwerp, 9 July.
Magiels, W. and De Hert, R. (eds) (2004), *Magie van de Cinema. Hollywood aan de Schelde*, Antwerp: Facet.

Maltby, R. (2006), 'On the Prospect of Writing Cinema History from Below', *Tijdschrift voor Mediageschiedenis*, 9, pp. 74–96.

—— (2011), 'New Cinema Histories', in R. Maltby, D. Biltereyst and P. Meers (eds), *Explorations in New Cinema History: Approaches and Case Studies*, Malden, MA: Wiley-Blackwell, pp. 3–40.

Maltby, R., Biltereyst, D. and Meers, P. (eds) (2011), *Explorations in New Cinema History: Approaches and Case Studies*, Malden, MA: Wiley-Blackwell.

Sedgwick, J. (2011), 'Patterns in First-Run and Suburban Filmgoing in Sydney in the Mid-1930s', in R. Maltby, D. Biltereyst and P. Meers (eds), *Explorations in New Cinema History: Approaches and Case Studies*, Malden: Blackwell, pp. 140–58.

Thompson, K. (1986), *Exporting Entertainment: America in the World Film Market, 1907–1934*, London: British Film Institute.

VKBB (1952), *Inlichtingsbulletijn/Information Bulletin, 7 (9)*.

—— (1953a), *Inlichtingsbulletijn/Information Bulletin, 8 (1–3)*.

—— (1953b), *Inlichtingsbulletijn/Information Bulletin, 8 (7)*.

Van de Vijver, L. (2011), 'Gent Kinemastad: Een multimethodisch onderzoek naar de onwikkeling van filmexploitatie, filmprogrammering en filmbeleving in de stad Gent en randgemeenten (1896–2010) als case binnen New Cinema History onderzoek', PhD thesis, Universiteit Gent.

Van Handenhove, C. (2002), 'Antwerpen Kinemastad', MA thesis, Universiteit Gent.

Zeguers, J. (2008), Interview with Kathleen Lotze and Philippe Meers, Antwerp, 4 July.

Notes

1 The quote in the title is from George Heylen about his spectacular survival of the bombing of the Rex cinema in December 1944. Quote in the national newspaper *De Morgen*, 23 July 1990 cited in Frederix 1995: 91.

2 At that moment, Antwerp's population was approximately 250,000. Unless indicated otherwise, with Antwerp we mean the city of Antwerp (current postcodes 2000 to 2060), without taking into account its outlying districts (postcodes 2100 to 2600), which currently belong to Antwerp as well.

3 The figures are based on the data published by the FOD Economie (Federale Overheidsdienst Economie/Belgian Federal Government Service for Economy) and the trade journal of the Vereniging der Kinemabestuurders van België/Belgian Association of Cinema Exhibitors (VKBB).

4 'The "Enlightened" City: Screen Culture between Ideology, Economics and Experience: A Study on the Social Role of Film Exhibition and Film Consumption in Flanders (1895–2004) in Interaction with Modernity and Urbanisation: Scientific Research Fund Flanders/FWO-Vlaanderen, 2005–08; promoters: Philippe Meers, Daniel Biltereyst and Marnix Beyen. The overall research project was based at the Universities of Antwerp and Ghent. The PhD project 'Antwerp Cinema City: A Media-historical Investigation into the Post-war Evolution of Film Exhibition and Reception in the City of Antwerp (1945–95) with a focus on the Rex group' is carried out at the University of Antwerp (2009–13 promoter: Philippe Meers, PhD candidate: Kathleen Lotze).

5 Our research is currently being expanded with 1982 and 1992 to cover the whole period of existence of the Rex cinema group.

6 Sources for this database were broad in range and consisted primarily of year books and annual reports, various theses, the original programming books of the Rex cinema group, as well as secondary literature about Antwerp's cinema history. In addition, interviews were conducted with historical key players within Antwerp's cinema sector.

7 It is quite remarkable that there was only one single cinema owned by one of the Hollywood majors: cinema Metro by MGM. However, its presence in Antwerp did not last long. Just 14 years after it had been opened by MGM, The Metro was taken over by Heylen in 1961. From this moment onwards, no cinema was exploited in Antwerp by an American major during the examined period. The cinema sector of the second largest Flemish city after Antwerp, Ghent, was marked by a similar fragmentation, and Hollywood majors were largely absent there as well (Van de Vijver 2011).

8 During that period, the average share of US productions at Flemish theatres was 81 per cent (VKBB 1952: 56; 1953a: 30, 35; 1953b: 9).

9 Former Secretary-General Zeguers: 'You needed sixteen or seventeen neighbourhood cinemas to make the revenues of one Metro, one Rubens or one Rex' (Magiels and De Hert 2004: 69).

10 Also compared with centre cinemas in Gent, the second Flemish city after Antwerp, the number of US productions there was considerably lower (Van de Vijver 2011: 160).

11 The Antwerp interviews were conducted by trained students under the supervision of Philippe Meers and researcher Gert Willems from the University of Antwerp. The interviews were transcribed in full and coded thematically. The researchers wish to thank Gert Willems and the many students at the University of Antwerp involved in this undertaking.

Chapter 14

From Out-of-town to the Edge and Back to the Centre: Multiplexes in Britain from the 1990s

Stuart Hanson

In 2010, Britain's first multiplex cinema, The Point in Milton Keynes, was 25 years old. The Point was one of the first purpose-built multiplexes in Europe, preceded only by developments in Sweden in 1980 and Belgium in 1982 (Delmestri and Wezel 2011), but significantly it was the first American multiplex in a foreign country. The Point was built and operated by the American Movie Corporation (AMC), with the benefit of 20 years' prior experience of the evolution in cinema-going in the United States – an evolution that had culminated in the development of the multiplex cinema in suburban and out-of-town shopping centres or malls. There was, however, no fanfare for this important and unique cinema as it reached a quarter of a century of operation. Indeed, it looks rather forlorn now, with its paint faded and metalwork rusty in places. Nevertheless, The Point is perhaps the most important cinema built in Britain since the heyday of the dream palaces in the 1930s, marking as it did a latter-day turning point in the fortunes of cinema-going in Britain.

By the start of World War II, there were over 4800 cinemas in Britain, and some 1.6 billion admissions were recorded in 1946 as over three-quarters of the population attended the cinema at least once a year, and one-third once a week or more (Box 1946). This was the zenith of cinema-going in Britain, as attendance declined every year thereafter until 1984, by which time cinema-going and cinemas were in a dire state. There were only 660 of them, half the number from ten years before, while annual admissions stood at 54 million (Hanson 2007). It was at this point – the nadir of cinema-going as a public entertainment – that the downward spiral of cinema attendance was reversed with The Point. From 1985, as the number of multiplexes increased, so did the number of cinema admissions – which rose steadily to reach 169 million in 2010 (BFI 2011: 9). Britain now has an excess of multiplex cinemas. In 2010, there were 278 of them, from a total of 716 cinemas, but multiplexes accounted for 75 per cent of screens (BFI 2011: 83–84). Three companies dominate the multiplex market in Britain – Odeon UCI, Cineworld and Vue – and they take some 70 per cent of the annual total box-office, which surpassed the significant £1 billion mark in 2009.

What happened between 1985 and now reveals much about the ways in which cinema-going in Britain has changed as a result of these new cinemas. Moreover, the story of the multiplex in Britain is linked inextricably to the fortunes of the city centre as a space for cultural and economic activity. Historically, the cinema has been an integral part of the urban landscape. When Milton Keynes was selected for Britain's first multiplex, the mould was cast for the development of a new cinema experience. Modelled on North America, the pattern of multiplex development was bound up with the shopping centre, and in particular the out-of-town shopping centre, at the expense of Britain's city and town centres. This chapter examines the development of the multiplex cinema from its inception in 1985, looking at the extent to which the development of the multiplex marked a break in this relationship with the city centre, only for it to be re-established in the first years of the twenty-first century. In doing so, consideration will be given to the complex interplay between planning, the market and the resurgence of the urban centre as the focus, both in Britain generally and more specifically via reference to the city of Leicester.

Post-war planning policy in Britain was concerned largely with accelerating the decentralization of populations in Britain's conurbations to new communities, notably in new towns and in the developing suburbs. The focus of developments in the new rebuilt and reshaped urban centres themselves was concerned with the commercial centre, which witnessed widespread rebuilding of shopping and business facilities in the 1950s and early 1960s. However, this was rarely accompanied by cinema development – especially outside London – and many cinemas destroyed by wartime bombing had not been replaced. For some ten years after the end of World War II, there were restrictions on luxury building, with housing the priority for planners. This meant that, notwithstanding some new cinemas built in the 1960s to replace those destroyed by bombing, there was no significant new building of cinemas in Britain until the multiplex in 1985. Nevertheless, Britain's town and city centres still contained most of the largest and most prestigious cinemas. The major exhibitors therefore concentrated on the modernization of these sites, including the dividing up of cinemas into multi-screen venues. This meant that the exhibitors' economic futures were tied largely to those of the city. Throughout this period, there was a steady fall in cinema attendance, and both ABC and Rank, the major cinema chains that dominated British exhibition, rationalized their operations, instigating subdivision of some cinemas and widespread closures of others. The number of cinema buildings fell from 1492 to 660, although the number of screens remained fairly constant due to the accelerated process of subdividing auditoria through what was referred to as 'twinning' and 'tripling' (Hanson 2007). For Britain's cinemas, this post-war metropolitan focus existed in the context of a steadily declining population in the city centre from the 1950s until the 1980s. For instance, in England and Wales between 1955 and 1985, 1.48 million houses were demolished and 3.66 million people displaced from city centres (Yelling 2000: 234).

The fortunes of the city and town centre were linked, Davis (1994) argues, to the issue of whether retail development should be allowed 'out of town' as distinct from 'in town', and this was the key issue that defined planning policy in Britain (Jones and Hillier 2000: 114). This resulted in a series of tensions amongst urban planners and developers following the 1970s, as Britain's provincial inner cities declined in relative importance as commercial and retail centres. The turning point was in part, according to Schiller (1986), the development of large out-of-town shopping centres, which he characterizes as the 'third wave' of retail decentralization in Britain. The 'first wave', in the 1970s, saw the development of large supermarkets outside of town centres, followed by the 'second wave' of what were called retail parks, primarily involving DIY centres, electrical retailers and furniture stores from the mid-1980s onwards.

This trend towards out-of-town developments in Britain was part of a general shift in favour of shopping and leisure in what was rapidly becoming a post-industrial economy, allied to the growing importance of the motor vehicle. In 1985–86, the proportion of households with access to a car was 62 per cent, rising to 75 per cent in 2010 (Department of Transport 2011). Throughout the post-war period, and especially into the 1980s, many people had moved to housing developments on the urban fringe, which led to greater demands for out-of-town shopping facilities. Moreover, many retailers – particularly the large chains – sought to reduce rents and combat the threat to business from city centre congestion by moving outwards. Increasingly, the pattern was extended to commercial and service sector industries, which sold off city-centre sites and built on the outskirts of cities and towns. Utilizing Garreau's (1992) conception of the 'Edge City', Barker (1996) refers to a process by which, for the preceding decade, Britain's cities had been 'turned inside out'. Barker observes that it is 'notable how many of the Conservatives' regeneration schemes end up pushing the Edge City phenomenon forward'.

During the 1980s, the Conservative government under Prime Minister Margaret Thatcher sought to encourage inward investment via a relaxed regulatory culture (see Gamble 1994), in which planning authorities had been instructed to be less rigid when considering applications for planning consent, in line with the government's free-enterprise philosophy. This much more *laissez-faire* approach to regional planning meant that there would be a presumption in favour of developments such as shopping centres (Crosby et al. 2005). The provision of new shopping facilities was a key element in the proposed regeneration of regional economies, in particular older industrial areas that effectively had become deindustrialized. The government proposed that the regeneration of these areas would come as a result of providing new jobs and better living conditions. This would not be achieved solely by direct government investment, but would require private capital.

For many of the developers, this inevitably meant the growth of the service sector in the form of retailing and leisure-based industries. Essentially, the Thatcher government's streamlining of planning procedures was a consolidation of the role of planning in supporting the market – indeed it was, according to Griffiths (2010: 5), nothing less than an effort to 'restructure for the market'. Some sense of the deeply ideological tenure of the government's proposals can be found in successive legislative changes to planning throughout the 1980s. In 1980, the *Local Government, Planning and Land Act* weakened the role of County Councils in favour of more district control, and introduced Enterprise Zones and Urban Development Corporations. In the Enterprise Zones, planning controls were relaxed with certain kinds of development, given what Guy (1994: 70) argues were 'in effect automatic planning permission'. Like Urban Development Corporations, which were created in order to regenerate former industrial areas, Enterprise Zones relied on private investment attracted by both this relaxed planning regime and a series of financial incentives. That ad hoc retail and leisure developments would dominate these areas was the outcome of a system in which no reference needed be made to a formal plan (Davies 1994: 233).

The result of such shifts in planning in the 1980s and early 1990s was that property markets became more speculative and the drive on part of retailers to get more efficient returns on capital meant that most proposals for major out-of-town shopping centres were approved, usually on the outskirts of major conurbations near to motorway junctions or major orbital roads. US cinema companies saw the parallel between these developments and those that had been so successful in the United States, especially since many catered for the car. This meant that the development of the multiplex cinema in Britain is intimately bound up with Schiller's (1994) 'third wave' of decentralized retail development.

Between 1986 and 1990, four major out-of-town shopping centres opened: the Metro Centre near Gateshead/Newcastle-on-Tyne; Merry Hill in the industrial West Midlands near Dudley; Lakeside near Thurrock on the M25 London orbital motorway; and Meadowhall near Sheffield. These centres were the location for the first round of multiplex developments. On three of these sites, UCI Cinemas[1] opened some of the first multiplexes in Britain, part of a boom in multiplex building that took place between 1985 and 1991, while Warner Bros opened one of its first multiplexes at Sheffield's Meadowhall in 1993. For the foreseeable future, one trade journal argued, the fate of the multiplex would 'be bound up with that of the shopping centre' (AIP & Co 1986: 30).

By the early 1990s, Britain had become the most developed multiplex market in Europe, with 42 new sites in the first five years and 82 in the first ten years after The Point opened (Dodona Research 2001). The construction that was undertaken in the initial building phase from 1985 to 1990 took place in areas carefully chosen using a range of criteria, including the multiplex's accessibility to the surrounding population, who could drive to the cinema, then park safely, conveniently and for free. The sites chosen were overwhelmingly, though not exclusively, in out-of-town locations around major cities. Very often, these were greenfield sites, cited frequently by developers as the only places on which multiplexes could be constructed, since with anything up to 12 screens and auditoria on a single floor, the new multiplexes –unlike traditional city-centre cinemas – needed large ground areas of 3000–4000 square metres, which along with car parking added up to some 15,000 square metres (Jones and Hillier 2000: 117).

A reliance on private rather than public transport was the corollary of these out-of-town developments, and this mobile population was one that the multiplex was able to court not only because the sites were convenient – near motorways, with free car parks – but also because many city cinemas had become an unattractive prospect precisely because they could not offer these facilities. In their study of the patronage of multiplex and non-multiplex cinemas, Collins et al. (2005) argue that those who travelled to out-of-town multiplexes were less sensitive to travel time and distance than those who went to cinemas in city centres. In part, this reflected a reliance on and necessity for private transport on the part of those who lived outside of city centres. This hypothesis seemed borne out by the CAVIAR 20 audience study, which indicated that 74 per cent of people who visited the cinema travelled there by car (Cinema Advertisers Association 2003).

Among many of the initial wave of US companies targeting Britain, the economic and political climate was both familiar to them and highly conducive to this new form of leisure-based industry. Moreover, the dominance of Britain's screens by Hollywood films reflected a broader climate of cultural connectedness with the United States. The speed with which Britain adopted the multiplex cinema was indicative of the extent to which what Delmestri and Wezel (2011: 831) call the 'cultural template of multiplexes' was less at odds with the 'cultural beliefs and practices' of Britain than it was of other countries in Europe. Implicit in this 'cultural template' was an acceptance that these new cinemas would be part of the central attraction of out-of-town leisure and shopping. The multiplex's location within, and in relation to, the shopping or leisure complex is indicative of a changed cinema culture in which, Smith (2005: 246) argues, there has been a 'discursive meshing of their spatial conditions and consumption practices and that this has been a deliberate strategy of the multiplex industry'. The consequences of out-of-town centres in terms of their impact on city centres seemed clear to many city councils – which, according to AMC's Bruno Frydman (1998), feared that the advent of multiplexes would take the cinema-going public away from town and city centres, with audiences irresistibly drawn by the leisure attractions that tended to spring up around cinemas.

Throughout the 1980s and 1990s, multiplex developments proceeded apace, with the majority of sites opened outside of the traditional city centres. This was not to say that cities did not see some new multiplex developments, especially those opened in Enterprise Zones and areas covered by Urban Development Corporations; however, many of these were in areas of the conurbation that competed with established commercial and retail centres.

In Leicester, a major city of some 280,000 people in the East Midlands region, the pattern of cinema developments has broadly followed national trends. In 1995, Warner Bros opened the city's first multiplex cinema – rebranded as Warner Village a year later, after the merger with Village Roadshow. With nine screens, it was part of a development called Meridian Leisure Park, 5 miles from the city centre, near the M69 and M1 motorways, with parking for several hundred cars and a range of chain-restaurants such as Burger King and Nandos, and a ten-pin bowling alley. Meridian Leisure Park was located away from the city centre but on a site that was characterized, according to revised *PPG6 Planning for Town Centres* (ODPM 2005) as 'out-of-centre'. In this context, 'out-of-centre' was defined as a 'location which is not in or on the edge of a centre but not necessarily outside the urban area' (ODPM 2005: 31). Although there was a bus service from the city centre to the site, and the surrounding neighbourhoods, it was irregular in the evenings and at weekends, meaning that the primary mode of transport would be the private car.

At this time, there were still three traditional cinemas located in the city centre – the Cannon, ABC and Odeon – all of which had been divided up into multi-screen venues in the 1970s. In January 1997, the Cannon closed, with construction of a new 12-screen Odeon multiplex underway on the site of the former cattle market at Freemans Park, just off the city's inner-ring road. With the new Odeon multiplex set to open in July 1997, the old Odeon cinema – first opened in 1938 – ceased operation. The ABC was sold to an independent exhibitor in May 1997; it was renamed the Belle Vue Cinema and began showing 'Bollywood' films (Johnson 2007). This meant that the new Odeon multiplex was the nearest cinema to the city centre that showed mainstream film releases. Though located within the central city core, the redeveloped Freemans Park was neither a 'town-centre' site (within the primary shopping area) nor an 'edge-of-centre' site, defined as 'a location that is well connected to and within easy walking distance (i.e. up to 300 metres) of the primary shopping area' (ODPM 2005: 31). Though situated less than a mile from the main shopping area, the existence of a large car park and the difficulty of walking easily from the city centre suggested that the developers still expected many cinema-goers to travel by car.

The only cinemas left in the city centre in the wake of these multiplex developments were the Phoenix Arts Centre, which showed predominantly art-house and speciality films alongside live performances and cultural events, and the Belle Vue Cinema. This meant that, according to Hubbard (2004), the two Leicester multiplexes 'accounted for 88 per cent of admissions in the city'. Hubbard's (2004) interviews with cinema-goers suggest that the Warner Village cinema attracted regular cinemagoers and those in groups – especially families – who saw going to the cinema as part of a whole night out that included eating before or afterwards. The Odeon multiplex was more popular with less frequent cinema-goers, students and those without access to a car, while the Phoenix's clientele attended cinema much more infrequently and had an older age profile.

Where the existing two largest chains, Rank (Odeon cinemas) and Cannon, opened multiplexes on the outskirts of towns and cities, they invariably closed their existing cinemas nearby. Moreover, they were also inclined to close these cinemas when other competitors opened a multiplex nearby. In 1991, UCI estimated that its cinemas had taken 10–35 per cent of business away from other cinema operators, while Rank insisted that the figure was nearer to 50 per cent in the case of many of its Odeon cinemas (*Screen Digest* 1991). In the ten years after the first multiplex opened in 1985, approximately 70 non-multiplex cinemas closed, which meant that for every multiplex opened at least one non-multiplex cinema closed. Dodona Research (2003: 16) was unambiguous in its assessment of cinema closures, stating that 'cinema closures generally represent a contribution to the process of moving cinemas from where they are not wanted to where they are, most often to somewhere with parking'.

Retail and leisure developments throughout the 1980s and early 1990s, then, were dominated to a large extent by an increase in car ownership; the long and steady process of urban decentralization; a lack of suitable sites for development in city centres; cheaper land and property rents in out-of-town sites; and the introduction of development zones with the concomitant relaxation in planning (see Jones and Hillier, 2000; Davies 1994; Fernie 1995). Wroe (1995) observes that it is 'no coincidence' that 'British leisure is joining British retailing in an exodus from the town centre to its edges'. However, among central government and local authorities, there were the beginnings of a shift – especially with a growing sense of unease about the impact of out-of-town leisure on the city centre and the introduction of more restrictive planning guidelines intended to rejuvenate Britain's neglected urban centres.

This renewed interest in city centres – a process called 'recentralisation' (Ravenscroft 2000: 2533) – reflects a change in planning priorities for leisure-based developments between 1993 and 1997 under John Major's Conservative government. In 1994, *Transport Planning Policy Guidance Note 13 (PPG13)* sought to reduce private car use and promote the use of public transport by encouraging planning authorities to 'make maximum use of the most accessible sites, such as those in town centres' (Department of the Environment 1994b, para. 21). In 1996, the new emphasis placed upon regenerating urban centres was explicitly signalled in *PPG6 Town Centres and Retail Developments* (Department of the Environment 1996), which sought to roll back the trend for out-of-town developments; while not outlawing them completely, it sought to encourage edge-of-centre or town-centre developments. Moreover, *PPG6* was the first to make special mention of multi-screen cinemas (see Pal and Jones 1996).

In 1997, the incoming Labour government under Prime Minister Tony Blair reinforced the commitment to developing urban centres and further discouraging out-of-town developments. The watchwords were increasingly 'sustainable development', with out-of-town developments increasingly seen as encouraging excessive use of motor cars, having a poor public transport infrastructure and building on valuable greenfield land. The pendulum swung decisively in 1999 with the publication of *A Better Quality of Life* (Department of Environment, Transport and the Regions 1999). In order to deliver sustainable development – defined as 'ensuring a better quality of life for everyone, now and for generations to come' (1999: para. 1.1) – planning regulations stressed the role leisure and shopping developments could have on sustaining the 'vitality and viability' of urban centres. Leisure – including bars, restaurants and multiplex cinemas – would encourage visitors into the urban centre outside of normal shopping and work hours, with the explicit aim of creating a more vibrant night-time economy (see Ennis-Reynolds 2002). The changes in planning regulations that sought to stimulate the growth of cinemas and other leisure sites in urban centres also saw an increase in the number of residential developments in the city centre, and an attempt to encourage – through planning and diversification of land use – an 'urban renaissance' (Office of the Deputy Prime Minister 2004).

Although the rhetoric of sustainable development was new, the importance of commercial interests was still paramount. The development of new spaces for retail and leisure, as part of a broad strategy of 'regeneration' in Britain's towns and cities, would rest ultimately on encouraging private developers in 'partnership' with local authorities (see Jones et al. 2003). Leicester, like several other localities, had begun to do this in 1994 when it introduced its Town Centre Management (TCM) programme. It was entirely in keeping with the discourse of public–private partnership, and among its four aims was one of enhancing 'the attraction of Leicester, not only for shopping but also for leisure activities, tourism, cultural activities and entertainment, year round, day and night' (Jones and Hillier 2000: 121).

Signalling what was clearly emerging as a shift of emphasis from out-of-town to city centres, AMC's head of European operations, Bruno Frydman (1998), observed that:

> On the basis of my experience so far, I would say that the new factor which we have had to come to terms with in Europe is the need to work with town and city centres. This is a continent-wide mentality: in Italy and Germany, for example, the vitality of urban centres has always been a priority. But now the United Kingdom has also introduced legislation making multiplexes proposed for the suburbs of major cities subject to approval by the local authorities and requiring such schemes to meet criteria set by central government.

In 2002, *Screen Finance* reported that multiplex building had slowed down, in part as a result of a series of takeovers. What was less clear from the article was that by 2000 the landscape for cinema development had literally and figuratively changed, in part as a result of changes to the prevailing planning culture in the 1990s, and a subsequent cultural and economic turn back towards the urban centre as a site of retailing and leisure. In a paper given in 2001 at a conference on Cinemas in the Community, Dodona Research's Karsten-Peter Grummitt informed delegates that for the first time the majority of new multiplex openings were in city centres, or what increasingly were referred to as 'out-of-centres' rather than out-of-town locations (cited in Ennis-Reynolds 2002: 318).

That year, AMC – reflecting the changes indicated by Frydman (1988) – re-entered the British multiplex cinema market. It opened two new multiplexes in mixed-use city centre developments in Manchester's Great Northern 16 development (a converted railway goods warehouse) and Birmingham's Broadway Plaza (a converted children's hospital and adjoining site). Another new entrant to the multiplex market, Ster Century (part of the South African Ster-Kinekor chain), also focused on town-centre sites, including The Light in Leeds, which incorporated a 13-screen cinema and a range of restaurants, bars and shops, as well as a health club. The building had formerly been the large inter-war office of a local building society. These cinema developments reflected a national trend as the number of screens in city centres or edge-of-centre cinemas increased by over 20 per cent between 2001 and 2004 (UK Film Council 2004: 40).

By the early part of the new millennium, local authorities across Britain were engaged in concerted efforts to engender what Ennis-Reynolds (2002: 327) identifies as a 'leisure-led renaissance' in their city centres. In Leicester, like other cities, this saw a variety of strategies, two of which – the designation of cultural zones or quarters and the identification of areas for redevelopment as shopping centres – were common. In both, the cinema would be seen as an important element in attracting people back to the city centre. In 1999, the city council designated what it saw as the rundown area of St Georges as Leicester's Cultural Quarter, in which it sought to create a group or cluster of creative and cultural industries as an engine for regeneration. In order to attract both business and residential development, the council improved streets and pavements, including the installation of new street furniture and art works.

The two principal attractions were a new £61 million theatre called The Curve and the £21 million Phoenix Square Digital Media Centre designed by Marsh Grochowski. Like the Curve, Phoenix Square was funded by the city council and a private developer, and opened in 2009. The centre incorporated two cinema screens with the capability to show 3D, digital and 35mm prints, in addition to a café bar, galleries, workshops, digital production facilities and office spaces, and over 60 residential apartments. Phoenix Square replaced the existing Phoenix Arts Centre in the centre of the city.

The second element of the city council's regeneration plan for Leicester's city centre was for an addition to the existing Shires shopping centre complex. The council itself could not fund such an ambitious project; however, it invested some £19 million in the 'Streets and Spaces' project, which was intended to improve the physical environment of the city centre, including pedestrianization, new seating and street furniture. This was seen as instrumental in encouraging the necessary inward investment from what would be a partnership between two private developers – Hammerson and Hermes. Built on former industrial brownfield land, the refurbishment of the existing centre and new extension cost £350 million. Renamed Highcross, it incorporated a multi-storey car park with 2000 spaces, two public squares and two anchor developments: a John Lewis department store and a 12-screen multiplex cinema operated by the American company Showcase.

Foreign Office Architects, most closely identified with Yokohama's iconic port terminal, designed the Showcase and adjoining John Lewis department store, working to a strict brief that entailed designing a two-part box that would be distinguished not by the interior but by the exterior. The rear of the two buildings faced the main thoroughfare in Leicester, with pedestrians approaching the development from a multi-storey car park across a glazed bridge, and was therefore intended to be a spectacle – especially at night. The Showcase cinema is clad in highly polished stainless steel panels, with curved and sinewy elevations, while the department store consists of two skins of glass etched with a fabric design pattern from John Lewis's back catalogue (Woodman 2008).

Leicester's Showcase was one of three such multiplexes opened in Britain, the others being in nearby Derby and in Bristol, newly branded by the company as 'Cinema de Lux'. All are marketed as more luxurious cinemas, and have two restaurants, one of which is part of a licensed cinema screen called the Director's Lounge. What is really significant about these developments, though, is that they are all located at the centre of the three cities, as anchors within new shopping developments. In seeking to explain the attraction of out-of-town multiplexes, Hubbard (2002: 1240) argues that what was occurring was a 'spatial switching' of cinema-going to these sites from those in the city centre. This was in part based on a perception of the city as a threatening and unsafe place, largely associated with the less affluent. Developments like Highcross are evidence of an observation Hopkins (1991 cited in Ravenscroft 2000: 3535) made about the ways in which town centres were 'moving indoors, both literally and metaphorically'. This was the corollary of a steady attempt to make safe the 'unsafe external environment' (Ravenscroft 2000: 3535) by recreating the controlled spaces of the out-of-town shopping centre.

Since 2000, there have been many town centre-based multiplex developments. Like leisure parks on the periphery of the city – such as Leicester's Meridian Leisure Park – the multiplex cinema is almost exclusively the anchor tenant to a mixed retail and leisure scheme. The multiplex's importance to developers is that they help guarantee visitor numbers and offset the increased construction and development costs – which, according to cost consultant Davis Langdon & Everest (2000), are approximately 20 per cent higher than comparable out-of-town sites. Unlike many leisure facilities that require large ground areas – such as health and fitness clubs and ten-pin bowling – multiplex operators have been able to adapt their designs to suit smaller ones by building multi-storey developments (Mintel Oxygen 2009). The attractions of a mixed-use complex extend beyond the possible cost savings to encompass many of the perceived advantages of the out-of-town site, including adjacent car parking, shelter from the elements, proximity of other leisure attractions and personal safety.

In 2010, the UK Film Council (2011: 89) reported that 47 per cent of Britain's 3671 cinema screens were in town/city centres, 14 per cent in edge-of-centre sites and 36 per cent in out-of-town sites. Given that the overwhelming majority of Britain's traditional cinemas are in town and city centres, the multiplex cinema is still located predominantly outside the urban centre. Nevertheless, the changes to planning laws over the past 15 years, and a developing culture of 'town centres first', have seen the re-emergence of the cinema as a key feature of the city centre. In part, the attractions of the multiplex cinema in both out-of-town or city centre rests with the relative attractions of both locations to cinema-goers, and these are determined by a range of demographic factors. According to research undertaken by Mintel Oxygen (2009), 'almost all types of consumers are more likely to have visited an out-of-town cinema than one in a city/town centre location, reflecting the greater prevalence of multiplex cinemas in out-of-town sites'. Nevertheless, cinema-going 'attracts more than half of all adults to town centres' (Mintel Oxygen 2009), suggesting the importance of cinemas to the developing urban leisure and retail economy. This is increasingly an economy that positions the cinema in relation to a series of other commercial and leisure enterprises, such as bars, nightclubs and restaurants, whose express appeal is to young people and non-car drivers. The concentration of such outlets in Britain's town and city centres has encouraged 'leisure grazing' (Ennis-Reynolds 2002: 326) and a bias towards those aged 16–34 (Mintel Oxygen 2009). If one considers that cinema's predominant audience is 15–34-year-olds (UK Film Council 2011), then one can see how the cinema assumes a key position in this new urban, leisure-based economy. Broadly speaking, where a city centre multiplex exists, it has proven popular with younger audiences and those unwilling to drive. Out-of-town and edge-of-centre multiplexes are popular with families and those wishing to park easily and for free (Mintel Oxygen 2009).

The four major multiplex operators – Odeon, Vue, Cineworld and Showcase –have been able to use their market dominance to maintain a strong presence in all categories of sites, especially via their inclusion in new prestigious city-centre developments across Britain. The much-vaunted resurgence of Britain's cities might, in the straitened financial circumstances of a recession, be premature. In many ways, though, the move from the out of town to the centre of towns and cities has not altered the one central feature of multiplex development in Britain: multiplexes continue to dominate the market in terms of box office, numbers of screens and cinema visits, and this looks set to continue in the foreseeable future.

References

AIP & Co (1986), 'The Point – Signalling a New Era in Cinema Exhibition?', *October*, 78, n.p.

Barker, P. (1996), 'The Future is Here and Now: Lots of Happy Smiling People Tripping to the Shopping Mall. But Does It Work?', *Guardian*, 8 October.

BFI (2011), *2011 Statistical Yearbook*, London: British Film Institute.

Box, K. (1946), *The Cinema and the Public* (An Inquiry into Cinema Going Habits and Expenditure made in 1946), London: Ministry of Information.

Cinema Advertisers Association (2003), *Cinema and Video Industry Audience Research (CAVIAR)*, London: Cinema Advertisers Association.

Collins, A., Hand, C. and Ryder, A. (2005), 'The Lure of the Multiplex? The Interplay of Time, Distance and Cinema Attendance', *Environment and Planning*, 37, pp. 483–501.

Crosby, N., Hughes, C., Lizieri, C. and Oughton, M. (2005), 'A Message from the Oracle: The Land Use Impact of a Major In-town Shopping Centre on Local Retailing', *Journal of Property Research*, 22: 2–3, pp. 245–56.

Davies, R. (1994), 'Retail Planning Policy', in P.J. McGoldrick (ed.), *Cases in Retail Management*, London: Pitman.

Davis Langdon & Everest (2000), 'Cost Model', *Building*, 5 May, http://www.davislangdon.com/upload/StaticFiles/EME%20Publications/CostModels/MultiplexCinemas_CM_5May00.pdf. Accessed 12 October 2011.

Delmestri, G. and Wezel, F. (2011), 'Breaking the Wave: The Contested Legitimation of an Alien Organizational Form', *Journal of International Business Studies*, 42, pp. 828–52.

Department of the Environment (1994a), *Sustainable Development: The UK Strategy*, London: HMSO.

—— (1994b), *Transport Planning Policy Guidance, PPG13*, London: HMSO.

—— (1996), *Town Centres and Retail Development, Planning Policy Guidance*, London: HMSO.

Department of Environment, Transport and the Regions (1999), *A Better Quality of Life – A Strategy for Sustainable Development*, London: DETR.

Department of Transport (2011), *National Travel Survey Statistical Release*, 28 July, http://assets.dft.gov.uk/statistics/releases/national-travel-survey-2010/nts2010-01.pdf. Accessed 8 October 2011.

Dodona Research (2001), *Cinemagoing 9*, Leicester: Dodona Research.

—— (2003) *Cinemagoing 11*, Leicester: Dodona Research.

Ennis-Reynolds, G. (2002), 'Sustainable Development and Multiplexes', *Journal of Leisure Property*, 2: 4, pp. 317–31.

Fernie, J. (1995), 'The Coming of the Fourth Wave: New Forms of Retail Out-of-town Development', *International Journal of Retail and Distribution Management*, 23: 1, pp. 4–11.

Frydman, B. (1998), 'Exporting the Multiplex Model to Europe: The Experience of AMC', paper presented at the MEDIA Salles round table, 'The Impact of Multiplexes on the Cinema Market and on their Environment', Amsterdam – Cinema Expo International, 15 June, http://www.mediasalles.it/expo98fr.htm. Accessed 10 September 2011.

Gamble, A. (1994), *Britain in Decline: Economic Policy, Political Strategy and the British State*, 4th edn, Basingstoke: Macmillan.

Garreau, J. (1992), *Edge City: Life on the New Frontier*, New York: Anchor Books.

Griffiths, R. (2010), 'Planning in Retreat? Town Planning and the Market in the Eighties', *Planning Practice and Research*, 1: 1, pp. 3–7.

Guy, C. (1994), *The Retail Development Process: Location, Property and Planning*, London: Routledge.

Hanson, S. (2000), 'Spoilt for Choice? Multiplexes in the 90s', in R. Murphy (ed.), *British Cinema of the 90s*, London: British Film Institute.

—— (2007), *From Silent Screen to Multi-screen: A History of Cinema-going in Britain Since 1896*, Manchester: Manchester University Press.

Hopkins, J.S.P. (1991), 'West Edmonton Mall as a Center for Social Interaction', *The Canadian Geographer*, 35, pp. 268–79.

Hubbard, P. (2002), 'Screen-shifting: Consumption, "Riskless Risks" and the Changing Geographies of Cinema', *Environment and Planning A*, 34: 7, pp. 1239–58.

—— (2004), '(Going Out (of Town): New Geographies of Cinema-Going in the UK', *Scope: An online journal of film and TV studies*, http://www.scope.nottingham.ac.uk/article.php?issue=feb2004&id=245&section=article&q=hubbard. Accessed 7 October 2011.

Johnson, B. (2007), *100 years of Leicester Cinema*, Chalford: Tempus.

Jones, P. and Hillier, D. (2000), 'Changing the Balance – the "Ins and Outs" of Retail Development', *Property Management*, 18: 2, pp. 114–26.

Jones, P., Hillier, D. and Comfort, D. (2003), 'Urban Regeneration Companies and City Centres', *Management Research News*, 26: 1, pp. 54–63.

Mintel Oxygen (2009), 'In- vs Out-of-town Leisure', *Leisure Intelligence Reports*, http://oxygen.mintel.com/index.html. Accessed 4 July 2011.

Office of the Deputy Prime Minister (2004), *Making it Happen: Urban Renaissance and Prosperity in our Core Cities: A Tale of Eight Cities*, Wetherby, West Yorkshire: ODPM.

—— (2005), *Planning for Town Centres, Planning Policy Guidance, PPG6*, London: HMSO.

Pal, J. and Jones, P. (1996), 'Multiplexes – What's the Picture?', *Town and Country Planning*, 65: 12, pp. 344–45.

Ravenscroft, N. (2000), 'The Vitality of Viability of Town Centres', *Urban Studies*, 37: 13, pp. 2533–49.

Schiller, R. (1986), 'Retail Decentralisation – The Coming of the Third Wave', *The Planner*, July, pp. 13–15.

—— (1994) 'Vitality and Viability: Challenge to the Town Centre', *International Journal of Retail & Distribution Management*, 22: 6, pp. 46–50.

Screen Digest (1991), 'United Kingdom: The Most Developed Multiplex Market Provides Pointers for European Developments', July, pp. 157–58.

Screen Finance (2003), 'Exhibition UK: Multiplex Numbers Fall for First Time in 2002', 26 March, pp. 4–5.

Smith, J. (2005), 'Cinema for Sale: The Impact of the Multiplex on Cinema Going in Britain, 1985–2000', *Journal of British Cinema and Television*, 2: 2, pp. 242–55.

UK Film Council (2004), *Statistical Yearbook/Annual Review 2004/05*, London: UK Film Council.

Woodman, E. (2008), 'Foreign Office Architects: No, It's Not a Guggenheim – It's a John Lewis', *Daily Telegraph*, 3 December.

Wroe, M. (1995), 'Pre-packed Fun in the Pleasure Dome', *Observer*, 8 October.

Yelling, J. (2000), 'The Incidence of Slum Clearance in England and Wales, 1955–85', *Urban History*, 27: 2, pp. 234–54.

Note

1   In December 1988, AMC announced that it would pull out of the British market. It sold its eight multiplexes to a partnership of CIC and United Artists Communications, which was renamed United Cinemas International (UCI).

PART IV

On the Margins

Chapter 15

The Place of Rural Exhibition: Makeshift Cinema-going and the
Highlands and Islands Film Guild (Scotland)

Ian Goode

The title of the seminal text *What is Cinema?* by André Bazin (1967) suggests an attempt to understand cinema as a relative totality, which takes into account the exhibition of film in the space of the cinema. Other theorists, such as Jean-Louis Baudry (1975) offer a more comprehensive theorization of the cinema apparatus. Despite these limitations, the achievement of *What is Cinema* is to set out some of the founding ideas on the aesthetics of film. The place of film exhibition in this examination of cinema is at best marginal, but Bazin's original question continues to invite responses as the geography of film history research expands beyond the urban context (Fuller-Seeley 2008: Maltby et al. 2007).

My concern here is to situate the exhibition of film in rural and culturally peripheral locations into the discussion of what cinema is and how it is historicized, using the example of Scotland's Highlands and Islands Film Guild during the post-World War II years. This provision of cinema to rural communities was made possible by the availability of the 16mm apparatus (Brown 2005; Lebas 2010; Slide 1992) and that broader definition of utility that Charles Acland has termed 'useful cinema' (Acland 2009; Acland and Wasson 2011). This cinema is described as 'institutionally functional deployments of moving image materials that exploited the relative mobility of the cinematic apparatus, and with it the conversion of sundry locations into screening sites' (Acland 2009: 152). Rural cinema in this case is useful and rural because there were no static, purpose-built cinemas close enough to be readily available to many of the often-remote communities in the Highlands and Islands of Scotland (Aveyard 2011). This framework of inquiry is motivated by exhibition history, but also considers what this cinema was and what cinema meant within this extended geography. I want to add to the dialogue that is currently revisiting Bazin, and also add to the work on peripheral cinemas (Andrew 2011; Fish 2007).

Bazin's interrogation of film is carried out comparatively through the related cultural forms of theatre and painting (Bazin 1967). In this example, the spatial dynamics of the theatre and the cinema screen are brought together in order to demonstrate their difference:

There can be no theater without architecture. Founded on the reciprocal awareness of those taking part and present to one another, it must be in contrast to the rest of the world in the same way that play and reality are opposed. The screen is not a frame like that of a picture but a mask which allows only a part of the action to be seen. There are no wings to the screen. There could not be without destroying its specific illusion, which is to make of a revolver or of a face the very center of the universe. In contrast to the stage the space of the screen is centrifugal. (1967: 105)

Bazin argues that, unlike theatre, the space of the cinema is extraneous to an understanding of its essence. This account of cinema emphasizes how the basis of theatre emerges out of the spatial relations between stage, actor and audience within the auditorium. The elimination of the conditions of film exhibition and the audience in the cinema from the comparison reveals the limits of the analysis.

A comparative account of theatre and cinema is also offered by Iain Mackintosh:

> Theatre is a three dimensional and three-way event, actor or actors communicating, not simply with you, the spectator, but with you and he, or she, over here and that group over there. All interact with the other. In cinema, which is a passive art form, you and your reactions are pre-programmed by the director, crew, cast and writer. The air conditioning must break down, the seats collapse or the man in the front row snore before you are made as aware of your surroundings as of the film. The cinema goer's communication with that ghostly image on the screen is one way: all he or she can do is listen or watch. (1993: 2)

This essentialist view of cinema assumes that the act of cinema-going and the experience of the exhibition space are secondary to the film projected on to the screen. In these accounts, the aesthetic and experiential relationship between cinema and theatre is antithetical. Historical research on film audiences shows that the exceptional circumstances that Mackintosh anticipates would generate awareness of surroundings in the cinema occur much more frequently than he assumes. Inquiries into the audience from the 1930s show how the unruly younger audience responded interactively to the cinema-going experience (Kuhn 2002: 100; Smith 2005: 77). Similar audience reactions are also likely to have occurred in the smaller, improvised spaces of village halls that hosted rural cinema. I want to suggest from this theoretical beginning, in combination with selected rural cinema-going memories and summative accounts gathered from my own research in the Scottish Highlands, that one of the consequences of the expansion of film history beyond the city is that the place of exhibition and its effect on the viewing experience can contribute to the understanding of what constitutes cinema. Historical research into cinema-going need not necessarily be positioned in methodological opposition to some of the suggestions of film theory represented here by Bazin (Kepley 1996).

The Highlands and Islands Film Guild

The Highlands and Islands Film Guild was formed in 1946 following the wartime success of other mobile cinemas in Scotland, particularly the Evacuees Film Scheme and the provision of 16mm cinema programmes to armed forces bases through the Entertainments National Service Association (ENSA) (Goode 2011). The exhibition of films outside cinema auditoriums had been championed previously by Scottish national John Grierson in 1936. Addressing the National Council of Women at the head post office in Manchester, Grierson (1935) referred to this practice as non-theatrical cinema, and implored the audience to 'look for the non-theatrical cinema in halls such as this, in YMCA halls, in church halls, rather than in the theatres' (Druick 2008).[1] The Scotsman anticipated that this form of exhibition, supported by the documentary film, could deliver a greater role for film in public education (Tallents 1955).

The Guild was formed as a result of a conference that gathered together the Scottish Agricultural Organisation Society, local authorities, government and social organizations, with the aid of a capital grant from the Carnegie UK Trust (Ross 1966: 269). Its functions were set out as follows:

(a) improving the educational, cultural and recreational amenities available to rural communities in the Highlands and Islands of Scotland by exhibiting and organising the exhibition of films on a non-profit-making basis;
(b) in close association with education authorities and other statutory or voluntary bodies concerned with the welfare of rural communities in Scotland, advising, assisting and co-operating with local organisations, such as community associations, whose objects might include the use and development of films for the purposes of education and recreation, and to promoting and encouraging the formation of such organisations and associations in areas where they did not already exist;
(c) assisting education authorities in furthering the educational use of films in rural schools and communities;
(d) producing or encouraging the production of films which might become permanent records of Scottish life etc. (1966: 271).

These functions clearly were civic rather than commercial. The rhetoric of informed provision allied with the instrumental use of film for education is clearly signalled. The organization of this service can be viewed as another means of countering depopulation from the rural communities of the Highlands and Islands to the cities in the south.[2] The operations of the Guild were coordinated from a central office based in Edinburgh, and from 1952 further north in Inverness. The operators were allocated cinema vans and areas where they would transport and deliver a predetermined programme of cinema on 16mm to the rural counties – from the Shetland Isles in the far north to Ross and Argyle in the South of the Highlands area (Ross 1966: 271).

The organization of the Film Guild and some of its more instrumental functions were informed by the previous decade and the growing discourse on the potential effects of cinema on the young. The 1933 Edinburgh Cinema Inquiry found that the cinema represented 'an influence of first importance in the lives of children' (Smith 2005: 93). Sarah Smith points out that the Edinburgh report does not replicate the moral panic evident in other inquiries carried out in other parts of the United Kingdom. However, it does note the importance of film certification and the role of the British Board of Film Censors in maintaining screen standards (Smith 2005: 92–93).[3]

The concern with the influence of cinema within the wider relations between young people, education and leisure is continued by the *Education Act* of 1944 (Tinkler 2001).

Educative paternalism advanced throughout the 1930s and 1940s is illustrated here by an Edinburgh schoolteacher. May Gordon Williamson is at pains to point out how 'more children go oftener to the cinema in Scotland than in any other country in the world' (Williamson 1956: 273). She goes on to argue for the necessity of children learning

> to distrust appeals directed solely to the emotions and to analyze the means by which the appeal is made. Only by educating them in the techniques of the cinema can this be achieved; and the first essential of all criticism, literary, artistic or musical, to be learned is the ability to discriminate between sham and sincerity, between sentimentality and sentiment. (Williamson 1956: 274)

This teacher recognized that the efforts being made to transport film to the scattered population of rural Scotland added to the importance of the Scottish Educational Film Association and British Film Institute initiatives already underway in the cities to cultivate film appreciation among young people (Williamson 1956: 275).

The delivery of non-theatrical cinema to the Highlands and Islands emerged from the institutionally governed relationship between education and film. Audience access was subject to the demand to impart a more critical disposition towards commercial cinema entertainment. The imperative of cultural enlightenment evinced by education policy was heightened by the prospect of this influential vehicle of modernity being made regularly available to rural communities. It is clear from the views of this teacher that young rural audiences could be prevented from going the same way as their urban equivalents with the correct direction, and the younger audience in general and the rural audience in particular both required influence and awaited improvement.

The children's matinees that allowed children in cities to go to the cinema without their parents, and were a response of the cinema industry to the burgeoning attendance of the young, were not a feature of rural cinema programming. The rural cinema operators screened educational films in schools, while later in the day the full Film Guild programme addressed the audience as a family with a typical evening bill consisting of a cartoon, a newsreel, the main feature film and a trailer (Ross 1966: 291). As Ross reports, 'prior to the advent of television in the late 1950s, 40 out of every 100 attending Film Guild evening shows were under the age of 16' (Ross 1966: 275). It is clear that the young people in the rural audience were a key consideration in the objectives of the Film Guild and in the education policy of the post-war years. What is less known is how young people both responded to and were involved in these developments in the cultural life of the Highlands and Islands.

The characteristics of rural cinema

The Guild depended on the dedicated work of its trained operators, who were responsible for delivering non-theatrical cinema to selected rural locations. The journey of the operator and the cinema van containing the 16mm cinema apparatus to the rural community was a precondition of exhibition. So too was the provision of a generator for power, in the days before electricity began to be made available to the Highlands and Islands by the Scottish Hydro-Electric Board in the 1950s (Miller 2002). The journey taken by this cinema and its operators through the less-than-accommodating landscape and harsh climate of northern Scotland informs the terms of its remembrance evident in the anecdotal narratives of local histories (Cameron 1993).

As the service expanded, transportation was complemented by static units where equipment would be dedicated to the more remote locations to remove the necessity for transportation. This was a cinema that was made rural, in part, by the geography of the area. The secretary T.S. Morris illustrates this in his account of the work of the Film Guild in 1955:

> It was a cold, wet day in February, 1952. A half-gale was blowing. The crofters and fisher folk crowded the jetty, watching anxiously. Would the generator arrive in time? Without it, Fetlar, in the north of Shetland and almost in the Arctic Circle, would not get its film show; without it the Highlands and Islands Film Guild, with the best of intentions in the world, could not supply the precious hours of happy entertainment to this outpost of Scotland. But it did arrive. And after a spell of feverish activity it was safely installed at the school. The engine was tested, and all awaited Willie Williamson the Guild's operator … And in spite of the bitter cold, sleet and shocking roads, the show went on with an audience of almost fifty – a very big crowd indeed on Fetlar. (Morris 1955: 28)[4]

The location of the far north and the journeys required to reach the Shetland Isles show how geography exerts its influence on this makeshift cinema. It is clear that Morris wanted to highlight the journeys and the conditions that defined the work of the Film Guild. This was cinema exhibition on the edge – often against the odds and in the face of meteorological adversity and geographical exigency.

A further example of the improvisation demanded by rural cinema is offered by Eshaness, a remote headland on the north western tip of the Shetland mainland:

> Eshaness, craggy and isolated, provides a rather special example of its appreciation. The hall there stands in the middle of what is almost a peat bog and there was no access road. The problem was a simple one – no road, no films. That was a challenge and the Shetlanders love a challenge: a common saying among these descendants of the hardy Vikings is 'Say du nawthin', but that does not mean they do nothing. The men set to, carted stones and rubble, dumped it into the old track and so made their road, whilst the women, equally anxious and willing, forgot their knitting and attended to the refreshments. In a day and a night the job was done and George Horne, the Guild's first operator, drove his van up for the show. (Morris 1955: 30)

The Shetland locations selected by Morris maximize the remoteness and unaccommodating character of the landscape and the response of the community to it. However, this account –

which typifies how this cinema is remembered and narrated by those closely involved with it – demonstrates how rural cinema in Scotland and its vital journeys were subject to both local geography and climate. The movement of the cinema apparatus and its operator from an administrative centre to peripheral locations in rural communities, where it was assembled for exhibition and later dismantled, rendered this mode of cinema makeshift, but also made it part of a cherished, communal experience. The narration of post-war cinema in these terms offers a contrast to the prevailing understanding of cinema after the early period as a fixture of urban modernity (Richards 1984).

It is less clear how the particular characteristics of exhibition influenced the audience experience of this mode of non-theatrical cinema. Given that the exhibition of this cinema was improvised, in what follows cinema-going experience is privileged, following Francesco Casetti's (2009) suggestion that this means something more than the reception of individual films; it also underlines Robert Allen's concern that film history should uncover the 'the sociality of the experience of cinema' (Allen 2010: 266).

The rural cinema-going experience

Empirical work on cinema audiences has shown that spectators remember the experience of going to the cinema more often than they do the individual film (Kuhn 2002: 100). Given the scarcity of cinema in the Highlands and Islands, the prospect of the Film Guild van and its operator delivering cinema into rural communities suggests a relationship with cinema that is different from the choice and permanence available to a metropolitan audience. I have selected three examples where the cinema experience offered by the Film Guild is recollected from the post-war years. Two come from my own research into memories of the Guild as part of a larger project – Rural Cinema in Scotland: Histories and Geographies (1946–1970) – and one from a previously published collection of cinema-going memories in Scotland (Martin 2000).

The selected memories confirm some of the key characteristics of rural cinema, and also reveal how the experience functioned as a catalyst for the expression of other forms of narrative about the community. The two later selections are not necessarily typical, but their expression gives a strong indication of the importance of this form of cinema-going to rural life in the post-war years.

The first memory comes from a resident of the northern Shetland island of Yell. Jeanette Nowak recalls from childhood how the physical conditions of exhibition influenced her experience of rural cinema and the terms of its remembrance:

My memories are not so much about the films themselves, more about the COLD! There was no electricity and no heating in the public hall – so it was a case of wrapping up well before you went – and also wrapped up – in paper to take with you – was a hot brick – straight out of the Rayburn oven! (Martin 2000: 50)

The exacting conditions remembered by this spectator illustrate the austerity of post-war life and the strategies designed to counter these conditions through the inventive use of domestic utilities. The determination to endure the conditions in the unheated local hall gives an indication of the appeal of makeshift cinema to the population of the Shetland Isles.

The following account comes from Elsie, who was resident in Glasgow and visiting the family holiday home in the village of Tighnabruaich in Argyll on the west coast of Scotland. Elsie's memories of rural cinema-going as a young 12-year-old who would be accompanied by her mother or other elder members of the family have enabled the realization of an adult ambition of becoming the author of her own short story, written for a creative writing course. This is an extract from a copy of 'A Night at the Cinema':

> I loved to carry the huge bunch of keys to unlock the many doors of the hall. Our first task was to sweep the hall and rid it of dust, an almost impossible task as many of the windows were sealed shut with too many years of paint. However, once the fog of dust disappeared, the next priority was organizing the seating. We pushed and pulled all the necessary seats stored in a large room at the back of the main hall. The seats were former pews from some long since disbanded church. The front three rows, on each side of the centre aisle, were long ridged benches, removed from a street-tram in a far off city. These special benches were reserved for the children who would attend the show. The hall had to be darkened, so large black drapes were placed over the windows. These were 'black-out drapes' left over from the last war, when sealing out light was mandatory in every household. (Habbick 2010)

Local materials were appropriated and reused to assemble the rural cinema exhibition space. The utilitarian space of the village hall was converted into a makeshift cinema, and Elsie clearly relished the opportunity to participate in the process of preparation. The sense of expectation, not only of going to see a film at the cinema but taking part in its construction, clearly contrasts with the more distant and discrete experience offered by the permanent environment of a purpose-built cinema. The involvement of members of the community is a recurring feature of the memories that I have gathered for this research, and it was clearly an important part of how cinema was made rural in Scotland during the post-war years. Such vernacular assemblage in a general space to accommodate the machinery of cinema was a regular facet of this cinema. Elsie's narrative continues:

> One particular night, the movie was *Nicholas Nickleby*, which was shown in black and white. Once the hall filled and the outside door closed, it was inky blank. Our black-out drapes worked very effectively, shutting out any light, and any hope of ventilation. Action – the projector purred into life and our movie started. Within the first thirty minutes I was bored, but instead of watching the screen I found something else on which to focus my attention. Directly in front of me was a portly farmer, dressed in a three-piece

dark suit, wearing a white shirt with a starched collar. He was absolutely bald. I watched fascinated as rivulets of perspiration ran from the top of his head, down his neck and over the back of his collar. I played mental races, watching them run down the back of his head. Sometimes the 'race' was interrupted as he dabbed the top of his head with a handkerchief. I conjured up all sorts of images where the perspiration accumulated and visualized him floating away! Despite the incredible heat, and his obvious discomfort, this patron continued to watch the movie without removing his jacket.

I was not the only one bored that evening. Very quickly there were sounds of movement and whispering from the front benches. Fidgeting around, somebody slid down and found the speaker cable running down the wall. With a few quick tugs on the cable, the sound on the screen was interrupted. The main character was suddenly stammering his lines, which ruined the seriousness of the scene. This continued long enough to completely destroy the ambiance of the movie. Adults and children alike started to giggle. Suddenly, all the lights switched on, as an agitated projectionist tried to catch the culprit. The guilty party was quicker than the projectionist, as all the children were safely seated on the front benches by the time a head count was made. The movie continued. (Habbick 2010)

The packed and level seating of the village hall in combination with what for Elsie was an unappealing film – *The Life and Adventures of Nicholas Nickleby* (Alberto Cavalcanti 1947) – meant that her attention wandered productively to the immediate environment of exhibition that she helped to assemble. This spectator chose to watch the audience in front of her as well as the films on the screen. The physical conditions of the hall and the lack of clear sight lines encouraged this formation, as did the disobedience of some in the audience. The film became subject to the conditions under which it was viewed and the film programme was part of an evening of entertainment that continued in the hall as a band arrived and a dance commenced (personal communication). The event of the Film Guild coming to the village was a cultural and social highlight for this community. The main feature film – a literary adaptation addressed to parents and children – typifies the educative purpose of the Highlands and Islands Film Guild in its early phase. Elsie makes narrative use of her experience of the cinema environment instead of the film in a way that provides an indication of her sense of ownership of the cinema when it periodically visited the village of Tighnabruaich.

Annette Kuhn contends from her research into British cinema in the 1930s that 'cinema provided a space for challenges to adult rules and for assertions of independence from parents, teachers and other authority figures' (2002: 62). In this post-war example, some of these possibilities still exist, but it also the specificity of rural cinema exhibition and Elsie's investment in it that render the intimate and transformed village hall space one of imaginative and irreverent possibilities for the subjectivity of this young spectator.

The next record of experience takes the form of a limerick poem written in 1947, which has been passed on and shared by the family and local friends of its author, Roderick

MacIntyre. The title of *The Village of Gairloch (Strath)* refers to the north-west coast of the Highland region, and this extract gives a vivid, humorous and insider's account of the arrival and impact of the Film Guild on a small village community:

The Village Called Strath
Then, all of a sudden a great big machine,
Was putting electric Light on a screen,
Till Marion Fraser stood up in its track,
And we saw a big lion looking out of her back.
Now the Devil was raging around in the hall,
You never knew next what would happen at all,
It was good to be thinking that out in the lobby,
Was standing the Sergeant and Sinclair the Bobby.
Well, what with the racket and what with the din,
Not one single person heard Beaton come in,
Quite speechless he stood as he gazed on the scene,
As an actress walked NAKED all over the screen.
His reason departed, he let out a roar,
As he carted the great big machine out the door,
And the last that we saw as he put it on fire,
Was DONALD DUCK climbing right up the church spire
(personal communication).

The reference to Beaton is to the surname of Reverend Archibald Beaton, the formidable minister of the local Free Presbyterian Church. The Reverend Beaton's church was next door to the Territorial Army Hall, where the pictures were shown (personal communication).

The reaction of the church to the arrival of cinema directly into the rural communities is an important element of the history of the Film Guild. In this example, the cinema offers Roddy a welcome opportunity to challenge through mockery the authority of the Church minister. The Free Presbyterian Church promulgated a strict code of conduct – particularly in relation to the Sabbath – and occupied an influential role in community life in the Highlands, as Callum Brown describes:

The Highlands and Hebrides had the most committed churchgoers, overwhelmingly drawn from relatively poor crofting communities … the dissenting clergy disapproved of sport, secular Gaelic song and dance, and even of religious voluntary organisations. Amongst adherents to the Free and Free Presbyterian Churches, there was a fierce grip on the outward face of popular culture … Sabbatarianism was strict with Sunday activities centred on Churchgoing and other tasks reduced to precisely catalogued acts of necessity (such as milking the cattle) and mercy. (Brown 1997: 15)

The arrival of the cinema and other leisure pursuits affected church attendance in this period, as this reflective quote from a rural minister illustrates:

> Forty years ago, everyone went to church; now no one goes because it is the thing to do; social convention that compelled the unwilling to come to church on Sunday now pushes them to the cinema on week nights. So preachers address congregations in which the aged and aging outnumber the young, but not as much as the women outnumber men; congregations, meagre in the morning, in the evening thin away to vanishing point, and disappear altogether as the day lengthens. (Brown 1997: 2)

The area represented by this minister was not as remote as the village of Strath, and had more small towns with permanent cinemas available within reasonable travelling distance for the local population. The representative of Forgan in the eastern county of Fife pinpoints how there is a seemingly irrevocable shift in the sources of culture able to attract younger members of the community.

Reverend Beaton's reaction – and that of the Free Presbyterian Church – to the arrival of the cinema in the village during the 1940s was much more disapproving than resigned. It is this disturbance of the cultural order and the attendant norms of community life that forms the context for the humour of Roddy's poem (personal communication). The members of the village audience form the role of a cast of potential characters to describe the arrival and impact of the cinema in the area. Imaginative licence is deployed to humorously and irreverently depict the impact of the illusion on the audience. The exhibition and viewing conditions encourage this spectator to see the image on the screen through the audience in front of the screen. The cinema also acts as a diversion from and disturbance of the assumed shared values of rural community, particularly regarding the codes of conduct decreed by the church. Cinema is represented by Hollywood stars such as Betty Grable, Victor Mature and its more general illusory, spectacular and sensual qualities, which combine to captivate the eager audience members – some of whom would be seeing cinema for the first time (personal communication).

The role occupied by the audience in the village of Strath is comparable with the knowable community that Raymond Williams identifies in nineteenth-century English literary fiction (Williams 1985: 166). The members of the rural audience are familiar to one another, and the proximity of the village setting defines them as a community for the writer to exploit. However, as the poem's irreverence indicates, the arrival of the cinema encourages an individual voice that is resistant to the implied equivalence and consensus of community.

Elsie's story and Roddy's poem offer examples of the experience of cinema-going in the general-purpose space of the hall, fostering an imaginative performativity in these spectators that is enhanced by recalling their experiences through writing. The experience of cinema is appropriated and moulded into what is not simply an intertext of rural cinema-going, but another individually authored narrative and cultural artefact of memory that exploits the intimacies of community for a more differentiated picture. The characteristics of rural cinema exhibition and its sociality feed the expression of other subjectivities that might not have been fully realized without its visiting presence.

Nicholas Hiley argues that there is evidence to suggest that, in the early period of British cinema, the auditorium was a proletarian public sphere, involving interplay between its working-class audience and the screened image (1995: 166). The interplay here is between cinema exhibition, community and the individual. The improvised space of rural cinema functioned as a space of possibility, where young people like Elsie and Roddy could assert and write their own individuality in the face of their elders, and the confining intimacy and outward conformity of community.

The isolated examples cited here suggest that the young rural spectator was not part of a compliant audience interested in taking up the offer of an improving or educational cinema. The exhibition of cinema in rural communities created the conditions for the interplay of the spectator with the cinema apparatus, suggesting that the environment of exhibition was important to the kind of experience audiences enjoyed. The intimacy of this environment meant that the smaller screened image became part of an improvised exhibition space rather than its *raison d'être*. The experiences described here are not necessarily exclusive to rural cinema, but the factors that influenced their occurrence are closely connected to the characteristics of a cinema that was made rural by the localized conditions of its exhibition.

Barbara Klinger wrote in 1989 of a practice of spectator digression prompted by intertexts related to the promotional discourses that circulate with the film (1989: 4). She points to a type of renarrativizing that shows how 'texts are prone to being restructured from "the outside"' (1989: 15). She goes on to suggest that 'cinematic detours or digressions constitute a significant socially-rooted dynamic within the film/spectator interaction' (1989: 4). The examples of rural cinema-going experience outlined show how the particularities of exhibition create the conditions for a digressing spectatorship. 'The Village of Strath' makes reference to cinema intertexts from Hollywood, but the key intertext is the knowable community audience, together with the familiar exhibition environment that stages the cinema. Similarly, Elsie's digression describes the rebellious interaction of the younger audience with the exhibition space and the projection equipment that is part of the space occupied by the audience.

Kuhn's (2002) research demonstrates how cinema can occupy the role of a transitional object. This psychoanalytic term refers to Sigmund Freud's account of the child's separation from the mother (Kuhn 2002: 36). In the selected experiences highlighted here, it is less the transitional than the *makeshift* nature of the cinema itself that conditions the interactions that occur in the local, communitarian exhibition spaces that characterized rural cinema in Scotland during the post-war years. These accounts of viewing experience reveal an appetite in some rural spectators for mischievous independence – contrary to the intentions of the educationalists. This is a cinema that is not already there, but it arrives in the area and is assembled by the operators and some volunteers for the community audience, then it departs. Film in this context is, as writer Iain Sinclair suggests, 'part of the occasion of its viewing. Part of the place where it is viewed' (Miller 2011).

This account of rural cinema demonstrates that if the parameters of *what* cinema is are extended to include *where* cinema is, and the spaces of its exhibition, then cinema can be viewed as much less centrifugal than Bazin (1967) suggests. The contrast that Bazin identifies between theatre and cinema is lessened in rural cinema. The restatement of Bazin's query within a changing – though still largely Anglo-American – geography of film history expands the discussion of what constitutes cinema beyond the city into the country (Andrew 2010).

The vocabulary available to describe rural cinema and cinema-going is less developed than its urban equivalent, but one of its key terms must be 'community', and in these selective examples, the relationship between the presence of cinema, the community and the individual is central. Judith Mayne's (1993) discussion of earlier disputes between theoretical accounts of the cinema apparatus and empirical studies of actual audiences warns against the tendency to overstate the agency of spectators in opposition to ideological structures (1993: 62). These isolated experiences of Highland and Islands audience take place against the background of the paternalistic and colonial culture of post-war British austerity, and can be expanded and placed in dialogue with the wider histories and geographies of cinema-going experience.

The question of what constitutes rural cinema in Scotland encourages a reconsideration of the significance of the environment of exhibition and its attendant geography, as well as the spectacle of cinema. The makeshift nature of this cinema influences the experience available to spectators and its significance. The consequences of a cinema that is by definition improvised, communal and localized mean that the place of exhibition is essential to understanding its function as cinema and the contribution of the rural audience to film history.

Acknowledgements

I would like to thank Elsie Habbick, Jeanette Nowak and the family of Roddy MacIntyre, who have allowed me draw on their rich memories and artefacts for the purpose of this article and my wider research project on the History of Rural Cinema in Scotland. I am also grateful to Dr Neil MacGillivray, who kindly passed on a copy of the poem to me and also put me in contact with Roddy's family.

References

Acland, C.R. (2009), 'Curtains, Carts, and the Mobile Screen', *Screen*, 50: 1, pp. 148–66.

Acland, C.R. and Wasson H. (eds) (2011), *Useful Cinema*, Durham, NC: Duke University Press.

Allen, R.C. (2010), 'Getting to *Going to the Show*', *New Review of Film and Television Studies*, 8: 3, pp. 264–76.

Andrew, D. (ed.) (2011), *Opening Bazin: Postwar Theory and Its After-life*, Oxford: Oxford University Press.

Aveyard, K. (2011), 'What the Country Tells Us: The Place of the "Rural" in Contemporary Studies of Cinema', *Media International Australia*, 139, pp. 124–32.

Baudry, J.L. (1975), 'The Ideological Effects of the Basic Cinematic Apparatus', *Film Quarterly*, 27: 2, pp. 39–47.

Bazin, A. (1967), *What is Cinema? Volume 1*, trans. H. Gray, Berkeley, CA: University of California Press.

Brown, C. (1997), *Religion and Society in Scotland Since 1707*, Edinburgh: Edinburgh University Press.

Brown, S. (2005), 'Coming Soon to a Hall Near You: Some Notes on 16mm Road-show Distribution in the 1930s', *Journal of British Cinema and Television*, 2: 2, pp. 299–309.

Cameron, I. (1993), 'The Orkney Rural Cinema Scheme: Reminiscences of a Part-time Operator', *Orkney View*, 47, pp. 11–15.

Casetti, F. (2009), 'Filmic Experience', *Screen*, 50: 1, 56–66.

Druick, Z. (2008), 'Mobile Cinema in Canada in Relation to British Mobile Film Practices', in W. Keller and G. Walz (eds), *Screening Canadians: Cross-Cultural Perspectives on Canadian Film*, Marburg: Universitatsbibliothek, pp. 13–33.

Fish, R. (ed.) (2007), *Cinematic Countrysides*, Manchester: Manchester University Press.

Fuller-Seeley, K. (ed.) (2008), *Hollywood in the Neighborhood: Historical Case Studies of Local Moviegoing*, London: University of California Press.

Goode, I. (2011), 'Cinema in the Country: The Rural Cinema Scheme Orkney (1946–67)', *Post Script: Essays in Film and the Humanities*, 30: 2, pp. 21–35.

Grierson, J. (1935), 'Art and the Film', *The Manchester Guardian*, 13 December.

Habbick, E. (2010), Interview with author, 12 August.

Hiley, N. (1995), 'The British Cinema Auditorium', in K. Dibbets and A. Hogenkamp (eds), *Film and the First World War*, Amsterdam: Amsterdam University Press, pp. 166–67.

Kepley, V. (1996), 'Whose Apparatus: Problems of Film Exhibition and History' in D. Bordwell and N. Carroll (eds), *Post-theory: Reconstructing Film Studies*, London: University of Wisconsin Press.

Klinger, B. (1989), 'Digressions at the Cinema: Reception and Mass Culture', *Cinema Journal*, 28: 4, pp. 3–19.

——— (2007), 'Cinema's Shadow: Reconsidering Non-theatrical Exhibition', in R. Maltby, M. Stokes and R.C. Allen (eds), *Going to the Movies. Hollywood and the Social Experience of Cinema*, Exeter: University of Exeter Press, pp. 273–90.

Kuhn, A. (2002), *An Everyday Magic: Cinema and Cultural Memory*, London: I.B. Tauris.

Lebas, E. (1995), 'When Every Street Became a Cinema: The Film Work of Bermondsey Borough Council's Public Health Department, 1923–1953', *History Workshop Journal*, 39, pp. 42–66.

——— (2010), *Forgotten Futures: British Municipal Cinema 1920–1980*, London: Black Dog.

MacKintosh, I. (1993), *Architecture, Actor and Audience*, London: Routledge.

Maltby, R., Stokes, M. and Allen, R.C. (eds) (2007) *Going to the Movies: Hollywood and the Social Experience of Cinema*, Exeter: University of Exeter Press.

Martin, A. (2000), *Going to the Pictures: Scottish Memories of Cinema*, Edinburgh: NMS Publishing.

Mayne, J. (1993), *Cinema and Spectatorship*, London: Routledge.

Miller, H. (2011), 'A Film Ride that Cuts to the Chase', http://www.guardian.co.uk/film/filmblog/2011/jul/20/film-ride-flying-down-rio?. Accessed 22 July 2011.

Miller, J. (2002), *The Dam Builders: Power from the Glens*, Edinburgh, Birlinn.

Richards, J. (1984), , London: Routledge. *The Age of the Dream Palace: Cinema and Society in Britain 1930–1939*

Ross, H. (1966), 'Showmen of the Crofter Counties', *Film User*, June, pp. 269–91.

Slide, A. (1992), *Before Video: History of the Non-theatrical Film*, London: Greenwood Press.

Smith, S. (2005), *Children, Cinema and Censorship: From Dracula to the Dead End Kids*, London: I.B. Tauris.

Tallents, S. (1955 [1932]), *The Projection of England*, London: Olen Press.

Tinkler, P. (1999), 'Youth's Opportunity? The *Education Act* of 1944 and Proposals for Part-time Continuation Education', *History of Education*, 30: 1 pp. 77–94.

Williams, R. (1985), *The Country and the City*, London: The Hogarth Press.

Williamson, M. (1956), 'Film Appreciation in Scottish Schools', *Quarterly Review of Film, Radio and Television*, 10: 3, pp. 273–80.

Notes

1 Barbara Klinger (2007) offers a useful discussion of the term 'non-theatrical' and its implications for reception studies and film studies more generally.

2 *The Scotsman* newspaper reported in 1947 that the previous year the loss of population by the drift south and migration overseas was approximately 57,000. See http://proquest.umi.com/pqdweb?did=1556971262&sid=2&Fmt=1&clientId=29134&RQT=309&VName=HNP1947. Accessed 20 November 2011.

3 The make-up of the Committee of the Edinburgh Cinema Inquiry of 1931–33 is revealing of the social agencies summoned to look at this influence on young people. The Inquiry was headed by The Very Rev. J.H. Miller, Warden of New College Settlement, Edinburgh, and former moderator of the United Free Church, and contained representatives of the Boys' Brigade, the Boys' Club Union, the Boy Scouts, the Church Lads' Brigade, the Church of Scotland, the Catholic Church, the Edinburgh Education Committee, The Educational Institute of Scotland, the Edinburgh Diocesan Social Services Board, The Howard League, the Mothers Union, the National Council of Women, The National Vigilance Association, the Scottish Temperance Alliance, the St Vincent de Paul society, the Girls' Club Union, the Girl Guides, the Girls' Association, the Girls' Friendly Society, the YWCA, the Women Citizens Association and the Juvenile Organisations Committee (Richards 1984: 70).

4 The operator referred to here was affectionately known by the community of Yell as 'Picter Billy': private correspondence with J. Nowak, 23 September 2011.

Chapter 16

'A Popcorn-free Zone': Distinctions in Independent Film Exhibition in Wellington, New Zealand

Ian Huffer

revious research has explored the way in which socio-cultural distinctions are articulated through art-house cinemas. The most developed of these studies is that of Wilinksy (2001), who shows how post-war art-house cinemas in the United States provided 'a sense of prestige and status' to an expanding middle class keen to 'distinguish themselves from one another and from other classes' (2001: 3, 82). Such prestige was established through the negation of mainstream cinema-going and the evocation of those cultural forms associated with high culture and the upper classes, such as the theatre, classical music and the opera (2001: 114). This was achieved by such means as the programming of foreign and independent films, 'refusing admission to children, charging high admission prices, and selling coffee instead of popcorn' (2001: 28, 106). Following Bourdieu (1984) and Gans (1974) she thus shows how these cinemas drew upon and contributed to hierarchies of taste that accorded the greatest prestige to those cultural forms most closely associated with higher socio-economic groups (2001: 82–96). She ends her study with a call for greater understanding of the distinctions articulated through contemporary art-house cinemas. In particular, she notes the need to consider the impact of developments such as the screening of art films with crossover appeal in mainstream theatres, and similarities in the theatre environments of new art-houses and multiplexes (2001: 136–37). For Wilinksy, these developments are indicative of 'the ambivalence of cultural values' (2001: 137–38). Postmodern theories take this cultural instability further, proposing a 'consumer culture based upon a profusion of information and proliferation of images which cannot ultimately be stabilized, or hierarchized into a system which correlates to fixed social divisions' (Featherstone 1991: 83). This consequently raises questions regarding the extent to which contemporary art-house cinemas continue to stabilize cultural flows in such a way that corresponds with social distinctions and hierarchies.

Research into contemporary art-house cinemas is limited; however, what does exist suggests that these sites continue to organize film exhibition around a clear set of cultural distinctions. While these studies acknowledge the movement of such cinemas into screening slightly more mainstream content, distinctions are still argued to be in place through the absence of blockbusters and the existence of a culture of film appreciation situated in opposition to the values of entertainment (Jones 2001: 126; Jancovich et al. 2003: 222). Analysing the comments of audiences for particular art-house cinemas and/ or the promotion and publicity surrounding them, these studies find evidence of a film culture that stresses the value of intellectual stimulation above more immediate emotional or physical pleasures. Such a film culture encourages a detached contemplation of a film's form over its function – 'the mode of representation over the object represented' – which may frame audiences' engagements with more mainstream films if they are screened (Jones 2001: 126; Jancovich et al. 2003: 220). This is consequently seen to position these cinemas as socially exclusionary, alienating those unaccustomed or unwilling to engage with film through these terms (Jones 2001: 125; Jancovich et al. 2003: 221–24). The precise form of these social distinctions remains ambiguous due to the absence of information about the identities of the audiences quoted in these studies. However, the fact that these studies use Bourdieu to support their definition of the taste formations articulated through these cinemas suggests the potential relevance of socio-economic status as a factor. For Bourdieu, the negation of 'immediate sensation' evident in the taste formations found in these cinemas is but a product of the 'distance from necessity' that characterizes the lives of dominant social classes (1984: 5, 486).

Despite these insights, these studies of contemporary art-house cinemas lack detailed consideration of the way in which distinctions may be articulated through the physical spaces of these cinemas and their programming. The position of these cinemas within the wider cultural geography of their respective cities is examined, but the physical environments of the cinemas themselves are left largely unexplored. Wilinksy reveals the important role played by theatre environments in setting the tone for audiences' encounters with films (2001: 104–14), as well as pointing towards this as a site of overlap between contemporary art-house cinemas and multiplexes. Analysis of these environments is thus essential in order to understand the distinctiveness – or not – of the cultural experience provided to art-house audiences today. In addition, while Jancovich et al. (2003) provide some consideration of the content screened at a festival held at their case-study cinema, there are no specific details of the cinema's programming outside of this festival, and Jones (2001) provides only two examples of films screened at the cinema that she examines. We need a full understanding of the range of films screened at such cinemas in order to gauge the way in which this content may complement or be in tension with any discursive formation evident in the promotion of these sites. Such an understanding also provides us with a point of comparison to look at the programming of mainstream cinemas, allowing us to consider the degree to which art-house cinemas provide an alternative.

This study consequently examines the physical spaces and programming of contemporary independent cinemas in Wellington, New Zealand, along with the promotion and publicity that intersects them. These sites have been discursively positioned as art-house cinemas through promotion and publicity (Positively Wellington Tourism 2011; Rose 1994; Saunders 2004). The term 'independent' is used to refer to them within this study due to ambiguities that arise around their categorization. The study asks whether the spaces, programming and promotion of these cinemas articulate cultural distinctions that appeal to social distinctions, or whether they provide evidence of their destabilization. In order to fully understand the differences articulated through these cinemas, the study also provides consideration of the spaces and programming of cinemas in Wellington operated by major chains. The study does not examine the political economy of film exhibition in Wellington, discussed in detail in Huffer (2011). Nor does the study utilize research into the audiences for the city's cinemas. This forms an essential area for further research in order to gauge how any appeals to social distinction are actually met.

Through its focus upon the cinemas of Wellington, this study responds to a lack of research on contemporary film exhibition in New Zealand. The study also expands our understanding of the specific relationship between class and culture within the nation. Despite the existence of an egalitarian myth rooted in the hopes of colonists fleeing the 'bad society of Europe' (Pitt 1977: 5), the centrality of capitalism to white settler colonialism ensured the division of New Zealand according to a socio-economic hierarchy (Roper 2005: 46). Importantly, the precise nature of this social hierarchy has been seen to shape cultural hierarchies in distinct ways. Sigley argues that the 'absence of a class of gentlefolk – who are not required to work', along with the cultural significance of the egalitarian myth, led to a distrust of high culture within New Zealand from the 1920s to the 1960s (2003: 20–21). The combination of this with a 'suspicion of popular culture in educated society' resulted in 'an affirmation of middlebrow culture as the dominant arbiter of taste' (2003: 352). Sigley adds that this cultural hierarchy began to break apart in the 1960s (2003: 346). This study grants us an insight into the extent of any such fragmentation.

The primary case studies for this chapter represent Wellington's independent cinemas as of September 2010 – namely, the Paramount, the Penthouse, and the Empire. In addition, the chapter examines the independent Light House Cinema, situated on the other side of Wellington Harbour in the town of Petone, but drawing significant business from the city (Anon 2006). Comparisons will also be made with Reading Cinemas' ten-screen Courtenay Central multiplex and the Embassy, owned by Wellington City Council but operated by Amalgamated Holdings Ltd (owner of the Australasian chains Event Cinemas, Greater Union and Birch Carroll and Coyle). Analysis of the programming of these cinemas has been based on the collation of all the films screened at these sites from 9 September to 6 October 2010. Information regarding the spaces, programming and promotion of these cinemas has been gleaned from newspaper publicity surrounding the cinemas, site visits, original interviews with exhibitors, material available via the cinemas' websites and the texts of the screened films.

Spaces

Publicity surrounding the physical environment offered by the city's independent cinemas is marked by an emphasis on their status as a 'popcorn-free zone' (Shouten 2002: A8). The cinemas thus follow in the tradition of the art-house cinemas analysed by Wilinsky (2001) while also underlining Bourdieu's suggestion that 'tastes are perhaps first and foremost distastes' (1984: 56). Elaborating on this distinction, Simon Werry, managing director of the Light House, explains that 'we offer a different product that is more enjoyable for the older clientele … There's no flashing lights, no popcorn …We sell stuff that doesn't make a noise in the theatre (Anon 2008). Kate Larkindale, manager of the Paramount, also points out that:

> A lot of people would prefer to come to a venue like this, because it's not full of rowdy children, it's not full of stinky popcorn, it's not dirty and sticky … it's an adult environment to come and see a film in. (Larkindale 2009)

In these comments, popcorn is associated with youth, noise and mess – and, by implication, the space of the multiplex – while the spaces of these independent cinemas are positioned as adult environments through the absence of these implied aspects of the multiplex cinema experience. This vision of popcorn-free adulthood is also implicitly intersected by notions of social class, revealed by the Penthouse's description of its target demographic as 'discerning customers in the 35 plus age group with a high disposable income' (Penthouse Cinema 2010). Popcorn and the multiplex are thus rejected due to the fact that they symbolize popular taste. In keeping with this, concession stands are replaced by cafés, again echoing an established tradition within art-house exhibition (Wilinsky 2001: 113). These cafés call into play oppositions between objects that are authentic or original and those that are mass produced, while also associating more economically inaccessible objects with refinement. Popcorn is thus replaced by individually prepared sweet and savoury foods and wine lists are foregrounded on menus and chalkboards. Online promotion may also reinforce this appeal, as evidenced in the Empire's declaration that its café offers 'fine wines' and 'real coffee' (Empire Cinema 2010). Cultural distinctions are thus articulated through the food and drink provided by these cinemas that are clearly designed to appeal to social distinctions and hierarchies.

The negation of the multiplex evident in this rejection of popcorn is articulated further through the 'intimate movie experience' provided by these cinemas (Positively Wellington Tourism 2011). The Light House, Empire and Penthouse all contain between three to five theatres seating between ten and 170 people. The exception is the Paramount, with a main theatre seating 480, though it also possesses two extra theatres seating between 40 and 60 people. In addition, the seating in all the theatres at the Light House and the Empire consists of two-person couches. This is also true of one of the Paramount's theatres, while the Penthouse draws attention to its 'luxurious armchair seats' (Penthouse Cinema 2010). The use of small theatres and couch or armchair seating echoes the aims of those post-war art-house exhibitors that attempted to convey the 'warmth of a home environment rather than a commercial public atmosphere' (Wilinksy 2001: 112). Such connotations are accentuated at the Light House through the presence of bookshelves and imitation log burners in the cinema's lounge areas, while the Empire's foyer is decorated with flowers arranged artfully in vases. As indicated in the quotation from the Penthouse, these home comforts are also promoted through terms relating to luxury. This luxury is, in turn, used to further distinguish such sites from mainstream cinema-going, with the Light House declaring that the cinema offers 'an environment of comfort and sophistication that transcends the multiplex' (Light House Petone 2010).

Wellington's independent cinemas also contrast with the spaces most associated with contemporary mainstream cinema-going through the age of their buildings and their exploitation of this heritage value. The Paramount has been in operation since 1917, the Empire first opened in 1925, the Penthouse began life as the Vogue Theatre in 1939 and, while the building in which The Light House is housed was not historically a cinema, it dates from 1926. This history is emphasized at the Light House and Empire via a dedicated noticeboard displaying images and information about the building's past, while the Light House and Penthouse also have specific pages on their websites detailing the history of the sites and the sympathetic nature of any changes that have been made. The Penthouse, for example, stresses that 'all the developments that have taken place at the [cinema] in recent years have been done with the original art deco style of the cinema in mind', enabling the cinema to retain 'its old-fashioned charm and elegance' (Penthouse Cinema 2010), while the Light House emphasizes that 'the façade remains and we have recycled a lot of timber' (Light House Petone 2010). However, the major structural transformations that have taken place in these buildings in order to accommodate extra screens or transform them into cinemas highlight the way in which these heritage values are, in part, a construction. This is particularly true of the Light House, given the fact that its main heritage value lies in its façade – literally embodying a 'veneer of pastness' (Davison 2008: 32).

This slight overstatement of difference is also evident in the overlap that exists between the spaces of Wellington's independent and mainstream cinemas. Reading Cinemas' Courtenay Central complex, for example, offers its own luxury experience, The Gold Lounge, granting patrons spacious armchair seating and the ability to order meals and wine from a fully licensed bar. This bar is situated at the top of the complex, allowing you to literally look down upon other patrons. It is also includes a number of the key spatial cues of distinction employed by the other cinemas, such as a chalkboard listing some of the day's specials. However, patrons have to navigate their way through the bustle of a neon-lit food court and shopping area before mounting the escalators to the concessions and ticket sales counter that allows them access to this special lounge. The luxury seating is also still within regular theatres of between 120 and 490 people – albeit segregated. Thus the cinema offers only pockets of luxury and exclusivity. The Embassy is potentially more challenging to the distinctiveness of Wellington's independent cinemas. An opulent picture palace, originally opened in 1924, the cinema is rich in the heritage values and/or luxury underpinning the appeal of Wellington's art-house cinemas. For example, patrons are welcomed by a tiled entranceway with marble staircases on either side leading up to an expansive foyer area, snack bar, café and jazz lounge. With 700 seats in the theatre, however, the cinema provides a contrast to the more intimate spaces of Wellington's independent cinemas, and popcorn is clearly foregrounded at the sales counter. The spaces of the city's independent cinemas are thus still distinguished from Reading and the Embassy by their ability to combine a degree of heritage and/or luxury with greater intimacy and more complete exclusivity due to their relative size and their rejection of certain popular tastes in food.

If the spaces of Wellington's independent cinemas still offer distinctions from those of the major chains, equivalence in the pricing of both the independents and majors alerts us to the relative luxury that all cinema-going represents in Wellington. Comparing weeknight adult tickets, for example, the Light House and Empire both charge $17, Reading charge $16.80, the Embassy charge $15.50, and the Paramount and Penthouse charge $15. In addition, Reading's Gold Lounge seats cost $33.20. This is in contrast to the standard cost of $8 for one night's rental of a newly released DVD at one of the city's Video Ezy stores. Such pricing parallels the high cost of cinema-going in the United Kingdom, which has made it a largely middle and lower middle-class leisure pursuit (Harbord 2002: 52; Bennett et al. 2009: 140). Thus we need to acknowledge the way in which Wellington's independent *and* mainstream cinemas may articulate distinctions within a heterogeneous middle class that is intersected by other formations of identity. Furthermore, the fact that the most expensive seats are found at Reading's multiplex points to the complexity of attempting to map cultural distinctions on to socio-economic positions. More specifically, it speaks to those members of society who are rich in economic capital and who may 'disregard traditional cultural hierarchies' (Stewart 2010: 60). In contrast, the reinforcement of social distinction through cultural distinction still appears to have some relevance to the spaces of Wellington's independent cinemas, due to the implicit rejection of contemporary mass production and consumption that is articulated through them. To what extent might such tendencies be borne out through the programming of these cinemas?

Programming

The programming of the majority of Wellington's independent cinemas is marked by an emphasis on film-making from beyond Hollywood. For the purposes of this study, Hollywood cinema is defined as those films with a US nationality and a major US distributor, eliminating independently distributed US films and non-US films with a major US distributor. Looking at their programming for one month, such Hollywood films form only one out of 35 films screened at the Paramount, two out of 14 films at the Penthouse, and three out of 19 films at the Lighthouse. This rejection of Hollywood cinema by the majority of Wellington's independent cinemas can be seen to imbue its programming with the connotations of art-house cinema due to the negations out of which this category of cinema is formed. With art-house cinema defined as not popular cinema, which is itself predominantly defined as Hollywood cinema, films from beyond Hollywood often acquire the status of art (Eleftheriotis 2001: 77). Such connotations complement the distinctions articulated through the spaces of these cinemas. However, the Empire is notable for screening 12 Hollywood films out of 14 films in total, producing tensions between its space and its programming that are discussed further below.

While the majority of the films screened at Wellington's independent cinemas (barring the Empire) are not Hollywood films, foreign-language films constitute only seven of the Light

House's 19 films, three of the Penthouse's 13 films, and five of the Paramount's 13 regular films. These are supplemented at the Paramount by the one-off screenings of a further 19 foreign-language films due to the cinema's hosting of the 'Reel Brazil Film Festival', the 'Reel Anime' festival, the 'Chilean Film Week' and the weekly screenings of the Wellington Film Society. As a result, on 13 September 2010, six out of nine films screened at the Paramount were foreign-language films, adding up to seven out of 14 screenings. If the Light House and Penthouse can be seen to foster a film culture of non-Hollywood films, then it is still one that is loaded towards English language film-making from Britain, Australia, New Zealand, Canada and the United States. The programming thus carries connotations of art cinema while minimizing potential barriers to accessibility, such as subtitles. Such a dynamic arguably points towards a somewhat middlebrow film culture defined by both 'immediate accessibility and the outward signs of cultural legitimacy' (Bourdieu 1984: 323). The same is also true of the Paramount's regular screenings, though this is balanced by the cinema's commitment to foreign language film festivals.

Connotations of middlebrow taste are expressed more clearly through the promotion of the films screened at these cinemas. This promotion is characterized in part by an emphasis on the films' cultural legitimacy. For example, the international awards and nominations these films have received are listed on posters hanging in the cafés of these cinemas and/or on promotional leaflets provided by the distributor that are available to pick up via dedicated racks or tables. This includes the success of films such as *El Secreto De Sus Ojos/The Secret in Their Eyes* (Campanella, 2009), *Un Prophète/A Prophet* (Audiard, 2009) and *Animal Kingdom* (Michôd, 2010) at the Academy Awards, Cannes and Sundance respectively. Audiences are also encouraged to appreciate the formal virtues of these films via stand-out quotes from reviews that are presented on the films' promotional leaflets. Performance is the formal quality most consistently emphasized. For example, 'Michael Caine is truly outstanding', offering a 'fine performance' in *Harry Brown* (Barber, 2009); Naomi Watts offers 'a blazing, faceted performance' in the 'exceptionally acted' *Mother and Child* (García, 2009); Jackie Weaver gives 'a magnificent performance' in *Animal Kingdom*; and Tilda Swinton gives 'a sensational performance' in *Lo Sono L'Amore/I Am Love* (Guadagnino, 2009), 'even by [her] standards'. Visual style is also picked out, though not to quite the same extent, centred largely upon the 'stylishly directed' *A Prophet* and 'elegant' *I Am Love*. This emphasis on performance and visual style in part conforms to the distanced appreciation of form associated with highbrow taste, those 'specifically artistic effects which are only appreciated relationally, through a comparison with other works' (Bourdieu 1984: 34). However, it is interesting that performance is the formal quality picked out most regularly. This is arguably due to its ability to be evaluated through the terms of believability as much as through detached comparison with other works. As such, it may be incorporated into more populist viewing strategies, as defined by Bourdieu, 'based on the affirmation of continuity between art and life' (1984: 32).

The accessibility of the films screened by Wellington's independent cinemas is further highlighted via an emphasis on their broader generic qualities. For example, *Flickan som*

Lekte Med Elden/The Girl Who Played with Fire (Alfredson, 2009), *The Secret in Their Eyes*, *Harry Brown, A Prophet* and *Animal Kingdom* are all described as 'thrillers' or 'thrilling'; *Le Concert/The Concert* (Mihăileanu, 2009) is a 'musical comedy'; and *Beneath Hill 60* (Sims, 2010) is a 'war movie' (Light House Petone 2010; Penthouse 2010). The promotion of these films thus mounts an appeal to middle-class audiences invested in cultural hierarchies but still wedded, in part, to populist pleasures. For Bourdieu, such audiences are marked by uncertainty, 'divided between the tastes they incline to and the tastes they aspire to' (Bourdieu 1984: 326). However, the historical distrust of high culture in New Zealand alerts us to this audience's potentially conscious and deliberate attachment of value to this cultural middle-ground.

In keeping with the target audience for the these cinemas, there is also a strong emphasis on middle-aged or older protagonists in those films screened by both the Light House and Penthouse (and in part by the Paramount and Empire): Michael Caine (born 1933) as the eponymous *Harry Brown*; Alexei Guskov (born 1958) as Andrey Filipov in *The Concert*; Patricia Clarkson (born 1959) and Alexander Siddig (born 1965) as Juliette and Tareq in *Cairo Time* (Nadda, 2009); Michael Nyqvist (born 1960) as Mikael Blomkvist in *The Girl Who Played with Fire*; Tilda Swinton (born 1960) as Emma Recchi in *I Am Love*; Annette Bening (born 1958) and Naomi Watts (born 1968) as Karen and Elizabeth in *Mother and Child*; Ricardo Darin (born 1957) as Benjamin Esposito in *The Secret in Their Eyes*; along with the crucial supporting role of Michael Douglas (born 1944) as Gordon Gekko in *Wall Street: Money Never Sleeps* (Stone, 2010) (IMDb 2010). The age of these protagonists is also not just incidental but is of key thematic importance, with a number of the films' plots pivoting upon crises of middle or old age. For example, *Harry Brown* represents a pensioner's battle against the lawless youth who have taken over his housing estate, and the protagonists of *The Concert, The Secret in Their Eyes* and *Mother and Child* are all haunted by their pasts (respectively, a ruined concert and career, an unsolved murder and unrequited love, and a baby given up for adoption). The lives of the middle-aged protagonists of *Cairo Time* and *I Am Love* are also reinvigorated and given new direction through romantic affairs. Such plots consequently offer potential resonance to the fears and fantasies of a middle-aged or older demographic.

Despite the middlebrow and middle-aged/older tendencies evident in the programming and promotion of Wellington's independent cinemas, it is overly reductive to explain the appeal of these cinemas' films solely through these terms. For example, *I Am Love* cultivates a distanced mode of engagement that appeals to highbrow taste formations via the heightened use of stylistic techniques. As Calhoun notes approvingly, the film's style encourages viewers to 'read the film rather than the characters' lips' (Calhoun 2010). This may be to such a degree that the film's accessibility is compromised. In particular, the decision to set the film to existing music by contemporary composer John Adams has led some critics to describe the score as 'distracting' and 'inappropriate' in places (Berardinelli 2010). However, if this 'refusal of what is ... easily decoded and culturally "undemanding"' (Bourdieu 1984: 486) challenges middlebrow engagement with the film, it further strengthens the extent to which these sites articulate a film culture in opposition to mainstream cinema-going. Only the Paramount explicitly promotes its films through reference to the challenge that they may present to audiences. For example, the cinema provides an in-house review of *Das Weisse Band/The White Ribbon* (Haneke, 2009) on its website that describes the film as 'disquieting', leaving the viewer 'with a sense of wrongness that you may not be able to shake or understand until long after leaving the cinema' (Paramount 2010). This reinforces the challenge to audiences represented by this cinema in a wider sense, embodied through its greater emphasis upon foreign-language cinema.

In addition to this greater emphasis on film as high culture, the Paramount is also marked by a greater emphasis on films that might appeal to a young adult audience. For example, it complemented *Exit Through The Gift Shop* (Banksy, 2009) (about street art) with the Reel Anime festival. The latter consisted of five films, all with young protagonists and action-based narratives. Furthermore, such films appear to complicate traditional cultural hierarchies. The documentary *Exit Through The Gift Shop* celebrates illegal street art while mocking its elevation within the art world via the success of the talentless (and seemingly fabricated) street artist Mr Brainwash. *Redline* (Koike, 2009) represents popular culture at its most immediate, while also possessing a heightened emphasis on form that evokes highbrow taste formations. The film, about a deadly car race, is described in promotion for the festival as a 'white knuckle ride to smash the senses' and 'one of the most … visually inventive films in years' (Madman 2011). Despite these signifiers of accessibility and cultural legitimacy, the film may strain the boundaries of what could be considered middlebrow – especially given the 'animated violence, nudity, drug use and coarse language' found in this film (Madman 2011). This is not in keeping with the rejection of vulgarity associated with middlebrow taste (Bourdieu 1984: 326). Nevertheless, due to its formal inventiveness and its subtitles, the film still complements the taste formation articulated through the Paramount. *Exit Through The Gift Shop* is also marked by formal experimentation, blurring the boundaries between documentary and mockumentary, and as such can be seen to reinforce the distinctions communicated through this cinema.

The manager of the Paramount draws the line at programming blockbusters and family films, citing *2012* (Emmerich, 2009) and *Cloudy with a Chance of Meatballs* (Lord/Miller, 2009) as examples of films 'that obviously wouldn't work here' (Larkindale 2009). Wellington's other independent cinemas, however, are marked by their movement precisely into this territory. For example, during the case study month, the Penthouse screened *Toy Story 3* (Unkrich, 2010), and the Light House screened *Despicable Me* (Coffin/Renaud, 2010) and *Avatar* (Cameron, 2009). While half of September consisted of the school holidays, the fact that the screening of these films coincided with the Light House's recent installation of 3D indicates that such a development represented more than a bit of seasonal opportunism. Such blockbusters may be recuperated from a middlebrow perspective, dependent on the degree of prestige attached to them in their critical reception (Roberts 2003). *Toy Story 3*, *Despicable Me* and *Avatar* arguably all have the potential to be approached through these terms via the reputation of Pixar, Steve Carell and the latter's Academy Awards. However, the array of immediate pleasures provided by these films may carry greater weight for audiences in the act of viewing them – be it their action, spectacle or visual comedy. These family films also disrupt the age-based distinctions otherwise articulated through these cinemas' spaces and programming. Such popular pleasures, and a child audience, are indulged to an even greater extent at the Empire. This cinema screened a host of Hollywood family films during September, including such critically derided movies as *Cats and Dogs: The Revenge of Kitty Galore* (Peyton 2010). The cinema's programme is thus largely indistinguishable from that of the city's mainstream cinemas, producing tensions between this content and the distinctions articulated through the cinema's space. It also renders the promotion of the film as an 'art-house' by Wellington's tourism website somewhat problematic.

The distinctions between the programming of Wellington's independent cinemas and that of the major chains are further muddied by the chains' screening of art-house content with mainstream crossover appeal. For example, in 2009 Reading introduced its Angelika brand 'for lovers of fine film', deriving from Reading's ownership of the successful Angelika Film Center art-house cinemas in New York and Texas (Reading Cinemas 2010; Reading International 2011). The Angelika brand does not relate to a specific screen in the complex, but is utilized to promote films screened that are in keeping with the brand. Angelika signage is also placed in close proximity to signage for the Gold Lounge Bar, though the Gold Lounge luxury seating was only available for one Angelika-branded film within the case study month – *Inception* (Nolan, 2010) — compared with five non-Angelika films. In addition to *Inception*, Angelika films in the case study month included *Beneath Hill 60*, *Animal Kingdom* and *Wall Street: Money Never Sleeps*, overlapping with the programming of the Light House, Penthouse and Empire. Such a choice of films represents the most accessible examples of those screened by Wellington's independent cinemas, specifically genre film-making from beyond Hollywood and Hollywood films with markers of quality (such as the return of Michael Douglas in his Oscar-winning role). This complements the dominance of Hollywood film-making across the cinema's programme as a whole, making up 25 of the 29 films screened in September. Foreign language cinema was noticeably absent, with no such films screened during this month. Overlap in the programming of Reading and Wellington's independent cinemas thus remains within clear boundaries and in keeping with Reading's primary emphasis on entertainment.

In contrast to Reading, the Embassy complemented newly released blockbusters with foreign cinema and even classics, undertaking the kind of repertory programming that has strong associations with art-house cinema but is largely absent from Wellington's independent cinemas today. For example, it screened *Les Enfants Du Paradis/Children of Paradise* (Carné, 1945) and *Le Salaire de la Peur/The Wages of Fear* (Clouzot, 1953) as part of its 'The Sunday Event' programme (Deluxe 2010). The Embassy screened six Hollywood films out of a total of 13 films. This reveals a greater weighting towards Hollywood cinema than Wellington's independent cinemas, though it falls some way short of Hollywood's dominance at Reading. The programming of the Embassy thus complements the way in which the space of this cinema problematizes simple distinctions between mainstream and non-mainstream cinema-going.

Conclusion

It is clear that the spaces of Wellington's independent cinemas mount an appeal that pivots upon their distinction from the space of the multiplex and contemporary mass production and consumption – albeit slightly overstated. When combined with their programming and promotion, a middlebrow and middle-aged film culture is prioritized across the cinemas as a whole. Such an emphasis on middlebrow taste can be seen to court middle-class audiences looking to distinguish themselves socially and culturally from the audiences for mainstream cinema. Middlebrow taste may also hold a particular appeal to the older audiences targeted by these cinemas due to the fact that their formative years were during, or relatively nearer, the period in which this taste formation held a privileged position in New Zealand society. Films characterized by more highbrow qualities can also be found at the Light House, Penthouse and Paramount, with the Paramount doing the most to draw attention to such qualities. This inclusion and/or cultivation of film as high culture further underlines how these cinemas establish cultural distinctions and hierarchies that are designed to appeal to social distinctions and hierarchies.

Such distinctions are complicated by the screening of films aimed at a young adult or child audience. Middlebrow and highbrow taste formations may be challenged by content that is more unruly in its combination of elements (such as *Exit Through The Gift Shop* or *Redline*), appealing to younger generations who have been shown to be less invested in traditional cultural hierarchies (Bennett et al. 2009: 178). Alternatively, such formations may be challenged by content that is resolutely popular (such as *Despicable Me* or *Avatar*). Nevertheless, some boundaries still seem to exist at the Paramount, Light House and Penthouse, programming films which can, in part, be incorporated into such taste formations. In contrast, the Empire takes the destabilization of social and cultural distinctions to an extreme through its juxtaposition of an art-house environment with a schedule given over almost completely to Hollywood films. The cinema thus emerges as an ambivalent site, avoiding easy categorization.

Rigid socio-cultural distinctions are also destabilized by the cinemas operated by major chains. This is particularly true of the ambiguous space and programming of the Embassy, reaching out to a diversity of audiences via its incorporation of a range of taste formations – albeit leaning more heavily towards Hollywood cinema. Reading's programming is less ambiguous, incorporating only the most mainstream of art-house content into its schedule. However, the socially exclusive but culturally popular pleasures provided by its Gold Lounge are notable for their dislocation of the relationship between social and cultural hierarchy.

Taken as a whole, these findings reveal the ways in which Wellington's cinemas both perpetuate and problematize the connection between cultural and social distinction. The fact that the perpetuation of this connection appears to be largely dependent upon an older demographic would suggest that such distinctions will continue to erode over time. Superficially, this would seem to be an egalitarian development, heralding an end to cultural elitism. However, given the increasing loosening of the connections between cultural and social hierarchies, the implications of this for social equality are unclear. Indeed, it is within the multiplex that the division of space according to a socio-economic hierarchy is at its most acute, via Reading's Gold Lounge. Furthermore, we need to recognize the way in which the appeal to cultural and social distinction mounted by Wellington's independent cinemas helps to sustain a degree of diversity within film exhibition that Reading's ten-screen multiplex fails to deliver in itself, and that is only partially provided by the Embassy. Such factors warn us from singling out Wellington's independent cinemas for their contribution to social stratification, and from overstating the positive effects of an end to the distinctions articulated through them.

Acknowledgements

Many thanks for the assistance of Kiri Griffin and Owen Mann at the New Zealand Film Archive, and to the exhibitors who agreed to be interviewed for this research.

References

The Academy of Motion Picture Arts and Sciences (2011), http://www.oscars.org/events-exhibitions/exhibitions/2009/anime.html. Accessed 30 June 2011.

Alfredson, D. (2009), *Flickan som Lekte Med Elden/The Girl Who Played with Fire*, Stockholm: Yellow Bird Films.

Anon (2006) 'Light House Cinema Casts Light on the Kapiti Coast', http://www.scoop.co.nz/stories/CU0604/S00086.htm. Accessed 8 June 2011.

——— (2008) 'Moving on', http://www.capitaltimes.co.nz/article/1735/Movingon.html. Accessed 1 July 2011.

Audiard, J. (2009), *Un Prophète/A Prophet*, Paris: France 2 Cinéma.

Banksy (2009), *Exit Through The Gift Shop*, London: Paranoid Pictures.

Bennett, T., Savage, M., Silva, E., Warde, A., Gayo-Cal, M. and Wright, D. (2009), *Culture, Class, Distinction*, London: Routledge.

Berardinelli, J. (2010), '*I Am Love* Review', http://www.reelviews.net/php_review_template.php?identifier=2103. Accessed 20 August 2012.

Bourdieu, P. (1984), *Distinction: A Social Critique of the Judgement of Taste*, London: Routledge.

Barber, D. (2009), *Harry Brown*, London: Marv Films

Calhoun, D. (2010), '*I Am Love* Review', http://www.timeout.com/film/reviews/88364/i-am-love.html. Accessed 20 August 2012.

Cameron, J. (2009), *Avatar*, Los Angeles: Lightstorm Entertainment.

Campanella, J.J. (2009), *El Secreto De Sus Ojos/The Secret in Their Eyes*, Madrid: Tornasol Films.

Carné, M (1945), *Les Enfant Du Paradise/Children of Paradise*, Paris: Société Nouvelle Pathé Cinéma.

Clouzot, H.G. (1953), *Le Salaire de la Peur/The Wages of Fear*, Paris: Compagnie Industrielle et Commerciale Cinématographique.

Coffin, P. and Renaud, C. (2010), *Despicable Me*, Los Angeles: Illumination Entertainment.

Davison, G. (2008), 'Heritage: From Patrimony to Pastiche', in G. Fairclough, R. Harrison, J.H. Jameson Jnr and J. Schofield (eds), *The Heritage Reader*, London: Routledge, pp. 31–41.

Deluxe (2010), http://www.deluxe.co.nz. Accessed 20 September 2010.

Eleftheriotis, D. (2001), *Popular Cinemas of Europe: Studies of Texts, Contexts and Frameworks*, London: Continuum.

Emmerich, R. (2009), *2012*, Los Angeles: Centropolis Entertainment.

Empire Cinema (2010), http://www.empirecinema.co.nz. Accessed 20 September 2010.

Featherstone, M. (1991), *Consumer Culture and Postmodernism*, London: Sage.

Gans, H. (1974), *Popular Culture and High Culture: An Analysis and Evaluation of Taste*, New York: Basic Books.

Garcia, R. (2009), *Mother and Child*, New York: Everest Entertainment.

Guadagnino, L. (2009), *Lo Sono L'Amore/I Am Love*, Rome: RAI Cinema.

Haneke, M. (2009), *Das Weisse Band/The White Ribbon*,

Harbord, J. (2002), *Film Cultures*, London: Sage.

Huffer, I. (2011) '"Wellywood's Cinemas": Theatrical film exhibition in "post-industrial" Wellington', *Studies in Australasian Cinema*, 5:3, pp. 251-264.

IMDb (2010), http://www.imdb.com. Accessed 20 September 2010.

Jancovich, M. and Faire, L., with Stubbings, S. (2003), *The Place of The Audience: Cultural Geographies of Film Consumption*, London: British Film Institute.

Jones, J. (2001), 'Finding a Place at the Downtown Picture Palace: The Tampa Theater, Florida', in M. Shiel and T. Fitzmaurice (eds), *Cinema and the City: Film and Urban Societies in a Global Context*, Oxford: Blackwell, pp. 122–33.

Koike, T. (2009), *Redline*, Tokyo: Madhouse.

Larkindale, K. (2009), Interview with author, 10 December.

Light House Petone (2010), http://www.lighthousepetone.co.nz. Accessed 20 September 2010.

Lord, P. and Miller, C. (2009), *Cloudy with a Chance of Meatballs*, Culver City: Sony Pictures Animation.

Madman (2011), http://www.madman.com.au/reelanime/redline. Accessed 30 June 2011

Michôd, D. (2010), *Animal Kingdom*, Sydney: Porchlight Films.

Mihăileanu, R. (2009), *Le Concert/The Concert*, Paris: France 3 Cinéma.

Nadda, R. (2009), *Cairo Time*, Toronto: Foundry Films.

Nolan, C. (2010), *Inception*, Burbank: Legendary Pictures.

Paramount (2010), http://www.paramount.co.nz. Accessed 20 September 2010.

Penthouse Cinema (2010), http://www.penthousecinema.co.nz. Accessed 20 September 2010.

Peyton, B. (2010), *Cats and Dogs: The Revenge of Kitty Galore*, Melbourne: Village Roadshow Pictures.

Pitt, D. (1977), 'Are There Social Classes in New Zealand?', in D. Pitt (ed.), *Social Class in New Zealand*, Auckland: Longman Paul, pp. 1–21.

Positively Wellington Tourism (2011), http://www.wellingtonnz.com/sights_activities/arts_culture. Accessed 8 June 2011.

Reading Cinemas (2010), http://www.readingcinemas.co.nz. Accessed 20 September 2010.

Reading International (2011), http://readingrdi.com. Accessed 30 June 2011.

Roberts, G. (2003), 'Circulations of Taste: *Titanic*, the Oscars and the Middlebrow', in J. Stringer (ed.), *Movie Blockbusters*, London: Routledge, pp. 155–66

Roper, B.S. (2005), *Prosperity for All? Economic, Social and Political Change in New Zealand Since 1935*, Melbourne: Thomson Dunmore Press.

Rose, J. (1994) 'Art-house Cinema Explosion', *City Voice*, 20 January.

Saunders, A. (2004), 'Grand Old Picture Palace is Making a Comeback', *The Wellingtonian*, 30 September.

Shouten, H. (2002), 'Werry Very Wary of New Cinema's Image', *The Dominion Post*, 15 July, p. A8.

Sigley, S. (2003), 'Film Culture: Its Development in New Zealand 1929–1972, PhD thesis, University of Auckland.

Sims, J. (2010), *Beneath Hill 60*, Sydney: Lucky Country Productions.

Stewart, S. (2010), *Culture and the Middle Classes*, Farnham: Ashgate.

Stone, O. (2010), *Wall Street: Money Never Sleeps*, New York: Edward R. Pressman Film.

Unkrich, L. (2010), *Toy Story 3*, Emeryville: Pixar.

Wilinsky, B. (2001), *Sure Seaters: The Emergence of Art-house Cinema*, Minneapolis, MN: University of Minnesota Press.

Chapter 17

Getting to See Women's Cinema

Julia Knight

During the 1970s and 1980s, a number of women's film and video distributors were set up in Europe and the United States. They played a key role in developing opportunities to see films made by women. With the media attention that surrounded Kathryn Bigelow's winning of the best director Oscar for *The Hurt Locker* (2008) – making her the first woman to do so in the then 82-year history of the Academy Awards – it is easy to forget that 40 years ago women directors were more notable for their virtual absence from cinema. Although Bigelow and other female directors have distanced themselves from gender issues (e.g. Bamigboye 2010; Savage 2010; Singh 2010; Weaver 2010), the emergence of women's distributors, such as Women Make Movies (set up in 1972) in the United States and Cinema of Women (set up in 1979) and Circles (set up in 1980) in the United Kingdom, helped pave the way for the greater visibility of women's contributions to cinema. Many of these distributors have since disappeared – the continuing existence of Women Make Movies is a rare exception – but their histories are indicative of the challenges involved in ensuring that non-mainstream work reaches audiences. This chapter focuses on the work of Cinema of Women in the United Kingdom during the 1980s, and explores the particular challenges the group faced in creating opportunities for feminist films to be seen by wider audiences.[1]

The invisibility of distribution

Traditionally, distributors have been the vital link between production and exhibition. Their acquisition decisions and the effectiveness of their promotional campaigns have helped determine what films audiences have had the opportunity to see, and thus distributors have played a key role in shaping film culture. Yet that role has tended to remain invisible to all but those in the industry. As a result, within film studies, distribution practices have until recently been critically neglected. Scholarly engagement has tended to be centrally concerned with the 'text' – so much so that introductory film studies books usually focus primarily on film genres, national cinemas, issues of representation, questions of authorship and the like (e.g. Bordwell and Thompson 2010; Cook 2007; Nelmes 2011). While this concern with the text is understandable, it has marginalized other factors that shape film culture.

Literature dealing with the distribution process, together with its associated promotional practices and links with exhibition, has been slowly emerging, and there is now a small body of work dealing with distribution practices in various areas of cinema. A cluster of books have addressed the distribution processes in commercial cinema, including Tiiu Lukk's *Movie Marketing: Opening the Picture and Giving it Legs* (1997), Jonathan Rosenbaum's *Movie Wars: How Hollywood and the Media Limit What Films We Can See* (2000), Tom Shone's *Blockbuster: How Hollywood Learned to Stop Worrying and Love the Summer* (2004) and Finola Kerrigan's *Film Marketing* (2010). Some books have also appeared that examine the rise of the more distinctive independent distributors, such as Angus Finney's *The Egos Have Landed: The Rise and Fall of Palace Pictures* (1996) and Peter Biskind's *Down and Dirty Pictures: Miramax, Sundance & the Rise of Independent Film* (2004).[2] More recently, others have examined the role of the film festival circuit, in particular Marijke de Valck's *Film Festivals: From European Geopolitics to Global Cinephilia* (2007) and Dina Iordanova's *Film Festival Yearbook* series (2009–12).

Work dealing with other areas of moving image distribution has been more sparse, relegated mostly to single book chapters in edited anthologies, or appearing as occasional journal articles (e.g. Brunsdon 1986: 179–231; Hines 1987b; Dickinson 1999: 210–23; Zryd 2006; Knight 2009). Notable exceptions have been Scott MacDonald's book *Canyon Cinema* (2008), on one of America's main distributors of experimental film, and Julia Knight and Peter Thomas' book *Reaching Audiences* (2011), examining the distribution of independent and artists' moving image work in the United Kingdom. Another British exception to the general paucity of literature dealing with the distribution of non-mainstream moving image work has been the multiple articles about women's moving image distribution and exhibition, many of which have appeared in journals such as *Screen* and the *Monthly Film Bulletin* (e.g. Imeson 1982; Root 1986; Cook 1986; Hines 1987a; Merz and Parmar 1987; Jenik 1987; Manning 1990a, 1990b; Knight 1992; Taylor 1999; Fowler 2002; Knight and Thomas 2008). Most of these have, however, been overviews aimed at highlighting the existence of feminist initiatives rather than analyses of the complexities of the distribution processes. Nevertheless, what is apparent in this limited literature is that distributors of non-mainstream material have always been inventive in creating exhibition opportunities. The concern of this chapter is the particular challenges Cinema of Women faced in ensuring that feminist films – with their focus on women as women and their lived experiences – had a place in the commercial cinema and on terrestrial television.

Getting feminist films into cinemas

In February 1983, Cinema of Women (COW) released a Dutch film, Marleen Gorris' *A Question of Silence* (1982). The film focuses on three women who meet for the first time while shopping in a boutique. When the male store manager accuses one of them of shoplifting, the other two join with her to attack and murder the manager. Although narrative based, the film has a non-realist style and offers an explicitly female perspective on how women experience patriarchal oppression. While the male judiciary can only understand the women's actions as a form of insanity, the women themselves experience their resulting bonding as a form of liberation from the oppressive nature of their previous existence, and are declared perfectly sane by a court-appointed female psychiatrist. The film clearly places women at the centre of its narrative, and is wholly concerned with the way in which they experience the world.

Founded four years earlier by a collective of six women, Cinema of Women (COW) was set up in part to ensure that such films could be seen by a wide audience of women, beyond the limited film festival and women's group circuit.[3] Achieving that goal essentially meant getting films into commercial cinemas and on to television. COW had released Leontine Sagan's *Maidens in Uniform* (Germany 1931) at a London repertory cinema two years earlier, but *A Question of Silence* was their first 35mm contemporary feature film release, and proved to be something of a learning curve.

The film was launched simultaneously at two central London first-run cinemas: the Screen on the Green in Islington and the Paris Pullman in Kensington. Although COW took out extensive advertising, the opening week's audience figures were disappointingly low. While a handful of film critics seemed to understand the feminist perspective that informed the film, many others did not and were damning in their assessment of it. One of the most extreme condemnations came from Milton Shulman (1983) in *The Standard*, who asserted:

[The film's resolution] is an argument that would have justified the Nazis exterminating the Jews, Herod's slaughter of babies and the lynching of blacks. Genocide is a comparatively modest moral device compared to the ultimate logic of this film's message, which is that the species should become extinct rather than survive in partnership with men.

In 1985, one of COW's workers, Jane Root (1986: 213), wrote an article detailing the strategies COW had employed to promote the film – one of the few articles to go beyond a mere overview – and suggested that the marketing of the film may have influenced the way it was received. Central to her analysis was COW's decision not to market *A Question of Silence* as a European art movie – even though the cinema at London's Institute of Contemporary Arts was keen to open the film[4] – because this would have focused attention on its 'difference from mainstream American film' (Root 1986: 215). While such a context might have drawn less scathing responses from the critics, COW wanted to target a wide female audience, and thus chose to highlight the film's potential to offer 'pleasurable experiences for specifically female cinema-goers' (1986: 214).

To its cost, COW discovered it had severely under-estimated the extent to which the (then largely) male film critics would either perceive the film as a threat or simply dismiss it as barely worth their attention. They also found that their target female audience did not expect to find the kinds of films that might interest them in commercial cinemas, and hence were not in the habit of frequenting them (Root 1986: 220–21; McNulty 2004).

To ensure *A Question of Silence* wasn't withdrawn from its opening cinemas prematurely, COW mounted an extensive grassroots campaign, which used volunteer labour and included leafleting across London, distributing posters and targeting feminist networks. Audience numbers did increase quite significantly, and the film was retained for a four-week run at both the Screen on the Green and the Paris Pullman.[5] Neither cinema would extend the film's run further, but the increased audience numbers enabled COW to get it transferred to another central London cinema, the two-screen Gate Bloomsbury – albeit known for showing art cinema and foreign-language films – for an additional eight-week run. It also went on to enjoy fairly extensive regional and repertory exhibition over the next two years. Through its sustained efforts, COW had at least ensured that the opportunity remained for audiences to see Gorris' film. As a result, the film became something of a *cause célèbre*, and COW regarded it as a victory for 'woman power'.[6]

Without COW's efforts and particular marketing strategy, it is likely that Gorris' film would have been seen by far smaller audiences, and many women in the United Kingdom would have remained unaware of an emerging body of feminist film-making. Indeed, although Gorris' next and more challenging feature, *Broken Mirrors* (1984), was picked up for distribution by the huge multinational Thorn-EMI, without COW's understanding of how to draw in the potential audience, it stayed in its opening cinemas for only three weeks and did not transfer to a follow-on venue.

COW went on to release further feminist feature films, including Margarethe von Trotta's *The Second Awakening of Christa Klages* (West Germany, 1979) and Lizzie Borden's *Born in Flames* (USA, 1983), both in 1984; Heiny Srour's *Leila and the Wolves* (UK/Lebanon, 1984) and Sheila McLaughlin and Lynne Tillman's *Committed* (USA, 1983), both in 1985; and Pat Murphy's *Anne Devlin* (Eire, 1984) in 1986. Like *A Question of Silence*, they were all released in central London cinemas, giving the films a national visibility and paving the way for their regional exhibition. It seems reasonable to expect COW to have benefited from the way in which *A Question of Silence*'s reception raised awareness of feminist film-making – that the film's *cause célèbre* status would make it easier to access audiences for their subsequent releases. But in fact COW continued to face a number of challenges in trying to get feminist films seen by wider audiences and, if anything, as the 1980s progressed, their task became even more difficult.

Indeed, on several occasions simply getting the films into cinemas was by no means straightforward. A few months after the release of *A Question of Silence*, COW managed to persuade Screen on the Green to take Lizzie Borden's *Born in Flames* (1983). Set in New York City, Borden's film takes place ten years in the future after a peaceful socialist revolution. Women find they have gained little from the revolution and still suffer harassment, exploitation and violence at the hands of men. As the situation deteriorates, four very different groups of women – a racially mixed Women's Army who campaign against female rape and assault; a black women's underground radio station, rooted in soul, gospel and reggae; a white women's underground radio station rooted in punk and rock; and a group of white female newspaper editors who disseminate the government line on the position of women – begin to work together across race and ideological lines to present united opposition to the oppression they experience. The film suggests that 'oppression against women is not eliminated automatically with "socialism" – not only do political values have to change, cultural values must change and become embedded in practice'.[7]

As with *A Question of Silence*, COW could see the potential of marketing the film to a wider audience of women rather than allowing it to be distributed in the context of 'art' or 'political' cinema. By the time COW made a formal approach to Borden in March 1983, she had in fact already agreed a UK contract with The Other Cinema (TOC), a small, independent distributor known for its catalogue of left-wing political films. However, Borden was keen to support feminist film distribution, and persuaded TOC to release her from her contract, enabling her to go with COW.[8] For COW, the Screen on the Green had particular appeal as an opening venue, since it was seen as 'perfectly poised between definitions of art and entertainment, showing a combination of mainstream releases … the occasional political film, music-related features and cult titles such as *Eraserhead*' (Root 1986: 217).[9] Although *Born in Flames* was only available on the non-theatrical format of 16mm, COW was able to convince the exhibitor to undertake the release – partly because the film had been well received at a number of international film festivals – but had to arrange for the installation of 16mm projection equipment at the cinema.[10] It opened in February 1984, but far from the release of Gorris' film making things easier, COW asserted that 'the problems associated with getting [*Born in Flames*] onto the screen have been very similar: a long grind of deals and negotiations, discussions over publicity, struggles to get it the kind of sympathetic press coverage that it deserves'.[11] Again, like *A Question of Silence*, it ran for four weeks at its opening cinema. While Borden's film didn't attract the savage reviews that Gorris' film did – possibly because, as Derek Malcolm (1983) observed, it had 'the saving grace of a sense of humour to temper its polemic' – when it transferred from the Screen on the Green, it was to a repertory cinema in South London, the Ritzy in Brixton, where it ran for only three weeks.

A few short months later, COW failed to interest Mainline, the company that ran the Screen on the Green, in giving any kind of release to another 16mm feminist feature film, Heiny Srour's *Leila and the Wolves* (1984), and had to settle for a repertory cinema instead.[12] COW had also hoped to open *Committed* (1983) – Sheila McLaughlin and Lynne Tillman's experimental film about the 1930s American movie actress Frances Farmer – there, but had to settle for the less desirable Electric Screen. Even when COW approached Mainline the following year, 1985, for a more conventional 35mm release of Pat Murphy's *Anne Devlin* (1984) – which had recently enjoyed a five-week run in Dublin and received largely positive reviews – they still failed to secure the Screen on the Green and met with only limited interest. Murphy's film is set in Ireland during the Republican uprisings of 1798. In the history books, Devlin is usually remembered – if at all – as the faithful housekeeper of the Republican leader Robert Emmet. Based on Devlin's prison journals, the film instead foregrounds her political commitment and personal strength, as demonstrated by her refusal to name her Republican companions while being interrogated and tortured after being arrested. Although the film's focus on a marginalized female figure is clearly informed by a feminist sensibility, it is also a historical costume drama, and arguably had greater commercial potential than *A Question of Silence*.

COW had been in contact with Murphy since August 1984, and it was finally agreed in November that they would distribute *Anne Devlin*. A lengthy process then followed during

1985, in which COW tried to find a suitable opening venue and date. Eventually, by the summer of 1985, they had started negotiations with Mainline to try to secure a month-long run at one of its London Screen cinemas – preferably either Screen on the Hill in Belsize Park or Screen on the Green in Islington. Mainline refused to open it at the more prestigious Screen on the Hill because they felt the film was 'not "big" enough', so discussion concentrated on Screen on the Green.[13] Since this was where both *A Question of Silence* and *Born in Flames* had opened, Mainline was aware of COW's ability to target audiences, but COW found this was not sufficient to secure them either a four-week run or even a firm commitment. As COW worker Eileen McNulty explained to Murphy:

> [I]n negotiating with the cinema owners/programmers we are in competition with what they consider to be more commercial, or 'less difficult' films than the ones we distribute, in terms of choice of cinema and length of run. With *Anne Devlin* we have had the basic problem that we are having to convince Mainline that the film is more commercial than they choose to think it is. They know from experience that we have authority in this field and have ensured the success of films they would not have thought of as being at all commercial, yet they are needing a lot of convincing, and indeed pushing.[14]

When pressed by Murphy for a firm opening date, McNulty went on to explain that Mainline had not yet confirmed a date, and asserted that 'this is where their lack of commitment to the film shows itself'.[15] But the reservations that Mainline had about the commercial viability of the film were also evident in its willingness to offer only a two-week run, rather than the four weeks it had given both A *Question of Silence* and *Born in Flames*. At the time of these negotiations, McNulty thought it likely that COW would be offered a two-week guaranteed run with an extension if the film did well. COW was willing to accept such an offer, but also intended to negotiate for a follow-on run at Mainline's Screen at Baker Street.

In the end, Mainline offered the Baker Street Screen as the opening venue, rather than the more desirable Screen on the Green sought by COW. However, the opening – scheduled for the end of January 1986 – in fact failed to materialize when Mainline enjoyed an unexpected box-office success with Chris Barnard's *Letter to Brezhnev* (UK, 1985), which looked likely to sit in the Baker Street cinema 'for months to come'.[16] As a result, COW was forced to shift the opening to the Hampstead Everyman – a repertory cinema – where it eventually opened in March 1986. In the light of these challenges, it is unsurprising that COW asserted:

> To anyone who has seen *Born in Flames* or *[A] Question of Silence* it might seem obvious that they can be watched in warm comfortable cinemas by large audiences. To us, at Cinema of Women it is a major achievement.[17]

Keeping them there

Clearly, getting the films into commercial cinemas was a challenge, but as demonstrated most forcefully by the reception of *A Question of Silence*, so too was keeping them there. For COW, this was equally important. Having a sustained presence on the commercial cinema circuit was the only way to reach large numbers of women. In order to have that presence, it was crucial to keep the films in the cinemas for as long as possible, to demonstrate to exhibitors that feminist films were viable. While COW would undoubtedly have preferred Gorris' film to continue longer at its opening venues, it recognized that its transfer to the Gate Bloomsbury was 'the next best thing' – even though it changed the context in which it was being screened.[18]

Viewed from a commercial perspective, however, it is possible to argue that Mainline was in fact justified in their reservations regarding the release of *Anne Devlin*. Just as COW was embarking on negotiations with Murphy in the autumn of 1984 to distribute *Anne Devlin*, it was also involved in discussions with Heiny Srour to distribute *Leila and the Wolves* (1984). Srour's film revolves around Leila, a Lebanese student dissatisfied with the official, colonial, male-dominated version of history. Through her eyes, the film reconstructs women's daily sacrifices and explores the hidden role of Arab women in the recent history of Palestine and Lebanon. Through the use of reconstruction and archived newsreel footage, the film takes Leila back in time, starting in Palestine under the British mandate in the 1920s, and ends with the Israeli invasion of Lebanon in 1982.

Although they were unable to interest Screen on the Green, COW was nevertheless able to tie up a release date relatively quickly – and indeed, releasing Srour's film was the reason COW gave Murphy for having to postpone a proposed April 1985 release date for *Anne Devlin*.[19] In January 1985, COW was able to confirm that Cinegate would open *Leila and the Wolves* in April 1985 at the Gate Notting Hill. According to COW, the terms agreed with Cinegate were that the film would stay there for four weeks:

> provided that it does not fall below your minimum running costs which need a weekly attendance of 1200. If during the first week, attendance is below this, but not below 1000 and it appears that word of mouth recommendation will increase attendance, then you will consider retaining it.[20]

The agreement with Cinegate also allowed for a longer run at Notting Hill and a transfer to the Gate Bloomsbury if the film did well. However, it ran for only three weeks because the film never reached the minimum weekly attendance figure and – in contrast to *A Question of Silence*, where audiences steadily increased over the first three weeks of its run at both opening cinemas – audiences for *Leila and the Wolves* steadily declined.[21]

Thus COW was unable to repeat the success it had with Gorris' film in terms of keeping their films in commercial cinemas. Yet COW undertook extensive advertising and marketing activities, including grassroots promotional campaigns, for all their releases. However, although an audience clearly existed for feminist films, such films were not to all women's taste. After a screening of *Committed* at a film society, for instance, the organizers reported: 'Audience violently disliked the film.'[22] During *A Question of Silence*'s run at the Screen on the Green, a parent was sufficiently outraged to write to the cinema, reporting that her 15-year-old daughter had gone to see the film with a friend and complaining that:

> It was not obvious from either the reviews in the *Gazette* nor from the hoardings outside the cinema that this was a feminist film nor that it had sub-titles. They sat through about a quarter of the film before leaving because they were surrounded by lesbians. I suggest that you have a public duty not to allow young people into your cinema unless it is pointed out to them exactly what is to be shown and what sort of people they are likely to be surrounded by.[23]

Furthermore, COW continued to have to contend with negative or dismissive reviewer responses. In 1984 it released Margarethe von Trotta's *The Second Awakening of Christa Klages* (1979), which follows a woman's attempt to keep a child-care centre open by robbing a bank to obtain much-needed funds. She had previously co-directed one feature with husband Volker Schlöndorff and acted in several New German Cinema films. While some reviewers did note von Trotta's directing talent (e.g. Andrews 1984; Gibbs 1984), Milton Shulman (1984) felt the film functioned at best as reassurance 'that women are much nicer than men'. Likewise ignoring the film's implicit feminist politics, *The Guardian*'s reviewer Tim Pulleine (1984) simply dismissed it as 'derivative' and 'muddled'. With regard to *Born in Flames*, John Coleman (1984) of the *New Statesman* suggested that 'Lizzie Borden didn't so much direct as ... take an axe', while Philip French (1984) of the *Observer* asserted: 'This angry film isn't poised enough to work as satire, but it has a wild jauntiness that takes the edge off its lunacy.' Jane Root (1986: 219) attributed the negative responses to *A Question of Silence* to the male reviewers' perception of the film 'as a threat', but it is equally possible to argue that the more dismissive reviews were a result of feminist films being deemed to be of marginal interest when measured against mainstream releases. When Coleman (1983) reviewed *A Question of Silence*, for instance, a woman reader wrote to him objecting to the brevity of the review, which was all of one sentence long and dismissed the film as 'simplistic and silly'. In his reply to the reader, he argued that he was in fact not unwilling to engage with a feminist film – and indeed wrote a two-page letter to the reader elucidating his views – but he had written too much on Sidney Lumet's *The Verdict* (USA), starring Paul Newman, and simply not left himself sufficient space to do so.[24] Rather than edit down his discussion of Lumet's film, Coleman had chosen to radically reduce his coverage of Gorris' film. Thus COW's releases had to compete with more commercial films for space in newspapers, just as they did in the cinemas.

Getting feminist films on television

The other way of accessing wider audiences was, of course, via television. Most film-makers were also extremely keen to secure a television sale because it generated additional income. Many had run up debts in the course of making their films, and looked to distribution income as a means of repaying those debts. While a number of directors expressed their support – as Borden had done – for a feminist distributor, they were also frequently desperate for any monies COW could get for them. Lynne Tillman, for instance, wrote to COW the year after the UK release of her film *Committed*, saying: 'We still have an $1,100 debt to be paid off, and monies from you would help.'[25] Since short cinema runs produced relatively low levels of revenue – which frequently yielded very little income for the film-maker after COW's recovery of its release costs[26] – television sales became all the more important, and film-makers were usually very interested in COW pursuing a broadcast deal on their behalf.

Such sales were invariably to Channel 4, since its remit to promote innovation and experiment opened up a highly appropriate broadcast outlet for the kinds of films that COW distributed. Indeed, in 1981 COW had been able to sell six titles to the new channel – including Michelle Citron's *Daughter Rite* (USA, 1979), Sally Potter's *Thriller* (UK, 1979) and Cristina Perincioli's *The Power of Men is the Patience of Women* (West Germany, 1979). This was not uncommon, since the channel began buying up substantial amounts of material to ensure it had enough programming to fill its schedules when it launched the following year.[27] Nevertheless, when quizzed by American film-maker Michelle Parkerson in 1985 about its track record in TV sales, COW was able to report a further seven sales in the past two years and said it was negotiating on another four.[28]

However, COW did not always get the TV rights, and even when it did, making TV sales – like getting films into commercial cinemas – was not always straightforward. When Pat Murphy agreed in November 1984 that COW was to distribute *Anne Devlin*, she was already in discussion with Channel 4 about the TV rights, but was happy to hand negotiations over to COW. Because – like Tillman and other directors – Murphy had debts to pay off, she was keen to maximize the broadcast licensing fee. In 1982, she had sold the rights to Channel 4 for one screening of her earlier film *Maeve* (co-directed with John Davies, UK/Ireland 1981) – about a 20-year-old woman returning to her native Belfast – for £17,500 and took that as a benchmark. Since she regarded *Anne Devlin* to have been 'a much more successful film in terms of theatrical impact and critical acclaim', she instructed COW to ask for a £50,000 fee for the rights to three transmissions.[29] Channel 4 responded by offering only £15,000, asserting that the fee paid for *Maeve* was 'indicative of occasional inconsistency and paying over the going rate in the early days of the Channel'.[30] Indeed, according to former deputy commissioning editor Rod Stoneman (2003), Channel 4 did not pay particularly high amounts for broadcast rights generally. For instance, the licence fee for Perincioli's *The Power of Men is the Patience of Women* (West Germany, 1978) – a feature film about domestic violence – had been a mere £5000.

Negotiations over *Anne Devlin* dragged on throughout 1985 and 1986, with Murphy reducing her price to £20,000,[31] while the channel increased its offer to £17,500 – initially still for three transmissions,[32] but revised it subsequently to only two transmissions since 'we have not repeated any feature more than once in the past'.[33] While Murphy felt the figure of £17,500 was 'still not enough',[34] she eventually was persuaded to accept the offer, since if she did not she risked missing the proposed transmission slot of spring 1987. As Channel 4 explained in December 1986, if the film was not screened in this slot, 'we would have to postpone acquisition for some time as the next relevant scheduling place would be a fiction season planned for Spring 1988'.[35]

Anne Devlin was indeed broadcast very soon after the contract was finalized, in April 1987, but this was not the case for all films purchased by the channel. By 1988, for instance, none of the six films COW had sold to Channel 4 in 1981 had been broadcast. To some extent this was a result of the channel over-purchasing prior to its launch, which had created a backlog of material waiting to be broadcast. However, in the case of Sally Potter's experimental short, *Thriller* (UK, 1979), the reason was more complicated. The film deconstructs Puccini's opera *La Bohème* to examine why the seamstress Mimi has to die, and makes extensive use of music from both the opera and Alfred Hitchcock's film *Psycho* (USA, 1960). Made when Potter was a student, the use of the music had never been cleared for television, and this was overlooked when Channel 4 bought the rights. Before finally committing to broadcasting it, the channel wanted to establish what the music clearance costs would be. When these, together with some other outstanding production payments, were estimated to total between £7100 and £8000, Channel 4 proposed 'that the remaining part of the licence fee which has not yet been paid by Channel 4 [£2,333.33] should be put towards clearance costs'.[36] Although the channel agreed to bear the balance of the costs, this arrangement – to which COW agreed[37] – meant that COW did not receive its full share of the licence fee.

The enormity and significance of the challenge

The low level of returns from short cinema runs and sales to Channel 4 produced relatively limited levels of resourcing for COW. Although COW was able to access some public funding – initially from the Greater London Council and subsequently the British Film Institute – the organization remained small in scale.[38] This compounded the challenges facing COW – not only were they trying to reach wider audiences of women, but they were trying to do so with very limited resources. As a result, the organization was frequently overstretched. Time and again, for instance, film-makers wrote to COW saying that they hadn't heard from them with regard to how their films were doing, where they were being shown and late payment of royalties.[39] Although inconceivable in the age of email, it was not unusual for COW to take two to three months to reply to letters, and on at least one occasion during 1985 a film-maker had to wait five months for a response.[40] Part of the reason the TV sale of *Anne Devlin* took so long to sort out was tardiness on COW's part in responding to

Channel 4's offer of £15,000 made in March 1985. The channel wrote to COW in April, June, August and October chasing up a response, before COW finally replied in November.[41] But COW's delay in responding to both the film-maker and Channel 4 in 1985 coincided exactly with the period when it was putting its energies into opening *Leila and the Wolves* at the Gate Notting Hill (April 1985) and negotiating a cinema opening for *Anne Devlin* with Mainline (the summer and autumn months of 1985). As a small organization, the need to juggle multiple demands with only minimal staffing levels meant that routine tasks – such as replying to correspondence – were often neglected.[42]

Unfortunately, COW's limited resources meant they were unable to meet all of their film-makers' expectations of what a distributor should do. This is particularly apparent in some of the correspondence between COW and film-makers Pat Murphy and Heiny Srour. In August 1985, when COW was in the middle of negotiating with Mainline to open *Anne Devlin* at one of its cinemas, Murphy wrote complaining of numerous postponements to the release date – with possible dates having been mooted for November 1984, April 1985 and September 1985. In particular, she stressed that:

> Surely you must realise that this continual postponement of the theatrical release is undermining whatever level of awareness has been built up around *Anne Devlin* over the past year and that this will make your task more difficult when you do manage to bring it on? … The success of the Dublin run was the result of a tremendous amount of concerted effort between myself and the Irish distributors.[43]

In a similar vein, Srour voiced on more than one occasion her feeling that COW should and could be doing more than they were to both promote *Leila and the Wolves* and bring about its speedy release. Three months after she had signed with COW, for instance, she complained that they hadn't shown the film to enough potential exhibitors, and said she also felt COW had not been sufficiently forceful in their approach to Mainline. Subsequently, according to COW, Srour threatened to 'take the film away from us if we weren't prepared to go far enough'.[44] Thus it is clear that neither film-maker was entirely satisfied with COW's efforts on behalf of her film. In this context, it is noteworthy that the second features from Borden (*Working Girls*, USA, 1986) and McLaughlin (*She Must Be Seeing Things*, USA, 1987), as well as that of Gorris, went to other distributors. While the specific reasons varied – and the decision was not necessarily in the hands of the director – in some cases it was partly because a more commercial distributor was deemed to be better placed to maximize exposure (and hence revenue) for the film. In the case of Gorris' *Broken Mirrors*, for instance, Thorn EMI – like COW – arranged to open the film at both the Screen on the Green and the Electric Screen, but also got it into a third central London cinema, the four-screen Cinecenta, for its second and third weeks.

The concerns of Murphy and Srour are, of course, perfectly understandable, but COW's efforts – in contrast to those of their commercial rivals – were necessarily constrained by its far more limited resources. It was always a very fine balancing act between doing as much as they could to promote their films they distributed, and being able to support that activity–whether via earned income, state subsidy or volunteer labour. It was not uncommon for film-makers to ask COW to arrange for prints to be made, subtitled or shipped to festivals, as well as expect them to commission publicity materials and advertising, and these costs would be deducted from distribution income before royalties were paid. However, as one COW worker was forced to explain to Srour when her expectations of COW's ability to undertake these tasks exceeded the organization's resources: 'COW couldn't invest beyond a certain point because we just don't have the money.'[45]

This exploration of COW's endeavours to reach a wider audience of women exposes both the enormity of the task it began with *A Question of Silence* and the scale of its achievement across subsequent releases. In 1985, Jane Root (1986: 222) asserted, with a touch of bitterness, that the three-week run of *Broken Mirrors* meant the film had disappeared from London cinemas 'with indecent haste'. But, given that *A Question of Silence*'s longer run proved to be exceptional, it is perhaps more important to note that COW demonstrated that releasing feminist films in commercial cinemas *at all* was indeed possible. That Thorn-EMI picked up on that and followed COW's lead by releasing Gorris' second feature – even if it did not share COW's commitment to securing follow-on runs – points to the magnitude of COW's achievement.

COW's endeavours are aspects of the distribution processes that are usually hidden from view, and have rarely been addressed by scholarly literature. When it released *Born in Flames*, COW astutely observed: 'We hope that the same kind of numbers of women who enjoyed *[A] Question of Silence* will like *Born in Flames*, but even if you don't we hope that you will appreciate *being able to see it at all*' (my emphasis).[46] It is difficult to over-estimate the significance of this, since 'being able to see' these films has played a crucial role in expanding the diversity of moving image culture in the United Kingdom. While the opportunities to see such films may have remained limited, those that COW created were hugely important, not only for making women's contribution to cinema more visible, but for helping nurture the careers of the women directors the organization championed.

References

Andrews, N. (1984), *Financial Times*, 20 January, p. 21.

Bamigboye, B. (2010), 'Oscars 2010: Kathryn Bigalow Becomes First Woman to Win Best Director as *Hurt Locker* Blasts ex-husband's *Avatar* with Six Gongs', *MailOnline*, 8 March, http://www.dailymail.co.uk/tvshowbiz/article-1256279/Oscars-2010-Kathryn-Bigelow-woman-win-best-director-Hurt-Locker-blasts-ex-husbands-Avatar-gongs.html. Accessed 28 October 2011.

Baupré, L. (1986), 'How to Distribute a Film', in P. Kerr (ed.), *The Hollywood Film Industry: A Reader*, London: Routledge & Kegan Paul, pp. 185–203.

Biskind, P. (2004), *Down and Dirty Pictures: Miramax, Sundance & the Rise of Independent Film*, London: Bloomsbury.

Bordwell, D. and Thompson, K. (2010), *Film Art: An Introduction*, 9th edn, Boston: McGraw-Hill.

Brunsdon, C. (ed.) (1986), *Films for Women*, London: British Film Institute.

Coleman, J. (1983), *New Statesman*, February, n.p.

—— (1984), *New Statesman*, 3 February, p. 30.

Cook, P. (1986), 'Breaking Down the Myths: Feminist Film Distribution Today', *Monthly Film Bulletin*, 53: 624, pp. 4–5.

—— (ed.) (2007), *The Cinema Book*, 3rd edn, London: British Film Institute.

Dickinson, M. (ed.) (1999), *Rogue Reels: Oppositional Film in Britain, 1945–90*, London: British Film Institute.

Drake, P. (2008), 'Distribution and Marketing in Contemporary Hollywood', in J. Wasko and P. McDonald (eds), *The Contemporary Hollywood Film Industry*, Oxford: Blackwell, pp. 63–82.

de Valck, M. (2007), *Film Festivals: From European geopolitics to Global Cinephilia*, Amsterdam: Amsterdam University Press.

Finney, A. (1996), *The Egos have Landed: The Rise and Fall of Palace Pictures*, London: William Heinemann.

Fowler, C. (2002), 'I'm Spartacus! On No Longer Seeing Films Made by Women', *Vertigo*, 2: 3, pp. 44–45.

French, P. (1984), *Observer*, 29 January, p. 54.

Gibbs, P. (1984), *Daily Telegraph*, 20 January, p. 13.

Grant, P. and Wood, C. (2004), *Blockbusters and Trade Wars: Popular Culture in a Globalized World*, Vancouver: Douglas & McIntyre.

Hines, S. (1987a), 'Feminist Distribution: A New Phase', *Independent Media*, 69, p. 9

—— (1987b), 'Independent Distribution: Changes for the 80s', *Independent Media*, 72, pp. 9–11.

Imeson, J. (1982), 'Women's Film Now', *Monthly Film Bulletin*, 49: 583, p. 184.

Iordanova, D. with Cheung, R. (eds) (2010), *Film Festival Yearbook 2: Film Festivals and Imagined Communities*, St Andrews, Fife: St Andrews Film Studies with College Gate Press.

—— (2011), *Film Festival Yearbook 3: Film Festivals and East Asia*, St Andrews, Fife: St Andrews Film Studies with College Gate Press.

Iordanova, D. with Rhyne, R. (eds) (2009), *Film Festival Yearbook 1: The Festival Circuit*, St Andrews, Fife: St Andrews Film Studies with College Gate Press.

Iordanova, D. and Torchin, L. (eds) (2012), *Film Festival Yearbook 4: Film Festivals and Activism*, St Andrews, Fife: St Andrews Film Studies with College Gate Press.

Jenik, A. (1987), 'Distribution Matters – "What Does She Want?"', *Screen*, 28: 4, pp. 70–72.

Kerrigan, F. (2010), *Film Marketing*, Oxford: Butterworth-Heinemann.

Knight, J. (1992), 'Cinenova: A Sign of the Times', *Screen*, 33: 2, pp. 184–89.

—— (2009), 'The "Alternative" End of Marketing: Building Audiences for Artists'/Community Film and Video in Britain Since 1980', *Historical Journal of Film, Radio and Television*, 29: 4, pp. 449–465.

Knight, J. and Thomas, P. (2008), 'Distribution and the Question of Diversity: A Case Study of Cinenova', *Screen*, 49: 3, pp. 354–65.

—— (2011), *Reaching Audiences: Distribution and Promotion of Alternative Film*, Bristol: Intellect.

Lukk, T. (1997), *Movie Marketing: Opening the Picture and Giving it Legs*, Beverly Hills, CA: Silman-James Press.

MacDonald, S. (2008), *Canyon Cinema: The Life and Times of an Independent Film Distributor*, Berkeley, CA: University of California Press.

Malcolm, D. (1983), 'Derek Malcolm Reviews the Best of the Edinburgh Festival', *Movie Guardian*, 1 September.

Manning, A. (1990a), 'Ten Glorious Years: Cinema of Women', *Independent Media*, 95, pp. 10–11.

—— (1990b), 'Sisters of Mercy', *Independent Media* 100, June, pp. 10–11.

McNulty, E. (2004), [Former COW worker] Interview with Julia Knight and Peter Thomas, 19 May.

Merz, C. and Parmar, P. (1987), 'Distribution Matters – Circles', *Screen*, 28: 4, pp. 66–69.

Nelmes, J. (ed.) (2011), *Introduction to Film Studies*, 5th edn, London: Routledge.

Pulleine, T. (1984), *The Guardian*, 19 January.

Root, J. (1986), 'Distributing "A Question of Silence" – A Cautionary Tale', in Charlotte Brunsdon (ed.), *Films for Women*, London: British Film Institute, pp. 213–23.

Rosenbaum, J. (2000), *Movie Wars: How Hollywood and the Media Limit What Films We Can See*, London: Wallflower Press.

Savage, M. (2010), 'Profile: Kathryn Bigelow', BBC News Channel, 8 March, http://news.bbc.co.uk/1/hi/entertainment/8491128.stm. Accessed 28 October 2011.

Shone, T. (2004), *Blockbuster: How Hollywood Learned to Stop Worrying and Love the Summer*, London: Simon & Schuster.

Shulman, M. (1983), *The Standard*, 17 February, p. 23.

—— (1984), *The Standard*, 19 January, p. 21.

Singh, A. (2010), 'Oscars 2010: Kathryn Below Profile', *The Telegraph*, 8 March, http://www.telegraph.co.uk/culture/film/oscars/7396349/Oscars-2010-Kathryn-Bigelow-profile.html. Accessed 28 October 2011.

Squire, J. (2006), *The Movie Business Book*, Maidenhead: Open University Press/McGraw-Hill Education.

Stoneman, R. (2003), [Former Assistant and Deputy Commissioning Editor, Channel 4] Interview with Peter Thomas, 2 July.

Tait, A. (1985), 'Distributing the Product', in M. Auty and N. Roddick (eds), *British Cinema Now*, London: British Film Institute, pp. 71–82.

Taylor, M. (1999), 'To Whom It May Concern. Please Note: Cinenova', *Filmwaves*, 8, pp. 16–19.

Weaver, M. (2010), 'Kathryn Bigelow Makes History as First Woman to Win Best Director Oscar', *The Guardian*, 8 March, http://www.guardian.co.uk/film/2010/mar/08/kathryn-bigelow-oscars-best-director. Accessed 28 October 2011.

Wyatt, J. (1998), 'The Formation of the "Major Independent": Miramax, New Line and the New Hollywood', in S. Neale and M. Smith (eds), *Contemporary Hollywood Cinema*, London: Routledge, pp. 74–90.

Zryd, M. (2006), 'The Academy and the Avant-Garde: A Relationship of Dependence and Resistance', *Cinema Journal*, 45: 2, pp. 17–42.

Notes

1 The research on which this chapter is based is part of a larger research project that was funded by the UK Arts and Humanities Research Council, 2002–05, and addressed artists' and independent film and video distribution in the United Kingdom from the late 1960s to 2000 (see http://alt-fv-distribution.net, accessed 20 September 2012). Our key research findings have been published in *Reaching Audiences: Distribution and Promotion of Alternative Moving Image* (Intellect, 2011, co-authored with Peter Thomas), while some of the primary research material has been made available through the Film and Video Distribution Database at http://fv-distribution-database.ac.uk (accessed 20 September 2012).

2 There have also been a handful of book chapters, mostly in edited anthologies. See, for instance, Tait (1985), Baupré (1986), Wyatt (1998), a chapter on theatrical distribution in Squire (2006) and Drake (2008).

3 Both Cinema of Women and the other UK women's film and video distributor, Circles, were set up partly to ensure that women film-makers could keep control of the distribution and circulation of their work. See, for instance, 'British Feminist Exhibition and Distribution: Three Statements' in Brunsdon (1986): 225–31.

4 Chris Rodley, Cinema Director, ICA Cinema, letter to Jane Root, Cinema of Women, 31 August 1982. Source: Cinenova (COW films, *A Question of Silence*, Correspondence). The following year, the ICA also expressed interest in opening Lizzie Borden's *Born in Flames* (USA, 1983), COW's second feature film release. See Chris Rodley, Cinema Director, ICA Cinema, letter to Jane Root, Cinema of Women, 10 August 1983. Source: Cinenova (*Born in Flames*, Correspondence with Lizzie Borden). Rodley was also one of the organizers of the 'Women's Own' festival, staged at the ICA Cinema in October 1980, which celebrated 80 years of women's work in film and television. Hence it is possible to argue that the ICA was known for showing women's films and would have been a logical venue for COW to use to open its films. This helps demonstrate the significance of choosing not to follow this route, and the enormity of the challenge COW faced in seeking out more mainstream venues.

5 Box office returns retained by COW show attendance figures at the Screen on the Green of 1171 in the first week, rising to 1453 in the second and 1802 in the third week; and at the Paris Pullman of 412 in the first week, rising to 449 in the second week and 641 in the third. Attendance figures then fell in the fourth week at both venues, to 1599 at the Screen on the Green and 629 at the Paris Pullman. Source: Cinenova (COW films, *A Question of Silence*).

6 Penny Ashbrooke, COW collective member, letter to Marie (Allod), 10 March 1983: 1. Source: Cinenova (COW films, *A Question of Silence*, press list).

7 *Born in Flames* promotional flyer, p. 2. Source: Cinenova (*Born in Flames*).

8 See Penny Ashbrook, Cinema of Women, letter to Lizzie Borden, 22 March 1983; Lizzie Borden, letter to Penny Ashbrook, Cinema of Women, 26 May 1983; Lizzie Borden, letter to Tony Kirkhope, The Other Cinema, 7 July 1983; Tony Kirkhope, The Other Cinema, letter to Lizzie Borden, 15 July 1983; Lizzie Borden, letter to Tony Kirkhope, The Other Cinema, 24 July 1983. Source: Cinenova (Correspondence with Lizzie Borden).

9 So, for instance, the release of Borden's film was followed by Lawrence Kasdan's *The Big Chill* (USA, 1983), starring Kevin Kline, William Hurt and Glenn Close, among others.

10 Penny Ashbrook, Cinema of Women, letter to Ian Christie, British Film Institute, 27 October 1983. Source: Cinenova (Correspondence with Lizzie Borden). As Ashbrook's letter points out, this also involved finding funding to finance the 16mm projection equipment.

11 Draft promotional flyer for *Born in Flames*, Cinema of Women, undated, p. 2. Source: Cinenova (Correspondence with Lizzie Borden).

12 Eileen McNulty, Cinema of Women, letter to Heiny Srour, 14 December 1984. Source: Cinenova (*Leila and the Wolves*).

13 Eileen McNulty, Cinema of Women, letter to Pat Murphy, 21 August 1985. Source: Cinenova (COW films, *Anne Devlin*), p. 2.

14 ibid, p. 1.

15 ibid.

16 Penny Ashbrooke, letter to Lesley Thornton, *The Observer Magazine*, 17 February 1986. Source: Cinenova (COW films, *Anne Devlin*, press screenings).

17 Draft promotional flyer for *Born in Flames*, Cinema of Women, undated, p. 1. Source: Cinenova (Correspondence with Lizzie Borden).

18 Penny Ashbrook, Cinema of Women, letter to Marie Allod, 10 March 1983. Source: Cinenova (COW films, *A Question of Silence*, Press Lists and Publicity Material).

19 See Pat Murphy, letter to COW, 12 August 1985, p. 1. Source: Cinenova (COW films, *Anne Devlin*, Communications with Pat + Contract + Channel 4).

20 Eileen McNulty, Cinema of Women, letter to David Stone, Cinegate, 31 January 1985. Source: Cinenova (*Leila and the Wolves*, Worker).

21 Box office returns retained by COW show attendance figures of 910 in the first week, 704 in the second and 678 in the third. Source: Cinenova (COW films, *Leila and the Wolves*, Returns).

22 Audience feedback sheet, St Andrews University. Source: Cinenova (COW films, *Committed*, Audience feedback). Although film societies are obviously not the same as commercial cinemas, they are attended by a paying public, and such non-theatrical screenings are one of the few instances where viewer reactions are reported back to the distributor.

23 Copy of letter sent to Screen on the Green, undated. Source: Cinenova (COW films, *A Question of Silence*, Correspondence).

24 John Coleman, *New Statesman*, letter to Julia Tozer, 4 March 1983. Source: Cinenova (COW films, *A Question of Silence*, Originals of reviews, synopsis and press release).

25 Lynne Tillman, letter to COW, 7 January 1986. Source: Cinenova (COW films, *Committed*, Correspondence). See also Pat Murphy, letter to Eileen McNulty, COW, 30 August 1987: 'I am writing in a state of urgency to ask you for the second installment of the Channel 4 licensing fee for *Anne Devlin* ... the previous payment went to the Film Board. This next sum is to come to me at Aeon Films. And it is badly, urgently needed.' Source: Cinenova (COW films, *Anne Devlin*, Communications with Pat + Contract + Channel 4).

26 Most usually, these were paid for advertising, press screenings, promotional leafleting, certification costs, freight charges and the like, but on occasions could also include print costs.

27 See Gail Patterson, Programme Acquisition Executive, Channel Four Television, letter to Jenny Wallace, Cinema of Women, 7 July 1988. Source: Cinenova (COW films, *Thriller*).

28 The four they were negotiating on at the time included *Committed* and *Anne Devlin*. See Jenny Wallace, COW, letter to Michelle Parkerson, 18 June 1985. Source: Cinenova (COW films, *Gotta Make This Journey*).

29 Pat Murphy, letter to Rod Stoneman, Commissioning Editor, Channel 4, 1 December 1986. See also Penny Ashbrook, COW, letter to Poonam Sharma, Programme Acquisition, Channel 4, 7 November 1985. Source: Cinenova (COW films, *Anne Devlin*, Communications with Pat + Contract + Channel 4).

30 Rod Stoneman, Assistant Commissioning Editor, Independent Film & Video, Channel 4, letter to Pat Murphy, 22 December 1986. Source: Cinenova (COW films, *Anne Devlin*, Communications with Pat + Contract + Channel 4).

31 Penny Ashbrook, COW, letter to Poonam Sharma, Programme Acquisition, Channel 4, 7 November 1985. Source: Cinenova (COW films, *Anne Devlin*, Communications with Pat + Contract + Channel 4).

32 Poonam Sharma, Programme Acquisition, Channel 4, letter to Penny Ashbrook, COW, 28 November 1985. Source: Cinenova (COW films, *Anne Devlin*, Communications with Pat + Contract + Channel 4).

33 Rod Stoneman, Assistant Commissioning Editor, Independent Film & Video, Channel 4, letter to Pat Murphy, 22 December 1986. Source: Cinenova (COW films, *Anne Devlin*, Communications with Pat + Contract + Channel 4).

34 Pat Murphy, letter to Rod Stoneman, Channel 4, 1 December 1986. Source: Cinenova (COW films, *Anne Devlin*, Communications with Pat + Contract + Channel 4).

35 Rod Stoneman, Assistant Commissioning Editor, Independent Film & Video, Channel 4, letter to Pat Murphy, 22 December 1986. See also, Eileen McNulty, COW, letter to Pat Murphy, 21 January 1987. Source: Cinenova (COW films, *Anne Devlin*, Communications with Pat + Contract + Channel 4).

36 Gail Pattinson, Programme Acquisition Executive, Channel 4, letter to Jenny Wallace, Cinema of Women, 26 August 1988. Source: Cinenova (COW films, *Thriller*).

37 Jenny Wallace, COW, letter to Gail Pattinson, Programme Acquisition Executive, Channel 4, 17 October 1988. Source: Cinenova (COW films, *Thriller*).

38 When that funding was withdrawn at the beginning of the 1990s, COW was forced to close down. For a discussion of this, and the challenges that come with being grant-aided, see Knight and Thomas (2011: Chapter 5).

39 See, for instance, Lynne Tillman, letter to COW, 7 January 1986, p. 1, saying 'Sheila and I haven't heard from you in a long time, so we'd appreciate your writing us to say how *Committed* is doing (where it's been screened, etc)'. Source: Cinenova (COW films, *Committed*, Correspondence etc). Pat Murphy, letters to COW, 12 August and 19 August 1985, complaining COW have not kept her informed about their progress with the film's release and that she always has to contact them. Source: Cinenova (COW films, *Anne Devlin*, Communications with Pat + Contract + Channel 4). Playpont films, letter to COW, 8 July 1983, complaining about not receiving an activity report for *A Question of Silence* and

threatening breach of contract and cancellation of contract if they do not receive one by 15 July. Source: Cinenova (COW films, *A Question of Silence*, Correspondence).

40 See Jenny Wallace, COW, letter to Michelle Parkerson, 18 June 1985, which is a very apologetic response to the film-maker's letter of 25 January 1985. Source: Cinenova (COW films, *Gotta Make This Journey*).

41 Poonam Sharma, Programme Acquisition, Channel 4, letters to Penny Ashbrook, COW, dated 29 April, 27 June, 6 August, 1 October, and 28 November 1985. Source: Cinenova (COW films, *Anne Devlin*, Communications with Pat + Contract + Channel 4).

42 On one occasion COW worker Eileen McNulty wrote (26 June 1986) to Pat Murphy, explaining she was going on three months' leave, which meant leaving the office staffed by only a new worker, one part-timer and one temporary worker. Source: Cinenova (COW films, *Anne Devlin*, Communications with Pat + Contract + Channel 4).

43 Pat Murphy, letter to The Collective, Cinema of Women, 12 August 1985, pp. 1–2. Source: Cinenova (COW films, *Anne Devlin*, Communications with Pat + Contract + Channel 4).

44 These observations come from notes made by COW from telephone conversations with Heiny Srour, 12 December and 16 December 1984, p. 1. Source: Cinenova (*Leila and the Wolves*, Leila Heiny).

45 Notes made by COW from telephone conversation with Heiny Srour, 16 December 1984, p. 1. Source: Cinenova (*Leila and the Wolves*, Leila Heiny).

46 Draft promotional flyer for *Born in Flames*, Cinema of Women, undated. Source: Cinenova (Correspondence with Lizzie Borden).

Chapter 18

Shifting Fandoms of Film, Community and Family

Tom Phillips

Introduction

> What is important to remember about [online fan] groups ... is that regardless of their online status, audience groups are significant examples of social activity being organized around cultural commodities. The syntax of that sentence is crucial. *The social interaction is the primary point of interest for most of the groups in the studies just listed, not the media text around which the community coalesced.* (Tuszynski 2008: 83)

In highlighting sociality as a key factor in the way fan communities operate, Stephanie Tuszynski identifies the way in which recent studies of fan cultures frequently have become drawn more to the relationships between fans themselves than to the object of the fandom. It is the social activity organized around these cultural commodities that becomes a signifier for fan practices at large. Such studies of fandoms have allowed opportunities to discuss the ways in which fans are categorized (by both themselves and others), with the labels developed helping in the processes of mapping fan activity. Some terms that have been adopted are 'Xenites' for fans of *Xena: Warrior Princess* (Stafford 2002), or 'X-Philes' for *X-Files* fans (Wooley 2001), with perhaps 'Trekkies' (rather than the more fan-friendly 'Trekkers') being the most well known in wider culture (Jenkins 1992).

Most explicitly with these examples, we can see the way in which the primary point of categorization is the cultural product that the fan culture supports. The fans are defined by their fandom regardless of the specificities of their activity. However where we begin to see the prevalence of socialization as identified by Tuszynski (2008) is within groups of fans who embrace a different kind of activity, where the cultural product in question becomes secondary to everyday interactions. This chapter is based on a case study of one such fan culture: the fans of film-maker Kevin Smith, who populate his official message board.

Beginning with his debut feature *Clerks* (1994), Smith's writing and directing attracted attention as part of his 'View Askewniverse' series (named for his production company View Askew). Spanning a further five films (*Mallrats*, 1995; *Chasing Amy*, 1997; *Dogma*, 1999; *Jay and Silent Bob Strike Back*, 2001; and *Clerks II*, 2006), the comedic dialogue-driven Askewniverse series was drawn together by the recurring appearance of stoner duo Jay and Silent Bob (the latter played by Smith), who became Smith's most famous characters. The comedic tone of his work has translated into his off-screen presence, and Smith has transposed the expletive-ridden content of the filmic dialogue into his everyday media output. Audiences are able to see this output in Q&A shows performed around the world (selling out venues from Carnegie Hall to the Sydney Opera House), or listening to one of the many recordings across Smith's own *SModcast* podcast network, comprising around 30 different shows and a live broadcast stream.

Owned and operated by Smith, the View Askew Message Board has existed in various guises since 1995, providing an official space where enthusiasts have expressed their thoughts on a number of subjects, both related to Smith and not. However, while the Message Board was initially primarily positioned around Smith's work, it has since changed markedly, with the emphasis shifting from Smith to the participants. This chapter examines such fan appropriation of the forum and their self-categorization as 'Boardies'. Despite being named for their location in cyberspace rather than the object of their fandom, this chapter suggests that the behaviour of fans does not necessarily reflect solely online practices, and can in fact represent behaviour that occurs in offline spaces as well.

In examining a fan culture that spans both online and offline practices, I address the broader question of whether a strictly online culture can be labelled a 'community'. In looking at the nature of the term in relation to the study of online fan cultures, Tuszynski observes that since Howard Rheingold (1993) began using the word to describe online groups, 'a small storm of controversy has raged ... over whether any online group merited the title of community or whether the term could not justly be applied to a social group that ... included no face-to-face element' (2008: 46). Complicating these delineations are online groups that also incorporate offline interaction. Such offline 'meet-ups' are a regular occurrence between members of the Board, and occur most often around specific Smith-related events, such as a Q&A show or film screening. As such, meet-ups can occur worldwide, correlating with Smith's international schedule.

In addressing the academic debate around notions of community, this chapter draws on my own experience of a meet-up from August 2010 where Smith performed a Q&A show in his hometown of Red Bank, New Jersey, rounding off a weekend filled with fan-organized meet-ups, hockey games and location tours. Here I highlight how meet-up culture helped to develop and maintain a sense of the communal, and what this means for one's Boardie status – particularly with regard to shifting the emphasis of the fan culture to one concerning the community itself.

Scholar-fandom

Having been a Kevin Smith fan since 2002, I had brief interactions on the Board in 2003 before becoming a lurker – one who '[watches] ... without actively participating – a kind of virtual [voyeur]' (Bell 2001: 198). I practised my fandom privately until 2010, when I began the doctoral research that forms the basis of this work. In attempting to adopt an appropriate methodology, I became aware of the ethically dubious choice of remaining a lurker while conducting the study – something that David Bell notes 'is not acceptable since it puts the researcher in a powerful and distant position' (2001: 198). In addition to the ethical ramifications, lurking as a method can also be detrimental to the interpretation of data. There can be a greater interest in *what* is being said rather than *who* is saying it. A researcher may find a desirable quote to use in their study, but if they do not understand who has said it, and that person's motivations and behaviour, the data will lose important contextual information.

Therefore, guided by Robert Kozinets' netnographic recommendation of entrée into the culture, where he recommends 'act[ing] like a new member, while also clearly stating … [you] are undertaking a research project' (2010: 93), I established my methodology as one of participatory scholar-fandom (Hills 2002). Matt Hills notes that scholar-fans must 'conform to the regulative ideal of the rational academic subject, being careful not to present too much of their enthusiasm while tailoring their accounts … to the norms of "confessional" (but not overly confessional) academic writing' (2002: 11–12). This tension between scholarship and fandom has remained a problematic issue for academic authors (Ford et al. 2011), and the distinction between 'professionalism' in academic work and portraying an active fan personality is a point I have addressed elsewhere (Phillips 2010).

What I have perhaps been most wary of, however, is that in attempting to tread the line between scholar and fan, there was a risk of alienating myself from both groups – something I have already experienced. For example, during one exchange with an (apparently hostile) fan on the Board, the motivations for my research were called into question (ethical considerations prevent me from citing the discussion here). In order to defend my work, I adopted a more formal tone of language than I had previously used online, and the poster reacted negatively to my descriptions of the processes of academic inquiry. While negative reaction was in the minority, taking an overly academic tone within a 'social' space seemed somewhat problematic.

Similarly, during my attendance at the August 2010 Boardie meet-up in Red Bank, I was careful to marshall my own scholar-fan behaviour during times of socialization. My first interaction with a fan in New Jersey was with Haar, who was staying at an adjacent hotel. We met with the intention of conducting an interview, but as we journeyed to a nearby restaurant, my scholarly intentions were tempered by my desire to connect with a fellow fan on an interpersonal level. It felt impolite to immediately launch into a more formal interview situation. I was not entirely familiar with Haar from the Board, and as such felt I should make an attempt to know more about him before asking him to divulge his thoughts and feeling to me 'on the record'.

In doing this, I was aware that the most obvious connection we shared was our Kevin Smith fandom – thus meaning we had an immediate conversation starter. However, by talking about our Smith fandom informally, I was also aware of the risk of the conversation slipping into areas I wanted to cover in the interview process. Therefore, my approach to this initial interaction with Haar – and subsequently the rest of my research participants on the trip – was to spend time getting to know him in a personal manner, separate from his

Kevin Smith fandom, in a manner that reflected Kozinets' belief that a researcher should be 'creative ... mindful and exacting' when crafting an entrance (2010: 93). This meant I subsequently categorized my behaviour and activity on the trip in scholar 'professional' and fan 'social' terms.

In contrast, allowing one's 'social' self to be made accessible to an academic audience has implicit connotations of unprofessionalism and the loss of academic authority. In so readily detailing my Boardie activities within my research, and with posts relatively easy to find, there is potential for my authority to be undermined when less appropriate details can be sought.

Despite this ever-present caution, however, my scholar-fandom of Smith heavily informs this research. The data accrued here are based on qualitative survey responses, email correspondence and face-to-face interviews from the Red Bank meet-up. In using data from both online and offline sources, this chapter examines the dynamics of Boardie identity. In particular, it considers the manner in which such face-to-face interactions challenge notions of the 'real' and the 'virtual', and how such interactions further impact my own scholar-fan experience.

Boardies and online 'community'

In describing the manner in which online groups categorize themselves, Nancy Baym notes that:

> Most online groups are not so tied to geographical space, yet people who are involved in online groups often think of them as shared places. The feeling that [such places] ... constitute 'spaces' is integral to the language often used to describe the internet. (2010: 75–76)

As one of these online spaces, the View Askew Message Board provides a platform for fans of Kevin Smith to define themselves as a collective group or, most frequently, a community. Baym goes on to note that: 'The sense of shared space, rituals of shared practices, and exchange of social support all contribute to a feeling of community in digital environments' (2010: 86). However, in adopting Baym's own use of the term 'community', one must be mindful of its contested nature accompanying 'ideological baggage' (Bell and Valentine 1997: 93), something similarly noted by Tuszynski (2008). Taking a more relativist approach, I instead turned to the Boardies' own use of the term to define their fan culture in search of understanding of the label.

During my initial survey, I asked respondents to discuss their conceptualization of the 'View Askew fan community'. My question was used in order to communicate with participants using succinct, familiar language that could enable responses to be elicited in a more informal manner free from academic constraints. The notion of 'community' was seemingly accepted and embraced as a method to describe the fan culture by fans when asked what led them to begin posting on the Board:

frick: When I started reading the Board in the current format it was easy to read and it seemed like [there] was a real sense of community between the regular posters. I liked that community and wanted to see if I could be a part of it even though my KS knowledge was not at 'superfan' level. (Survey response, 27 June 2010)

Ruth: I think the sense of community is developed via the Board, and would be less developed without it. (Survey response, 12 May 2010)

slithybill: I think the Board has created a stronger sense of community and has fostered stronger friendships and relationships that will last entire lifetimes. (Survey response, 12 May 2010)

During face-to-face interviews, respondents offered interpretations that built on the online responses, again focusing on participation and interaction between fans. For example, JordanFromJersey likened the structure of the fan culture to a school's social order, noting that the community was 'a little bit of everything … the jocks, the preps, the geeks, the nerds. Mostly the nerds! But the jockier nerds, the preppier nerds' (Live interview, Red Bank NJ, 2 August 2010). Haar similarly described the social interactions between fans, observing: 'Oh, it's like any kind of community, there's gonna be neighbours that don't get on, you know – "Your dog's shitting on my yard again, and your kid's got his radio too loud"' (Survey response, 31 July 2010).

The findings from both the survey and interviews suggest that Boardies think of themselves as a community – a point perhaps more important than whether or not their interactions conform to a definition of community devised by scholars. This is further reinforced in the responses from JordanFromJersey and Haar who, in instilling their replies with reference to 'real-life' social structures, demonstrate an opposition to the popular notion that 'the community debate is merely the surface level of a deeper issue: the presence of an oppositional binary with "the real" on one side and "the virtual" on the other' (Tuszynski 2008: 52). The responses here show that the View Askew community need not be thought of in terms of a real/virtual opposition. Instead, it can encapsulate both online and offline fan practices, challenging the way in which 'Boardie' may initially be thought of as categorizing merely the online aspect of Kevin Smith fan culture.

Throughout the articulation of these practices, both online and offline responses to the culture not only feature aspects of the 'communal', but also use language that begins to emphasize a shift from Kevin Smith fandom to Boardie fandom. First, it is notable that when asked to define the fan community, none of the respondents mentioned the binding force of Kevin Smith. Although frick mentions her capital regarding Smith knowledge, it is done so sparingly, and in relation to the 'sense of community' that she perceives exists between Boardies. Furthermore, slithybill notes that lifelong relationships have been forged, and yzzie, who notes that 'My love of Kevin Smith movies brought me to the board. My love of the people and community made it into an online home,' (Survey response, 12 May 2010) demonstrates that although Kevin Smith was an instigative factor in bringing her to the Board, what made her a *Boardie* was the connections made with others. In not categorizing their fan community with references to Smith, but rather with references to other fans, the Boardies here present an opposition to the previously cited Xenites or X-Philes, and signal a fan community not defined by its fandom, but rather by the interpersonal relationships within that community.

Cult geographies, meet-ups, and offline 'community'

One such example of offline fan practices that can strengthen interpersonal ties within the fan community occurred during the aforementioned Red Bank Boardie meet-up. As a Smith fan, travelling to New Jersey was an exciting prospect for me. Not only is it Smith's hometown, but also the filming location for scenes from most of the Askewniverse films. It is also home to Jay and Silent Bob's Secret Stash, Smith's own comic book and film merchandise store.

I had previously visited some of these locations in 2004 while still a lurker on the Board, but my fan experience had been largely insular, stemming from the fact that I was still a lurker, and made no claims to be a fully fledged Boardie. The insular feeling of my fan experience came from the fact that I was aware at this time that meet-ups took place, and although my companion on the trip was similarly a Smith fan, I had no channel with which to further share stories about where I had been. By (choosing to have) no outlet with which to articulate and demonstrate my fan 'social' behaviour, I was unable to fulfil the cultivation of my own Boardie identity, nor have that identity ratified by other fans.

Yet for me in 2004 and again in 2010 – and indeed for many other fans – the journey to Red Bank is one of pilgrimage. In order to capitalize on the importance of these locations, and to more fully integrate my 'social' self, prior to the 2010 trip I helped to organize a location tour taking in notable View Askew landmarks, such as the Quick Stop convenience store (featured in *Clerks*, *Chasing Amy* and *Clerks II*). Much like X-Philes and their relationship to the Vancouver shooting location of *The X-Files*, the New Jersey sites were subject to a 'tourist gaze', which is 'at once both familiar ... and exotic ... The 'tourist gaze' is thereby transformed into a focused and knowledgeable search for authenticity and "reality"' (Hills 2002: 147–48). My experience on the New Jersey location tour – particularly in contrast to my 2004 visit – indicated that these places were subject to a similar tourist gaze, with Smith fans imbibing these regular locales with an exotic aura readily consumed by the communal group, despite the fact they may be coded as 'everyday places' (Brooker 2006: 13).

Prior to the trip, my online survey data revealed that Board meet-ups held some importance for fans, and certainly helped in the cultivation of a Boardie identity. Although Princess Muse noted 'I guess other groups have meet ups and events and such' (Survey response,

12 May 2010), there seemed to be a general feeling that meet-ups were a significant milestone in Board interaction, and potentially aided in the heightened feelings of community and togetherness felt between Boardies:

> *syracuselaxfan:* In early 2008 [at] … my first 'meet-up' with other members of the Board … I introduced myself to some people and was welcomed in with open arms. It was quite a wonderful feeling. (Survey response, 27 June 2010)

> *Graham Cracker:* I think I really began to feel as part of the community after attending a meetup. And really since then I have never felt more at home with other Internet people. (Survey response, 27 May 2010)

> *Fenderboy:* The Board truly is an awesome group of people. I went to my first meet up back in March [2010] and it was one of the best experiences I've ever had. (Survey response, 12 May 2010)

Armed with this prior knowledge, I was apprehensive about attending the meet-up because of a concern of the 'professional'/'social' tension in my reasons for attending. Meet-ups appeared to be a situation where significant bonds were formed, and I was wary of my first face-to-face offline interaction with other fans being dominated by my status as a researcher. As a result, I decided to ask attending fans about their previous meet-up experience, and what they expected from the weekend, in order to gauge both their opinions on meet-up culture, and whether any of my underlying fears might be confirmed. Haar appeared to echo my apprehension, albeit in a different context:

> I'm kind of curious to see just the whole spread of people that show up, and see how they compare face-to-face versus online. Cos a lot of people, you know, they like to preach, go, 'Well I'm the same here as I am in person', and then you see them in person and they either don't talk or they're total dicks. (Live interview, Red Bank, NJ, 31 July 2010)

However, the tension shared by myself and Haar seemed to be unwarranted, as in a similar fashion to the above meet-up testimonials, I too felt welcomed due to the efforts of fans such as TearsInRain, who noted, 'Whenever I go to events I try to make sure everybody's included, has a good time, the same way I did [at my first meetup], the same way Kevin does for all of his fans …' (Live interview, Red Bank, NJ, 2 August 2010)

In contrast to my 2004 trip, in 2010 fellow fans went out of their way to make others feel included in their culture, no matter what their motivations for being there may have been, so my tourist gaze of Red Bank became influenced by the shared communal fan experience – something I had previously not experienced. As noted above, Baym believes that: 'The sense of shared space, rituals of shared practices, and exchange of social support all contribute to a feeling of community in digital environments' (2010: 86). Through the experiences of myself and the other fans, it is possible to see a digital community transferring into the physical, motivated by the shared experience of space, practice and support. Following the 2010 trip, these experiences allowed me to cultivate an active Boardie identity. Here my online sense of community was informed directly by my tangible offline experience of the trip.

The (Kevin Smith?) fan family

In keeping with slithybill's observation that the fan community has instigated lifelong relationships, I wanted to investigate whether Kevin Smith fandom was necessary in order for the community's continued functionality to be maintained. My own fan experience had been that online Boardies were not dependent on Smith discussion to function, with topics discussed ranging from soccer to *Doctor Who* to Broadway musicals. In addition, my aforementioned offline Smith-free conversations in Red Bank had been largely successful from a social standpoint. Ming, webmaster of the Board, similarly noted that Kevin Smith fandom was largely irrelevant to the overall sense of community:

Ming: The same people from the community come back [to meet-ups], they all become my friends … I think a lot of people come … when Kevin has a thing … They don't really come out for him, it's just an excuse to come out. They just want to hang out with each other.

Tom Phillips: Does it even matter being a Kevin Smith fan anymore?

Ming: No I don't think so, I think it's, they all like each other – it's just something they have in common. It's kinda, you know, when you meet your wife or girlfriend, you have something in common initially, but you stick together probably for other reasons. (Live interview, Red Bank, NJ, 2 August 2010)

Ming's comparison of the fan community to a strong romantic relationship is telling, as it suggests a level of devotion to others within the community, regardless of their 'fan cultural capital' – the knowledge that a fan has about their object of fandom (Fiske 1992: 33) – proving that frick's earlier trepidation was unwarranted.

Similarly, TearsInRain feels the relationship between fans is not entirely dependent on Smith fandom being a primary communicative structure, noting that 'some of … [the other fans] are like family to me – it's not just community. I flew to Ireland to stay with somebody … I've gone to LA to stay with people. I'll go to Florida, we go all over the place with or without Kevin' (Live interview, Red Bank, NJ, 2 August 2010). By noting the strong relationship between fans as one of 'family', and placing that term within a hierarchal structure above 'community', TearsInRain demonstrates how the conceptualization of the fan family becomes a significant appeal of the Kevin Smith fan culture. In the same manner, ima_dame also categorizes her definition of the fan community in this way:

The community … [is like] a family. Totally. … [W]e're a family that lives everywhere in the world and we come together for … reunions … I'm really terrible with putting Boardie names and real names together … It's like those cousins you don't quite know their name but you know they're related, you know?! It all comes back to that family thing for me. (Live interview, Red Bank, NJ, 3 August 2010)

TearsInRain and ima_dame's continued discourse of 'family' demonstrates the level of perceived intimacy between Boardies, regardless of fan cultural capital. The notion of fan family – seemingly transcending that of fan 'community' in terms of intimacy – demonstrates that, in this instance, the general conception of the nature of community can be seen to be false. For instance, Sarah Gatson and Amanda Zweerink note that when conceptualization transfers from the 'real' to the 'virtual', 'strong' ties are thought to become 'weak' (2004: 41), yet in the relationship between Boardies, at times 'reality' paves the way for the strengthening of 'virtual' interpersonal ties. As Boardie Roguewriter notes:

I think [off-Board communication] strengthens groups within the main community group – it enhances the relationships you treasure most among the VA community, so perhaps there's a danger that it reinforces cliques or exclusive small clubs within the whole. But overall, I think it enhances more than it segregates. It enriches great online friendships to be able to carry them away from the message board, elsewhere on the internet – and eventually out into the real world. It's an added bonus, and a great way to turn great conversations with interesting people into lifelong friendships. (Email interview, 22 December 2010)

Taking Roguewriter's testimony into account, the distinction between real and virtual in the practices of Boardies appears cyclical in nature, with initial online relationships leading to stronger face-to-face interpersonal ties, which can then in turn pave the way for the strengthening of 'virtual' communication – a product of the Kevin Smith fan culture that I would term the online and offline sociality cycle.

In attending meet-ups and becoming part of the fan family, Boardies are able to build upon their 'fan social capital' – the network of fan friends and acquaintances that a fan possesses (Hills 2002: 57) – in their interaction with others. Furthermore, there is an opportunity to gain further 'access to media producers and professional personnel linked with the object of fandom' (2002: 57) by having the opportunity to meet Smith and others associated with his media output. For example, in addition to meeting fellow fans in Red Bank, I was also able to meet Smith as well as individuals who had been involved in Smith's professional (and personal) lives, such as Jennifer Schwalbach Smith, Bryan Johnson and Walter Flanagan.

Hills notes that 'it is likely that fans with a very high fan cultural capital … will therefore possess [a] high level of fan social capital. But while high fan social capital is likely predicted by high fan cultural capital, this relationship need not follow' (2002: 57). This can be seen in way frick was able to cultivate a Boardie identity, for although she initially stated that her

Kevin Smith knowledge 'was not at "superfan" level', she later noted that 'I'm on [the Board] nearly every day and talk to the international friends I have made every day on the phone/ IM/facebook/etc' (Survey response, 27 June 2010). However, more broadly applicable to the fan family, fan social capital is a commodity attainable by all, rather than exclusive to a particular few, regardless of fan cultural capital. Following the lead from Smith's open relationship with his fans (Smith 2009), TearsInRain notes the way in which he and others, as members of the fan family, attempt to welcome others into that social group:

> I've seen some amazing displays of generosity and compassion on The Board ... I do try to go out of way to make people happy, but it's the same stuff that Kevin, or Ming ... or Jen [Schwalbach Smith – Smith's wife] does for me. They've given me some of my most happy, memorable moments of my life, and in turn, why not do it for other people? It makes me happy that other people are happy. (Live interview, Red Bank, NJ, 2 August 2010)

The behaviour of fans, as exemplified here by TearsInRain, becomes a democratizing process for the fan family, as fan social capital is extended to all, and despite this apparently only being accessible to those who attend meet-ups, participation is dependent on being part of the online and offline sociality cycle, and therefore actually being a member of the Board in the first instance. TheManWhoLikesSMod notes that 'to get the full Kevin Smith experience, you should join the board and become part of the family' (Email interview, 23 January 2011), with the 'family' categorization reflected in the questionnaire responses of Zeebadaboodee, Rocco, Graham Cracker, JaniceM, Quantum Leap and chubtoad01, among others. This demonstrates that family and Boardie status are as accessible a commodity online as offline, and fan social capital is a malleable process that negotiates, and therefore eradicates, the supposed binaries of 'real' and 'virtual'.

Conclusion

In demonstrating the online and offline practices of Kevin Smith fans in this chapter, the cyclical nature of the familial and communal relationship between Boardies is made apparent. Such a relationship between fans demonstrates that, ultimately, fan cultural capital is largely irrelevant, as members are seemingly welcomed regardless of the extent of their Kevin Smith knowledge – a knowledge that ultimately becomes secondary to the function of the community. In categorizing the 'View Askew fan community' – and therefore what constitutes a 'Boardie' – in ways that suggest both online and offline practices, the fans demonstrate repeatedly that the oppositional binaries of 'real' and 'virtual' are being broken down, much in the same way that my own binaries of scholar and fan, professional and social, were negotiated throughout the Red Bank trip.

Ultimately, through this trip, my own experience as a Smith fan contributed to my research, as my experience of meet-up culture as well as my own feelings of heightened fan social capital helped me to understand the processes by which one can begin to self-identify as a Boardie. Post-Red Bank, thanks to the togetherness and spirit I felt at the meet-up, my perception of the Smith fan 'community' (as well as my scholar and fan identities) was altered, as I became friends on Facebook with a number of the people I had met, welcoming them into my online social and personal, rather than professional, life – fully cementing my own place in the fan family, and demonstrating that being a 'Boardie' is not dependent on communicating via the Board. KTCV notes that in meeting fellow fans in person, 'You get to pick up their senses of humor and speech patterns, so online communication is easier to decipher' (Email interview, 21 December 2010), demonstrating the online and offline sociality cycle in practice, and suggesting that perhaps the concepts of fan cultural capital, as well as 'real' and 'virtual', are supplanted – if not made redundant – by the experience of meet-ups and the categorization of Boardies as fan family.

The move from a fandom of Smith to a fandom of each other demonstrates the shifting and malleable nature of fan cultures, meaning that although labels such as 'Xenites', 'X-Philes', 'Trekkers' and 'Boardies' seemingly allow us to easily '[incorporate] a whole range of networks into a specific social dynamic' (Pickerill 2003: 16), it is perhaps more apt to unpack these terms within the specific context of their respective fan cultures, and the discourses within which they operate.

References

Baym, N.K. (2010), *Personal Connections in the Digital Age*, Cambridge: Polity Press.

Bell, D. (2001), *An Introduction to Cybercultures*, London: Routledge.

Bell, D. and Valentine, G. (1997), *Consuming Geographies: We are Where We Eat* London: Routledge.

Brooker, W. (2006), 'The *Blade Runner* Experience: Pilgrimage and Liminal Space', in W. Brooker (ed.), *The Blade Runner Experience: The Legacy of a Science Fiction Classic*, New York: Columbia University Press.

Fiske, J. (1992), 'The Cultural Economy of Fandom', in L.A. Lewis (ed.), *The Adoring Audience: Fan Culture and Popular Media*, London: Routledge, pp. 30–49.

Ford, S., Kustritz, A. and Stein, L. (2011), 'Acafandom and Beyond: Week One, Part One', *Confessions of an Aca/Fan*, 13 June, http://henryjenkins.org/2011/06/acafandom_and_beyond_week_one.html. Accessed 20 May 2012.

Gatson, S.N. and Zweerink, A. (2004), *Interpersonal Culture on the Internet: Television, the Internet, and the Making of a Community*, New York: Edwin Mellen Press.

Hills, M. (2002), *Fan Cultures*, London: Routledge.

Jenkins, H. (1992), *Textual Poachers: Television Fans and Participatory Cultures*, New York: Routledge, 1992.

Kozinets, R.V. (2010), *Netnography: Doing Ethnographic Research Online*, London: Sage.

Phillips, T. (2010), 'Embracing the "Overly Confessional": Scholar-Fandom and Approaches to Personal Research', *Flow*, 13: 5, http://flowtv.org/2010/12/embracing-the-overly-confessional. Accessed 20 May 2012.

Pickerill, J. (2003), *Cyberprotest: Environmental Activism Online*, Manchester: Manchester University Press.

Rheingold, H. (1993), *The Virtual Community: Homesteading on the Electronic Frontier*, Reading, MA: Addison-Wesley.

Smith, K. (2010), 'Kevin Smith, Taking questions While baked.' *A.V. New York*. Available from: <http://newyork.decider.com/articles/kevin-smith-taking-questions-while-baked,29171. Accessed 15 December 2010.

Stafford, N. (ed.) (2002), *How Xena Changed our Lives: True Stories By Fans for Fans*, Toronto: ECW Press.

Tuszynski, S. (2008), 'IRL (In Real Life): Breaking Down the Binary Between Online and Offline Social Interaction', PhD thesis, Bowling Green State University Press.

Wooley, Christine A. (2001), 'Visible Fandom: Reading *The X-Files* Through X-Philes', *Journal of Film and Video*, 53: 4, pp. 29–53.

PART V

Just Watching Movies?

Chapter 19

Watching Popular Films in the Netherlands, 1934-36

Clara Pafort-Overduin

Introduction

In his provocative essay 'The Stress Test', Dutch director and former film commissioner Ate de Jong claimed that 'success can be predicted'. De Jong developed a method that he claimed was capable of predicting accurately the ticket sales of yet-to-be-made films. He had tested his model on 20 Dutch film projects in the domestic market, and in almost all cases actual and estimated ticket sales were closely aligned. In his model, De Jong combines a quantitative and qualitative approach involving target group analysis establishing the possible size of the box office, and cultural analysis answering the question of what specific Dutch feeling the film aims to evoke (De Jong 2011). His essay shows that hard empirical numbers and soft elucidations are both equally important when it comes to understanding why some types of film are more popular than others.

Over the last few years, I have been trying to combine these two approaches in my research on the first Dutch sound films released in the 1930s. While working on the reception of the second Dutch talkie, *The Sailors*, (*De Jantjes*, Jaap Speyer, 1934), I was struck by the aphorism 'a true Dutch film with a true Dutch heart', which was used by the film critic of the national Amsterdam-based newspaper *De Telegraaf* in his review of the film on 10 February 1934. What did this maxim mean, and was this truly a nationally felt emotion or rather the musings of a bourgeois city dweller? Answering these questions led to a far larger project, and resulted in me compiling a very large dataset containing the programme information of 145 cinemas in 22 Dutch cities and towns between 1934 and 1936. With this dataset, a much broader range of issues than just the popularity of this one film could be addressed – such as, for example, distribution patterns, differences in national and local popularity and differences in the profiles of Dutch cinemas. To answer my question fully, however, I also needed a qualitative (content) analysis to understand what it was to which audiences had been responding, and how producers had tried to tap into perceived national preferences.

In this chapter, the case study of *The Sailors* will function as a demonstration of how I tried to combine quantitative and qualitative analyses. It is not my ambition to discuss all facets and outcomes of this case in detail, but to lay out my thoughts on how different approaches can be combined fruitfully in analyzing film popularity.

Film as a cultural commodity

The starting point for both quantitative and qualitative analysis is the understanding that film is a cultural commodity on which audiences can choose to spend money – or not. Each film has to build its own audience, and even though Hollywood – along with all other commercial film producers – strives for habitual cinema-goers, thus guaranteeing a constant box-office stream (Maltby 2011: 7–8), it is also clear that huge differences exist between the audiences that individual films attract, implying that audiences have preferences and make choices. As John Sedgwick (2000) demonstrates, cinema-going as a habitual practice cannot explain why film attendances are statistically spread in the form of a long-tail pattern, meaning that only a few films are box office hits and most films attract much smaller audiences and bring in far less revenue. I am not claiming that I have found the decisive answer to explain differences in popularity, but I believe it should be possible to identify factors that can help us understand these differences.

In my view, the film itself should be considered as part of the explanation too. Much as we should avoid a too film-centric approach, we should also not fall into the trap that the film is not important at all. Though viewers may not remember much about the films they watched (Kuhn 2002) and the measurable effects these might have had on their world-view, ultimately they do represent a positive decision. Even in a one-cinema town, there is always the choice between entering and passing by.

The ways in which people select films are complex, with many different factors influencing this process. For instance, social factors like peer group influences may well affect people's choices of what film to see or what cinema to attend, and even what seats to sit in. From interviews conducted by students in the Film Studies Department of Utrecht University, it would seem that as late as the 1950s, class was an important factor in the way people chose which cinema to visit and where they were seated once there.[1] Also, examples of how political, religious or other authorities tried to guide audiences in making 'the right' choices are countless. In 1930, the Reformed Protestant Church (Gereformeeerde Kerk) officially stated that its members should refrain from watching fiction films – in the same fashion as they should refrain from theatre-going. Only documentaries, newsreels and animation films were permitted– a ban that was lifted in 1957 (Hes 1972: 93–94, 127–28). Catholic priests commonly advised their congregations about which films should be avoided, while other titles were recommended (Van Oort 2007: 137–91). In 1933, Dutch socialists called for a boycott of German films because of the anti-Semitic politics of Germany (Nederlandschen Bioscoop Bond 1933: 17–18).

Of course, it is up to the marketing departments of commercial film producers and distributors to deal with particular social, ideological and religious attitudes, and to convince as many people as possible to buy a ticket by means of countering strategies such as the promotion of film stars, the creation of novel film content and the deployment of clever marketing strategies. Thus, to understand the popularity of a film, it is necessary to analyse the subject-matter, cinematographic characteristics and production features, as well as the marketing and distribution strategies adopted by its distributor – all within a general context of the circumstances in which audiences live their lives, including their ideological orientation. This is a daunting task, and while it may be true that a complete picture may never emerge, it is still relevant to ask questions about the popularity of particular films with the purpose of understanding what they meant for an audience at a certain place and point in time, as part of a broader study of social and cultural history.

Before we can even begin to explain and understand the popularity of certain films, we have to determine which films were popular. As with this project, one of the common problems film historians encounter is the lack of specific box-office data, forcing them to reconstruct this data. To establish which films were popular and which were not, we cannot rely solely on film reviews in newspapers and journals; we also need to go deeply into the programming of the films. Only if we know which titles were programmed in what cinemas and for how long can we start ascertaining patterns of popularity.

John Sedgwick (2000) has developed a method to measure relative popularity, the Popularity Statistic (hereafter POPSTAT).[2] I have used his insights to establish the popularity of the Dutch films in which I was interested. To be able to perform a POPSTAT analysis, I built a very elaborate database – as mentioned earlier – with programme information of all films shown in the cinemas in 22 cities and towns in the Netherlands between1934 and 1936, covering over 40 per cent of all existing Dutch cinemas for that period.[3] The dataset comprises 26,059 records of individual film screenings, including the total number of screenings in any one week during the period of films in each of the 144 cinemas in the survey.[4] (Especially in smaller towns, the number of screenings per week changed, depending on the demand for a particular film.) In addition, supplementary information was added to all films in the dataset about the production year, the producer the director, the country of origin derived from the International Movie Database and the Dutch distributor, derived from the Cinema Context database. Finally, data was recorded about the size and location of all cinemas.

With a dataset of this nature, it is possible to compare film programming on the local, regional and national levels, in order to determine at each level the nature of product competition between cinemas. It is also possible to compare the programming in rural areas with that in urban areas and to determine whether films were popular nationwide or just in certain places. As John Sedgwick (2000) has shown in his work on local popularity, the POPSTAT methodology allows the possibility of contrasting the popularity of international stars like Shirley Temple or Marlene Dietrich against that of national film stars, and in so doing to determine audience preferences (2000: 102–42). As Garncarz (1994), Pafort-Overduin (2011), Sedgwick (2000, 2011) and Sedgwick et al. (2012) have shown, indigenous productions – however poor their production values might have been – often were very popular with national audiences, to the point where they rivalled big-budget Hollywood films.

Furthermore, distribution strategies can be mapped out. Not only can we follow the life and death of a film; we can also establish its penetration in the market – was it shown everywhere or just in the big cities? The answers to these kinds of questions and the (national) comparisons of the answers give film historians a better understanding of how film markets worked, and will make it possible to distinguish patterns and peculiarities. However, to explain these, we need both an economic and cultural analysis.

A notion that can help us structure the cultural aspects of popularity is *appropriation*. In the Netherlands, it was used by historian Willem Frijhoff (1992, 2003) to analyse cultural practices like customs and (religious) rituals. Appropriation starts from an active understanding of culture, and shows how individual cultural practices relate to and influence each other. Frijhoff identifies three phases in a dialectical process of appropriation: representation, recognition and incorporation. For any particular group, representation is manifest in accounts of those characteristics that identify it. Each group then recognizes itself in (part of) this account and incorporates this into a new representation after which the cycle starts again (Frijhoff 1992: 614). Film production and reception can be analysed in the same way. The producers of a film can be seen as creating a representation and presenting that to audiences, who then in turn respond by coming to watch the film. Popular representations will thus lead to similar representations. As commercial producers need to earn back their investments, production decisions will be determined by what they believe audiences will like.

Because historical records have been lost, in many cases it is impossible to find out what exactly caused producers to take the decisions they took. However, from the evidence presented by the film itself, it is possible to infer the kind of decisions that were made. In case of *The Sailors*, for example, the film script was based on a theatre play that was extant at the time. The choices made by the scriptwriter and producer are reflected in their reconceptualization of the play into a film commodity and their assumptions of what they thought audiences would and would not like. After all, we can assume they wanted to attract as many cinema-goers as possible. The analysis of how the theatre play was transformed into the film is a first line of inquiry in terms of unravelling its popularity.

A second line of inquiry maps the distribution and exhibition of *The Sailors*. The analysis of the distribution firstly focuses on the expectations of the distributors by looking first at the number of copies with which the film premiered, and second at how the film was diffused through the territory, involving a count of the number of copies of the print in circulation. This pattern tells us how supply was connected to demand – the greater the level of demand became, the more copies were in circulation.

Third, the programming of *The Sailors* is analysed, showing where and for how long the film was shown and how these figures compared with the average number of screenings at each cinema in each locality. From this breakdown, it is possible to measure whether the film was more popular in one place than in another. This data are then related to the ideological and religious orientation of Dutch audiences by comparing the geographical spreading of the outcomes of the general election of 1933 with the local popularity of *The Sailors*.

A final facet of the investigation concerns the written reception of the film. Reviews of *The Sailors* in 26 Dutch newspapers were analysed. In this case study, the results are not discussed separately but will be referred to when necessary.

Production of *The Sailors*

There was no system of film subsidy or quota protection in the Netherlands in the 1930s (*Film Daily Yearbook* 1938: 1243). Given that Dutch language films had difficulty building markets outside of the Netherlands, that the Dutch nation was small (8.29 million inhabitants in 1933 (Centraal Bureau voor de Statistiek 1934: 11) and that it had fewer cinema seats per capita than almost every country in the then developed world, the absence of state involvement meant that making profits was particularly difficult for Dutch film entrepreneurs (Sedgwick et al. 2012). Further, the small scale of the market militated against film entrepreneurs pooling risks across a range of film outputs, requiring them to finance their films one at a time, making it essential to produce films that were attractive to Dutch audiences (Dittrich 1986: 139–41)

Alex Benno, the first producer of *The Sailors*, tried to diminish these risks by choosing one of the most successful Dutch theatre plays from the interwar period, hiring an experienced director and popular actors. He even decided to shoot a German version of the film (with the same Dutch actors now speaking German), with the aim of making the film accessible to Germany audiences, as was announced in the newspaper *De Gelderlander* on 27 September 1933. Unfortunately, he was forced into bankruptcy after three-quarters of the film had been shot. On 28 November 1933, the newspaper *Algemeen Handelsblad* heralded that *The Sailors* had been saved by its Dutch distributor Loet Barnstijn.

The theatre play *The Sailors* – hereafter referred to as *The Sailors, 1920* (*De Jantjes* 1920) – was written by Herman Bouber, and its sensational success brought him national fame. This popular play about ordinary Amsterdam citizens was spoken in a specific Amsterdam dialect, called 'Jordaans', and initially was performed in the small neighbourhood theatre *Plantage Schouwburg*. After a hundred or so performances, a wider, more affluent audience started to take an interest in the play. Theatre reviewers had been charmed by the authenticity of *The Sailors* and the realistic performances of the actors, leading audiences who normally frequented the grand city theatre The Stadsschouwburg to visit this local theatre.

An essential feature of *The Sailors, 1920* was songs written by Louis Davids and Maggie Morris. Davids was a popular entertainer, and his songs were widely recorded, played on the radio and printed as sheet music. The powerful songs of the theatre play were incorporated in the film and advertisements of *The Sailors*, where they frequently were referred to as 'those well known songs' (e.g. see *Twentsch Dagblad Tubantia*, 22 February 1934).

From theatre play to film script: content adaptation of *The Sailors*

The social and political elements of *The Sailors* as filmed entertainment were severely curtailed, with passages that might have been interpreted as political statements and pejorative references to class differences removed. For example, scenes were cut that depicted the disappointment of the colonial soldier who learned that there was an unbridgeable gap between the higher and lower ranks, preventing him from moving up through the ranks. Unlike in the play, the film does not depict real poverty and none of the characters is in need. This does not mean that class is totally absent from the film, but the ways in which class differences are perceived by the characters are more cohesive. Rich men are no longer represented as unreliable and untrustworthy; instead, they have turned into ethically worthy characters who support women from the lower classes. This change is closely linked to the way in which one of the two principal female characters is affected by her visits to places of entertainment. In the theatre play, Jans frequents the so-called cabaret, hoping she will find a rich man to marry her.[5] The man she meets turns out to be a pimp, and a disappointed Jans returns home and marries a simple sailor instead. In other words, Jans is punished for her visits to the cabaret. In the film, however, Jans manages to find a rich man through the cabaret who introduces her to a life of luxury. Through his contacts, he even helps Greet (Jans' friend) find a free lawyer to defend her falsely accused fiancé. The film goes against the more common representation of the cabaret as an immoral space; instead, it stands for a place where a woman can find a reliable friend (Pafort-Overduin 2004; Pafort-Overduin et al. 2006). Class differences still exist in the film, but there is no real partition between classes in relation to social goals such as justice, and the cabaret functions as the place where all sorts of people can meet. What makes this observation important is that the scenes in the cabaret were added by Loet Barnstijn after he took over the production. He invested extra money to enable a huge cabaret scene to take place, as he believed that this was necessary to increase the films' appeal (*Haarlemsch Dagblad*, 13 December 1933) Most film reviewers later on stated that the scenes in the cabaret had given the film an 'international quality' (e.g. *Nieuwsblad van het Noorden*, 17 February 1934).

The Sailors was shot partly in the studio and partly on location. Shots of the Dutch coast, with its dunes and lighthouses, picturesque images of Amsterdam and shots stressing the bustle and grandeur of Dutch harbours, figure prominently in the film. These images of well-known Dutch locations, reinforced by song, are linked to intensive emotional moments in the narrative, and evoke a feeling of solidarity. A good example of this clever editing is the parting scene in the Amsterdam harbour when crying mothers and girlfriends wave goodbye to the sailors who are leaving for six years to be colonial soldiers. This emotional scene became the 'must see' moment of the film, one mentioned by all reviewers.

To summarize, negative references to social inequality were replaced by positive ones, and with a montage of recognizable Dutch images accompanied by emotional songs to which the audience could hum along, allowing the film to tap into feelings of national belonging.

Distribution and exhibition

In the same way that film producers tried to make films that accommodated the preferences of Dutch audiences, distributors and exhibitors also searched for the perfect match between film and audience. Dutch distributors deployed a conservative strategy through which they responded to audience interest, so that between 1934 and 1936, 84 percent of all new films in my dataset were launched with one copy, 13 per cent with two, and only 2 per cent with two or more copies; depending on demand, more copies could be made during the course of a film's distribution. For exhibitors, the limited number of prints meant that it could take a long time before a new film reached their theatres, but it also meant that direct competition between two local cinemas screening the same film title was very rare.

It is telling that, of the Dutch films, 74 per cent premiered with two or more copies, whereas this was true for only 10 per cent of American films and 30 per cent of German films, indicating that distributors had high hopes of Dutch films; clearly, they expected Dutch audiences to express a preference for Dutch films.[6] *The Sailors* was only the second Dutch sound feature made, and premiered on 9 February 1934 in Amsterdam and The Hague, suggesting that the distributor, Barnstijn, expected a more than average appeal. Soon after its premiere, it became clear that *The Sailors* was going to be a hit. Even local newspapers in remote parts of the Netherlands reported its success, preparing local audiences for the arrival of *The Sailors* in future weeks.[7] Rising demand must have be the reason why Barnstijn decided to make more and more copies. Table 19.1 shows the development of the number of copies during 16 weeks after *The Sailors* premiered. To contextualize this, the distribution pattern of the other film titles that premiered at the same date are added as well.

Apart from the total number of exhibition weeks that each film title accumulated during the 16 weeks following its première (the sum of all individual exhibition weeks per copy), Table 19.1 also lists the ranking of each of the films based on their POPSTAT scores generated during the following year. The close correlation between the two suggests that the total number of exhibition weeks is indicative of film rank. *The Sailors* was by far the most popular using either category.

A second interesting aspect of Table 19.1 is that different distribution strategies become visible. Not only is it evident when and in what quantities distributors adapted the films' supply (the number of copies circulating at once), it also shows whether the expectations of distributors had been accurate. Of the seven films that premiered together with *The Sailors*, five were released with just one print, with the last three listed films not generating sufficient audience interest to warrant the expenditure on a second print.

The Sailors and *La Maternelle* accumulated the highest number of exhibition weeks and also have the highest POPSTAT score. Both films only reached their peak after eight and 12 weeks respectively, indicating that its distributors were cautious. *La Maternelle* started with one copy in the first week; a second copy was added in the third week, but it was not until the eighth week that it circulated with four copies. *The Sailors* premiered with two copies and this number rose steadily until it reached its peak with ten copies. The distribution patterns of *The Sailors* and *La Maternelle* are alike, but differ in magnitude. After its first week, the number of simultaneously circulating copies of *The Sailors* never dropped below four; even in Week 16 there were five copies on the market. As a consequence, the total

Table 19.1: Number of copies circulating per week during 16 weeks of films that premiered on 9 February 1934.

Film	1	2	3	4	5	6	7	8	9	10	11	12	13	14	15	16	Total no of circ. weeks	POPSTAT ranking	Greatest no. of copies in circ.
The Sailors (NL, 1934)	2	4	6	5	6	5	4	10	10	7	5	6	4	4	6	5	89	1	10
La Maternelle (FR, 1933)	1	1	2	2	2	2	2	4	2	1	4	5	3	2	1	2	36	12	5
Cette vieille canaille (FR, 1934)	1	1	1	1	2	0	0	2	2	2	1	2	0	1	0	1	17	41	2
Schön ist jeder Tag den Du mir schenkst, Marie Luise (DE, 1934)	2	3	1	2	0	1	0	0	0	1	0	0	1	0	0	0	11	110	3
Dans les rues (FR, 1933)	1	1	0	0	1	0	0	1	1	0	0	0	0	0	0	0	5	525	1
Air Hostess (USA, 1933)	1	0	0	0	0	0	1	0	0	0	1	0	0	0	0	0	3	652	1
Love, Honour and Oh Baby (USA, 1929)	1	1	0	0	0	0	0	0	0	0	0	0	0	0	0	0	2	783	1

number of screening weeks for *The Sailors* was more than twice that for *La Maternelle* – 89 versus 36.

Different distribution patterns can be seen with the other films listed in Table 19.1. *Cette vieille canaille* illustrates that, even with a small number of copies continually travelling the country, a reasonable success could be attained: the film ranked 12th in the POPSTAT of new films. An extra copy of this title was made after a few weeks (Week 5). This seemed to have been a good decision, as there was a constant demand, even though the film was out of circulation for four of the 16 weeks investigated. The data for *Schön ist jeder Tag den Du mir schenkst, Marie Luise* suggest that high expectations for this film were not met at the box office. The film started out with two copies and a third was added in the second week, but by the fourth week the film was screened in only two theatres, and thereafter barely screened at all – in nine of the 16 weeks the film does not appear on the cinema programs in the dataset. Unlike *Cette vieille canaille*, which had a low but stable distribution pattern, *Schön ist jeder Tag den Du mir schenkst, Marie Luise* only generated returns during the first four weeks after its release.

The other three films, *Dans les Rues*, *Air Hostess* and *Love Honor and Oh Baby*, attracted virtually no interest, finishing up at the tail end of the POPSTAT ranked order of new films. All three received highly negative assessments by the Central Film Censorship Committee (Centrale Commissie voor Filmkeuring) and were given restrictive certificates that allowed only adults over 18 years of age to watch them. *Air Hostess* was given three cuts because of salacious scenes. *Love, Honor and Oh Baby* was considered a threat to morality. The distributor of *Dans les rues* appealed the 'over 18' decision – a judgment based upon the criminal milieu among which the film was set. After a second appeal, the film was again ruled 'over 18'.[8]

To establish whether the distribution patterns of the films analysed above differed from the pattern of all new films released on to the Dutch market, an analysis was made of the average number of copies of all 744 new films that premiered between 1 January 1934 and 1 January 1936 for the 52 weeks following their first screening. Of these 744 films 409 titles were produced in the United States, 58 in France, 17 in the Netherlands, 192 were German spoken (169 German films and 23 Austrian films) and 68 films were produced in other countries. Figure 19.1 captures this data, showing that Dutch films not only premiered with more copies but maintained this ascendancy during their life-cycle.

The dataset allows us to microscopically investigate the diffusion of *The Sailors* in order to establish whether local differences in the popularity were commonplace. Was the film just as popular in a big city like Amsterdam as in a small town with a population slightly under 10,000, like Culemborg? Relative local popularity is a measure that should reflect local circumstances. For example, a small town with a single small cinema will contribute much less to the national POPSTAT Index than the multiple cinemas of, say, Amsterdam. However, this does not mean that the film was any less popular in the small locality. To correct for this, the actual number of film screenings of each film shown in a town was

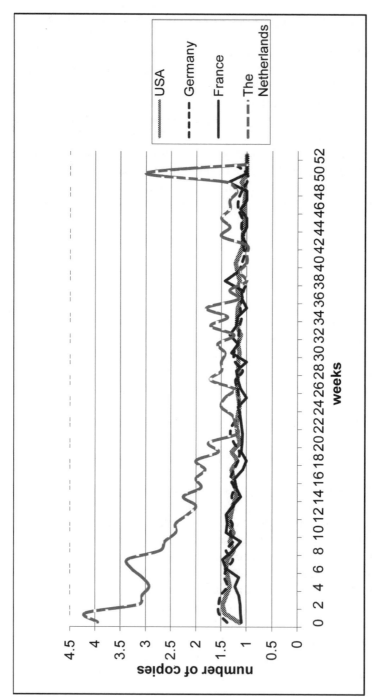

Figure 19.1: The mean number of copies in circulation 52 weeks after release.

Relative local popularity of The Sailors

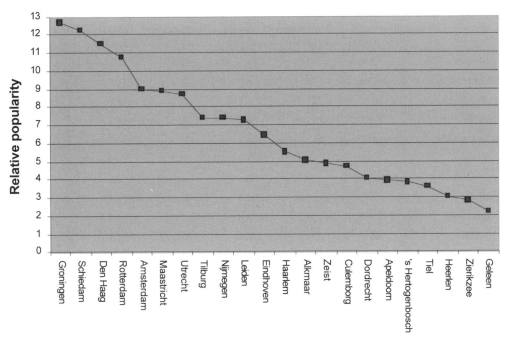

Figure 19.2: Relative local popularity of *The Sailors*.

counted and compared with the average number of screenings a film received in that town. Figure 19.2 presents the results.

Differences in the relative popularity of *The Sailors* are evident. For instance, in Amsterdam – the city where *The Sailors* is set – the film received nine times the average number of screenings of 74, but was even better received in northern Groningen, where the multiplication factor was 13. Also, in The Hague and Schiedam, the film scored more than ten times the average number of screenings of new films. In Rotterdam, Amsterdam and southern Maastricht, the multiplication factor was close to nine. Relatively low numbers of screenings were recorded in the towns of Heerlen and Geleen, and in Zierikzee, located in the south-west of the country. In all cases, *The Sailors* was more popular than the average film.

An underlying question that emerges from these results is whether there is a correlation between the ideological and/or religious orientation of a local population and the local popularity of a film. Although these kinds of correlations should always be treated with utmost care, as the reasons why a film appealed to audiences cannot be reduced to one or two variables, they can point to a direction where we could search for an explanation for the high or low popularity of a film For the analysis of the interrelation between religious

Table 19.2: Places represented in the dataset with the number of inhabitants, the voting percentages of each compartment and the percentage of wealthy taxpayers.

City	Population	Protestant vote (%)[1]	Catholic vote (%)[2]	Social Democratic vote (%)[3]	Liberal vote (%)[d]	Wealthy taxpayers (%)
Apeldoorn	68,590	42.2	10.1	24.5	15.0	14.0
Dordrecht	60,131	31.2	9.2	37.3	18.1	8.4
Groningen	115,185	28.2	8.0	38.0	16.6	13.6
Haarlem	131,257	17.1	26.7	35.3	16.4	9.8
Amsterdam	781,645	17.1	15.3	46.9	15.2	6.3
Schiedam	61,845	28.3	25.3	30.4	9.9	5.4
Heerlen	49,724	6.8	60.4	20.0	1.8	5.3
Utrecht	161,093	24.5	27.3	31.3	13.1	9.1
Rotterdam	595,448	23.7	15.6	40.7	13.4	6.6
Leiden	73,612	31.8	20.9	33.0	10.4	9.2
Tilburg	88,890	2.7	80.6	11.0	1.4	8.7
Zeist	29,691	44.5	12.3	20.5	17.6	18.8
The Hague	482,397	24.8	18.2	32.7	16.5	13.0
Eindhoven	103,030	6.5	68.1	18.4	3.5	6.3
Maastricht	65,929	2.2	60.4	27.5	2.2	8.9
Nijmegen	90,739	8.6	62.8	18.7	6.3	14.3
Culemborg	9,359	15.1	39.0	28.5	15.2	14.0
Geleen	14,289	5.4	66.8	14.8	0.7	4.8
Zierikzee	6,944	37.0	12.4	20.1	26.8	21.8
's-Hertogenbosch	46,212	4.2	68.7	10.7	2.6	8.3
Alkmaar	30,467	12.8	31.5	31.2	21.1	14.3
Tiel	12,730	14.3	21.9	37.6	19.1	12.8

Sources: Cinema Context Collection; Beekink et al. (2003). ARP, CHU, SGP, CDU en Hervormd Gereformeerde Partij.
2. Rooms-Katholieke Staatspartij en Rooms-Katholieke Volkspartij.
3. SDAP, CPH en Revolutionair-Socialistische Partij.
4. Vrijzinnig Democratische Bond en Vrijheidsbond.

and/or ideological characteristics of local audiences and local popularity, the results of the 1933 general election were paired with the local popularity results of *The Sailors*. During this time, the Netherlands could be characterized as a so-called compartmentalized society, in which four pillars were distinguished: Catholic, Protestant, Liberal (the Dutch term Liberal could also be translated as Conservative) and Socialist (Sedgwick et al. 2012). These four compartments were constructed in a top-down fashion by political parties that tried to direct the lives of their members by offering compartmentalized newspapers, trade unions, schools, social clubs, sporting clubs and so on. The Catholic compartment was the best organized due to the strict hierarchical organization of the Catholic Church. The conservative compartment has also been called the 'rest compartment', as it was the least organized of the four. It was commonly assumed that each compartment strictly separated its members to prevent them from meeting individuals of the competing compartments. Local research has shown that this was not the case, and that people could mix in normal life (Blom and Talsma 2000). One of these places was the cinema, as exhibitors strove for a neutral image in order to attract as many people as possible (Dibbets 2006: 47).

There was however a kind of geographical demarcation because of the way Catholics and Protestants were spread through the country: the south was dominated by the Catholics, while the Protestants were clustered in the so called Bible Belt that spread from mid-west to mid-east. This makes it possible to distinguish differences in the popularity of *The Sailors* between these two compartments. In Table 19.2 the towns and cities included in the dataset are listed together with the number of inhabitants and the voting percentages for each compartment.

From Figure 19.2 we learn that *The Sailors* was most popular in Groningen, Schiedam, The Hague, Rotterdam and Amsterdam. All of these were cities or larger provincial towns with populations ranging between 59,000 and 778,000, suggesting that *The Sailors* was better appreciated in urban than in rural areas. Also noticeable is the fact that in these five cities, the Socialists received more votes than the political parties of the other three compartments. This strong level of preference is probably rooted in the earlier popularity of *The Sailors* as a play originally written for the common theatre. The reviewer of the socialist newspaper *Voorwaarts* hinted at those roots in his appraisal of the film on 18 February 1934: 'The simple, heartily subject is indeed one the very best examples of Bouber's sensitive popular romance, that deploys the procedure of a laugh and a tear most skilfully without reaching for disreputable methods.' (Translation CPO) It would appear that the 'common' and 'popular' ethos of *The Sailors* helped attract larger audiences in areas with relatively more Socialist voters.

Another possible explanation for the relative local popularity can be traced by asking the opposite question: Where did *The Sailors* catch on least? Figure 19.2 shows this to be in the towns of Tiel, Zierikzee, Heerlen, Geleen and 's-Hertogenbosch. The last three were strongly Catholic-oriented places, as can be read from Table 19.2: the Catholic vote in 1933 was 60.4 per cent, 66.8 per cent and 68.7 per cent respectively. Zierikzee can be characterized as a rich, Protestant-oriented town, as the Protestant parties received 37 per cent of the vote and the percentage of wealthy taxpayers was the highest in the dataset, at almost 22 per cent. The combination of Protestants and wealthy taxpayers seems to have had a negative influence on the popularity of *The Sailors*.

The low score in Tiel initially appears contra-intuitive, as the number of Socialist votes is quite high. However, the percentage of Liberals was also very high (the third highest score in

345

the dataset), as was the relatively high percentage of wealthy taxpayers (12.8 per cent); this combination probably caused a negative effect on attendances of *The Sailors*.

Heerlen is an interesting case. Not only was *The Sailors* poorly received relative to the other locations in the investigation, but this applied to all Dutch films: only one Dutch title featured in the local top ten of most popular films in the research period 1934–36. The top ten films in Heerlen included five German spoken titles. This is possibly explained by the composition of its residents. Heerlen had the highest percentage of foreign workers of the Limburg mining area: 21.9 per cent versus the Limburg average of 10.7 per cent. German workers made up the largest share, with 6253 of a total population of 46,885 in 1930 (Dieteren 1959: 33). Although this result is very local and cannot be generalized, it points to an audience preference for indigenous films – in this case, a mining town with a high proportion of German workers expressed a preference for German films.

The preference for indigenous films is also apparent in most of the reviews I have collected. The novelty that audiences could hear their own language was perceived as an important reason to watch *The Sailors*. The reviewer of the northern-based *Leeuwarder Courant* even claimed on 17 March 1934 that it was only now that audiences could really experience and fully understand film, and that the language of foreign films had always been a barrier to a truly felt film experience.

Conclusion

The case study of *The Sailors* has shown that qualitative and quantitative data can reinforce one another. An analysis of the production and adaptation process of a film can help to explain its national and local popularity. The widespread popularity of *The Sailors*, shown in its distribution pattern and POPSTAT ranking, suggests that its makers successfully tapped into the shared emotions of the nation by cleverly combining images of Dutch landmarks and landscapes with touching songs and recognizable dramatic moments. A further analysis of relative local popularity uncovered differences in local preferences. In the case of *The Sailors* – a film that depicts working-class people – local differences point towards a preference for the film among working-class urban audiences – those who formed the vast majority of the Socialist pillar.

The results also hint at the importance of language, as observed by other scholars including Garncarz (1994) and Sedgwick (2000, 2011). Not only is this demonstrated by the number of national productions listed in the top ten of the most popular films screened in the Netherlands between 1934 and 1936, it is also traceable on a local scale such as in Heerlen, where the appeal of German films might be explained by the presence of German mining workers. These inferences all need a more thorough empirical underpinning, but they do indicate the direction towards which our efforts should be aimed.

References

Beekink, E., Boonstra, O., Engelen, T. and Knippenberg, H. (eds) (2003), *Nederland in verandering. Maatschappelijke ontwikkelingen in kaart gebracht 1800–2000*, Amsterdam: Aksant.

Blom, J.C.H. and Talsma, J. (eds) (2000), *De verzuiling voorbij. Godsdienst, stand en natie in de lange negentiende eeuw*, Amsterdam, Het Spinhuis.

Centraal Bureau voor de Statistiek, (1934), *Bevolking en bevolkingsdichtheid der gemeenten van Nederland op 1 januari 1934*, 's-Gravenhage: Martinus Nijhoff.

—— (1938), *Statistiek van het bioscoopwezen 1937 waarin mede opgenomen gegevens omtrent filmkeuring*, 's-Gravenhage: Rijksuitgeverij.

Dibbets, K. (2006), 'Het taboe van de Nederlandse filmcultuur. Neutraal in een verzuild land', *Tijdschrift voor Mediageschiedenis* 9: 2, pp. 46–64.

Dieteren, P.R. (1959), De migratie in de mijnstreek 1900–1935. Een sociaal-historische studie, PhD thesis, Katholieke Universiteit Leuven.

Dittrich, K. (1986), 'De speelfilm in de jaren dertig', in K. Dibbets and F. van der Maden (eds), *Geschiedenis van de Nederlandse film en bioscoop tot 1940*, Houten: het Wereldvenster, pp. 105–44.

De Jong, A. (2011), *Succes is voorspelbaar! Stress-test voor Nederlandse speelfilms,* Dutch Directors Guild, http://www.directorsguild.nl/articles/view/1259. Accessed 3 December 2011.

Film Daily Yearbook (1938), Amsterdam: Film Daily Yearbook.

Frijhoff, W. (1992), 'Identiteit en identiteitsbesef. De historicus en de spanning tussen verbeelding, benoeming en herkenning', *Bijdragen en mededelingen betreffende de geschiedenis der Nederlanden,* 107: 4, pp. 614–34.

Frijhoff, W. (2003), 'Toeëigening als vorm van culturele dynamiek', *Volkskunde*, 104: 1, pp. 3–17.

Garncarz, J. (1994), 'Hollywood in Germany: The Role of American Films in Germany', in D.W. Ellwood and R. Kroes (eds), *Hollywood in Europe. Experiences of a Cultural Hegemony*, Amsterdam: VU University Press, pp. 94–137.

Hes, J. (1972), *In de ban van het beeld. Een filmsociologisch-godsdienstsociologische verkenning*, Assen: Van Gorcum.

Kuhn, A. (2002), *Dreaming of Ginger and Fred: Cinema and Cultural Memory*, New York: New York University Press.

Maltby, R. (2011), 'New Cinema History', in R. Maltby, D. Biltereyst and P. Meers (eds), *Explorations in New Cinema History: Approaches and Case Studies*, Malden, MA: Wiley-Blackwell, pp. 3–40.

Nederlandschen Bioscoop Bond (1934), *Jaarverslag 1933*, Amsterdam: n.p.

Pafort-Overduin, C. (2004), '"De Jantjes": Hogerop via het cabaret?', in M. de Keizer and S. Tates (eds), *Moderniteit. Modernisme en massacultuur in Nederland 1914–1940*, Zutphen, Walburg Pers, pp. 165–83.

—— (2011), 'Distribution and Exhibition in the Netherlands, 1934–1936', in R. Maltby, D. Biltereyst and P. Meers (eds), *Explorations in New Cinema History: Approaches and Case Studies*, Malden, MA: Wiley-Blackwell, pp. 125–39.

Pafort-Overduin, C., De Jong, F., Van Oort, T. en Van der Velden, A. (2006), 'Cinema Context en onderzoek naar sociale netwerken binnen de filmgeschiedschrijving: een aanzet tot discussie', *Tijdschrift voor Mediageschiedenis*, 9: 2, pp. 28–45.

Sedgwick, J. (2000), *Popular Filmgoing in 1930s Britain: A Choice of Pleasures*, Exeter: University of Exeter Press.

—— (2011), 'Patterns in First-Run and Suburban Filmgoing in Sydney in the Mid-1930s', in R. Maltby, D. Biltereyst and P. Meers (eds), *Explorations in New Cinema History. Approaches and Case Studies*, Malden, MA: Wiley-Blackwell, pp. 140–58.

Sedgwick, J., Pafort-Overduin, C. and Boter, J. (2012), 'Explanations for the Restrained Development of the Dutch Cinema Market in the 1930s', *Enterprise and Society*, 13: 3, pp. 634–71.

Van Oort, T. (2007), *Film en het modern leven in Limburg*, Maaslandse Monographieën, 70, Hilversum: Uitgeverij Verloren.

Notes

1 One of the assignments in my Film History classes between 1995 and 1999 was an oral history interview with an elderly person about his or her cinema-going habits in the 1950s. We found many examples of men or women who only went to, or avoided, a particular cinema. For example, a Catholic woman told us that she only went to the so-called White Cinema (Witte Bioscoop) in Amstelveen, as its film programme was approved by the Catholic Church.

2 The POPSTAT formula I used is derived from the formula described in Sedgwick (2000: 55–73). My version of the POPSTAT score is calculated as follows. A film scores a total number of screenings in a certain cinema (each single bill performance scores 1, each double bill performance scores 0.5). That total number of screenings is multiplied by the seating capacity of that cinema, and then divided by the average number of seats from all cinemas in the dataset (this is to correct for differences in cinema size). The sum of the results of all cinemas where the film was shown make up the total POPSTAT score for a film.

3 In 1937, the Central Bureau of Statistics in the Netherlands counted 333 cinemas. (Centraal Bureau voor de Statistiek 1938).

4 The data were collected as part of my PhD investigation. The programme data for 14 of the 22 places was found in local newspapers; the Cinema Context database provided the programme information for the other eight towns. The Cinema Context data was refined by adding the number of screenings per day. This information was also found in local newspapers. The Cinema Context database is developed by Karel Dibbets with the support of the Netherlands Organisation for Scientific Research (NWO): http://www.cinemacontext.nl (accessed 20 May 2012).

5 A Dutch cabaret in the 1930s was a place of entertainment where audiences could alternately watch variety like performances and dance.

6   Pafort-Overduin (2011: 129–34) reaches the same conclusion. The numbers in that article are slightly different from those ones mentioned in this chapter, as the database was expanded later on, but they show the same pattern.

7   This happened, for example, in the northern town of Groningen. On 17 February 1934, the reviewer of the *Nieuwsblad van het Noorden* reported the success of *The Sailors* in Amsterdam while the film only arrived eight weeks after its première in Groningen on 30 March 1934.

8   From the Cinema Context database, it can be read that the first ruling was on 12 January 1934; the second on 22 January 1934 and the third on 8 February 1934. See www.cinemacontext.nl (accessed 20 February 2012).

Chapter 20

Contemporary Italian Film-goers and Their Critics

Alan O'Leary and Catherine O'Rawe

Qualcuno, prima o poi, dovrà fare anche un'analisi del pubblico di certi film oltre che del film stesso.

[Someone, sooner or later, will also have to do an analysis of the audience for certain films and not just of the film itself.]

– Marco Giusti (2003: 6)

The Italian film audience has famously been sentimentalized in films such as Giuseppe Tornatore's *Cinema Paradiso* (1988) and *Baarìa* (2009), yet it would be fair to say that it remains a relatively unknown object. The turn to historical reception studies that has taken place within film studies in the last 25 years or so, marked by the works of Janet Staiger (1992) and Robert Allen and Douglas Gomery (1985), among many others, has left only a faint imprint on Italian film studies, which is still largely text-centred. In this context, Mariagrazia Fanchi and Elena Mosconi (2002: 9) have noted the 'marginalità … delle forme di spettatorialità e le esperienze di visione' ('marginality … of the forms of spectatorship and the experience of viewing') in Italy.

Still, a closer look at the Italian context shows us that, at least since World War II, regular attempts have been made by both the cinema industry and film magazines to investigate Italian audiences. These surveys were supplemented by audience 'inchieste' (investigations or inquiries) in left-leaning film journals, which generally had the purpose of discovering popular taste only in order to correct or elevate it, thus exposing the gap between cineastes and intellectuals and the popular audience, conceived as an homogeneous mass.[1] The lament that the popular Italian audience remains a mystery is a familiar one, and was repeated by illustrious film historian Gian Piero Brunetta in the introduction to his 1997 account of Italian cinema-going, *Buio in sala*, when he asked:

Perché i tempi dello storico e del critico non hanno quasi mai punti di contatto o di congruenza con quelli del pubblico? Perché nessuno ha mai voluto studiare nella sua specificità il tempo biologico del pubblico, la curva delle emozioni, le modifiche dei ritmi sociali prodotte dal rito della visione cinematografica? … Come si può organizzare una ricerca sistematica 'dalla parte dello spettatore'? (Brunetta 1997: xx)

[Why is the experience of the historian and the critic so rarely congruent with that of the audience? Why has nobody ever wanted to study in all its specificity the lived experience of the audience, the emotional fluctuations and the changes to social patterns that are produced by the ritual of film-viewing? ... How can systematic research be organized 'from the point of view of the spectator'?]

The sources used by Brunetta for his reconstruction of cinema-going are, however, exclusively texts by novelists and intellectuals; this is symptomatic, we believe, of an enduring discursive divide in Italy between auteur or art-house cinema and mass or popular cinema. Intellectuals approaching Italian popular cinema and its audiences have tended to lay bare their own anxieties and prejudices about the popular. As the following lament by Carlo Tagliabue suggests, audiences for popular cinema are often seen as passive ideological dupes lacking political acumen and cultural discernment. Tagliabue is commenting on the results of one of the few empirical studies of Italian cinema-goers, undertaken at the turn of this century:[2]

> Non ci resterebbe che prendere atto della totale passività del pubblico italiano di fronte a scelte e proposte fatte da altri: uno spettatore che subisce, in sostanza, quanto gli viene proposto e che si fa modellare nei suoi gusti, dimostrando una scarsa capacità reattiva ... Quell'oscuro, ma necessario e fondamentale, oggetto del desiderio che è lo spettatore ha davanti a sé un panorama univoco: un panorama che lo ha cambiato nel corso degli ultimi decenni, togliendogli, in maniera indotta, il gusto delle scelte con cui nutrire il proprio immaginario, intossicandolo con una serie di prodotti di basso profilo qualitativo (Tagliabue 2000: 51).[3]
>
> [All one can do is acknowledge the complete passivity of the Italian public when faced with choices and proposals made by others. This is a spectator who fundamentally accepts anything put before him [sic] and who allows his tastes to be dictated, showing a scant ability to resist ... That obscure but necessary and fundamental object of desire that is the spectator has been changed by the monotone cinematic landscape that has faced him over the past decades, forcefully depriving him of choices with which to nourish his imagination, and poisoning him with a series of low-quality products.]

The image of toxic products being consumed by a spectator too passive or unreactive to know better connects audience and genre in a particular way: the 'serie di prodotti di basso profilo qualitativo' ('series of low-quality products') no doubt refers to the popular comedies and dramas that make up the bulk of Italian domestic production. In this chapter, we examine two examples of these popular genres and their audiences, both much despised but rarely scrutinized: first, the teen film genre and its presumed audience, the teenage girl fans of heart-throb actor Riccardo Scamarcio; and second, Italy's Christmas comedies – the so-called *cinepanettoni* ('film-Christmas-cakes'). We outline some of the pervasive critical discourses around both the films and their spectators, and close by arguing that both these films and these groups of viewers are a central, though repressed, part of Italy's cinematic imaginary.

Riccardo Scamarcio and the female audience

Riccardo Scamarcio shot to fame in the 2004 film *Tre metri sopra il cielo/Three Metres Above the Sky*, directed by Luca Lucini and adapted from the cult 1992 novel by Federico Moccia. He reprised the role of the attractive protagonist Step in the sequel, *Ho voglia di te/I Want You* (Prieto, 2007). Step is a brooding James Dean-type rebel, whose penchant for motorbike racing involves him in the death of his best friend, and whose relationships with girls (Katy Louise Saunders in the first film and Laura Chiatti in the second) involve grandiose gestures of commitment. The films mix melodrama, romance and comedy, and the second film in particular attracted a large audience, taking over €14 million at the Italian box office. Although Scamarcio was trained at the prestigious Centro Sperimentale in Rome, and his subsequent career has been impressively varied – with prominent roles in middlebrow dramas such as *Mio fratello è figlio unico/My Brother is an Only Child* (Luchetti, 2007) and *Il grande sogno/The Big Dream* (Placido, 2009) – he has been dogged by the 'stigma' of having been a teen heart-throb, and having had an ardent young female fan base in the earlier part of his career.

For male actors, heart-throb status is often complicated and unwelcome: as Nash and Lahti write in relation to Leonardo Di Caprio's stardom post-*Titanic*, 'the proximity to both feminized iconography and to female consumers carries with it certain degrading connotations for male stars' (1999: 71). The persistence of the twin ideas of teenage girls as being both pathologically hysterical and 'uncritical consumers' (Click 2009) has meant that the female teenage audience has enjoyed very little cultural prestige. To focus on *Ho voglia di te*, the review of the film in the left-wing daily *L'Unità* displaces its anxiety about the popularity of the film on to its spectators, finding the girls in the audience to be renouncing traditional feminist symbols for a facile technology:

> Otto marzo, festa delle donne. Ma al pubblico, nettamente femminile, della première di *Ho voglia di te* a Roma, il particolare sembra essere sfuggito. Sono giovani, giovanissime, capelli lunghi e lisci (un po' come le protagoniste dei libri diventati film di Moccia), telefonini in mano pronte a scattare foto e nessuna mimosa in vista. (Battisti 2007)
>
> [8th of March: International Women's Day. But that detail seems to have slipped the minds of the predominantly female audience at the Rome premiere of *Ho voglia di te*. They are young, very young, with long straight hair (a little like the female characters in the Moccia books), with mobile phones at the ready to take pictures, and not a mimosa [the traditional flower of Women's Day] in sight.]

The author of the review goes on to offer paternalistic advice to the girls in the cinema (although with a box-office intake of over €14 million, we might presume some boys and adults are also going to see the film):

> Lungi dal giudicare, sommessamente ci permettiamo di dare due suggerimenti al teen-pubblico: 1) o voi ragazze che amate l'idolo Scamarcio riccioluto e motorizzato, provate a

noleggiare *I diari della motocicletta*, protagonista un giovanissimo Che Guevara, anche lui moro e riccioluto, magretto e su una moto spericolata. La sua, oltre tutto, è anche storia vera. 2) alle giovani coppie innamorate: piuttosto che inquinare l'ambiente con i lucchetti, adottate e/o piantate un albero a simbolo del vostro amore eterno. Non si arrugginisce, non forma mucchi informi con altri amori/lucchetti, e ogni primavera tornerà a fiorire. (Battisti 2007)

[Far from judging them, let us humbly make two suggestions to these teen spectators: 1) oh all you young girls who love the curly-haired heart-throb Scamarcio on his motorbike, why not rent *Motorcycle Diaries*, whose main character is a young, dark and curly-haired Che Guevara, who is also a slim daredevil on a motorbike. Besides anything else, his is a true story. 2) to all you young couples in love: rather than polluting the environment with padlocks, why not adopt and/or plant a tree as a symbol of your eternal love. It won't get rusty, it won't create unsightly heaps of padlocks, and every spring it will flower again.]

The reference to the *lucchetti*, or padlocks, that Step attaches to the Ponte Milvio in Rome as proof of his love for the heroine, Gin, is interesting: the film encouraged a copycat custom (originally generated by the 2006 novel) of affixing symbolic padlocks, not just on the Ponte Milvio, but on many bridges in Italian cities.[4]

One critic does at least declare his incapacity to review the film, distant as he is from its presumed teenage audience:

Perché quando uno, avendo una certa età e per di più trovandosi lì con il ruolo sempre un po' antipatico di 'critico', prova un vago imbarazzo a vedere film come *Ho voglia di te*? Perché non riconosce, non può riconoscere il valore banale quanto volete ma eterno di racconti così. È probabilissimo che Scamarcio e [Laura] Chiatti comunichino a chi ha gli anni giusti lo stesso emozionato tremore che, non so, trentacinque anni prima comunicavano Warren Beatty e Julie Christie (*I compari* di Altman). (D'Agostini 2007)

[Why does a person of a certain age, finding himself in that slightly distasteful role of critic, feel a slight sense of embarrassment in watching films like *Ho voglia di te*? Because he doesn't, he cannot recognize the banal yet timeless quality of stories like this. It is highly probable that Scamarcio and Laura Chiatti are communicating to those young viewers the same flutter of excitement that Warren Beatty and Julie Christie gave spectators 35 years earlier in Altman's *McCabe and Mrs Miller*.]

This question of whether middle-aged critics are able to review a film aimed at a youth audience, and whether their reviews actually have any impact on that audience, is repeated in broadsheet reviews: Paolo Mereghetti, writing in the *Corriere della Sera*, implicitly acknowledges this when he says that 'Ci sono dei film che evitano il confronto con la critica. La bypassano, la superano d'un balzo, la ignorano. *Ho voglia di te* di Luis Prieto (ma sarebbe giusto aggiungere 'e di Federico Moccia') è uno di questi' ('there are films that escape all critical judgement. They bypass it, they leap beyond it, they ignore it. *Ho voglia di te* by Luis Prieto (but it would be correct to add "also by Federico Moccia") is one of these.') (Mereghetti 2007).

We tend to agree with the British journalist Marina Hyde, who in discussing critical responses to the *Twilight* films starring global heart-throb Robert Pattinson, notes the inability of negative reviews to affect the films' success. For Hyde, the critical anguish provoked by films such as this, which have defied critical panning, is expressed as an 'impotence metaphor': 'Every single thing any middle-aged man writes is useless – powerless! meaningless! – in the face of a gazillion teenage girls' (Hyde 2009). Something like Hyde's analysis is found in Italy in Massimo Benvegnù's dissection of the hand-wringing over *Ho voglia di te*:

> Il problema è come sempre quello dei ruoli: sentendosi bypassati, i critici cercano di mettere in scena la loro protesta e guadagnare faticosamente il centro della scena, sgomitando contro i rivali. Dobbiamo dedurre che anche loro son gelosi del successo di Scamarcio e della Chiatti? (Benvegnù 2007)
>
> [The problem, as always, is about status: critics, aware that they are being bypassed, try to rehearse their protests and take centre-stage, elbowing their rivals out of the way. Should we deduce from this that they are jealous of the success of Scamarcio and Chiatti?]

Although it is difficult to establish the precise make-up of the audience for a film like *Ho voglia di te*, the assumption that it is female underwrites much criticism of the film.[5] Furthermore, various prejudices about the response of that audience persist. In order to challenge the idea of female spectators as passive recipients of material we need only look briefly at the phenomenon, mentioned above, of the symbolic *lucchetti* generated by *Ho voglia di te*. This phenomenon, whereby fans of the film (and book) have imitated its protagonists and left their mark on the surface of the city by attaching padlocks to bridges, may be understood as an example of what Henry Jenkins (2006) famously dubbed 'convergence culture' – that is, the contemporary reception culture in which types of 'participatory' fandom interact with new patterns of media distribution and flow. Jenkins argues that convergence 'does not occur through media appliances, no matter how sophisticated they may become. Convergence occurs within the brains of individual consumers and through their social interaction with others' (2006: 3). The shift in cultural practices around fandoms enables analysis to focus on the spectator as an active participant in the reception both of stars and of film texts. The *lucchetti* are a fascinating material example of this 'active' fandom: textual elements are, in Jenkins' words, 'extracted from the media flow and transformed into resources through which we make sense of our everyday lives' (2006: 3–4), and this occurs both on the streets of Rome and Milan, and in the YouTube fan videos dedicated to Step and his on-screen partners. The paternalistic and ecologically friendly advice given to the young fans by the critic from *L'Unità* that instead of tying a padlock to a bridge they should plant a tree ignores the fact that the former act is an assertion by the young spectators of their presence – a presence routinely read as troubling.[6]

However, it is when these young spectators enter the cinema to view more highbrow films (as advised, after all, by the *Unità* critic) that they are seen to become both dangerous and endangered. We witness this in responses to Scamarcio's role as ex-terrorist Sergio Segio in the recent film *La prima linea/The Front Line* (Renato De Maria, 2009), an account of the activities of clandestine left-wing armed group Prima Linea, in which Segio was a leading figure between 1976 and 1983. Aside from worrying that the casting of Scamarcio (and Giovanna Mezzogiorno as his partner in politics and romance, Susanna Ronconi) was glamorizing terrorism, Pier Luigi Battista worries that an impressionable young audience, drawn in by their love of Scamarcio, will be incited to follow the wrong path: 'non si sa che impressione ne possa ricavare chi, con qualche anno di meno (anzi, con parecchi anni di meno) stravede per Scamarcio e la Mezzogiorno' [we don't know what impression the young fan who is crazy for Scamarcio and Mezzogiorno might get from it] (Battista 2009). Similarly, Roy Menarini talks of 'il rischio di identificazione dei giovani spettatori verso attori come Riccardo Scamarcio e Giovanna Mezzogiorno' (the risk that young spectators might identify with actors like Riccardo Scamarcio and Giovanna Mezzogiorno), but emphasizes how the figure who is really problematic for critics is Scamarcio rather than Mezzogiorno:

> chi si chiede come uno stesso attore – Scamarcio – possa interpretare in pochi anni l'idolo delle ragazzine nei film tratti da Federico Moccia, il fascista di *Romanzo criminale*, il militante divenuto brigatista di *Mio fratello è figlio unico*, il poliziotto di sinistra in *Il grande sogno*, e infine l'estremista armato Sergio Segio, non ha tutti i torti (Menarini 2009).
>
> [Those who wonder how the same actor – Scamarcio – can, within a few short years, take on the roles of teen heartthrob in the films based on Moccia books, the fascist in *Romanzo criminale*, the left-wing activist-turned terrorist in *Mio fratello è figlio unico*, the left-wing policeman in *Il grande sogno*, and finally the armed extremist Sergio Segio, are not entirely mistaken.]

This anxiety about *La prima linea* was expressed particularly in the heated debate around the film's qualification for government subsidy as 'film d'interesse culturale' (a film of cultural importance): in an extraordinary meeting, the government's 'Commissione per la cinematografia – sottocommissione per il riconoscimento dell'interesse culturale' ('Committee for cinema – sub-committee for the recognition of cultural interest') met the director, writer (Sandro Petraglia) and producer (Andrea Occhipinti), and various groups representing families of terrorist victims. Fears were expressed repeatedly by the victims' associations, and by the committee itself, that the choice of actors described as 'di fascino' ('attractive'), and 'beniamini delle giovani generazioni' ('favourites of the younger generation'), might risk creating both 'idealizzazione romantica' ('romantic idealization') and 'identificazione' ('identification') with the plot and protagonists (Commissione per la cinematografia 2008).[7] Young spectators are regarded as at risk of being misled into sympathy with Segio and Ronconi's actions: the report quotes the opinion of Paolo Bolognesi, president of the Unione Vittime per Stragi (Union of Massacre Victims):

[R]itiene che tale progetto comporti effettivamente un rischio di idealizzazione romantica anche considerando la scelta degli attori protagonisti e lo ritiene pertanto un'operazione estremamente negativa per le nuove generazioni, ribadisce la necessità, quale punto fondamentale della riflessione, di una particolare attenzione al messaggio trasmesso alle nuove generazioni. (Commissione per la cinematografia 2008)

[He believes that such a project carries a risk of romantic idealization, especially taking into account the choice of actors, and he therefore thinks it is an extremely negative undertaking with regard to young audiences; he emphasizes that it is fundamental to consider the need for particular attention to be paid to the message sent out to young people.]

In short, the young female audience has to be redeemed, via more political films, as when it is instructed to view *The Motorcycle Diaries*: however, this raises a further anxiety – is such an audience capable of reading more difficult films correctly, or indeed, of telling the difference between film and reality? Will its members be seduced by the attractive face of Riccardo Scamarcio into a belief that extra-parliamentary violence in the 1970s and 1980s was justified? The difficulty posed by the young female audience seems to reside partly in this anxiety over its members' incompetence as spectators, which places them at risk of becoming seduced by bad messages. As Buckingham and Bragg argue in relation to their work with young viewers in the UK: 'invoking concerns about children, sex and the media seems to serve as a powerful means of mobilizing more general anxieties about social and moral decline' (2004: 9). Buckingham and Bragg's own work produced interesting findings: they argue that young people are media-literate, and are often highly critical media consumers.[8] It would seem strange if this were not also the case in Italy, and it would certainly be interesting to find out what young viewers actually thought of *La prima linea*, or to know more about their views in general on how they are viewed as spectators.

The *cinepanettone* and its audiences

The *cinepanettoni* are a 'filone' (sub-genre) of farcical comedies, one or sometimes two of which are released annually in Italy for the Christmas period with titles like *Vacanze di Natale '90/Christmas Vacation 1990* (Oldoini, 1990) and *Natale a Rio/Christmas in Rio* (Parenti, 2008). They date back to Carlo Vanzini's 1983 (*Vacanze di Natale/Christmas Vacation*), and have been produced for the most part by Aurelio de Laurentiis' Filmauro company.[9] The series is strongly associated with the actor Christian de Sica (son of the actor and filmmaker Vittorio), but the films are ensemble comedies featuring stock comic types and regional stereotypes, and the humour they contain describes a range from social satire to slapstick and grotesque. Their roots are found in the comic tradition that has been a constant in Italy (the first film was a kind of remake of the 1959 *Vacanze d'inverno/Winter Vacation*, directed by Camillo Mastrocinque), as it has been in other countries, but the films can also be remarkably hybrid texts that include, for example, thriller or travelogue elements in order to appeal to a variegated audience. Indeed, what is particularly significant about the *cinepanettone* is that it has been successful enough to have become part of the annual festive rituals for large numbers of Italians – an untested commonplace has it that many Italians go to the cinema, often as a family, only once a year, and then it is to see a *cinepanettone*. What is certain is that these are films made for the cinema itself (as distinct from home viewing). They are characterized by unusually multiple address and are designed to be enjoyed in company; in any case, the annual *cinepanettone* is regularly among the most successful releases of the year.[10]

Despite this, the *cinepanettone* and its audiences remain almost unstudied, and the films have suffered a critical disdain from those representing authoritative film criticism and scholarship. The *cinepanettone* is regarded as a base and 'vulgar' product; it is seen to be politically unsound, and has become a byword for low quality as well as a metonym for the degraded tastes of the Italian public – or at least that part of it that has never learned to be discerning. Giorgio Simonelli, for example, writes of the *cinepanettone* as 'quello che è ormai un imbarazzante fenomeno italiano', that which 'indigna ogni volta al suo apparire buona parte della società, che è diventato antonomasia della superficialità, della banalità, della volgarità, della mancanza di progetti del nostro cinema' ('is by now an embarrassing Italian phenomenon [which] causes indignation at its every appearance to a good part of society and which has become synonymous with superficiality, with banality, with vulgarity, and with the absence of ideas in our cinema') (Simonelli 2008: 185). Negri and Tanzi write of the thoughtless consumption of the films: that they are 'un'offerta che cattura migliaia (o meglio milioni) di spettatori che non vanno mai al cinema, se non una volta all'anno per gustarsi il loro *cinepanettone*' ('A product that captures thousands (or better, millions) of spectators who never go to the cinema if not once a year in order to savour their *cinepanettone*') (Negri and Tanzi 2009: 189–90).

Negri and Tanzi elaborate on their theme of the uncritical tastes of the *cinepanettone* audience: 'Stordito dagli eccessi alimentari e sentimentali del periodo natalizio,' they write, 'il consumatore assorbe meglio' ('Stupefied by the alimentary and sentimental excesses of the Christmas period the consumer absorbs more readily') (2009: 191). They continue:

L'euforia delle feste, la smania collettiva di evasione e divertimento, il desiderio inconscio di ritrovare sul grande schermo qualcosa di familiare producono un curioso effetto placido. Si entra nel cinema già con la voglia di ridere. E si riderà comunque, anche se i tempi comici sono sballati e le situazioni triviali o ai limiti dell'imbarazzante. (2009: 190)

[The euphoria of the celebrations, the collective frenzy of escapism and enjoyment, the unconscious desire to recognize something familiar on the big screen – all produce a curious pacifying effect. One already enters the cinema with the yen to laugh. And one laughs regardless, even if the comic timing is clumsy and the situations trivial or at the limits of embarrassment.]

What strikes Roy Menarini (2010) as particularly regrettable is the fact that so many Italians place such value on seeing these films year after year, and he wonders why the *cinepanettone* should be so successful when similar low and exploitative humour can be found elsewhere: 'Si tratta, con tutta evidenza, di un appuntamento sociale, di un comportamento rituale, di una traccia che, a vederla con ottimismo, ci parla di una funzione di massa del cinema.' ('One is dealing, evidently, with a social appointment, with ritual behaviour, with a vestige which, to take the most positive view, speaks of a mass function of cinema') (2010: 80). Menarini is surely correct to point to the ritual aspect of the film-going that attends the *cinepanettone*, but he denies any complexity to the potential relationships the audiences for the films have with them; for him, attendance is but a 'riflesso pavloviano' ('Pavlovian reflex') (2010: 81).

The negative characterization of the *cinepanettone* and its audience is not restricted to criticism and scholarship; it is also proverbial in the wider culture, and seems to be a pre-eminent means of establishing distinction among those with aspirations to cultural capital. Forums like YouTube feature amateur filmmakers or budding critics distinguishing themselves from the common horde by declaring their disdain for the series of films,[11] and one episode of the satirical TV show *Mai dire Martedì/Never Say Tuesday*, broadcast on Italia1 in 2007–08) featured a spoof trailer for a film entitled *Natale al cesso/Christmas on the Toilet*.[12] What is striking about this parody version of the *cinepanettone* is its exclusive focus on the so-called 'vulgar' aspects of the series: dialectal obscenity, fart jokes, slapstick and humiliating sexual situations. Capping this partial and hypocritical (if perfectly amusing) portrayal is the implied sense of shame that films like these could be seen elsewhere and Italian culture judged on the basis of them – something signalled by the ironic tag line that accompanies the spoof trailer: 'Il genere di film che il mondo ci invidia' ('The Italian film genre envied by the world').

Inasmuch as the *cinepanettone* is considered in relation to the rest of Italian film culture, it tends to be understood as a threat, seen to represent an aesthetic risk for Italian filmmakers and to coach audiences to expect the worst. In *Boris: il film/Boris: the Film* (Ciarrapico and Torre, 2011), the feature offshoot of the cult satirical television series *Boris* (2007–10), the *cinepanettone* is employed to connote the lowest point to which Italian cinema can fall. The plot of *Boris: il film* concerns a maladroit television director, René, who for his first feature hopes to adapt *La casta*, the (real) 2007 book by Gian Antonio Stella e Sergio Rizzo, which denounces the corruption and arrogance of the Italian political class. René begins with a model like *Gomorra/Gomorrah* (2008) – Matteo Garrone's denunciation of the Neapolitan mafia – in mind, but constructed entirely from long takes, only to end up begging for production money by promising to make a *cinepanettone* (the word is introduced and pronounced very deliberately, almost like the breaking of a taboo), and his film is ultimately entitled *Natale con la casta/Christmas with the Caste*.

The tone of the humour in the spoof trailer 'Natale al cesso' is reprised in *Boris: il film*, in the scene where René's 'Natale con la casta' is previewed. In this case, a cabaret performer shown in an earlier scene to greatly entertain a theatre audience with obscene catchphrases is crudely edited into the austere *plan-sequence* we have seen being painstakingly filmed by Renè and his crew: 'sti cazzi!' ('Who gives a fuck!') interjects the *caberista* at intervals to the public's general mirth. The point being made is the by-now familiar one of the uncritical character of the Italian audience for these films. And if Boris is explicitly a satire of Italian television and film production processes and personnel, its most trenchant mockery is reserved for the Italian public itself, which is seen to demand the propagandistic and sentimental television mini-series we see being made about the early life of the then pope (entitled 'The Young Ratzinger'), and seen to be satisfied with the lowest common denominator entertainment of the *cinepanettone* in the caricature version constructed in *Boris: il film* itself.

The satire of the *cinepanettone* in *Mai dire Martedì* and *Boris: il film* risks toothlessness because it distils the films to a 'vulgarity' that is just one of the genre's features (one gleefully enjoyed and recycled by the satirists), a vulgarity that is also regularly – even ritualistically – deplored in scholarship and criticism. What further links the satire with the content of authoritative critical discourse is the yoking of a simplistic characterization of the films to a condescension towards and distaste for their audience. The simplistic characterization of the films is matched by the crude characterization of its spectator.

There seems to be widespread agreement that the *cinepanettone* appeals to a particular type of person, despite the films' multiple address to a variegated holiday audience, which must range across age, gender and class. We present here a brief analysis of some of the responses to an online questionnaire about the *cinepanettone*, designed by Alan O'Leary to analyse the consumption, utilization, circulation and discursive construction of the films.[13] Responses to this questionnaire suggest take-up to have been skewed to those with a low opinion of the *cinepanettone*. Respondents were asked whether they believed there was a typical spectator for the *cinepanettone* and, if so, to provide a description of that person. The descriptions (mostly a single phrase) include the following, which may be taken as representative of the first 200 responses. The expression 'l'Italiano medio' (the average Italian) recurs frequently, often alone but sometimes often linked to social class or status:

> Un italiano medio e poco intelligente e ironico.
> L'italiano medio, ovvero cultura medio/bassa.
> [An average Italian of low intelligence and irony.
> The average Italian, that is, low/average culture.]

The *cinepanettone* has often been seen as simultaneously symptom and cause of the success of Silvio Berlusconi and the Italian right in the past two decades. Descriptions of the spectator make this link:

> Tipico Berlusconiano.
> I truzzi, gli arricchiti e i Berlusconiani.
> L'italiano ignorante, l'italiano stupido e l'italiano di destra (più del 50%).

Una persona senza cultura, che non legge e non si informa, non va al cinema abitualmente e non conosce la storia del cinema, probabilmente di centro-destra, con pregiudizi e priva di gusto e con la soglia dell'attenzione e la capacità di concentrazione bassissime.
[Typical Berlusconi type.
The boors, the *nouveaux riches* and the Berlusconi types.
The ignorant Italian, the stupid Italian and the right-wing Italian (more than 50 per cent). A person without culture, who doesn't read and doesn't keep himself informed, doesn't go to the cinema regularly and doesn't know the history of cinema, probably a supporter of the centre right, bigoted and tasteless and with an extremely short attention span and low capacity for concentration.]

In contrast to the female spectator of Riccardo Scamarcio, the imagined spectator for the *cinepanettone* seems to be a man:

Maschilista e volgare.
Un uomo porco a cui piace vedere culi e tette al vento … e che si diverte con volgarità e espressioni dialettali e che si masturba ripensando alla battona di turno che ha recitato nel film.
[Male chauvinist and vulgar.
A pig of a man who likes to see tits and ass all over the place … and who amuses himself with vulgarities and phrases in dialect and who masturbates while he thinks about the latest slag who has acted in the film.]

It is notable that where typically it might be the feminized spectator who bears the brunt of authoritative denunciation or complaint, here it is the figure of the middle- or lower-class male who incarnates the abject spectator. The success of the *cinepanettone* with a variegated audience that includes families and persons of all ages and both sexes implies that that the spectator really cannot be so confidently characterized or gendered. Of course, a delimited characterization is required ('led') by the questionnaire rubric itself, but the remarkable strength of the language in these responses points to a perceived cultural and political divide in Italy. It seems that the questionnaire respondents are not simply laying bare anxieties and prejudices about the popular and its appeal in their descriptions of the 'typical' spectator, but are also revealing how the popular form of the *cinepanettone* itself is employed as metaphor and scapegoat for political disappointment.

Conclusion

The celebrated Italian novelist and intellectual Italo Calvino once wrote:

Cinema vuol dire sedersi in mezzo a una platea di gente che sbuffa, ansima, sghignazza, succhia caramelle, ti disturba, entra, esce, magari legge le didascalie forte come al tempo del muto; il cinema è questa gente, più che una storia che succede sullo schermo. Il fatto caratteristico del cinema nella nostra società è il dover tener conto di questo pubblico incommensurabilmente più vasto ed eterogeneo di quello della letteratura: un pubblico di milioni in cui le benemerite migliaia di lettori di libri esistenti in Italia annegano come gocce d'acqua in mare. E questo pubblico ha con la creazione cinematografica un rapporto dialettico: si lascia imbottire il cranio dal cinema, ma s'impone a sua volta al cinema. Tutto dipende da come questa dialettica funziona: male, quasi sempre, ma comunque gli splendori e le miserie del film nascono da lì. (Calvino 1953: 262)

[Cinema means sitting in the stalls among people who huff and puff, guffaw and suck sweets, who disturb you coming in and going out, who may even read the titles out loud like in the era of the Silents. The cinema is these sorts of people before it is any story that happens on the screen. The distinguishing feature of cinema in our society is the fact that you have to pay attention to an audience that is immeasurably more vast and varied than the audience for literature: an audience of millions which drown the admirable thousands of book readers in Italy like drops of water in the sea. And this audience has a dialectical relationship with cinematic creation: it allows its brain to be stuffed full by the cinema, but it imposes itself in turn on the same cinema. All depends on how this dialectic functions: almost always badly, but one way or another both the splendours and the squalor of film are born from it.]

Calvino summarizes and exemplifies two important and contradictory ideas about the Italian audience: first, the need to account for it, to factor it into discussions of cinema as an essential component of the filmic experience; and second, the perception of its passivity and defencelessness against the power of the mass medium ('si lascia imbottire il cranio'). Encompassing both these ideas, however, is the construction of the audience as 'other': the audience surrounds 'you', with the 'you' presumably referring to the hapless intellectual or cinephile spectator looking to improve him or herself, who has to contend with the mass of confectionary-munching spectators disturbing his experience.

As the two case studies discussed above demonstrate, certain types of popular audience become a focus for opprobrium, and are even treated as symptom of a diseased or decaying political and civic consciousness. No doubt it is easier to assert that certain groups of filmgoers tend to be 'bad' Italians is than it is to discern what kind of cultural work films actually do for their audiences, and what use they make of these films in their own lives. The 'problem' posed by Italian spectators – whether as mass presence or as imagined lone voyeur – can only be addressed by the type of project imagined by Gian Piero Brunetta, cited at the beginning of this chapter – a project undertaken on behalf of the Italian spectator. In seeing Italian cinema from the point of view of the spectator, both the perspective of the spectator, and the films he or she watches, might begin to make more sense.

References

Allen, R. and Gomery, D. (1985), *Film History: Theory and Practice*, New York: McGraw-Hill.

Anon (2011), 'I lucchetti dell'amore saranno rimossi', *Corriere della Sera*, 12 December.

Battista, P. (2009), 'Quei volti troppo belli per il male', *Corriere della Sera*, 13 November.

Battisti, R. (2007), 'Ho voglia di … Scamarcio', *L'Unità*, 9 March.

Benvegnù, M. (2007), 'Ho voglia di.. una critica cinematografica seria!', *Il Riformista*, 14 March.

Boero, D. (2009), *Chitarre e lucchetti: Il cinema adolescente da Morandi a Moccia*, Genoa: Le Mani.

Brunetta, G.P. (1997), *Buio in sala*, Venice: Marsilio.

Buckingham, D. and Bragg, S. (2004), *Young People, Sex, and the Media: The Facts of Life?*, Basingstoke: Palgrave Macmillan.

Calvino, I. (1953), 'Il realismo italiano nel cinema e nella narrativa', in *Cinema nuovo*, 10, 1 May.

Click, M. (2009), *'"Rabid" "Obsessed", and "Frenzied": Understanding Twilight Fangirls and the Gendered Politics of Fandom'*, http://flowtv.org/2009/12/rabid-obsessed-and-frenzied-understanding-twilight-fangirls-and-the-gendered-politics-of-fandom-melissa-click-university-of-missouri. Accessed 3 January 2012.

Commissione per la cinematografia, sottocommissione riconoscimento interesse culturale (2008), Report of Extraordinary Meeting, 19 September.

D'Agostini, P. (2007), 'Basta essere adolescenti per apprezzare i lucchetti', *La Repubblica*, 9 March.

Eco, U. (1964), *Apocalittici e integrati: comunicazioni di massa e teorie della cultura di massa*, Milan: Bompiani.

Fanchi, M. and Mosconi, E. (2002), *Spettatori: forme di consumo e pubblici del cinema in Italia 1930–1960*, Rome: Bianco e Nero.

Giannelli, E (1953), *Indagini di mercato sul cinema in Italia 1950–1953*, Rome: ANICA.

Giusti, M. (2003), 'Preface' in F. Spicciarello, A. Pallotta and S. Sirianni (eds), *'Vacanze di Natale' di Enrico e Carlo Vanzina,* Rome: Un Mondo a Parte, pp. 4–6.

Guidacci, L., MacLean, M. and Pinna, L. (1958), *Due anni col pubblico cinematografico*, Rome: Bianco e Nero.

Hipkins, D. (2012), 'Who wants to be a TV showgirl? Auditions, talent and taste in contemporary popular Italian cinema', in *The Italianist*, 32: 2, pp. 154–90.

Hyde, M. (2009), 'The *Twilight* Saga: *New Moon* – Why Resistance is Futile', *The Guardian*, 27 November.

Jenkins, H. (2006), *Convergence Culture: Where Old and New Media Collide*, New York: New York University Press.

Menarini, R. (2009), '*La prima linea* e il tabù del terrorismo', *Il corriere di Bologna*, 25 November.

────── (2010), *Il cinema dopo il cinema: dieci idée sul cinema italiano 2000–2010*, Genoa: Le Mani.

Mereghetti, P. (2007), '*Ho voglia di te*', *Corriere della Sera*, 9 March.

Negri, G. and Tanzi, R. (2009), *Natale al cinema: da 'La vita è meravigliosa' a 'A Christmas Carol'*, Alessandria: Falsopiano.

Nash, M. and Lahti, M. (1999), '"Almost Ashamed to Say I am One of Those Girls": *Titanic*, Leonardo Di Caprio, and the Paradoxes of Girls' Fandoms', in K. Sandler and G. Studlar (eds), *Titanic: Anatomy of a Blockbuster*, New Brunswick, NJ: Rutgers University Press, pp. 64–88.

O'Leary, A. (2011), 'The Phenomenology of the Cinepanettone', *Italian Studies*, 66: 3, pp. 431–43.

——— (2013), *Fenomenologia del cinepanettone*, Soveria Mannelli: Rubbettino.

O'Rawe, C. (2008), '"I padri e i maestri": Genre, Auteurs, And Absences in Italian Film Studies', *Italian Studies*, 63: 2, pp. 173–94.

Repetto, M. and Tagliabue, C. (eds) (2000), *La vita è bella? Il cinema italiano alla fine degli anni novanta e il suo pubblico*, Milan: Il Castoro.

Simonelli, G. (2008), *Cinema a Natale: da Renoir ai Vanzina*, Novara: Interlinea.

Staiger, J. (1992), *Interpreting Films: Studies in the Historical Reception of American Cinema*, Princeton, NJ: Princeton University Press.

Tagliabue, C. (2000), 'Lo spettatore italiano: quell'oscuro oggetto del desiderio', in M. Repetto and C. Tagliabue (eds), *La vita è bella? Il cinema italiano alla fine degli anni novanta e il suo pubblico*, Milan: Il Castoro, pp. 43–51.

Vitali, A. (2007), 'Step è tornato, ora deve scegliere: *Ho voglia di te*, al cinema è ressa', *La Repubblica*, 8 March.

Notes

1 Examples are Giannelli (1953), and Guidacci et al. (1958). See also O'Rawe (2008) for discussion of the investigation by the communist paper *L'Unità* in 1955–56.

2 The study was intended to cast light on the condition of the Italian cinema industry at the turn of the century. Questionnaires were distributed to a sample of Italians between the ages of 14 and 64 who had been to the cinema at least once in the previous two months. See Repetto and Tagliabue (2000).

3 Tagliabue's discourse is in the tradition of the Italian 'apocalyptic' intellectual, as characterized by Umberto Eco (1964).

4 At the time of writing, the borough council in Rome was trying to have the *lucchetti* removed, despite counter-arguments about how much tourism they attract to the area. See Anon (2011).

5 The youth audience itself is subject to prejudice in Italy, as in Boero's remark that 'gli spettatori under twenty non hanno gusti particolarmente complicati' ['spectators under 20 don't have particularly complicated tastes'] (Boero 2009: 9).

6 The mass physical presence of the young spectators can clearly be disturbing to the critic: 'Orde di ragazzine si aggirano rapaci, jeans a vita bassissima e pancette traballanti, videofonini pronti all'azione' (Vitali 2007) ['Hordes of marauding young girls mill around, their wobbling bellies visible above low-rise jeans, mobile phones ready to take videos'].

7 De Maria himself clarified that the actors were required to read through extensive background material 'per entrare correttamente nel personaggio' ['to get fully into the character'], and several steps were taken to reduce the risk of 'identificazione', including the promotion of a restrained and affectless performance style.

8   Danielle Hipkins (2012) discusses the moral panics around young spectators in Italy in an important article on contemporary Italian cinema.

9   See O'Leary (2011) for a more complete description and list of the *cinepanettoni*.

10 The success has tailed off in recent years, and the 2011 *cinepanettone*, *Vacanze di Natale a Cortina*/*Christmas Vacation in Cortina* (Parenti) performed distinctly less well at the box office, though still earning a substantial (in Italian terms) €11.7 million.

11 See, for example, http://youtu.be/FbGLQCw7xbY. Accessed 23 February 2013.

12 Available at various web addresses, including http://youtu.be/glDlBbACGbw. Accessed 20 November 2011.

13 The questionnaire was available at https://www.survey.leeds.ac.uk/cinepanettone until March 2012. A full analysis of the responses is given in O'Leary (2013).

Chapter 21

Imagining a 'Decent Crowd' at the Indian Multiplex

Adrian Mabbott Athique

Introduction: the multiplex in India

It was in marked contrast to the 'downshifting' trends in the exhibition sector over the previous two decades that the luxury multiplex cinema first appeared in India's urban landscape in 1997. The multiplex had previously made an important intervention in urban leisure elsewhere in the world, but the appearance of the format in India has, if anything, had an even more dramatic impact upon the cinematic culture. In part, this stems from the primary role still played by cinema in Indian popular culture. Much more than this, however, the multiplex format has been deployed strategically against the backdrop of massive social change taking place in an era of economic liberalization. India's new chrome and glass multiplexes have been much appreciated by middle-class cinema-goers seeking a 'better' standard and wider choice of entertainment than that provided by the older large-capacity halls.

Owing to smaller auditoriums, much higher admission prices and the inherent rationale of providing an entertainment menu, the multiplex has served to elevate the box office value of the middle-class public. During the decade of its existence, the multiplex has thus been very much a sign of the times – both a symptom and a symbol of new social values. In particular, the multiplex has been indicative of a broader agenda to create a 'globalized' consuming middle class and a new urban politics. The multiplex cinema in India must therefore be understood as part of a sustained attempt to create dedicated 'public' spaces for the middle-class family. In order to understand the lived experience of the multiplex somewhat better, this chapter provides a qualitative account of the multiplex audience found in two locations: the mega-city of Bangalore in south India and the smaller ('tier two') city of Baroda in the Western state of Gujarat. The major focus of my inquiry is upon the social imagination of multiplex patrons as manifested through descriptions of the multiplex and who (and what) goes there.

Imagining audiences

In terms of the human experience of leisure, it is the articulation of a social imagination that provides the broadest expression of our relation with the consumption of media. Benedict Anderson famously postulated that it was the fundamental nature of the print media that produced the social imagination of modern nationalism by fostering a deep sense of fraternity amongst its readership (1991: 1998). Elsewhere, other scholars have also taken up this idea of media encouraging larger and more abstracted social formations and applied it to television and the Internet (Appadurai 1996; Castells 1996). Given the undeniable complexities of quantifying such imaginative relations between media forms, their communicative content, their creative professionals and their consumers, it is not surprising that the advent of the mass media has instigated a rich debate across the humanities for almost a century, almost every aspect of which remains unresolved to date. What is beyond doubt is that our engagement with the modern media is inherently a social practice, one that links us practically and symbolically – if not always physically – with others. Following this lead, this chapter will seek to explore the social imagination that is being constructed around the multiplex, ultimately providing a rich speculative, descriptive and analytical account of the multiplex crowd (Walsh 2010).

I begin with the observation that any mediated social imagination necessarily extends beyond media consumers themselves. Crucially, those who speculate in the cultural industries (for themselves or on behalf of others) do so on the basis of their own interpretation of a potential market that is conceptualized in the form of an audience. This notion of an audience as an inhabited market is conceived of in terms of an interdependency between media providers and consumers – a relationship that attributes agency (albeit unequally) to both. Naturally, the limitations of any market-based definition of community arise from the restriction of social agency to choices based upon consumption. As such, this framing will always attribute more weight to the decisive act of consumption than to the production of meanings or pleasures. Nonetheless, this is undeniably imaginative work that is social in nature. It is also important work, whether it is undertaken by children's entertainers, classical musicians or film professionals focusing on the successful exploitation of public taste. It is the capacity for imagining large numbers of plausible – but fictitious and essentially unknowable – consumers upon which commercial success often depends. For this reason, it comes as no surprise that the management staff I interviewed at the Indian multiplex chains were very conscious of their desired audience:

> I can definitely speak about our audiences, and they would be 18–34 age group, basically the college kids, and what we call the younger, the newly married people. I think that the younger crowd, basically, they want to go out and have a nice time on evenings and enjoy themselves. In India we call them 'dinks', double-income no kids. It is that category that really is pushing it. Disposable income is going up. People are making more money so people want to spend that money and enjoy themselves. (Shriram Krishnan, Chief Financial Officer, PVR Cinemas Ltd, interview 20 January 2007)
>
> Primarily we do 15 to 35. Somebody who earns around more than 120,000 rupees. Typically someone who is at least a graduate, and who has money to spend but doesn't have time. So it is more of disposable time as a business person I am after, than disposable money. Today if you build something which deserves somebody's attention, people are

ready to pay. (Tashur Dhingra, Chief Operating Officer, Reliance-Adlabs, interview 8 January 2007)

The logic of the imaginative associations made here is readily apparent. The first component is the identification of a demographic with the requisite spending capacity and few financial commitments, which can hypothetically be translated into the desired spending behaviours, and thus company profits. Needless to say, the nature of this projection is somewhat arbitrary. Nonetheless, this capacity to rhetorically assume the role of an ideal consumer is a common feature of the way that media professionals describe their audiences. What it also represents in this particular case is an attempt to bridge the perceived disconnect between the wealth of India's middle classes and their desire to spend that wealth. While the blue-sky projections of the purchasing power of India's middle classes provoked a frenzy of interest in the Indian market during the 1990s, the growth in consumption has lagged markedly behind its perceived potential (Fernandes 2006: 78). According to William Mazarella (2003), the major problem faced by India's advertising industry (itself perhaps the major beneficiary of the new economy) has been that household incomes have been a relatively poor indicator of propensity to spend. However, according to the multiplex chains, their high admission prices dictate a clientele drawn from a much more select segment of the middle classes. By its very definition, these people can afford to spend above the odds on non-essentials and, more importantly, have already shown their willingness to do so. Advertising incomes for the multiplex chains are significant for this reason, constituting 5 per cent of overall incomes and growing steadily, according to Snehal Chitneni, Corporate Communications Manager at INOX Leisure Ltd:

Corporates look at multiplexes as a very attractive venue for advertising, simply because of the kind of audience we attract. Most multiplexes are located in premium locations. The audiences that they attract are similarly SEC A+, SEC B. So basically, the upper to the middle classes are the ones who frequent multiplexes. Plus, we have a captive audience. When you run your ads in the interval or before a film, the audience are just sitting there because they have nowhere else to go. Plus a lot of corporates also do a lot of their product launches, setting up of kiosks. For example, if they are launching a skincare range they will have a counter where patrons can go and test it. So we have a lot of huge brands like Mercedes, Philips, Sony. The Levers of the world use INOX. (Snehal Chitneni, interview, 9 January 2007)

The multiplex crowd is thus not only selected for its own spending capacity within the confines of the mall-multiplex combine, but also for its on-sale value to advertisers. The multiplex crowd is thus both imagined and traded as a commodity. For the purposes of advertisers, the multiplex crowd is posited as an entirely different proposition from the regular cinema crowd, as Parveen Kumar at Wave Cinemas (on the outskirts of New Delhi) explains:

You know we advertise a normal good car in normal cinemas. OK, their clientele are like that, so they can put a more impact on local clientele. But if you are advertising for Nokia N Series, you have to play this thing in multiplexes because these people can afford Nokia N Series. Or let it be Windows Vista, in normal halls it doesn't matter any difference if we are advertising Windows Vista or Nokia because both things are out of their reach. So multiplex clientele matters, because Pepsi, Nokia, LG, Samsung, big business houses, we are investing more on their promotion or sales part, and we are their biggest consumers in that way. (Parveen Kumar, Operations Manager, 9 March 2007)

The explicit construction of the multiplex crowd as a 'consuming commodity' is a useful example of instrumental rationality at work in the social imagination. However, if we take into account the environmental conditions created by the visual impact of advertising at the multiplex, and the bridging effect of the older tradition of the star-hoarding meeting the newer one of the film star as a clothes-horse for innumerable consumer brands, then we cannot help but be aware of how the multiplex patron is interpellated by a particular set of ideological conditions that equate leisure with consumption. Iconicity aside, the physicality of the multiplex remains important here. The historical trajectory that is commonly marked out in metanarratives of the public sphere inspired by Anderson, Habermas and others, beginning with small-scale physical assembly and culminating in the virtual mass publics of television and the Internet, tends to sideline the particular operating conditions of cinema (Habermas 1989). Despite being a mass media, cinema continues to require public assembly within specifically constructed physical environments. Cinema is therefore implicated not only in the discursive functions of a symbolic virtual gathering but also in the continuing material production of public space and public assembly. As such, the cinema continues to represent a unique interface between the mythic-symbolic and the architectural and biological dimensions of public culture.

This is why the designers and operators of the multiplex are not only interested in what Indian English would designate as the 'creamy layer', but also in attracting the 'decent crowd'. This is because 'ambience' is an important component of the environmental conditions seen as conducive to consuming behaviours. Ambience, of course, has a human element, in which social mores and manners are emphasized. Thus, for some operators, the high prices charged at the multiplexes are not only about maximizing revenue streams, and certainly not about maximizing occupancy. Rather, they are designed to ensure that only particular kinds of people (and not others) go to the multiplex:

This is why they don't want to reduce the prices, because we also have the fear that once I reduce the prices, you know – I can understand that even if I reduce the prices I cannot get that much of impact on my general business – but I don't want to reduce my prices because then there's a chance that I'll get people which I don't want to be in the cinema … [In this multiplex] You will not find anyone hooting and shouting. It's very important. So being a manager it is my responsibility to give a sense of security to my customers. I don't want a couple of guys who can spoil the whole experience of the cinema for the rest of 50 or 60 people. (Parveen Kumar, 9 March 2007)

The inculcation and preservation of a sense of ontological security among patrons is an important behavioural aspect of the management of the multiplex chains, an imperative that goes beyond prioritizing the successful application of modern advertising techniques. In both respects, however, we might argue that the goal of the multiplex in India is to fashion a very particular kind of public through dynamic pricing, physical location and the architectural and paramilitary management of the built environment. This is a programme of social engineering with fairly concrete material methods (placement, catchment, architecture, stop-and-search). Accordingly, the multiplex can be accused of 'audiencing' – that is, of consciously seeking to shape its own clientele. What is less obvious is the extent to which these artificial conditions of existence actually reflect the social reality of the multiplex crowd. Thus it becomes necessary to gauge the extent to which members of this new public are actually aware of or identify with the *ideal type* of the multiplex spectator – the mould into which they are being placed.

Assessing the multiplex crowd: findings from attitudinal surveys

In making an assessment of the multiplex public, a range of small-scale survey studies and focus group exercises were conducted in sites across India in the early part of 2007 by myself and Douglas Hill (Athique and Hill 2010). Here, I will make reference to the surveys and focus groups that I conducted in the cities of Bangalore and Baroda. This pairing provides a useful comparative between a leading metropolis with a population of 5.5 million and a provincial 'tier two' city with only 1.5 million inhabitants. Bangalore has, of course, become well known internationally as the 'silicon valley' of India, being home to the country's major concentration of IT and call centre operations (Athique 2012: 90–111). Baroda, by contrast, enjoys an established position as an industrial city within one of India's most industrialized states (Gujarat). In that sense, Baroda is a good example of the urban development model followed during the decades when 'heavy industry' enjoyed privileged status, while Bangalore has been placed at the forefront of India's attempts to materialize a 'global' city via the post-industrial paradigm. Interestingly, both cities had three multiplexes in operation at the time when this fieldwork was conducted, with the major difference being one of scale. Baroda's new leisure landmarks had three screens on average, while Bangalore hosted the largest facility in India, the 11-screen PVR Cinemas at Forum Mall in the suburb of Koremangala, a focal point for the IT boom.

Functionally, the initial survey exercise was designed to encourage qualitative responses as well as basic demographic data. The questions were designed to address three primary lines of inquiry: (1) What was the primary motivation for visiting a multiplex? (2) How accurate were claims made by the industry that the multiplex crowd was socially (and socio-economically) distinct from the regular cinema audience? (3) To what extent did the social imagination of multiplex patrons reflect the ethos of the multiplex and of new regimes of consumption in general? The survey exercises were followed up with invitations to attend focus group discussions. These sessions expanded upon the embodied and symbolic nature of the multiplex experience, with an emphasis on the motivations that drove participation as well as individual perceptions of the multiplex audience.

Bangalore sample

In describing their motivations for visiting a multiplex, the survey respondents in Bangalore identified a range of factors that corresponded broadly with the operating logic of the multiplex format, such as distance, timings of shows and choice of films. However, the greater attention to patron comfort in Indian multiplexes, and the greater contrast of these conditions with the existing theatrical infrastructure, made environmental conditions a much more significant factor for patrons choosing to visit the multiplex. The following are some indicative samples of survey responses:[1]

20Mu: The sound quality was better compared to other theatres. I like the environment and basically the crowd is good.

21Mu: I couldn't watch films in other theatres 'cos the environment of the other theatres wouldn't be as good as that of the multiplex and also the comfort of watching movies in the multiplex is very good. Environment consists of people, the cleanliness of the place, etc.

21Fu: The good and decent crowd.

22Fu: Because of the picture quality, sound effects and especially the comfort. I prefer English movie in the multiplex. Indian movies have too many songs which are not suited to be played in multiplex.

18Fu: Because the crowd isn't very cheap. It is more comfortable. What I see as comfort is my basic priority for entertainment.

18Mu: There are a lot of choices offered. I could make last minute decisions. Also, there's the cool factor involved. People like to be seen in multiplexes. I would be too.

What becomes immediately apparent from these responses is that the environmental conditions that make the multiplex attractive to this audience have a human dimension. In this respect, the responses of this survey group echoed Parveen Kumar's concern with maintaining the selectivity of the multiplex audience, with respondents identifying the human make-up of the multiplex audience as a motivational factor for their own participation. At the same time, it was immediately apparent that film choice was a relatively weak factor in making a decision to visit a multiplex – a surprising result that underscored the importance of 'ambience' as the major drawcard:

17Mu: As multiplexes are more comfortable than a normal theatre. It is very much organized. Especially, 90 per cent of the crowd will be decent. Multiplexes are a huge advantage for ladies as ladies won't prefer to get squashed between a group of gents which usually occurs in a normal theatre. So to avoid the chaos, it's better everyone choose multiplex. Even the sound quality is better. Ambience is more and it is very, very clean.

Of the sample group of 40 respondents, 32 people stated that they were regular visitors to the multiplex, with 14 respondents visiting every month and eight visiting three to four times per month or more. However, only a quarter of respondents identified themselves as 'multiplex only' patrons. Nonetheless, despite the large proportion of the sample group who identified themselves as visiting normal cinema halls in addition to multiplexes, the image of Bangalore's regular theatres that emerged from their description of them was overwhelmingly negative, as the following examples demonstrate:

17Mu: There is too much of crowd left at a time. It is too dirty. No ambience. No proper parking. Dirty toilets.

21Mu: The sound, the crowd (generally cheap) the ambience.

21Fu: Cleanliness. All local people will come. Too much crowded.

21Mu: The seating quality is not good. The place is generally not clean and the washrooms and restrooms need more maintenance.

23Fu: Rats, cost, cheeking, etc.

27Fu: The choice of food/snacks at canteen – not like multiplex and – sometimes – bugs on seats.

21Mu: Not clean and hygienic. Too crowded. Crowd not good.

This almost dialectical representation between multiplex and cinema hall bears a very strong resemblance to the claims made by the multiplex industry, suggesting that they have successfully identified the major concerns of their target audience. From this perspective, it is hard to see why a greater supply of multiplex screens in the city would not instantly translate into a much greater 'multiplex only' audience. There were, however, some detractors from the overall polarity of this description. Two (older, male) viewers explicitly stated that they disliked the multiplex crowd, and while film choice was given as a positive factor by a respondent who liked watching 'English' movies, it was given as a negative feature of the multiplex by two others who preferred Indian regional-language movies. Similarly, for one respondent the major drawback of the normal cinema was 'bad food', while for another the multiplex experience was diminished by the fact that 'They won't let us take the snacks we want to take'. However, the only major inversion of the 'bad' normal cinema versus the 'good' multiplex took place around the issue of cost. One-third of respondents thought that multiplexes were far too costly, variously stating that multiplexes were 'Too heavy on the pockets' and that the ticket prices were 'a little too high for the Indian economy', and therefore 'the price becomes a matter of concern'.

This reticence surrounding the cost of visiting the multiplex was reflected in the spending patterns that this group attributed to their multiplex visits. The vast majority of the group who specified their spending claimed to spend less than 300 rupees (US$6.12) on a visit to the multiplex, including ticket and refreshments (27 respondents from 38). Just under half (16 from 38) spent less than 200 rupees (US$4.08). These are, of course, significant sums when compared with the average ticket cost of 40 rupees for a regular theatre in Bangalore, but they represent a fairly modest level of expenditure for a crowd imagined as the 'crème de la crème' of Indian society. Indeed, despite the degree of emphasis that has been placed upon their consumer aspirations by the operators, only half this group (21 respondents) indicated that they spent money on anything other than their movie ticket and basic refreshments when visiting a multiplex.

It is worth noting, however, that the modest spending of this sample was not necessarily indicated by the consuming 'firepower' of the group as measured by the traditional benchmarks commonly used by the market research industry. For example, almost two-thirds of the sample owned a two-wheeler (26 from 40). More than a third claimed to own a car (15 from 40) and just over a quarter (11 from 40) held a credit card. Three-quarters of the sample had completed a tertiary qualification, and the remaining quarter had completed 12th Standard and were attending college. In all these respects, the sample group appeared commensurate with the profiles prepared by the industry for its advertising clients. Despite this, however, this small-scale study appeared to suggest that only a relatively small proportion of the multiplex crowd – even in a major metropolitan centre like Bangalore – was likely to be of interest to Mercedes or Sony in the immediate future.

Baroda cohort

Multiplex patrons in the Baroda sample were much more concerned overall with the quality of the cinematic facilities (sound, projection) and the co-location of retail and restaurant facilities than the Bangalore sample when making their choice to visit the multiplex. In part, this reflected the far greater presence of large-scale mall developments in Bangalore, where they have become more or less ubiquitous, as opposed to Baroda, where the presence of Central Mall's Baroda site is comparatively recent and still considered novel. Where the responses of the two survey groups reinforced each other most strongly was in the emphasis on environmental conditions, and the relatively low importance of the theatrical offerings in motivating patrons. In terms of the multiplex 'ambience' as a draw for this group, the human aspect (that is, the 'crowd') appeared to be an even more decisive factor for the Baroda sample. It was a consistently important factor for female respondents, as can be seen from a selection of sample responses:

> *F16u:* I choose the multiplex because of its ambience. The comfortable seating arrangements, good sound system and also good quality foodstuffs. And even to some extent in a multiplex there are good crowd too. I choose any multiplex which is closer to my home, like INOX.

> *F18u:* I chose multiplex because multiplexes are comfortable. The crowd there is good. Security system is well-organized, no nuisance is involved over there. We can do window shopping or regular shopping along with watching the movie.

> *F20u:* I choose INOX multiplex because INOX being a multiplex that offers a lot of facilities. One can visit Pantaloons, have food at McDonalds and of course watch a movie. So it's like having everything under one roof. Moreover, the gentry at multiplexes is better.

> *F20u:* Initially, I was enamoured by the luxury and ostentatiousness of a multiplex. As a school kid, when the multiplex euphoria began to catch up, it suddenly became uncool to watch movies in a normal cinema hall. One can also enjoy watching a movie in a multiplex without all the hooting and disturbance, that was the main attraction for me.

The importance of the multiplex to the group's cinema habits was clearly substantial, with three-quarters of respondents describing themselves as regular visitors. Compared with the Bangalore sample, there was a more substantial proportion of 'multiplex only' patrons in Baroda, constituting around half of the sample. In order to contextualize this, it is worth noting that Baroda had three operational multiplexes at the time of the survey, the same number as Bangalore (albeit with only half the screen capacity). If we consider that the population of Baroda is less than a third of the population of Bangalore, then it becomes clear that the former is far better serviced than the latter. Where we approach the survey group in gendered terms, male respondents displayed a 50/50 split between 'multiplex only' patrons and those who also visited 'normal cinemas'. Female respondents showed a nominal bias towards exclusive use of the multiplex. However, when these preferences were arranged by age, there was a marked bias amongst the youngest cohort (16–21 years) towards exclusive multiplex use. This suggests that the recent advent of the multiplex craze may have successfully captured the younger cohort, while older multiplex patrons were more likely to also continue visiting the cinemas that they had been using before the multiplexes arrived.

The disjuncture between generational perspectives can be most bluntly illustrated by comparing the two responses below, one from a younger, female patron and one from a male patron who was the oldest survey respondent:

F18u: Multiplexes are having wide space to move around. Its ambience is good, the whole premises are bright. Good crowd – that is, people are sober, sophisticated – the premises are clean. There are many theatres, shopping malls are there. Eatables are good. Good facility of entertainment and good security arrangements and no havoc created.

M44u: I don't like multiplexes. They are too artificial. Eatables (junk food) are priced unreasonably. The aura around the multiplexes puts a strain to conform.

This male respondent claimed that, despite being a regular visitor to multiplexes, he visited the multiplex primarily due to 'peer pressure'. It would be erroneous, however, to imply that all the older respondents who also visited single-screen theatres actually preferred them to the multiplex. One of the older female respondents (F35u), identified that she visited normal cinemas primarily for reasons of cost, and that she greatly preferred the multiplex due to: 'Cordial surroundings, and to a certain extent, the viewers. As far as India is concerned there are categories of viewers. At multiplex, yes, the difference can be noted.' As with the Bangalore survey group, when we compare the overall description of the multiplex with the descriptions offered of the single-screen cinemas in Baroda, we can see clearly how one functions as the negative inverse of the other. The crowd at the multiplex was 'decent' or 'good', while the crowd at the normal cinema was 'dirty', 'cheap' or 'bad'. The seats at the multiplex are a drawcard, while at the normal cinema they are a drawback.

There were some significant differences between the two survey sites, however. Although cleanliness was still a selling point for the multiplex in Baroda, there were no specific complaints in Baroda about the dirtiness of the single-screen cinemas, which was the most common complaint of the Bangalore group. Another difference was that in Baroda 'security' (and its negative inverse of anti-social behaviour at the normal cinemas) was a more significant factor. For one young female respondent, the traditional cinema hall was described as a dark and sexually threatening space. For a male respondent, the regular cinema crowd demonstrated a lack of appreciation for the cinema as an art form. Another female respondent specified that the noisy behaviour of regular cinema patrons was off-putting:

F18u: Normal cinemas are not having wide space. Crowd is not good, has cosy premises, very crowded. Indecency is seen, the whole premises are not bright. Nuisances and havocs are created.

M22u: What I like is the prices for the tickets is damn low here. What I don't like is the crowd it attracts. Not that I am against the lower classes but they don't appreciate good work.

F20u: The hooting and screaming is one of the main reasons why I don't like normal cinema halls.

Some other respondents were more equivocal in their comparison of the multiplex with its architectural predecessor. For one male respondent, it was less a case of normal cinemas being dreadful *per se*, but multiplexes simply being better. The older male in the group claimed to prefer the 'atmosphere' of the regular cinema, even though he disliked the behaviour of patrons there as much as he did the behaviour of those at the multiplex:

M23u: Normal cinemas can also provide quite good facilities, but they are not in match with those of multiplex, and their quality is of no match to the multiplex.

M44u: I like the relaxed atmosphere of normal cinemas, though the rats, spitting, smoking and lovers may be sometimes irritating. The crass crowd of the multiplex also uses their mobiles with a kind of unconcern for the other.

Even for those who found the presence of the 'cheap/dirty crowd' less of a problem, it was clear that visiting a normal cinema was seen as an uncomfortable and inconvenient experience. While Baroda's single-screen cinemas were not described as unhygienic, they were still considered far from satisfactory venues for enjoying movies. When we take note of the fact that the average Indian multiplex is a good deal more comfortable than its counterpart in many developed countries, the enormous disparity between this exaggerated luxury and the hard and cramped seating found at the older cinemas is of major significance to the viewing experience. Even for those who enjoy taking part in, or simply observing, the raucous collective rituals of audiences in regular theatres, complaints about the quality of seating have to be taken seriously when the average running length of an Indian film is over three hours. As one respondent (F37m) put it: 'In normal cinema, watching movie is like doing a work of watching. It's not leisure.' A younger respondent agreed:

F18u: I chose INOX to watch the movie because it is the most happening place. Movie at a regular theatre is a chore but at a multiplex it is an experience. The lightings, ambience, the smell of popcorn, the acoustics, add and enhance the whole experience of watching a movie. You feel sort of pampered and special. At other theatres, there are dirty chairs, tobacco-stained walls, scruffy employees and horrible visuals. Who in their right mind would go elsewhere?

While enjoying the relatively greater comforts of the multiplex, those respondents who were prepared to detail their spending appeared to spend fairly modestly. Only one respondent spent more than 500 rupees (US$10.20) on a trip to the cinema, and half of the group spent less than 200 rupees (US$4.08). However, this group did appear inclined to spend on ancillary activities while visiting the multiplex, with just one respondent spending nothing and two spending less than 100 rupees (US$2.04). The remainder of the group claimed to spend between 200 and 500 rupees outside of the cinema during visits to the multiplex. In demographic terms, the 'consumer profile' of the Baroda group was remarkably similar to the survey group in Bangalore. One-third had their own credit card; over half had a two-wheeler and almost one-third had a private car at their disposal. Three-quarters had completed some tertiary education, and the reminder were engaged in tertiary studies. This profile matched the Bangalore cohort closely and, needless to say, is far above the national average in every respect.

Safety, sociability and congeniality

Lakshmi Srinivas (2002) describes the established practices of viewing *masala* movies in India's older cinema halls as actively participatory in nature – a tendency she attributes to overwhelmingly group-oriented social relations in India, a collectivity that she juxtaposes with the atomized, disciplined spectators of American cinemas. The cinema halls are thus closely associated with raucous acts of mass participation, such as screaming, applauding, whistling and singing. However, for much of the multiplex clientele, this 'active' mode of spectatorship (where audiences boo the arrival on screen of the villain, sing and dance during the film songs, and throw coins at the screen) was actually seen to devalue their own experience of going to the cinema. A large component of the eagerness of multiplex viewers not to mix with the 'cheap crowd' in traditional cinema halls appeared to stem from a rejection of the latter's emotionally demonstrative and 'undisciplined' watching of films:

> *M:* If you compare it to any normal cinema, you go there you have bad seats, you have bad lighting, you have a bad crowd, you have bad everything … You basically have people who basically start to hooting and howling at anything and everything that just comes up on screen. They can't sit quietly and appreciate the movie that's going on.

By contrast with regular Indian cinema halls, the film-viewing experience in the multiplex is odour-free and marked by relative silence. The sporadic call tones of mobile phones and the subsequent mumbled one-sided conversations provide the only major distraction from the screen, with laughter at appropriate points in the film narrative (and only those points) being the only audible sign of shared participation. To be part of this 'decent crowd' was seen by multiplex patrons as a marker of both affluence and good manners, and it allowed them to put themselves at a distance from the general movie-going public.

In his writings on Indian cinema halls in the 1990s, Steve Derne (1999) emphasizes the highly sexualized atmosphere of the cinema. For Derne, both the thematic content of the Hindi film and the traditions of spectatorship that surround it encourage the objectification of women. The practice of watching films thus engenders a state of aggressive collective sexual excitement amongst mostly male audiences, a state of mind that spills over into lewd advances towards female patrons and threatening sexual behaviour outside the cinema hall. Derne notes that women were confined to more expensive balcony seats and, without the presence of male chaperones, were unsafe even there from harassment. In the Bangalore focus group, the female members of the group stated that that their parents would not allow them to attend normal cinemas in Bangalore, which were considered unsafe. The cause of this danger was the disruptive presence of 'locals'. The male members of the focus group also recognized that there was a gendered dimension that marked out the difference between the multiplex and the normal theatre environment for female viewers:

M: I was watching a movie in a normal theatre recently and all drunkards came and it wouldn't be safe for a girl. They were smelling of booze and all that. You know we guys are used to … we are more used to that crowd.

F1: It is not just a theatre. Even if it is a restaurant or anywhere, it always depends. If there is more of a local crowd there, we don't hang out there.

F2: That influences us a lot. It influences our thinking. If there are a lot of people, local people in any place, then we wouldn't go there. As simple as that.

This account provides a marked contrast to Lakshmi Srinivas's (2002) assertion that trips to the cinema in India are highly social in nature, broadly representative of the entire social spectrum and essentially represent an outing for the entire family. Without having enough evidence to endorse either position, it did appear that safety was a major issue for female patrons – particularly the younger ones – and that the multiplex was widely perceived to be 'safer' than a regular cinema hall. Taking a broader perspective on the multiplex as a 'safe' environment, one male focus group member was also highly critical of what Phil Hubbard has called the 'ontological security' of the multiplex (2003). There was no doubt in this respondent's mind that multiplexes engendered a sense of security amongst their audiences. For him, however, the safety offered by new leisure architectures was as ephemeral as the sense of prosperity that it is intended to articulate:

M: Maybe the multiplexes make us think that India is shining when actually it is still not. Right, and I think that's very, very important because there are people who are much below the poverty line now, so-called poverty like, you know what the poverty line is, right, and what's happening to them? And they are just being forgotten ... people feel safe because they feel they belong to a higher income bracket and they can afford to see movies in safety and I think this is an illusion that we have, and people live with this kind of illusion that there is something called 'safety' here but in the old theatres there was none, 'OK so I am safer here', but I think it is just an illusion.

A 'decent crowd'

As this chapter has demonstrated, the audience research conducted in these two cities indicated the general preoccupation of multiplex patrons with hygiene, security and shopping. However, it was the presence of an appropriate (or 'decent') crowd that was consistently seen as the definitive factor in choosing to attend the multiplex, as well as being the most critical factor in constructing the 'ambience' of the multiplex and the most valued aspect of the multiplex experience. The 'decent crowd' of the multiplex was consistently articulated throughout these audience studies as an imagined community strongly differentiated from the general cinema audience. The modes of viewing at the multiplex were similarly constructed in an inverse manner to the perceived norms of cinema spectatorship in India, and this difference was overwhelmingly attributed to the audience demographic. The multiplex crowd was defined by its exclusive nature, which was widely considered the price that had to be paid for enjoying cinema in a manner that was not simply luxurious but, most importantly, disciplined and non-threatening. To be part of the 'decent crowd' was seen as a marker of both affluence and good manners, and it allowed multiplex patrons to put themselves at a distance from the general movie-going public.

At the same time, despite seeing themselves as moving amongst an 'decent' crowd characterized by good manners and affluence, most multiplex patrons also demonstrated personal consternation with the high costs of visiting the multiplex. In this sense, the actual multiplex audience appeared to be much more variegated in its spending capacity, habits and attitudes towards consumption than the imaginative description offered by the industry itself. As such, the remarkably consistent description of the multiplex audience (among both executives and patrons) as the most wealthy, high-status and free-spending members of Indian society was not reflected by the actual audience that we encountered. Rather, it appears that the multiplex functions as a major site for middle-class aspiration, and that multiplex operators are capable of marketing its socially exclusive nature to a wide cross-section of the middle classes. Finally, what is at once obvious about the primacy of 'decency' in this case, but nonetheless needs to be restated here, is that the content of multiplex programming was far less important to the multiplex audience than the quality of seats and who they were sitting with.

References

Anderson, B. (1991), *Imagined Communities: Reflections on the Origins and Spread of Nationalism*, London: Verso.

—— (1998), *The Spectre of Comparisons: Nationalism, Southeast Asia and the World*, London: Verso.

Appadurai, A. (1996), *Modernity at Large: Cultural Dimensions of Globalization*, Minneapolis, MN: University of Minnesota Press.

Athique, A. (2012), *Indian Media: Global Approaches*, Cambridge: Polity Press.

Athique, A. and Hill, D. (2010) *The Multiplex in India: A Cultural Economy of Urban Leisure*, London: Routledge.

Castells, M. (1996), *The Rise of the Network Society*, Oxford: Blackwell.

Derne, S. (1999), 'Making Sex Violent: Love as Force in Recent Hindi Films', *Violence Against Women*, 5: 5, pp. 548–75.

Fernandes, L. (2006), *India's New Middle Class: Democratic Politics in an Era of Democratic Reform*, Minneapolis, MN: University of Minnesota Press.

Habermas, J. (1989), *The Structural Transformation of the Public Sphere: Inquiry into a Category of Bourgeois Society*, Cambridge, MA: MIT Press.

Hubbard, P. (2003), 'A Good Night Out? Multiplex Cinemas as Sites of Embodied Leisure', *Leisure Studies*, 22, pp. 255–72.

Mazzarella, W. (2003), *Shoveling Smoke: Advertising and Globalization in Contemporary India*, Durham, NC: Duke University Press.

Shrinivas, L. (2002), 'The Active Audience: Spectatorship, Social Relations and the Experience of Cinema in India', *Media, Culture & Society*, 24, pp. 155–73.

Note

1   Respondent identifier key = age (numeral) gender (capital) marital status (lower case).

Chapter 22

The VHS Generation and their Movie Experiences

Janna Jones

Introduction

This chapter examines the cinema memories and reflections of a group of university students who were born in the early 1990s, and grew up watching movies at home and at the mall. The early movie experiences of the tail-end members of the VHS generation (approximately 1980–2000) are in some ways dramatically different from those of earlier generations of movie watchers. Prior to the mass marketing of VCRs and DVD players, children most often spent their formative years sitting in front of big screens at movie theatres situated in their communities. These university students are part of the first generation of film watchers who grew up experiencing movies in both private and public spaces. They were practically weaned on VHS tapes, but they also experienced the theatrical spectacles of fantasy film premieres. Many of their earliest memories of movie watching focus on obsessive viewing of Disney VHS tapes, but they also recount the wonders of attending *Star Wars*, *Lord of the Rings*, and *Harry Potter* premieres at the multiplex.

Most of them grew up in homes where solitary watching was a normalized activity. In 2005, when they were 15 years old, the average American home had 2.62 television sets, and 41 per cent of American homes owned three or more television sets. In the same year, 76 per cent of American families had at least one computer in their homes, and 38 per cent of American families owned an Xbox or a similar video game (PhysOrg.com 2005). Yet they were also raised in the multiplex – almost all of them remember attending movie premieres targeted towards their demographic. They were approximately nine years old when first film of the *Star Wars* prequel trilogy was released in 1999; the last film of the trilogy was released in 2005 when they were 15. *The Lord of the Rings* trilogy and the first *Harry Potter* film were released in 2001. Subsequent *Harry Potter* films were released in 2002, 2004, 2005, 2007, 2009, 2010 and 2011. *Toy Story*, Pixar's first film, was released in 1995; other Pixar films – *A Bug's Life* (1998), *Toy Story 2* (1999) *Monsters Inc.* (2001) and *Finding Nemo* (2003) – were also released when members of the VHS generation were young. The movie industry clearly catered to the children of the 1990s, both in their homes and at the theatre, and as a result this generation learned to fluidly navigate both kinds of cinema space. Their movie memories of small and big screens suggest that this generation's movie-going practices are tightly woven into their everyday lives.[1]

In this chapter, I interpret essays written by 20-year-old college students, which detail their most significant cinema memories. My analysis focuses on four themes that I discovered in many or all of the essays: obsessive and solitary watching; family watching and parental control; the navigation of the social space of the movie theatre; and the movie spectacle. My analysis of these four themes leads me to conclude that, like generations of movie-goers before them, these members of the VHS generation view sociability as the most meaningful part their movie experiences. Even those chronicling early obsessive and solitary watching swiftly shift to relational stories once they have accounted for their initial movie experiences.

For two semesters, I required my History of Television and Film students to write essays detailing their most significant memories surrounding watching television and/or film, prior to entering the university.[2] My students are Electronic Media and Film (EMF) majors, and they are unselfconscious consumers and enthusiastic producers of various forms of media. Most of my students grew up in small towns or cities (like Phoenix, Tucson or Las Vegas) in the United States southwest. Quite a few of them are the first of their families to attend a university. Like their peers across the United States, many of my students' parents are divorced, and as a result they have lived in various familial configurations – with two parents, a single parent, their grandparents and step-parents. My intention with the assignment is to provide them with the time and space to reflect on the impact of television and/or film on their lives. Writing their essays, I reasoned, might bring them insights into the experiential nature of media consumption that could serve them well both personally and professionally. Of the 69 essays I collected, 35 focus on television memories.[3] Five of the essays emphasize film texts that inspired the authors to study filmmaking. My analysis focuses on the predominant themes in the remaining 24 essays. To be sure, the analysis of this small set of essays cannot provide us with any definitive conclusions; nonetheless, they do shed light on the ways in which members of the VHS generation experienced the movies in their homes and at the cinema.

Solitary watching

Thirteen of the student essays begin by detailing what some of the essayists describe as their obsession with watching movies on VHS tapes when they were young children. Their recollections focus on the naming of their favourite films, the pleasures that accompanied watching them and their ability to have some control over their viewing experiences. Essayists remember an intense desire to watch their favorite films repeatedly. One student, for example, remembers his fascination with The Beatles' film *The Yellow Submarine*:

> One of my earliest memories as a child stems from The Beatles' movie *The Yellow Submarine*. I can remember sitting on the couch in our knotty-pine den before elementary school. My parents had both left for work, and my grandma was watching me. I sat and watched the movie over and over again. This actually became a motif throughout my

childhood with many movies. I would constantly watch movies multiple times until they were memorized.

Another student remembers repeatedly watching *The Little Mermaid* and *Mary Poppins*:

> If I had to guess, it was the colors, music, and characters in these movies that engaged me at such a young age. I doubt the ability of my little brain to follow a story very well, as I remember that each time I watched it felt like something new was happening.[4]

Most of the university students recounting their initial experiences watching movies on the family's VCRs do not include any mention of other family members or friends. In these recollections, they speak mainly of the film itself and the pleasures it brought them. One student explained:

> I don't remember my parents at all. I remember the moments when I was watching alone. I was in my own world, it seemed, no one was around to enjoy the moments I thought were fantastic as a child. Back then it didn't bother me that I was watching the films alone, until now when I really think about it. It seems sad, but it was a moment in my childhood that I experienced, where I was able to enjoy films in a quiet and independent environment.

If parents were mentioned in the detailing of their earliest movie memories, it was usually because they were remembered as potential or real obstacles to their viewing pleasures. One student remembers his obsession with the movie *Space Jam*, claiming that he watched in every day for a month when it came out on VHS.

> What I didn't understand was that adults got tired of the same movies. I would say, 'Dad! *Space Jam!*' and he would reply, 'Isn't there a different movie you want to watch today?' to which I would just give a big smile and say, 'Nope!' And I would sit there, laughing hysterically at the same parts, almost quoting the entire movie.

Another student recalls making do with parental constraints that kept her from her favourite film. Her mother grew tired of renting the same movie, *My Girl*, and refused to do it anymore. 'I convinced her to get it one more time,' the student remembers, 'I used my tape deck to record the sound of the movie on cassette tapes, and I would listen to it all the time. I was absolutely enamored with the film.'

Since they were toddlers, researchers and influential thinkers have been anxious that this generation would grow up alienated and disconnected, in part because of the ubiquity of screens in their lives. When they were ten years old or so, Robert D. Putnam's influential book *Bowling Alone: The Collapse and Revival of American Community* (2000) was published to great acclaim (Putnam 2000). Drawing on his extensive research, including nearly

500,000 interviews, Putnam argued that the United States had become an increasingly socially disconnected society. Americans' social capital had plummeted, Putnam explained, due in part to suburban lifestyles, long commutes, changes in family structure and work habits, and most importantly for our purposes, over-dependency on television screens and computers. Society's incessant staring at screens, Putnam argued was contributing to the country's feelings of alienation, and made it difficult for individuals to connect with families, friends and community members. The students' chronicles of obsessive movie watching with little memory of the people around them might strike Putnam as evidence of alienation; even some of these students are startled at the solitary nature of their earliest movie experiences. But they tend to speak to the significance of solitary obsessive movie watching only when they are addressing their very first cinema memories. Their remembrances after the age of eight or so detail movie experiences entangled in their relationships with family, friends and sometimes strangers. It is likely that solitary movie watching persisted as they matured; however, the memories of such viewing were apparently not significant enough to include in their essays.

Kuhn's (2002) valuable and important analysis of 1930s British movie-goers' early memories enables a comparison between an earlier generation's memories and those of the VHS generation. The movie theatres of the 1930s British children were often situated in the middle of villages, towns or city centres. Kuhn explains that their journey – on foot – to and from the theatre is an important part of their remembered movie experiences, and is vital to the structure of their memories:

> For this generation, going to the pictures was the occasion for the very earliest ventures into the world, beyond the home. Close to the home, almost an extension of the home and yet not home, 'the pictures' is remembered as both daring and safe. (Kuhn 2002: 36)

Members of the VHS generation are most likely to remember watching their earliest movies on the couch; their memory maps detail their family living room, not theatres and city streets. Their earliest memories of movies suggest a secure and isolated experience that required little more from them than the engagement of their imagination and the ability to adjust the tracking on the VCR. Their later remembrances, however, are surprisingly similar to those of the 1930s British movie-goers. Both groups remember using the movie screen as a backdrop for experimentation with the rules of the adult world; both groups focus on their own performances of independence and interconnection.

Family viewing

All the student essays suggested that movies, both at home and at the theatre, were important relational tools for their families. In fact, some of essays claimed that movie watching was an anchor for their happy childhood memories, as it was a pleasurable and important ritualized event that had the capacity to improve and enhance amicable family dynamics. Few essays detailed the content of the films or even the titles, but the students do remember the satisfaction and comfort they felt with their families, and for some, the relief they experienced when underlying tensions and arguments temporarily ceased while the movie was playing. Sociability is a vital part of the movie-going phenomenon, and cinema-going scholars argue that it was as significant to early movie audiences as what they saw on the screen. As Robert Allen (2006) contends:

> There is an argument to be made that the history of 'reception' during the classical era is best understood not as the aggregate of specific acts of reception but rather as patterns of movie-going within which textual 'reception' in its most narrow sense is a part but not necessarily the most important part for many people. (2006: 58)

The sociability of the movies and its dynamic, pleasurable communicative practices has been a key component in analysing the historic 'patterns of movie-going' – those intermingling forces of commerce, culture and audience agency. My students' essays suggest that sociability, a fundamental characteristic of the movie experience, endures in cinema's domesticated age.

Some of the them take great care to reflect on the moment in time when they remember transitioning from a solitary to a relational viewer. While watching a dinosaur movie at home with her cousins, one student recounts how the experience helped her to frame the concept of movie watching at an early age:

> I learned that the term 'movie' was not only what I was watching, but also *how* I was watching. Viewing this movie with my cousins, I was able to enjoy their company and share with them the emotional responses that forever changed my cinematic experience.

Another student detailed the period when movie watching evolved from a solitary experience to a collective one:

> Up until this point, watching movies had been a private activity. As I said before, it was as much a babysitting tool for my parents as it was entertainment for me. But then my brother became of [an] age to where we could sit and watch movies together and my dad started a routine where every Friday after work he would rent movies for my brother and me. It started to become a shared experience.

Others carefully detail particular relational episodes that have little to do with specific movies, but were significant memories that took place while their families were watching movies together. One student remembers that her sister's behaviour was more compelling than the highly anticipated movie her family was watching:

As the movie played on I remember my older sister taking my aunt's stress ball from a coffee table. Only a few seconds after she picked it up and played around with it, it exploded in her face. Flour went everywhere and a sudden burst of laughter erupted from the adults in the room. My sister cried as she tried to wipe the white powder off her face. Although Jabba the Hut was an extremely interesting character, I found that my sister having flour blast in her face was more entertaining. I think the biggest reason for this recollection was because I remember how I felt in that moment, when we were around the family and all had something to laugh about.

Of course, cinema's sociability is not confined to domestic viewing. Most of the students' essays chronicle the relational dimensions of watching a movie at the theatre. The most dramatic difference between the two sorts of viewing is that the memories of *going* to the movies are written with more descriptive flourish than the tales of home viewing:

The floors were still sticky and full of popcorn from the showing before, but I didn't care because I was there to see *Star Wars* with my dad. The seats quickly filled up, and I remember there were people even sitting in the aisles. The movie started and the cheers from the crowd rang out, and my dad and I looked at each other and smiled. The room was buzzing with energy and even though the movie wasn't that great and everyone laughed at most of it, it was still one of the best times I had, and it is one of the greatest memories of my father.

As will be discussed further, the essayists remember the *Star Wars*, *Harry Potter* and *Lord of the Rings* premieres as significant, singular and spectacular events that enabled their families to share in the holiday-like rituals of opening nights:

The most memorable times were when my dad pulled us out of school and we went as a family to wait in line at the theater to see *The Lord of the Rings* movies the day they came out. We sat in line and talked, played games, snacked, and if mom was looking, we would pretend to do homework so that she felt better about pulling us out of school for the day. After the movie was over and we were in the car driving home, we talked about the movies – what we liked and didn't like, questions about things that didn't make sense, and even how they differed from the books (which my dad read to us because he loves Tolkien and wanted us to know the books before the movies).

As some reflected on their family viewing practices, they concluded that watching movies with loved ones was an important activity that organized family leisure time and helped to foster familial cohesiveness. 'The main thing is – it isn't the actual films,' one student explained, 'but the people I watch the movies with and the bonds that are created through spending time together.' Another student concluded that media served as both a backdrop of everyday life and a social catalyst, allowing for special connections between loved ones and helping to foster important memories:

Making connections with people can be difficult, but sometimes the things we take for granted can bring us together. Television, music, film and even video games are commonplace in our society, and are integrated into our everyday lives, but they can act as a device to bring people together and create bonds. I never would have thought of film as a social catalyst, but upon reviewing my life I see that it isn't really about the actual TV program, film or game; it is about the experiences and memories that are created when people spend time together forming bonds. Films serve as a backdrop to my memories.

Recounting many pleasurable memories of togetherness with their families, 15 of the students also remember significant movie experiences that fostered personal anxieties and family discord. Usually these narratives stressed the tensions of subscribing to or ignoring parental rules that forbade R-rated, horror or *Harry Potter* movies. The students remember that peer pressure often took precedence over the power of their parents' demands. Essayists remember that defying their parents was not hard to do because illicit movies were easily accessible on cable television:

When I was 11 or 12, I recall seeing a *Batman* movie on TV. It was much more violent, fast paced, and darker than the kinds of movies my mother let me watch. My mother discovered me watching it and quickly turned off the TV and forbade me from watching shows like it in the future. As a result of not being able to watch the *Batman* movie, I started to become defiant towards my mother for the first time in my life. I often secretly watched R-rated films late at night without my mother or father finding out.

R-rated films were not the only forbidden cinema fruit. Because it was a popular film with her friends, one student remembers feeling obligated to sidestep her father and his church's banning of a *Harry Potter* film. 'When my parents were divorced he relied on the church for parenting skills, some of which came a little too late,' the student writes. 'I remember going against my father's wishes and seeing the movie. It wasn't just because my father told me not to do it; I think a lot of it had to do with the fact that all my other friends had seen it.' While they spoke more often of the cohesiveness of family viewing, their descriptions of parental control and the tensions it created suggest that their movie experiences sometimes challenged their families and did not always unify them. The essays more often recounted tensions when they focused on the social space of the movie theatre. Unlike the comfort and security they described when watching Disney movies at home, their memories of experiences at movie theatres are sometimes fraught with anxiety due to the social pressures they recalled feeling in the theatre's public space.

Navigating the social space of the theatre

The VHS generation's first experiences with films were rarely in movie theatres. When they were judged mature enough to be taken to theatres, their parents drove them to the multiplex, which was generally outside of the city centre. Kuhn's (2002) 1930s filmgoers' memories and careful descriptions of their routes to and from the theatres were a significant part of their narratives. Kuhn writes: 'In their memory maps, local picture houses figure as stopping-off points in familiar everyday foot-passages from home through remembered streets' (2002: 35). The university students, on the other hand, don't mention – much less provide any detail about – the landscape between home and the theatre.

The automobile contributes to the eradication of the landscape between the home and the theatre, and the theatre and home, attenuating the essayists' sense of how the movie theatre was situated in their communities. Car rides were rarely mentioned unless the drive was insufferably long, there was a rush to get to the theatre or they remember awkward drop-offs at the theatre:

> About four blocks away from the theater, I asked my Dad to pull over and if he would drop me off here. He exclaimed, 'no way, the theater is over there, why would I drop you off here?' He continued up the block and dropped me off in front of the theater. Not too happy, I tried to escape from the car without being seen. Just as I closed the door my friend spotted me, yelled my name and began to walk over. As quickly as possible I said 'Bye, Dad,' and slammed the door shut, only to hear my dad reply with a 'Call me later, Boo!' I was officially embarrassed.

Awkward drop-offs took place between the ages of 12 and 16, when the essayists remember being old enough to go the theatre without adult supervision but were still too young to drive. During this period, the theatre was a critical space for their maturation, for it served as a safe public space where they could enjoy social interaction with their peers without the hassles of parental surveillance. A drop-off is awkward because the worlds of autonomy and dependence collide when a parent drives up to the front of the theatre. Others remember grasping for their autonomy even when their parents were in the theatre with them:

> I sat ten rows in front of my parents and did not speak to them until we got into the car and left the movie theatre. I look back at that situation now and realize I was just being childish, but I'll never forget that one time I watched an entire movie sitting by myself. I felt so 'grown up' sitting by myself.

The movie theatre is remembered as a stage for performing the delights and struggles of identity and interpersonal relationships. Their parents are primary players in their narratives, but they also detail the complexities of interacting with friends, sweethearts and strangers – in line, in the lobby (foyer) and in the theatre auditorium. One poignant memory is a reminder of the racial discrimination that minority filmgoers experienced during the twentieth century:

> Dionne and I, being close in age, were playing around when one of the kids behind us exclaimed, 'Dad, why is that nigger with them?' At first I didn't realize what had been said

until my mom turned around and said a stern 'Fuck you' to the man. This was the first time I heard my mom curse in front of me, and it was also the first time I had seen her stand up to someone like that. My mom grabbed us, and we left the theater.

The Dionne narrative is also a reminder that the movie theatre has always been a space for interacting with strangers, as it has been since its earliest days, but it also a space where intimate relationships are created, sustained and derailed. The dim lighting of the auditorium complicates surveillance, much to the delight of romantically inclined couples. As Mark Jancovich explains, 'teenagers are particularly drawn to places free of parental supervision. The cinema has therefore been a key site for courting and dating' (2011: 90). Eight of the essays – all written by young men, explain the significant role the movie theatre played in teenage dating experiences. Their stories of first dates and first kisses suggest that the romantic rituals at the theatre can be complicated performances fraught with anxiety. One student remembers the painful self-doubt of initiating his first kiss:

The middle of the movie starts, and it is a long romantic scene with music in the background. I swear it was designed for the sole purpose of making out with your significant other. I knew it, my girlfriend knew it, it seemed like everyone in the theater knew it. Suddenly I cursed the makers of the movie for leading me into such an obvious trap without any warning. I wasn't ready for the kiss. I had no idea what I was doing. Do I start it now? What if the scene ends right as I move in?

While discussions about the messages of specific movies are rare, one essayist did speak to the vulnerability he felt as he experienced the emotional pull of *Up* while sitting in a theatre with his new girlfriend:

Another thing about *Up* was that it was so sad. This was an issue because I was on a date with a girl and the last thing I wanted to do was to tear up next to her. Well unfortunately, *Up* was the first movie since *The Green Mile* that made me shed tears. I was just so emotionally moved by it. Thankfully it was dark, so I just kept turning away to wipe the tears.

While the VHS generation's earliest movie experiences were usually at home and their topographic relationship with the movie theatre was fragile at best, as they matured, they used the movie theatre space in many of same ways as Kuhn's 1930s filmgoers. The secure space of the mall theatre, as well as the story on the movie screen, served as backdrops for these movie-goers' public performances of autonomy and interconnectedness. Kuhn writes:

For the 1930s generation, cinema provided a safe space for challenges to adult rules and for the assertions of independence from teachers and other authority figures. It also offered a safe space for the explorations of fears and horrors. (2002: 62)

The essays suggest that the many of fundamental aspects of cinema's sociability endure into the twenty-first century, despite the radical changes in film technology, distribution and exhibition.

The movie spectacle

Twenty of the accounts recall the excitement and wonder of attending *Star Wars*, *Harry Potter* and *Lord of the Rings* premieres. Many of the students claim that the movie spectacle – by which I mean a movie opening that attracts large crowds and has a carnival-like atmosphere – was their most significant movie memory. Some readers may be unfamiliar with the movie spectacle, so I offer one recollection of a *Star Wars* opening night.

> Even though I considered myself to be a *Star Wars* fan, I was put to shame in comparison to the other people who stood alongside me. People dressed up in amazing outfits having saber duels and playing music; others having *Star Wars* marathons before the final event; it was a circus. For one night, I was part of this group, even though I was not dressed up or knew all the intricate details these people knew, I was part of a different type of society; I was part of a cult. Eventually the clock struck midnight and the door opened and we managed perfect dead center seats in a completely packed theater. What I saw in that room was unmatched. Never before had I heard people cheering in the theaters. There was so much energy, and even if you didn't like the movie in comparison to the original classics, you couldn't help but be sucked into this fantastic world. That night is still probably my highest and best movie experience to date.

The VHS generation was raised on opening night spectacles of fantasy films at the mall. There were 14 *Star Wars*, *Lord of the Rings* and *Harry Potter* opening nights between the years of 1999 and 2011, which means it was possible for them to attend at least one big movie event a year between the ages of nine and 21 (not taking into account Pixar films). More like a holiday than going to a movie at the mall, many of them remember that opening night meant the ordinary routines of daily life were suspended, which helped to shape the extraordinary event shared with family and friends. While it is likely that many of the essayists' families purchased VHS or DVD copies of these films, only two of the students mention watching these films at home. The films' significance is directly related to the big events at local theatres.

The movie premiere is, of course, nothing new in Hollywood. During the 1920s, film premieres usually took place in Hollywood. Like today's Academy Awards, opening night was an explosion of light, stars and enthusiastic fans. In 1929, *Collier's* accurately described the film premiere when it claimed that 'the picture about to be shown for the first time may be just another seven thousand feet of film; the audience is the show' (quoted in Karnes 1986: 555). During the Depression, opening night extravaganzas were no longer exclusive to Hollywood, as the film industry began to migrate them to local movie theatres across the United States. During the 1930s, the studios recognized that hundreds of simultaneous opening nights could help to secure the idea of Hollywood and increase profits. 'By mobilizing these energies on a new nationwide scale, Hollywood could retain its potent glamour, while making it more acceptably and squarely all-American,' writes David Karnes 'And by exchanging their early image of carnival splendor for a Depression-era spirit of civic festival, Hollywood movie premieres not only overcame hard times, but set the stage for a new interplay between movie fantasy and American culture' (1986: 356). Depending on the economic and creative well-being of the film industry, the movie premiere's relevance to popular culture has waxed and waned since the 1930s. The movie premiere experienced a renaissance during the 1990s because of the onslaught of fantasy films and the film industry's push to reconnect audiences with movie theatres. The simultaneous big opening nights around the country, and the loyalty and playfulness of the films' fans, helped to make the movie spectacle a collective childhood memory unique to the VHS generation. While these students comment favourably on the films, most of their recollections focus on the carnival-like atmosphere outside the movie theatre and the rituals they enjoyed with their families and friends.

The movie spectacle experience approximates the excitement of city streets that earlier generations of filmgoers encountered and most often enjoyed. For the students, the film premiere turns the ordinary and nondescript atmosphere of the multiplex on its head. Hours before the movie's starting time, friends, families and strangers stand in long lines, rubbing elbows with fans dressed in costumes, enjoying video games and saber fights, speaking to strangers, and suffering the commotion and inconveniences of public life. Of course, critics have been telling us for decades that the suburbs, the mall and the multiplex are unsatisfying and sterile replicas of city life. The mall theatre, Anne Friedberg (1991) explains, delivers a fabricated experience: 'Like tourism, which mass publicity and cliché prepare, the shopping mall cinema encodes the foreign in the familiar, introduces the new and exotic from the vantage of comfort and safety' (1991: 424). Critics grimly explain that the suburban mall is a policed space that offers none of the freedoms of the city. William Sharpe and Leonard Wallock write: 'With its travertine "boulevards" that serve as sanitized streets, the mall is a controlled, artificial environment that screens out undesirable persons and weather and even the passage of time' (1994: 12). The VHS generation – or at least those who grew up wandering mall corridors – likely understand the constraints of the shopping mall as well as, or better than, critics. Perhaps this is why the movie spectacle is such a significant memory for them: during these seldom and special times, throngs of movie attendees seem to joyfully command the space in and around the theatre. The mundane gives way to the unexpected – mostly off but also on the screen. For this generation, who grew up experiencing movies in the privacy of their homes and the controlled environment of the mall, the movie spectacle offers a glimpse of the unpredictable nature of the lively city street that generations of filmgoers before them likely took for granted.

Conclusion

Robert Allen (2011) writes that during the last century, the experience of movie-going has involved a distinctive though highly variable social practice:

> For one hundred years, individual films were the most ephemeral and most transitory aspect of movie-going. Movies had to share the same space with bodies, furniture, architecture, food and, for a lot longer and a lot more theaters than most film histories have acknowledged, human performers. (2011: 81)

Allen states that such performances are on the wane or are already a thing of the past, but these recollections suggest otherwise. Though their earliest movie experiences usually took place in their homes and their subsequent experiences were often anchored in the shopping mall multiplex, these students' memories of autonomy, interdependence and sociability share much in common with the movie experiences of the generations of movie-goers who came before them. Allen seems amenable to the enduring nature of the movie experience when he argues that it is open-ended, and should not be spatially or temporally bracketed:

> The relations that constitute the experience of cinema are not fixed; the character of its heterogeneity cannot be predicted or assumed. The experience of cinema is a product of relations … (2011: 86)

Today, as in the past, audiences necessarily navigate their way through the constraints and pleasures of commercial film, its exhibition and the cinematic environments that commerce helps to create. The accounts – like the experiences of filmgoers before them – have adapted to and helped to shape the unique and localized movie cultures of which they are a part. Their memories of the adventure, subtle dangers and mysteries of public life, and the equally inexplicable dynamics of family and home, suggest that we need not declare the demise of the movie experience any time soon.

References

Allen, R.C. (2011), 'Reimaging the History of the Experience of Cinema in a Post-Movie-Going Age', *Media International Australia*, 139, pp. 80–87.

—— (2006), 'Relocating American Film History: The "Problem" of the Empirical', *Cultural Studies*, 20: 1, pp. 48–88.

Friedberg, A. (1991), 'Flaneurs du Mal(l): Cinema and the Postmodern Condition', *PMLA*, 106, pp. 419–31.

Jancovich, M. (2011), 'Time, Scheduling and Cinema-Going', *Media International Australia*, 139, pp. 88–95.

Jones, J. (2011), 'When the Movie Started We All Got Along: Generation Y Remembers Movie Night', *Media International Australia*, 139, pp. 96–102.

Karnes, D. (1986), 'The Glorious Crowd: Hollywood Movie Premieres Between the Wars', *American Quarterly*, 30, pp. 553–72.

Klinger, B. (2006), *Beyond the Multiplex: Cinema, New Technologies, and the Home*, Berkeley, CA: University of California Press.

Kuhn, A. (2002), *Dreaming of Fred and Ginger: Cinema and Cultural Memory*, New York: New York University Press.

PhysOrg.com (2005), 'Americans in Love with "Terabyte Lifestyle"; Study Finds Nearly all Own Products with Digital Technology', 11 August, http://www.physorg.com/news5759.html. Accessed 20 February 2012.

Putnam, R. (2000), *Bowling Alone: The Collapse and Revival of American Community*, New York: Simon and Schuster.

Sharpe, W. and Wollock, L. (1994), 'Bold New City or Built-Up 'Burb? Redefining Contemporary Suburbia', *American Quarterly*, 46, pp. 1–30.

Notes

1 For an analysis of these essays focusing solely on family viewing, see Jones (2011).

2 Kate Bowles, at the University of Wollongong, NSW brought to my attention the website 'Life History and The Media Project'. She suggested that the limited life history would be an excellent way for our students to think about their own media practices. My students submitted their essays to their classroom Vista website. They signed consent forms allowing their essays to be used in future scholarly research. No students are identified in this chapter.

3 There is rich research potential for comparing the essays about television with the essays about film, but I have not begun this analysis.

4 For an outstanding analysis of repeat viewing, see Klinger (2006).

Index